ANNUAL EDITIONS

Child Growth and Development

02/03

Ninth Edition

EDITORS

Ellen N. Junn
California State University, Fullerton

Ellen Junn is an associate dean at California State University, Fullerton. She received a B.S. in experimental psychology from the University of Michigan and an M.A. and Ph.D. in cognitive and developmental psychology from Princeton University. In addition to her work on educational equity issues, Dr. Junn's research and publications focus on developments in children's conceptions regarding adult social relationships and on college teaching effectiveness.

Chris J. Boyatzis
Bucknell University

Chris Boyatzis is an assistant professor of psychology at Bucknell University. He received a B.A. in psychology from Boston University and an M.A. and Ph.D. in developmental psychology from Brandeis University. Many of his research interests lie at the intersection of social and cognitive development in early childhood. Dr. Boyatzis has published research on children's nonverbal and social status, media effects on children, symbolic development, and play and art. He has also written on the use of literature and film to teach developmental psychology.

McGraw-Hill/Dushkin
530 Old Whitfield Street, Guilford, Connecticut 06437

Visit us on the Internet
http://www.dushkin.com

Credits

1. **Conception to Birth**
   Unit photo—Middlesex Hospital photo.
2. **Cognition, Language, and Learning**
   Unit photo—© 2002 by Cleo Freelance Photography.
3. **Social and Emotional Development**
   Unit photo—Courtesy of Robin Gallagher.
4. **Parenting and Family Issues**
   Unit photo—Courtesy of Addie Raucci.
5. **Cultural and Societal Influences**
   Unit photo—United Nations photo by John Isaac.

Copyright

Cataloging in Publication Data
Main entry under title: Annual Editions: Child Growth and Development. 2002/2003.
1. Child psychology—Periodicals. I. Junn, Ellen N., *comp.* II. Boyatzis, Chris J., comp. III.
Title: Child growth and development.
ISBN 0–07–250713–6   658'.05   ISSN 1075–5217

Ninth Edition

Cover image © 2002 by PhotoDisc, Inc.
Printed in the United States of America   1234567890BAHBAH5432   Printed on Recycled Paper

Editors/Advisory Board

Members of the Advisory Board are instrumental in the final selection of articles for each edition of ANNUAL EDITIONS. Their review of articles for content, level, currentness, and appropriateness provides critical direction to the editor and staff. We think that you will find their careful consideration well reflected in this volume.

EDITORS

Ellen N . Junn
California State University Fullerton

Chris J. Boyatzis
Bucknell University

ADVISORY BOARD

Michael S. Becker
York College

Linda S. Behrendt
Concordia College

Mary Belcher
Orange Coast College

Catherine Crain-Thorenson
Western Washington University

Patrick M. Drumm
Ohio State University, Lancaster

JoAnn M. Farver
University of Southern California

Kathy E. Fite
Southwest Texas State University

Trisha Folds-Bennett
College of Charleston

Betty K. Hathaway
University of Arkansas

Charles D. Hoffman
California State University, San Bernardino

Dene G. Klinzing
University of Delaware

Marcia Lasswell
California State Polytechnic University

Nancy G. McCarley
Mississippi State University

Joann Montepare
Emerson College

Karen L. Peterson
Washington State University

Derek Price
Wheaton College

Lauretta Reeves
Rowan University

Nadia A. Sangster
Wheelock College

Sally M. Sentner
Clarion University

Daniel D. Shade
University of Delaware

Mary Helen Spear
Prince George's Community College

Connie Steele
University of Tennessee

Harold R. Strang
University of Virginia

Gloria Wellman
Santa Rosa Junior College

Staff

EDITORIAL STAFF

Ian A. Nielsen, Publisher
Roberta Monaco, Senior Developmental Editor
Dorothy Fink, Associate Developmental Editor
William Belcher, Associate Developmental Editor
Addie Raucci, Senior Administrative Editor
Robin Zarnetske, Permissions Editor
Marie Lazauskas, Permissions Assistant
Diane Barker, Proofreader
Lisa Holmes-Doebrick, Senior Program Coordinator

TECHNOLOGY STAFF

Richard Tietjen, Senior Publishing Technologist
Jonathan Stowe, Executive Director of eContent
Angela Mule, eContent Developer
Joe Offredi, Technology Developmental Editor
Janice Ward, Software Support Analyst
Ciro Parente, Editorial Assistant

PRODUCTION STAFF

Brenda S. Filley, Director of Production
Charles Vitelli, Designer
Mike Campbell, Production Coordinator
Laura Levine, Graphics
Tom Goddard, Graphics
Eldis Lima, Graphics
Nancy Norton, Graphics
Juliana Arbo, Typesetting Supervisor
Karen Roberts, Typesetter
Jocelyn Proto, Typesetter
Cynthia Vets, Typesetter
Cathy Kuziel, Typesetter
Larry Killian, Copier Coordinator

048001

To the Reader

In publishing ANNUAL EDITIONS we recognize the enormous role played by the magazines, newspapers, and journals of the public press in providing current, first-rate educational information in a broad spectrum of interest areas. Many of these articles are appropriate for students, researchers, and professionals seeking accurate, current material to help bridge the gap between principles and theories and the real world. These articles, however, become more useful for study when those of lasting value are carefully collected, organized, indexed, and reproduced in a low-cost format, which provides easy and permanent access when the material is needed. That is the role played by ANNUAL EDITIONS.

We are delighted to welcome you to this ninth volume of *Annual Editions: Child Growth and Development 02/03.* The amazing sequence of events of prenatal development that lead to the birth of a baby is an awe-inspiring process. Perhaps more intriguing is the question of what the future may hold for this newly arrived baby—for instance, will this child become a doctor, a lawyer, an artist, a beggar, or a thief? Although philosophers and prominent thinkers such as Charles Darwin and Sigmund Freud have long speculated about the importance of infancy on subsequent development, not until the 1960s did the scientific study of infants and young children flourish. Since then, research and theory in infancy and childhood have exploded, resulting in a wealth of new knowledge about child development.

Past accounts of infants and young children as passive, homogeneous organisms have been replaced with investigations aimed at studying infants and young children at a "microlevel" as active individuals with many inborn competencies, who are capable of shaping their own environment, as well as at a "macrolevel" by considering the larger context surrounding the child. In short, children are not "blank slates," and development does not take place in a vacuum; children arrive with many skills and grow up in a complex web of social, historical, political, economic, and cultural spheres.

As was the case for previous editions, we hope to achieve at least four major goals with this volume. First, we hope to present you with the latest research and thinking to help you better appreciate the complex interactions that characterize human development in infancy and childhood. Second, in light of the feedback we received on previous editions, we have placed greater emphasis on important contemporary issues and challenges, exploring topics such as understanding development in the context of current societal and cultural influences. Third, attention is given to articles that also discuss effective, practical applications. Finally, we hope that this anthology will serve as a catalyst to help students become more effective future professionals and parents.

To achieve these objectives, we carefully selected articles from a variety of sources, including scholarly research journals and texts as well as semiprofessional journals and popular publications. Every selection was scrutinized for readability, interest level, relevance, and currency. In addition, we listened to the valuable input and advice from members of our advisory board, consisting of faculty from a range of institutions of higher education, including community and liberal arts colleges as well as research and teaching universities. We are most grateful to the advisory board as well as to the excellent editorial staff of McGraw-Hill/Dushkin.

Annual Editions: Child Growth and Development 02/03 is organized into five major units. Unit 1 focuses on conception, prenatal development, and childbirth. Unit 2 presents information regarding developments in cognition, language, learning, and school. Unit 3 focuses on social and emotional development, while unit 4 is devoted to parenting and family issues such as child care issues, fathering, moral development, and discipline. Finally, unit 5 focuses on larger cultural and societal influences (such as after-school care and violence among youth) and on special challenges (such as poverty, childhood victimization and abuse, resilience, and children with autism).

Instructors for large lecture courses may wish to adopt this anthology as a supplement to a basic text, whereas instructors for smaller sections might also find the readings effective for promoting student presentations or for stimulating discussions and applications. Whatever format is utilized, it is our hope that the instructor and the students will find the readings interesting, illuminating, and provocative.

As the title indicates, *Annual Editions: Child Growth and Development* is by definition a volume that undergoes continual review and revision. Thus, we welcome and encourage your comments and suggestions for future editions of this volume. Simply fill out and return the comment card found at the end of this book. Best wishes, and we look forward to hearing from you!

Ellen N. Junn
Editor

Chris J. Boyatzis
Editor

Contents

UNIT 1
Conception to Birth

Three articles discuss the development of the child from the prenatal state to birth.

UNIT 2
Cognition, Language, and Learning

Ten selections consider the growth of children's cognitive and language abilities and their experiences in the learning process in school.

The concepts in bold italics are developed in the article. For further expansion, please refer to the Topic Guide and the Index.

The concepts in bold italics are developed in the article. For further expansion, please refer to the Topic Guide and the Index.

UNIT 3
Social and Emotional Development

Six articles follow a child's emotional development into the larger social world.

The concepts in bold italics are developed in the article. For further expansion, please refer to the Topic Guide and the Index.

UNIT 4
Parenting and Family Issues

Seven articles assess the latest implications of child development with regard to attachment, marital transitions, day care, and the moral development of children.

The concepts in bold italics are developed in the article. For further expansion, please refer to the Topic Guide and the Index.

UNIT 5
Cultural and Societal Influences

Nine selections examine the impact that society and culture have on the development of the child.

The concepts in bold italics are developed in the article. For further expansion, please refer to the Topic Guide and the Index.

Topic Guide

This topic guide suggests how the selections in this book relate to the subjects covered in your course. You may want to use the topics listed on these pages to search the Web more easily.

On the following pages a number of Web sites have been gathered specifically for this book. They are arranged to reflect the units of this *Annual Edition.* You can link to these sites by going to the DUSHKIN ONLINE support site at *http://www.dushkin.com/online/.*

ALL THE ARTICLES THAT RELATE TO EACH TOPIC ARE LISTED BELOW THE BOLD-FACED TERM.

World Wide Web Sites

The following World Wide Web sites have been carefully researched and selected to support the articles found in this reader. The easiest way to access these selected sites is to go to our DUSHKIN ONLINE support site at *http://www.dushkin.com/online/*.

AE: Child Growth and Development 02/03

The following sites were available at the time of publication. Visit our Web site—we update DUSHKIN ONLINE regularly to reflect any changes.

General Sources

American Academy of Pediatrics
http://www.aap.org

This organization provides data for optimal physical, mental, and social health for all children.

CYFERNet
http://www.cyfernet.mes.umn.edu

The Children, Youth, and Families Education Research Network is sponsored by the Cooperative Extension Service and USDA's Cooperative State Research Education and Extension Service. This site provides practical research-based information in areas including health, child care, family strengths, science, and technology.

KidsHealth
http://kidshealth.org

This site was developed to help parents find reliable children's health information. Click on the topic bars: Baby's Development, Nutrition, Pediatric News, Safety and Accident Prevention, and Childhood Infections.

National Institute of Child Health and Human Development
http://www.nichd.nih.gov

The NICHD conducts and supports research on the reproductive, neurobiological, developmental, and behavioral processes that determine and maintain the health of children, adults, families, and populations.

UNIT 1: Conception to Birth

Babyworld
http://www.babyworld.com

Extensive information on caring for infants can be found at this site. There are also links to numerous other related sites.

Children's Nutrition Research Center (CNRC)
http://www.bcm.tmc.edu/cnrc/

CNRC, one of six USDA/ARS (Agricultural Research Service) facilities, is dedicated to defining the nutrient needs of healthy children, from conception through adolescence, and pregnant and nursing mothers. The *Nutrition and Your Child* newsletter is of general interest and can be accessed from this site.

Zero to Three: National Center for Infants, Toddlers, and Families
http://www.zerotothree.org

This national organization is dedicated solely to infants, toddlers, and their families. It is headed by recognized experts in the field and provides technical assistance to communities, states, and the federal government. The site provides information that the organization gathers and disseminates through its publications.

UNIT 2: Cognition, Language, and Learning

Educational Resources Information Center (ERIC)
http://www.ed.gov/pubs/pubdb.html

This Web site is sponsored by the U.S. Department of Education and will lead to numerous documents related to elementary and early childhood education, as well as other curriculum topics and issues.

I Am Your Child
http://iamyourchild.org

Information regarding early childhood development is provided on this site. Resources for parents and caregivers are available.

National Association for the Education of Young Children (NAEYC)
http://www.naeyc.org

The National Association for the Education of Young Children provides a useful link from its home page to a "parent information" site.

Results of NICHD Study of Early Child Care
http://156.40.88.3/publications/pubs/early_child_care.htm

This study indicates that the quality of child care for very young children does matter for their cognitive development and their use of language. Quality child care also leads to better mother-child interaction, the study finds.

Vandergrift's Children's Literature Page
http://www.scils.rutgers.edu/special/kay/sharelit.html

This site provides information about children's literature and links to a variety of resources related to literacy for children.

Project Zero
http://pzweb.harvard.edu

Harvard Project Zero, a research group at the Harvard Graduate School of Education, has investigated the development of learning processes in children and adults for 30 years. Today, Project Zero is building on this research to help create communities of reflective, independent learners, to enhance deep understanding within disciplines, and to promote critical and creative thinking. Project Zero's mission is to understand and enhance learning, thinking, and creativity in the arts and other disciplines for individuals and institutions.

UNIT 3: Social and Emotional Development

Max Planck Institute for Psychological Research
http://www.mpipf-muenchen.mpg.de/BCD/bcd_e.htm

Several behavioral and cognitive development research projects are available on this site.

National Child Care Information Center (NCCIC)
http://www.nccic.org

Information about a variety of topics related to child care and development is available on this site. Links to the *Child Care Bulletin,* which can be read online, and to the ERIC database of online and library-based resources are available.

www.dushkin.com/online/

Serendip
http://serendip.brynmawr.edu/serendip/

Organized into five subject areas (brain and behavior, complex systems, genes and behavior, science and culture, and science education), Serendip contains interactive exhibits, articles, links to other resources, and a forum area for comments and discussion.

UNIT 4: Parenting and Family Issues

Facts for Families
http://www.aacap.org/publications/factsfam/index.htm

The American Academy of Child and Adolescent Psychiatry here provides concise, up-to-date information on issues that affect teenagers and their families. Fifty-six fact sheets include issues concerning teenagers, such as coping with life, sad feelings, inability to sleep, getting involved with drugs, or not getting along with family and friends.

Families and Work Institute
http://www.familiesandworkinst.org

Resources from the Families and Work Institute, which conducts policy research on issues related to the changing workforce and operates a national clearinghouse on work and family life, are provided.

The National Academy for Child Development
http://www.nacd.org

This international organization is dedicated to helping children and adults reach their full potential. Its home page presents links to various programs, research, and resources in topics related to the family and society.

National Council on Family Relations
http://www.ncfr.com

This NCFR home page will lead you to articles, research, and a lot of other resources on important issues in family relations, such as stepfamilies, couples, and divorce.

The National Parent Information Network (NPIN)
http://ericps.ed.uiuc.edu/npin/

The National Parent Information Network contains resources related to many of the controversial issues faced by parents raising children in contemporary society. In addition to articles and resources, discussion groups are also available.

Parenting and Families
http://www.cyfc.umn.edu/Parenting/parentlink.html

The University of Minnesota's Children, Youth, and Family Consortium site will lead you to many organizations and other resources related to divorce, single parenting, and step-families, as well as information about other topics of interest in the study of children's development and the family.

Parentsplace.com: Single Parenting
http://www.parentsplace.com/family/singleparent/

This resource focuses on issues concerning single parents and their children. Although the articles range from parenting children from infancy through adolescence, most of the articles deal with middle childhood.

Stepfamily Association of America
http://www.stepfam.org

This Web site is dedicated to educating and supporting stepfamilies and to creating a positive family image.

UNIT 5: Cultural and Societal Influences

Ask NOAH About: Mental Health
http://www.noah-health.org/english/illness/mentalhealth/mental.html

This enormous resource contains information about child and adolescent family problems, mental conditions and disorders, suicide prevention, and much more, all organized in a "clickable" outline form.

Association to Benefit Children (ABC)
http://www.a-b-c.org

ABC presents a network of programs that includes child advocacy, education for disabled children, care for HIV-positive children, employment, housing, foster care, and day care.

Children Now
http://www.childrennow.org

Children Now focuses on improving conditions for children who are poor or at risk. Articles include information on education, influence of media, health, and security.

Council for Exceptional Children
http://www.cec.sped.org

This is the home page for the Council for Exceptional Children, a large professional organization that is dedicated to improving education for children with exceptionalities, students with disabilities, and/or the gifted child. It leads to the ERIC Clearinghouse on disabilities and gifted education and the National Clearinghouse for Professions in Special Education.

National Black Child Development Institute
http://www.nbcdi.org

Resources for improving the quality of life for African American children through public education programs are provided at this site.

Prevent Child Abuse America
http://www.preventchildabuse.org

Dedicated to their child abuse prevention efforts, PCAA's site provides fact sheets and reports that include statistics, a public opinion poll, a 50-state survey, and other resources materials.

We highly recommend that you review our Web site for expanded information and our other product lines. We are continually updating and adding links to our Web site in order to offer you the most usable and useful information that will support and expand the value of your Annual Editions. You can reach us at: *http://www.dushkin.com/annualeditions/*.

UNIT 1

Conception to Birth

Unit Selections

1. **The End of Nature Versus Nurture**, Frans B. M. de Waal
2. **How Old Is Too Old to Have a Baby?** Judith Newman
3. **Fetal Psychology**, Janet L. Hopson

Key Points to Consider

- Where do you stand on the nature/nurture issue? Does it comfort you—or unsettle you—to know that the genes you inherited influence your mental health or sexual orientation, and so on? Given the information in the article "The End of Nature Versus Nurture," how would you respond to someone who claimed that a person's mental health or sexual orientation is "determined" by their genes?

- Although not altogether commonplace, there have always been reports of men over the age of 50–70 years fathering children with younger women. Recently medical and technological advances have now made it possible for women in their 50s and sometimes 60s to bear healthy children. Do you feel that the heightened level of media attention, and sometimes disapproval, directed toward women as opposed to men, is fair or warranted? Do you think it is wrong or problematic for older women to want to bear and raise babies? Why or why not? What about a child born into a family where both parents are in their 50s or early 60s? Do you think there should be some limit to the age at which people are told they cannot or should not be able to have or raise children? Defend your answer.

- Does knowing that a fetus can hear, taste, or feel change your position on abortion? Why or why not? If not, in what way is fetal research beneficial?

 **Links: www.dushkin.com/online/**
These sites are annotated in the World Wide Web pages.

Babyworld
http://www.babyworld.com
Children's Nutrition Research Center (CNRC)
http://www.bcm.tmc.edu/cnrc/
Zero to Three: National Center for Infants, Toddlers, and Families
http://www.zerotothree.org

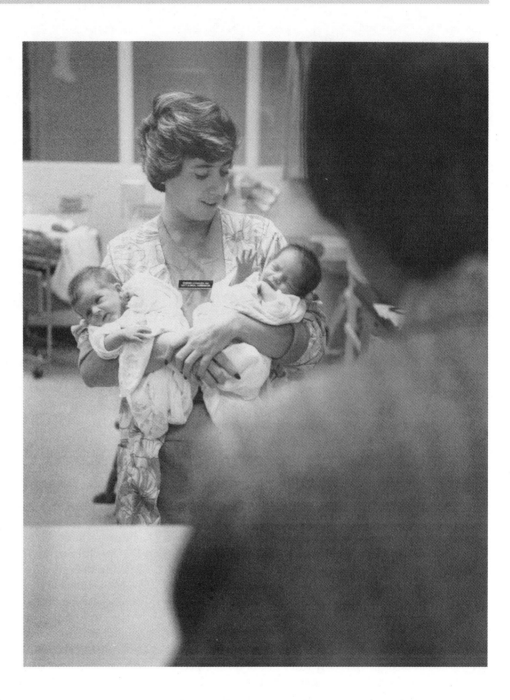

Our understanding of conception and prenatal development is not what it used to be. We are now witness to dramatic changes in reproductive technology. Advances in this new "prenatal science" include fertility treatments for couples who have difficulty conceiving and a host of prenatal diagnostic tests, such as amniocentesis and alpha-fetoprotein testing, which assess the well-being of the fetus as well as detect genetic or chromosomal problems.

Perhaps the oldest debate in the study of human development is the "nature versus nurture" question. Scientists have moved beyond thinking of development as due to either genetics or environment, now recognizing that nature and nurture interact to shape us. Each human is a biological organism, and each is surrounded, from the moment of conception, by environmental forces. According to "The End of Nature Versus Nurture," author Frans de Waal argues for breaking down the dichotomy and instead building research programs that integrate developmental, genetic, evolutionary, and cultural approaches and theories to better understand human behavior.

Amazing new fertility techniques now make it possible for women and couples who have postponed childbearing to have the chance to have children in their 40s, 50s, and even into their 60s. While these technological advances have done much to permit women and older professional couples with the opportunity to bear children, author Judith Newman discusses the significant personal, ethical, and medical risks and gains that medical advances now afford in "How Old Is Too Old to Have a Baby?"

Recent research on prenatal development continues to yield new and startling data. For example, "Fetal Psychology" describes new abilities of the fetus such as prenatal hearing, personality, and dreaming and the critical brain developments that underlie these skills.

The End of Nature versus Nurture

Is human behavior determined by genetics or by environment? It may be time to abandon the dichotomy

by Frans B. M. de Waal

The defenders of nature and nurture have been at each other's throats for as long as I can remember. Whereas biologists have always believed that genes have something to do with human behavior, social scientists have flocked en masse to the opposite position: that we are fully and entirely our own creation, free from the chains of biology.

I felt the heat of this debate in the 1970s whenever, in lectures for general audiences, I mentioned sex differences in chimpanzees, such as that males are more aggressive and more ambitious than females. There would be howls of protest. Wasn't I projecting my own values onto these poor animals? Why did I even bother to compare the sexes? Did I perhaps have a hidden agenda?

Nowadays the same sort of information makes people yawn! Even direct comparisons between human and ape behavior, something that used to be taboo, fail to get anyone excited. Everyone has heard that men are from Mars and women from Venus. Everyone has seen, in *Time* and *Newsweek*, PET scans of the human brain engaged in various tasks, with different areas lighting up in male and female brains.

This time, however, it is my turn to be troubled. Instead of celebrating the victory of the biological approach, I regard some of the contemporary dichotomies between men and women as gross simplifications rendered politi-

cally correct by a fashionable amount of male-bashing (for example, when normal hormonal effects are referred to as "testosterone poisoning"). We remain as far removed as ever from a sophisticated understanding of the interplay between genes and environment. Society has let the pendulum swing wildly back from nurture to nature, leaving behind a number of bewildered social scientists. Yet we still love to phrase everything in terms of one influence or the other, rather than both.

It is impossible to explore where we may be heading 50 years from now without looking back an equal number of years at the charged history of the nature/nurture controversy. The debate is so emotional because any stance one takes comes with serious political implications. Positions have ranged from an unfounded faith in human flexibility by reformists to an obsession with blood and race by conservatives. Each in their own way, these positions have caused incalculable human suffering in the past century.

Learning and Instinct

Fifty years ago the two dominant schools of thought about animal and human behavior had opposite outlooks. Teaching animals arbitrary actions such as lever-pressing, American behaviorists came to view all behavior as the product of trial-and-error learning. This process was considered so universal that differences among species were irrelevant: learning applied to all animals, including humans. As B. F. Skinner, the founder of behaviorism, bluntly put it: "Pigeon, rat, monkey, which is which? It doesn't matter."

In contrast, the ethological school in Europe focused on naturalistic behavior. Each animal species is born with a number of so-called fixed-action patterns that undergo little modification by the environment. These and other species-specific behaviors represent evolutionary adaptations. Thus, no one needs to teach humans how to laugh or cry; these are innate signals, universally used and understood. Similarly, the spider does not need to learn how to construct a web. She is born with a battery of spinnerets (spinning tubes connected to silk glands) as well as a behavioral program that "instructs" her how to weave threads together.

Because of their simplicity, both views of behavior had enormous appeal. And although both paid homage to evolution, they sometimes did so in a superficial, arm-waving sort of way. Behaviorists stressed the continuities between humans and other animals, attributing them to evolution. But because for them behavior was learned rather than inborn, they ignored the genetic side, which is really what evolution is all about. While it is true that evolution implies continuity, it also implies diversity: each animal is adapted to a specific way of life in a specific environment. As is evident from Skinner's statement, this point was blithely ignored.

Similarly, some ethologists had rather vague evolutionary notions, emphasizing phylogenetic descent rather than the processes of natural selection. They saw behavioral traits, such as the inhibition of aggression, as good for the species. The argument was that if animals were to kill one another in fights, the species would not survive. This may be true, but animals have perfectly selfish reasons to avoid the escalation of fights that may harm themselves and their relationships. Hence, these ideas have now been replaced by theories about how traits benefit the actor and its kin; effects on the species as a whole are considered a mere by-product.

Behaviorism started losing its grip with the discovery that learning is not the same for all situations and species. For example, a rat normally links actions with effects only if the two immediately follow each other. So it would be very slow to learn to press a bar if a reward followed minutes later. When it comes to food that makes it sick, however, a delay of hours between consumption and the negative sensation still induces food aversion. Apparently, animals are specialized learners, being best at those contingencies that are most important for survival.

At the same time that behaviorists were forced to adopt the premises of evolutionary biology and to consider the world outside the laboratory, ethologists and ecologists were laying the groundwork for the neo-Darwinian revolution of the 1970s. The pioneer here was Dutch ethologist Nikolaas Tinbergen, who conducted ingenious field experiments on the survival value of animal behavior. He understood, for instance, why many birds remove eggshells from the nest after the chicks have hatched. Because the outside of a shell is colored for camouflage but the inside is not, predators such as crows easily locate eggs if broken shells are placed next to them. Throwing out the pieces is an automatic response favored by natural selection because the birds that practice this behavior have more surviving offspring.

Others developed theories to explain behavior that at first sight does not seem to help the actor but someone else. Such "altruism" can be seen in ant soldiers giving their lives in defense of their colony or dolphins lifting a drowning companion to the surface. Biologists assumed that natural selection will allow for assistance among relatives as a means of promoting the same genes. Or, if two animals are unrelated, the favor granted by one must be returned at some future time.

The scientists felt so confident about their explanations of cooperative animal societies that they could not resist extending these ideas to our own species. They saw the hugely cooperative enterprise of human society as based on the same premise of family values and economic tit-for-tat.

It fell to an American expert on ants, Edward O. Wilson, to deliver the news in 1975 that a great deal of human behavior was ripe for the Darwinian perspective and that the social sciences should prepare themselves to work together with biologists on this endeavor. Thus far the two disciplines had led separate lives, but from the perspective of a biologist social science is not much more than the study of animal behavior focused on a single species: ours. Because this is not how social scientists see their work, proposals for a united framework were not kindly received. One of Wilson's outraged opponents even poured cold water over Wilson's head after he gave a lecture. For reasons explained below, his new synthesis, dubbed "sociobiology," was equated with the race policies of the past and ultimately with the Holocaust.

Although the criticism was patently unfair—Wilson was offering evolutionary explanations, not policy suggestions—we shouldn't be surprised that the topic of human biology arouses strong emotions.

Burdens of the Past

It is generally believed that some human behavior can easily be changed because it is learned, whereas other behavior resists modification because it is part of our biological heritage.

Ideologues of all colors have grasped this division to argue for the innate nature of certain human characteristics (for example, purported race differences in intelligence) and the plasticity of others (such as the ability to overcome gender stereotypes). Thus, Communism was founded on great confidence in human malleability. Because people, unlike social insects, resist submerging individuality for the greater good, some regimes accompanied their revolutions with massive indoctrination efforts. All of this proved in vain, however. Communism went under because of an economic incentive structure that was out of touch with human nature. Unfortunately, it did so only after having caused great misery and death.

Even more disastrous was the embrace of biology by Nazi Germany. Here, too, the collective (*das Volk*) was placed above the individual, but instead of relying on social engineering the method of choice was genetic manipulation. People were classified into "superior" and "inferior" types, the first of which needed to be protected against contamination by the second. In the horrible medical language of the Nazis, a healthy *Volk* required the cutting out of all "cancerous" elements. This idea was followed to its extreme in a manner that Western civilization has vowed never to forget.

Don't think that the underlying selectionist ideology was restricted to this particular time and place, however. In the early part of the 20th century, the eugenics movement—which sought to improve humanity by "breeding from the fitter stocks"—enjoyed widespread appeal among intellectuals in both the U.S. and Great Britain. Based on ideas going back to Plato's *Republic*, sterilization of the mentally handicapped and of criminals was considered perfectly acceptable. And social Darwinism—the idea that in a laissez-faire capitalist economy the strong will outcompete the weak, resulting in general improvement of the population—still inspires political agendas today. In this view, the poor should not be aided in their struggle for existence so as not to upset the natural order.

Given these ideologies, it is understandable why suppressed categories of people, such as minorities and women, fail to see biology as a friend. I would argue, however, that the danger comes from both directions, from biological determinism as well as its opposite, the denial of basic human needs and the belief that we can be everything we want to be. The hippie communes of the 1960s, the Israeli kibbutzim and the feminist revolution all sought to redefine humans. But denial of sexual jealousy, the parent-child bond or gender differences can be carried only so far before a counter-movement will seek to balance cultural trends with evolved human inclinations.

What makes the present era different is that the genocide of World War II is fading into memory while at the same time the evidence for a connection between genes and behavior is mounting. Studies of twins reared apart have reached the status of common knowledge, and almost every week newspapers report a new human gene. There is evidence for genes involved in schizophrenia, epilepsy and Alzheimer's and even in common behavioral traits such as thrill-seeking. We are also learning more about genetic and neurological differences between men and women, as well as between gay and straight men. For example, a small region of the brain in transsexual men (who dress and behave like women) resembles the same region in women's brains.

The list of such scientific advances is getting longer by the day, resulting in a critical mass of evidence that is impossible to ignore. Understandably, academics who have spent their life condemning the idea that biology influences human behavior are reluctant to change course. But they are being overtaken by the general public, which seems to have accepted that genes are involved in just about everything we do and are. Concurrently resistance to comparisons with other animals has dissipated because of a stream of television nature programs that has brought exotic wildlife into our homes while showing animals to be quite a bit smarter and more interesting than people used to believe.

Studies of chimpanzees and bonobos, such as those by Jane Goodall and myself, show that countless human practices and potentials, from politics and child-rearing to violence and even morality, have parallels in the lives of our closest animal relatives. How can we maintain the dualisms of the past—between humans and animals and between body and mind—in the face of all this evidence to the contrary? Current knowledge about our biological background simply doesn't permit a return to the tabula rasa views of the past.

This doesn't solve the problem of ideological abuse, however. If anything, it makes things worse. So long as people have political agendas, they will depict human nature one way or another for their own purposes. Conservatives like to point out that people are naturally selfish, whereas liberals argue that we have evolved to be social and cooperative. The obvious correctness of both influences goes to show what is wrong with simple-minded genetic determinism.

The Best of Both Worlds

Because genetic language ("a gene for x") plays into our sound-bite culture, there is all the more reason to educate the public that genes, by themselves, are like seeds dropped onto the pavement: powerless to produce anything. When scientists say that a trait is inherited, all they mean is that part of its variability is explained by genetic factors. That the environment usually explains at least as much tends to be forgotten.

As Hans Kummer, a Swiss primatologist, remarked years ago, to try to determine how much of a trait is produced by genes and how much by the environment is as useless as asking whether the drumming that we hear in the distance is made by the percussionist or his instrument. On the other hand, if we pick up distinct sounds on different occasions, we can legitimately ask whether the variation is caused by different drummers or by different drums. This is the only sort of question science addresses when it looks into genetic versus environmental effects.

I foresee a continued mapping of the links between genes and behavior, a much more precise knowledge of how the brain works and a gradual adoption of the evolutionary paradigm in the social sciences. Charles Darwin's portrait will finally decorate the walls of departments of psychology and sociology! But one would hope that all of this will be accompanied by continued assessment of the ethical and political implications of behavioral science.

Traditionally, scientists have acted as if it is none of their business how the information they produce is being used. During some periods they have even actively assisted in political abuse. One notable exception was, of course, Albert Einstein, who may serve as a model of the kind of moral awareness needed in the behavioral and social sciences. If history teaches us anything, it is that it is critical that we remain on the alert against misinterpretations and simplifications. No one is in a better position than the scientists themselves to warn against distortions and to explain the complexities.

In which direction the thinking may develop can perhaps be illustrated with an example from the crossroads between cultural and evolutionary anthropology. Sigmund Freud and many traditional anthropologists, such as Claude Lévi-Strauss, have assumed that the human incest taboo serves to suppress sexual urges between family members. Freud believed that "the earliest sexual excitations of youthful human beings are invariably of an incestuous character." Hence, the incest taboo was seen as the ultimate victory of culture over nature.

In contrast, Edward Westermarck, a Finnish sociologist who lived at about the same time as Freud, hypothesized that early familiarity (such as between mother and child and between siblings) kills sexual desire. Little or no sexual attraction is found, he argued, between individuals who have grown up together. A fervent Darwinian, Westermarck proposed this as an evolved mechanism designed to prevent the deleterious consequences of inbreeding.

In the largest-scale study on this issue to date, Arthur P. Wolf, an anthropologist at Stanford University, examined the marital histories of 14,400 women in a "natural experiment" carried out in Taiwan. Families in this region used to adopt and raise future daughters-in-law, which meant that intended marriage partners grew up together from early childhood. Wolf compared these marriages with those arranged between men and women who did not meet until the wedding day. Using divorce and fertility rates as gauges of marital happiness and sexual activity, respectively, the data strongly supported the Westermarck effect: association in the first years of life appeared to compromise adult marital compatibility. Nonhuman primates are subject to the same mechanism. Many primates prevent inbreeding through migration of one sex or the other at puberty. The migratory sex meets

new, unrelated mates, whereas the resident sex gains genetic diversity from the outside. But close kin who stay together also generally avoid sexual intercourse.

Kisaburo Tokuda first observed this in a group of Japanese macaques at the Kyoto zoo in the 1950s. A young adult male that had risen to the top rank made full use of his sexual privileges, mating frequently with all the females except for one: his mother. This was not an isolated case: mother-son matings are strongly suppressed in all primates. Even in bonobos—probably the most sexually active primates on the earth—this is the one partner combination in which sex is extremely rare or absent. Incest avoidance has now been convincingly demonstrated in a host of primates, and the mediating mechanism is thought to be early familiarity.

The Westermarck effect serves as a showcase for Darwinian approaches to human behavior because it so clearly rests on a combination of nature and nurture. The framework includes a developmental component (learned sexual aversion), an innate component (the effect of early familiarity), a cultural component (some cultures raise unrelated children together, others raise siblings of the opposite sex apart, but most have family arrangements that automatically lead to sexual inhibitions among relatives), a sound evolutionary reason (suppression of inbreeding) and direct parallels with animal behavior. On top of this comes the cultural taboo, which is unique to our species. An intriguing question is whether the incest taboo merely serves to formalize and strengthen the Westermarck effect or whether it adds a substantially new dimension.

The unexpected richness of a research program that integrates developmental, genetic, evolutionary and cultural approaches to a well-circumscribed phenomenon demonstrates the power of breaking down old barriers between disciplines. Most likely what will happen in the next millenium is that evolutionary approaches to human behavior will become more and more sophisticated by explicitly taking cultural flexibility into account. Hence, the traditional either/or approach to learning and instinct will be replaced by a more integrated perspective. In the meantime, students of animal behavior will become more interested in environmental effects on behavior and especially—in animals such as primates and marine mammals—the possibility of cultural transmission of information and habits. For example, some chimpanzee communities use stones to crack nuts in the forest, whereas other communities have the same nuts and stones available but don't do anything with them. Such differences are unexplained by genetic variation.

These two developments together will weaken the dichotomies popular today to the point of eliminating them. Rather than looking at culture as the antithesis of nature, we will be gaining a much more profound understanding of human behavior by silently carrying the old nature/nurture debate to its grave.

FURTHER INFORMATION

SOCIOBIOLOGY: THE NEW SYNTHESIS. Edward O. Wilson. Belknap Press (Harvard University Press), 1975. 25th anniversary edition (in press).

SEXUAL ATTRACTION AND CHILDHOOD ASSOCIATION: A CHINESE BRIEF FOR EDWARD WESTERMARCK. Arthur P. Wolf. Stanford University Press, 1995.

THE MISMEASURE OF MAN. Revised edition. Stephen Jay Gould. W. W. Norton, 1996.

GOOD NATURED: THE ORIGINS OF RIGHT AND WRONG IN HUMANS AND OTHER ANIMALS. Frans de Waal. Harvard University Press, 1997.

FRANS B. M. DE WAAL was trained as a zoologist and ethologist in the European tradition in his native country, the Netherlands. He has been in the U.S. since 1981 and is currently director of the Living Links Center at the Yerkes Regional Primate Research Center in Atlanta and is also C. H. Candler Professor of Primate Behavior in the psychology department at Emory University. His research includes social interactions in primates as well as the origins of morality and justice in human society.

How Old Is Too Old to Have a Baby?

Fertility technology is advancing at such an astonishing pace that couples who fail to have children in their forties could realistically wait until their sixties to try again

BY JUDITH NEWMAN

TO BECOME A FATHER at 52 is unusual. To become a mother at 52 is to defy nature. Alan and Deirdre, both 52, don't want to let many of their friends and colleagues in on their secret yet, in case something goes wrong. But they are doing everything in their power to have a baby. They have the money, and they have the will. Deirdre, a trim, athletic researcher at a medical school in Connecticut, has three adult children from a previous marriage; Alan, a college English professor, has never had kids. "I always wanted children," he says. "Three years ago, when I found this woman I loved who was my own age, I thought, 'Well, that's one dream I'll have to relinquish.'"

Deirdre had already gone through menopause. By supplying the correct amounts of estrogen and progesterone via hormone therapy, it is relatively easy to make the uterus of a post-menopausal woman hospitable to a fetus. But even then, the chance of a woman Deirdre's age getting pregnant with her own eggs is non-existent. So doctors suggested the couple consider implanting a donor egg fertilized with Alan's sperm. Egg donation is no longer considered cutting-edge medicine, but using the procedure to impregnate a woman over 50 is. Still, Alan and Deirdre

were overjoyed. "I thought, 'Isn't science great?'" Alan says.

In a few weeks, Machelle Seibel, a reproductive endocrinologist at the Fertility Center of New England, will mix the eggs of a much younger woman with Alan's sperm and introduce the resulting embryos to Deirdre's uterus. Her chances of giving birth will then rocket from less than 1 percent to 50 percent. "I would have considered doing this even if I hadn't remarried," Deirdre says with a lopsided grin. "The idea of having another child at this stage is compelling."

Not that Deirdre and Alan are unaware of the problems of being older parents. They worry about how they'll function with little sleep—"although I needed a lot of sleep even when I was in college," Alan says—and they are concerned that they might not be around to see their child come of age. If Deirdre gets pregnant, they plan to move to the Midwest to be near Alan's four brothers and sisters. "As a hedge against possible early death, we want our child to be surrounded by as much family as possible," Alan says.

Deirdre's three children, all in their twenties, are trying to be supportive. But they're skeptical. "Independently they came to me and said they thought it would be weird to be their age and have parents in

their late seventies," Deirdre says. "But I look at it like this: Our definition of 'family' has expanded. Now there are gay and adoptive and single-parent families who've used assisted technology. So although an 'older-parent family' is what we'll be, it's only one of several variations."

Twenty-two years after the world's first test-tube baby was conceived through in vitro fertilization, science is giving men and women—at least those who can afford the steep medical fees—increasing flexibility to alter the seasons of their lives. Infertility treatments once considered revolutionary are now commonplace: If a man has a low sperm count, sperm cells can be retrieved from a testicle for direct injection into an egg's cytoplasm. If the shell of an egg has hardened because of age, doctors can hatch it in the lab and then implant it on the uterine wall. If a woman has stopped producing eggs, she can avail herself of drugs to induce ovulation, as well as donor eggs or donor embryos. These days, the science of assisted reproductive technology is advancing at such a rapid rate that laboratory researchers say it will soon be medically possible for even a centenarian to give birth. But such tinkering with the biological clock begs a commonsense question: How old is too old to have a baby? And this seemingly straightforward question trickles into a cascade of other questions: How old is too old for parents? For children? For society?

When it comes to treating women for infertility, the American Society for Reproductive Medicine would like to draw its line in the sand at menopause. "Around 50, that's when reproductive processes have physiologically stopped, and therefore the intervention and treatment by physicians should also stop," says Robert Stillman, a former member of the society's board of directors. "Infertility is a medical disorder, affected by the reproductive life span. Just as we wouldn't consider inducing a prepubescent individual to conceive—although we could—we shouldn't induce pregnancy in someone who's gone through menopause."

In recent years, an increasing number of women have chosen to spend more time building a career, or looking for the right mate, before having children. Some have been shocked to belatedly discover there is no denying a fact of nature. Without any scientific intervention, childbearing is out of the question for most women by the time they reach their early forties. Between the ages of 35 and 40, fertility tapers off, and after 43 it pretty much plummets off the cliff. That is because something about the aging process upsets the process of meiosis, the nuclear division of the ovum or sperm in which chromosomes are reduced to half their original number. Sex cells do not divide properly, and there are too many or too few chromosomes in the egg or sperm. For women in their mid-forties, there is a dramatic increase in the risk that their eggs will have the wrong number of chromosomes after ovulation. Hence the difficulty in getting, and staying, pregnant. And unlike a man, whose sperm supply is constantly renewing itself, a woman is born with all the eggs she'll ever have. In fact, ovaries start aging before a woman's birth. A 20-week-old fetus has about 7 million eggs. Eighteen weeks later, at birth, that number has been decimated to less than 2 million. Even though the eggs remain unused throughout childhood, by puberty the egg supply has dropped to 400,000—less than 6 percent of what the child started with. By menopause, the egg larder is close to empty.

Even when an older mother manages to get pregnant, she and her baby face additional medical hurdles. With mothers over 35, there is a greater risk of hypertension and diabetes for themselves, and likely a greater risk of juvenile diabetes for the children. A 1995 Swedish study found that women born to mothers age 45 or older had a slightly higher chance of developing breast cancer than women born to younger mothers. Most well known is the increased risk of certain chromosomal abnormalities such as Down's syndrome, in which there is an extra set of genes in each cell.

Studies suggest that being the child of an older father also carries risk. Because older sperm tend to have more chromosomal mutations—ranging in seriousness from harmless to lethal—there is among older fathers a higher rate of kids born with certain rare tumors, neural-tube defects, congenital cataracts, and upper limb defects. Curiously, there's also a higher rate of homosexual children born to older dads.

While men experience some decline in the number of sperm, motility, and morphology—the number of normal sperm—after age 40, it's generally not enough to prevent them from becoming fathers. There are typically 150 to 300 million sperm released in one ejaculation. Even if the number drops by 50 percent, there are still pretty good odds there will be some keepers.

And now, technology has advanced to the point where even men with extremely poor sperm quality can father children. With intracytoplasmic sperm injection, an embryologist can inject a single sperm into the cytoplasm of an egg with a microscopic needle while bypassing the normal cascade of chemical reactions necessary for fertilization. The procedure, which has only been around since 1992, is a primary reason for the speed-of-light development of fertility treatment for aging would-be parents—because it's not only sperm that can be injected into the egg. The processes of microinjection and micromanipulation of egg and sperm are making a wider array of new treatments possible.

For example, embryologist Jacques Cohen, scientific director at the Institute for Reproductive Medicine and Science of Saint Barnabas in Livingston, New Jersey, has developed a procedure called cytoplasmic transfer that shows promise for assisting women approaching their early forties who either can't get pregnant through in vitro fertilization or have embryos of such poor quality they don't survive. Doctors take the cytoplasm of a youthful and healthy egg—containing not the DNA but the proteins and enzymes for healthy cell growth—and inject it into the problematic egg to boost its quality. Possible health risks with the procedure have not yet been conclusively studied and there are troubling ethical questions. (See box "Can a Baby Have Three Parents?") But out of 26 attempts, the technique has resulted in 12 live births.

Jamie Grifo, director of New York University's reproductive endocrinology unit, is further refining another technique to assist women between 42 and 45, whose chances of having a child with their own eggs hover around 5 percent. He takes an older woman's egg and extracts the nucleus, which contains the DNA. Then he removes the nucleus from the donor egg of a much younger woman and in its place microinjects the genetic material of the older woman. The procedure, attempted on two women last year, resulted in fertilized embryos but not babies. Grifo and his team went back to the lab, perfecting the process on mice. The result: baby mice.

Double Trouble

Since the advent of in vitro fertilization two decades ago, there has been an explosion in the number of multiple births, particularly among women over 40. Statistics released last September by the Centers for Disease Control reveal a 52 percent increase overall in twin births between 1980 and 1997. Among women between 40 and 44, the increase in the number of twins born was 63 percent, and among women between 45 and 49 it was a staggering 1,000 percent. The ages of the mothers had less effect on the health or survival of the infants than the pregnancy complications generally associated with multiple births. For example, the risk of a very low birth weight is eight times higher for twins than for single births. The ultimate impact of multiple births on the lives of older parents is immeasurable. "Keeping up with two kids instead of one is a real challenge," says Machelle Seibel. "The increase in energy required is exponential rather than additive."

Grifo's groundbreaking work could provide the answer women like Alison Carlson are looking for. Carlson is a golden girl: blond, sunny, a former professional tennis coach in San Francisco. When she got married last year to a younger man and started trying to get pregnant at 42, she assumed she'd succeed quickly. "I was an athlete," she says. "I felt

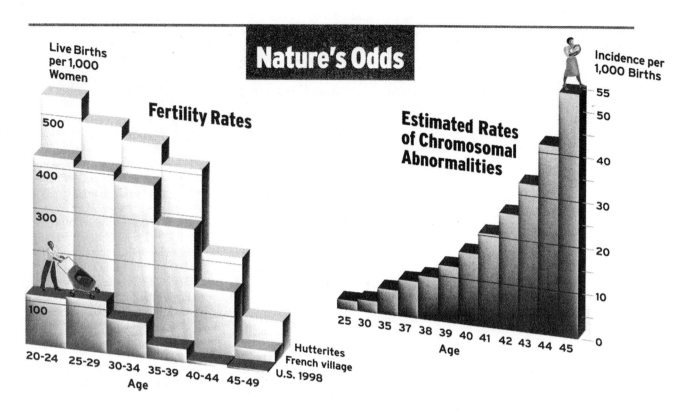

Nature's Odds

Fertility Rates

Live Births per 1,000 Women

Age: 20-24, 25-29, 30-34, 35-39, 40-44, 45-49

Hutterites
French village
U.S. 1998

Estimated Rates of Chromosomal Abnormalities

Incidence per 1,000 Births

Age: 25 30 35 37 38 39 40 41 42 43 44 45

Dale Glasgand

LEFT: Contemporary birth records of the Hutterites, a religious sect in the western U.S. and Canada that does not practice birth control, and seventeenth-century birth records from a French village reveal a similar pattern: Natural fertility rates among women drop off precipitously around age 40. The latest available overall birthrates for U.S. women follow the same downward trend but are lower across the board because of the prevalence of birth control and a tendency of women to marry later in life. RIGHT: Statistics indicate that the risk of women having children with chromosomal abnormalities, including Down's syndrome, rises steadily from 2.1 per thousand births at age 25 to 53.7 per thousand births at age 45.

the normal rules wouldn't apply to me." At first it seemed she would be right. In her initial round of in vitro fertilization, Carlson produced an impressive 27 eggs, and 25 were fertilized: "I was a champ." She got pregnant but quickly miscarried. Forty-five percent of women over 40 do, usually because of chromosomal abnormalities in their eggs. "Suddenly I felt like I should buy one of these T-shirts that say 'I Can't Believe I Forgot to Have Children.'" Carlson says that when she tried again, she failed to get pregnant at all.

Intellectually, Carlson knows the problem is age, but emotionally she cannot accept it. Like so many men and women over 40 who begin fertility treatments, she feels pressure to keep trying. "I'm embarrassed because, first, I felt I was being so arrogant," she says. "Like, here we all are, a bunch of baby boomers who went to college in the second wave of feminism, dedicated to having important careers before having

babies, and then paying gobs of money so science can give us what we want. I'm appalled at my own sense of entitlement."

Given the anguish many aging baby boomers now experience trying to get pregnant, it's hard to fathom that the future holds no less than the end of infertility. Doctors recently discovered how to freeze a woman's eggs when she's young and then thaw them when she's ready to get pregnant. A woman could finish college and graduate school, launch a career, and then start a family with eggs she parked on ice at age 18.

Banking individual eggs is just the beginning. Recently Kutluk Oktay, the chief of reproductive endocrinology and infertility at New York Methodist Hospital in Brooklyn, has been experimenting with freezing and transplanting swatches of ovarian tissue. Each bit of tissue contains thousands of immature follicle eggs. While individual, already-developed eggs die

easily when frozen, immature follicle eggs embedded in the ovarian tissue fare a lot better. Oktay has already tried the technique on a 30-year-old dancer from Arizona who'd had her first ovary removed at 17 because of cysts but had the foresight to have her second ovary frozen. Last fall, Oktay sewed 80 small pieces of the tissue back into her pelvis and revived her menstrual cycle. The woman is not trying to conceive. But Oktay's colleague, Roger Gosden, now reproductive biology research director of McGill University's Royal Victoria Hospital in Montreal, has removed the ovaries of sheep, frozen them, thawed them, sutured them back in the sheep—and gotten lambs aplenty.

Of course cryopreservation will not help those whose eggs are already sitting on the porch in little rocking chairs. But researchers have found ways to keep old eggs alive. Jon Tilly, the director of the Vincent Center for Reproductive Biology at Massachusetts General Hospital in Boston, has been studying genetically altered mice to better understand the process of apoptosis, or natural cell death. Cells are programmed to die: Fifty or sixty genes, maybe more, regulate their expiration. One specifically involved in the death of immature eggs in the ovaries is known as the bax gene. When Tilly and his researchers studied mice that lacked the bax gene, they found that 24-month-old females—the equivalent of 80- to 100-year-old humans—still have functioning, estrogen-producing ovaries. "We were pretty amazed," says Tilly. "And the bax gene has a precise counterpart in humans that appears to be responsible for the decimation of eggs during menopause." Silencing of one of the "cell death" genes may be the first step in finding treatments to help woman delay menopause or avoid the health problems—osteoporosis, heart disease—associated with the cessation of estrogen production. Tilly also believes that in the not-wildly-distant future the ability to suppress the bax gene in women's ovaries may prolong their fertility too. He is quick to add, however, that even though the old female mice with newly viable eggs were allowed to cavort with young, studly mice, they did not produce offspring. This is because older mice lose the capacity to excrete adequate levels of two hormones: one that stimulates egg follicles to grow and mature and another that causes the ripened egg to be released from the ovary into the reproductive tract.

Another approach to ending infertility involves beating the numbers game. What if a woman had an unlimited number of eggs? This may someday be possible if researchers can get somatic cells—that is, cells from anywhere in the body—to act like sex cells. Normal cells are diploid, with 46 chromosomes—23 from one's father and 23 from one's mother. The gonads (testicles and ovaries) divide the chromosomes to create haploid cells, namely spermatozoa and eggs. As the eggs age, most suffer from aneuploidy, the uneven division of the chromosomes. Anything other than 23 sets of chromosomes makes the egg either entirely unviable, or viable but resulting in abnormalities like Down's syndrome. It is not that the eggs, in their undeveloped state, are abnormal; it's that something about the machinery of meiosis—the chromosomal division at ovulation—goes awry as women age. The key to fixing this problem is to make faux eggs—normal body cells that behave like eggs by undergoing meiosis. Thus, anyone 18 to

100 would have an unlimited supply of easily harvested "sex cells."

This is exactly what Cohen and some other researchers are working on now. Bioethicists balk, because the process sounds like a kissing cousin to cloning. But it's not. The resulting cell has half its mother's chromosomes and, when united with sperm, could be expected to create a bona fide, half-his, half-hers human. The catch is that the parents could theoretically be 100 or more years old. "This is going to involve some major discussions about what's clinically acceptable and what's socially acceptable," Cohen says.

Can a Baby Have Three Parents?

One new fertility treatment called cytoplasmic transfer involves taking a younger woman's "egg white," which contains the proteins and enzymes necessary for proper growth, and microinjecting it into the egg of an older woman. The idea is to restore healthy components to the older woman's egg, making fertilization and pregnancy more likely. The problem, says Machelle Seibel, is that mitochondria—tiny football-shaped structures in the cytoplasm that are the energy powerhouses of a cell—also contain some DNA. And scientists know that there are a number of inherited mitochondrial DNA diseases, resulting in health problems that range from the mild to the fatal. (Problems as varied as sudden infant death syndrome and Alzheimer's are thought to stem from genetic defects in the mitochondria.) Theoretically, the young woman giving her cytoplasm becomes the third parent, capable of passing along some genetic information, including her family diseases. "I don't think this component of the procedure is completely appreciated by the providers or the receivers," says Seibel. "Cytoplasmic transfer may be fine, but its safety is unproven. This makes me a little uncomfortable."

Of course, even if they have all the financial resources in the world, most couples past the age of retirement probably won't want to start raising children. "This won't be some huge public policy issue," says Arthur Caplan, director of the Univer-

sity of Pennsylvania's Center for Bioethics. "It's not like you'll see all these people running from nursing homes to birthing centers." But, Caplan adds, the very fact that 50-year-old mothers and fathers could become relatively commonplace raises another issue. "One of the ethical questions becomes: What's in the best interest of the child? And the answer is simple: It's good not to be an orphan. A good, loving environment requires one parent. So if a father is 20 and a mother 80, that's not a problem. If the father is 60 and the mother 40, well, one should think about the implications of depriving a child of grandparents. It's not morally reprehensible, but it's an issue. Now, if both parents are in their sixties"—as was the case in 1996 with Arceli Keh, the 63-year-old Filipino who gave birth after lying about her age to her fertility specialists in California—"that's a problem."

Contemplating their own untimely demise won't deter truly determined older parent wanna-bes, like Eileen and Charles Volz of Millbury, Massachusetts. Eileen, a certified public accountant, was 42 and had just married Charles, a digital commerce executive, in 1992 when she was diagnosed with breast cancer. Radiation and chemotherapy put her into immediate menopause, but she overcame the cancer. Four years passed before she and her husband heard about egg donation. "People thought we were a little nuts," says Charles Volz. "I mean, I already had three children, and she had survived breast cancer—why should we tempt fate?"

One look at their son, C.J., answers the question. On her first try at Machelle Seibel's clinic, she got pregnant with a donor egg and had C.J. at 48. "I never for a moment felt he wasn't mine," Eileen says. "Genetics is the smallest part of being a mother."

Eileen Volz is now 50; her husband is 48. They tried a second round of egg donation, which failed, but they are contemplating a third. Sure they'll be collecting Social Security by the time C.J. is ready to head off to college. But Charles Volz speaks for older parents everywhere when he offers this Pollyannaish view of his midlife adventure: "It's not a problem at all. Hey, I'm going to live forever."

Perhaps the biggest question for science and society will not be answered for a number of years, until the first generation of children born to older parents through assisted reproductive technology enters their teenage years: What happens when children nature did not intend to create become adults? Already there are some troubling questions about the 20,000 children conceived throughout the world by intra-cytoplasmic sperm injection. Aggressively injecting a sperm into an egg manually has been found to change a whole sequence of molecular events in fertilization; for example, the DNA packaged in the head of the sperm unravels more slowly than in normal fertilization, throwing off the timing of the process. Scientists worry that although there hasn't been an obvious increase in birth defects so far, sex chromosome abnormalities may show up when the children reach puberty. One 1998 study in Belgium showed that of 1,082 prenatal tests on intracytoplasmic sperm injection pregnancies, one in 120 had sex chromosome abnormalities, as compared to a general population figure of one in 500 pregnancies.

"Fertility is a unique field in some respects," says Massachusetts General's Jon Tilly. "In most fields of scientific inquiry, most of the problems are worked out in an-imal models. But here, technology is moving so fast, and people are so desperate for answers, that work on humans is paralleling work on animals. That may turn out to be good, because we are accelerating the application of our knowledge. But it may be bad, because we don't know what's safe. We don't know about unforeseen problems. There may be reasons the body is not designed to be reproducing after its early forties."

FETAL PSYCHOLOGY

Behaviorally
speaking, there's little
difference between a newborn
baby and a 32-week-old fetus.
A new wave of research suggests
that the fetus can feel, dream, even
enjoy *The Cat in the Hat*. **The
abortion debate may never
be the same**.

By Janet L. Hopson

The scene never fails to give goose bumps: the baby, just seconds old and still dewy from the womb, is lifted into the arms of its exhausted but blissful parents. They gaze adoringly as their new child stretches and squirms, scrunches its mouth and opens its eyes. To anyone watching this tender vignette, the message is unmistakable. Birth is the beginning of it all, ground zero, the moment from which the clock starts ticking. Not so, declares Janet DiPietro. Birth may be a grand occasion, says the Johns Hopkins University psychologist, but "it is a trivial event in development. Nothing neurologically interesting happens."

Armed with highly sensitive and sophisticated monitoring gear, DiPietro and other researchers today are discovering that the real action starts weeks earlier. At 32 weeks of gestation—two months before a baby is considered fully prepared for the world, or "at term"—a fetus is behaving almost exactly as a newborn. And it continues to do so for the next 12 weeks.

A fetus spends hours in the rapid eye movement sleep of dreams.

As if overturning the common conception of infancy weren't enough, scientists are creating a startling new picture of intelligent life in the womb. Among the revelations:

• By nine weeks, a developing fetus can hiccup and react to loud noises. By the end of the second trimester it can hear.

• Just as adults do, the fetus experiences the rapid eye movement (REM) sleep of dreams.

• The fetus savors its mother's meals, first picking up the food tastes of a culture in the womb.

• Among other mental feats, the fetus can distinguish between the voice of Mom and that of a stranger, and respond to a familiar story read to it.

• Even a premature baby is aware, feels, responds, and adapts to its environment.

• Just because the fetus is responsive to certain stimuli doesn't mean that it should be the target of efforts to enhance development. Sensory stimulation of the fetus can in fact lead to bizarre patterns of adaptation later on.

The roots of human behavior, researchers now know, begin to develop early—just weeks after conception, in fact. Well before a woman typically knows she is pregnant, her embryo's brain has already begun to bulge. By five weeks, the organ that looks like a lumpy inchworm has already embarked on the most spectacular feat of human development: the creation of the deeply creased and convoluted cerebral cortex, the part of the brain that will eventually allow the growing person to move, think, speak, plan, and create in a human way.

At nine weeks, the embryo's ballooning brain allows it to bend its body, hiccup, and react to loud sounds. At week ten, it moves its arms, "breathes" amniotic fluid in and out, opens its jaw, and stretches. Before the first trimester is over, it yawns, sucks, and swallows as well as feels and smells. By the end of the second trimester, it can hear; toward the end of pregnancy, it can see.

FETAL ALERTNESS

Scientists who follow the fetus' daily life find that it spends most of its time not exercising these new abilities but sleeping. At 32 weeks, it drowses 90 to 95% of the day. Some of these hours are spent in deep sleep, some in REM sleep, and some in an indeterminate state, a product of the fetus' immature brain that is different from sleep in a baby, child, or adult. During REM sleep, the fetus' eyes move back and forth just as an adult's eyes do, and many researchers believe that it is dreaming. DiPietro speculates that fetuses dream about what they know—the sensations they feel in the womb.

Closer to birth, the fetus sleeps 85 to 90% of the time, the same as a newborn. Between its frequent naps, the fetus seems to have "something like an awake alert period," according to developmental psychologist William Fifer, Ph.D., who with his Columbia University colleagues is monitoring these sleep and wakefulness cycles in order to identify patterns of normal and abnormal brain development, including potential predictors of sudden infant death syndrome. Says Fifer, "We are, in effect, asking the fetus: 'Are you paying attention? Is your nervous system behaving in the appropriate way?' "

FETAL MOVEMENT

Awake or asleep, the human fetus moves 50 times or more each hour, flexing and extending its body, moving its head, face, and limbs and exploring its warm wet compartment by touch. Heidelise Als, Ph.D., a developmental psychologist at Harvard Medical School, is fascinated by the amount of tactile stimulation a fetus gives itself. "It touches a hand to the face, one hand to the other hand, clasps its feet, touches its foot to its leg, its hand to its umbilical cord," she reports.

Als believes there is a mismatch between the environment given to preemies in hospitals and the environment they would have had in the womb. She has been working for years to change the care given to preemies so that they can curl up, bring their knees together, and touch things with their hands as they would have for weeks in the womb.

By 15 weeks, a fetus has an adult's taste buds and may be able to savor its mother's meals.

Along with such common movements, DiPietro has also noted some odder fetal activities, including "licking the uterine wall and literally walking around the womb by pushing off with its feet." Laterborns may have more room in the womb for such maneuvers than first babies. After the initial pregnancy, a woman's uterus is bigger and the umbilical cord longer, allowing more freedom of movement. "Second and subsequent children may develop more motor experience in utero and so may become more active infants," DiPietro speculates.

Fetuses react sharply to their mother's actions. "When we're watching the fetus on ultrasound and the mother starts to laugh, we can see the fetus, floating upside down in the womb, bounce up and down on its head, bum-bum-bum, like it's bouncing on a trampoline," says DiPietro. "When mothers watch this on the screen, they laugh harder, and the fetus goes up and down even faster. We've wondered whether this is why people grow up liking roller coasters."

FETAL TASTE

Why people grow up liking hot chilies or spicy curries may also have something to do with the fetal environment. By 13 to 15 weeks a fetus' taste buds already look like a mature adult's, and doctors know that the amniotic fluid that surrounds it can smell strongly of curry, cumin, garlic, onion and other essences from a mother's diet. Whether fetuses can taste these flavors isn't yet known, but scientists have found that a 33-week-old preemie will suck harder on a sweetened nipple than on a plain rubber one.

"During the last trimester, the fetus is swallowing up to a liter a day" of amniotic fluid, notes Julie Mennella, Ph.D., a biopsychologist at the Monell Chemical Senses Center in Philadelphia. She thinks the fluid may act as a "flavor bridge" to breast milk, which also carries food flavors from the mother's diet.

FETAL HEARING

Whether or not a fetus can taste, there's little question that it can hear. A very premature baby entering the world at 24 to 25 weeks responds to the sounds around it, observes Als, so its auditory apparatus must already have been functioning in the womb. Many pregnant women report a fetal jerk or sudden kick just after a door slams or a car backfires.

Even without such intrusions, the womb is not a silent place. Researchers who have inserted a hydrophone into the uterus of a pregnant woman have picked up a noise level "akin to the background noise in an apartment," according to DiPietro. Sounds include the whooshing of blood in the mother's vessels, the gurgling and rumbling of her stomach and intestines, as well as the tones of her voice filtered through tissues, bones, and fluid, and the voices of other people coming through the amniotic wall. Fifer has found that fetal heart rate slows when the mother is speaking, suggesting that the fetus not only hears and recognizes the sound, but is calmed by it.

FETAL VISION

Vision is the last sense to develop. A very premature infant can see light and shape; researchers presume that a fetus has the same ability. Just as the womb isn't com-

What's the Impact on Abortion?

Though research in fetal psychology focuses on the last trimester, when most abortions are illegal, the thought of a fetus dreaming, listening and responding to its mother's voice is sure to add new complexity to the debate. The new findings undoubtedly will strengthen the convictions of right-to-lifers—and they may shake the certainty of pro-choice proponents who believe that mental life begins at birth.

Many of the scientists engaged in studying the fetus, however, remain detached from the abortion controversy, insisting that their work is completely irrelevant to the debate.

"I don't think that fetal research informs the issue at all," contends psychologist Janet DiPietro of Johns Hopkins University. "The essence of the abortion debate is: When does life begin? Some people believe it begins at conception, the other extreme believes that it begins after the baby is born, and there's a group in the middle that believes it begins at around 24 or 25 weeks, when a fetus can live outside of the womb, though it needs a lot of help to do so.

"Up to about 25 weeks, whether or not it's sucking its thumb or has personality or all that, the fetus cannot survive outside of its mother. So is that life, or not? That is a moral, ethical, and religious question, not one for science. Things can behave and not be alive. Right-to-lifers may say that this research proves that a fetus is alive, but it does not. It cannot."

"Fetal research only changes the abortion debate for people who think that life starts at some magical point," maintains Heidelise Als, a psychologist at Harvard University. "If you believe that life begins at conception, then you don't need the proof of fetal behavior." For others, however, abortion is a very complex issue and involves far more than whether research shows that a fetus hiccups. "Your circumstances and personal beliefs have much more impact on the decision," she observes.

Like DiPietro, Als realizes that "people may use this research as an emotional way to draw people to the pro-life side, but it should not be used by belligerent activists." Instead, she believes, it should be applied to helping mothers have the healthiest pregnancy possible and preparing them to best parent their child. Columbia University psychologist William Fifer, Ph.D., agrees. "The research is much more relevant for issues regarding viable fetuses—preemies."

Simply put, say the three, their work is intended to help the babies that live—not to decide whether fetuses should.—*Camille Chatterjee*

pletely quiet, it isn't utterly dark, either. Says Fifer: "There may be just enough visual stimulation filtered through the mother's tissues that a fetus can respond when the mother is in bright light," such as when she is sunbathing.

A fetus prefers hearing Mom's voice over a stranger's—speaking in her native, not a foreign tongue—and being read aloud familiar tales rather than new stories.

Japanese scientists have even reported a distinct fetal reaction to flashes of light shined on the mother's belly. However, other researchers warn that exposing fetuses (or premature infants) to bright light before they are ready can be dangerous. In fact, Harvard's Als believes that retinal damage in premature infants, which has long been ascribed to high concentrations of oxygen, may actually be due to overexposure to light at the wrong time in development.

A six-month fetus, born about 14 weeks too early, has a brain that is neither prepared for nor expecting signals from the eyes to be transmitted into the brain's visual cortex, and from there into the executive-branch frontal lobes, where information is integrated. When the fetus is forced to see too much too soon, says Als, the accelerated stimulation may lead to aberrations of brain development.

FETAL LEARNING

Along with the ability to feel, see, and hear comes the capacity to learn and remember. These activities can be rudimentary, automatic, even biochemical. For example, a fetus, after an initial reaction of alarm, eventually stops responding to a repeated loud noise. The fetus displays the same kind of primitive learning, known as habituation, in response to its mother's voice, Fifer has found.

But the fetus has shown itself capable of far more. In the 1980s, psychology professor Anthony James DeCasper, Ph.D., and colleagues at the University of North Carolina at Greensboro, devised a feeding contraption that allows a baby to suck faster to hear one set of sounds through headphones and to suck slower to hear a different set. With this technique, DeCasper discovered that within hours of birth, a baby already prefers its mother's voice to a stranger's, suggesting it must have learned and remembered the voice, albeit not necessarily consciously, from its last months in the womb. More recently, he's found that a newborn prefers a story read to it repeatedly in the womb—in this case, *The Cat in the Hat*—over a new story introduced soon after birth.

DeCasper and others have uncovered more mental feats. Newborns can not only distinguish their mother from a stranger speaking, but would rather hear Mom's voice, especially the way it sounds filtered through amniotic fluid rather than through air. They're xenophobes, too: they prefer to hear Mom speaking in her native language than to hear her or someone else speaking in a foreign tongue.

By monitoring changes in fetal heart rate, psychologist Jean-Pierre Lecanuet, Ph.D., and his colleagues in Paris have found that fetuses can even tell strangers' voices apart. They also seem to like certain stories more than others. The fetal heartbeat will slow down when a familiar French fairy tale such as *La Poulette* ("The Chick") or *Le Petit Crapaud* ("The Little Toad"), is read near the mother's belly. When the same reader delivers another unfamiliar story, the fetal heartbeat stays steady.

The fetus is likely responding to the cadence of voices and stories, not their actual words, observes Fifer, but the conclusion is the same: the fetus can listen, learn, and remember at some level, and, as with most babies and children, it likes the comfort and reassurance of the familiar.

FETAL PERSONALITY

It's no secret that babies are born with distinct differences and patterns of activity that suggest individual temperament. Just when and how the behavioral traits originate in the womb is now the subject of intense scrutiny.

In the first formal study of fetal temperament in 1996, DiPietro and her colleagues recorded the heart rate and movements of 31 fetuses six times before birth and compared them to readings taken twice after birth. (They've since extended their study to include 100 more fetuses.) Their findings: fetuses that are very active in the womb tend to be more irritable infants. Those with irregular sleep/wake patterns in the womb sleep more poorly as young infants. And fetuses with high heart rates become unpredictable, inactive babies.

"Behavior doesn't begin at birth," declares DiPietro. "It begins before and develops in predictable ways." One of the most important influences on development is the fetal environment. As Harvard's Als observes, "The fetus gets an enormous amount of 'hormonal bathing' through the mother, so its chronobiological rhythms are influenced by the mother's sleep/wake cycles, her eating patterns, her movements."

The hormones a mother puts out in response to stress also appear critical. DiPietro finds that highly pressured mothers-to-be tend to have more active fetuses—and more irritable infants. "The most stressed are working pregnant women," says DiPietro. "These days, women tend to work up to the day they deliver, even though the implications for pregnancy aren't entirely clear yet. That's our cultural norm, but I think it's insane."

Als agrees that working can be an enormous stress, but emphasizes that pregnancy hormones help to buffer both mother and fetus. Individual reactions to stress also matter. "The pregnant woman who chooses to work is a different woman already from the one who chooses not to work," she explains.

She's also different from the woman who has no choice but to work. DiPietro's studies show that the fetuses of poor women are distinct neurobehaviorally—less active, with a less variable heart rate—from the fetuses of middle-class women. Yet "poor women rate themselves as less stressed than do working middle-class women," she notes. DiPietro suspects that inadequate nutrition and exposure to pollutants may significantly affect the fetuses of poor women.

Stress, diet, and toxins may combine to have a harmful effect on intelligence. A recent study by biostatistician Bernie Devlin, Ph.D., of the University of Pittsburgh, suggests that genes may have less impact on IQ than previously thought and that the environment of the womb may account for much more. "Our old notion of nature influencing the fetus before birth and nurture after birth needs an update," DiPietro insists. "There is an antenatal environment, too, that is provided by the mother."

Parents-to-be who want to further their unborn child's mental development should start by assuring that the antenatal environment is well-nourished, low-stress, drug-free. Various authors and "experts" also have suggested poking the fetus at regular intervals, speaking to it through a paper tube or "pregaphone," piping in classical music, even flashing lights at the mother's abdomen.

Does such stimulation work? More importantly: Is it safe? Some who use these methods swear their children are smarter, more verbally and musically inclined, more physically coordinated and socially adept than average. Scientists, however, are skeptical.

"There has been no defended research anywhere that shows any enduring effect from these stimulations," asserts Fifer. "Since no one can even say for certain when a fetus is awake, poking them or sticking speakers on the mother's abdomen may be changing their natural sleep patterns. No one would consider poking or prodding a newborn baby in her bassinet or putting a speaker next to her ear, so why would you do such a thing with a fetus?"

Als is more emphatic: "My bet is that poking, shaking, or otherwise deliberately stimulating the fetus might alter its developmental sequence, and anything that affects the development of the brain comes at a cost."

Gently talking to the fetus, however, seems to pose little risk. Fifer suggests that this kind of activity may help parents as much as the fetus. "Thinking about your fetus, talking to it, having your spouse talk to it, will all help prepare you for this new creature that's going to jump into your life and turn it upside down," he says—once it finally makes its anti-climactic entrance.

UNIT 2
Cognition, Language, and Learning

Unit Selections

Key Points to Consider

- If you have not already had a child, imagine yourself a parent of a newborn; based on the information in "The World of the Senses," what sorts of measures would you consider to optimize the sensory environment for your new baby?

- Why do you think parents are increasingly interested in trying to create geniuses?

- If sex differences between boys and girls are based on evolutionary principles, should we still teach boys to be less aggressive and girls to be more independent?

- What is your definition of giftedness and how does it differ from what the article on giftedness describes?

- According to Howard Gardner, there are eight intelligences. Do you think there are more? Which other abilities might you nominate as another possible intelligence and why?

- In "Where the Boys Are," the article suggests that boys are being shortchanged by our schools. How do you reconcile this trend, given the research in recent years implicating greater discrimination and negative effects for girls rather than boys?

 **Links: www.dushkin.com/online/**
These sites are annotated in the World Wide Web pages.

Educational Resources Information Center (ERIC)
  http://www.ed.gov/pubs/pubdb.html

I Am Your Child
  http://iamyourchild.org

National Association for the Education of Young Children (NAEYC)
  http://www.naeyc.org

Results of NICHD Study of Early Child Care
  http://156.40.88.3/publications/pubs/early_child_care.htm

Vandergrift's Children's Literature Page
  http://www.scils.rutgers.edu/special/kay/sharelit.html

Project Zero
  http://pzweb.harvard.edu

We have come a long way from the days when the characterization of cognition of infants and young children included phrases like "tabula rasa" and "booming, buzzing confusion." Infants and young children are no longer viewed by researchers as blank slates, passively waiting to be filled up with knowledge. Today, experts in child development are calling for a reformulation of assumptions about children's cognitive abilities, as well as calling for reforms in the ways we teach children in our schools. Hence, the articles in the first subsection highlight some of the new knowledge of the cognitive abilities of infants and young children.

Recent brain development research indicates that newborns possess a number of impressive abilities. The essays "The World of the Senses" and "Categories in Young Children's Thinking" describe how scientists are discovering, by employing ingenious experimental techniques, that infants possess many heretofore unrealized skills that are heavily influenced by both nature and early experiences.

Parents today seem increasingly concerned with raising the "perfect" child. As a result, more parents have begun to question whether or not their infant or toddler is learning to crawl or walk on time. Author Joan Raymond in "Kids, Start Your Engines" provides sound research advice on the achievement of various physical milestones and discusses individual variations among children. Similarly, of greater concern is the increasing need felt by some parents to pressure their toddlers and children into becoming "geniuses." "The Quest for a Super Kid" helps to debunk some of these potentially harmful myths and provide parents with healthier perspectives and alternatives.

What accounts for sex differences between boys and girls? Are boys and girls programmed by their genes to behave in certain ways or are these behavioral differences the result of socialization and culture? David Geary, in "Evolution and Developmental Sex Differences," argues that an evolutionary perspective along with cultural factors may help to explain some of these differences.

Learning to understand the thoughts and feelings of others is an important developmental milestone for children. The authors of "Do Young Children Understand What Others Feel, Want, and Know?" describe research showing how children often initially begin with intuitive or folk understandings and how parents and their culture can influence this progression.

How do you know if your child is gifted or not? Harvard psychologist Dr. Ellen Winner summarizes some of the research findings about the qualities and characteristics of gifted children and raises important future questions about the respective contributions of genetics and environment in creating and supporting gifted children.

As Erik Erikson noted, from about age 6 to 12 years, children enter the period of "industry versus inferiority" and become preoccupied with learning the tools of their cultures. In our own culture, these tools are the "three R's": learning to read, write, and do arithmetic in school. For parents, teachers, and the public alike, the debate surrounding IQ or intelligence continues to draw considerable interest. Famed author Howard Gardner in

"The First Seven… and the Eighth" explains his theory of multiple intelligences that now includes an eighth component—naturalist intelligence—and how these abilities are influenced by teaching and learning.

One important factor in a child's success in school involves parental involvement in their schooling. In "Parental Engagement That Makes a Difference," Jeremy Finn describes research showing that specific kinds of parental involvement in both the home and the school are key in helping children excel in school.

Recent controversy abounds on the topic of whether girls or boys are being shortchanged by our schools. Cathy Young in "Where the Boys Are" reviews the various camps on whether boys or girls are at more educational risk in elementary, secondary, and college settings and makes the case for balancing the record and rhetoric on this hot issue.

The World
Of the
Senses

From the moment of birth, babies respond to their mothers' voices, distinguish shapes and have definite taste and aroma preferences.

By Joan Raymond

IT'S TUESDAY AFTERNOON AT THE Epsteins' Philadelphia apartment. Seven-month-old Ana Natalia is sitting up, smiling, waiting for her favorite midafternoon activities: snack time, featuring a lovely sweet-potato purée, accompanied by a gentle back rub. When her mother, Lucia, puts some world music on the CD player, Ana Natalia arches her 15-pound body in delight. Life doesn't get any better than cool times, good food and a massage.

REACH OUT
At birth the sense of touch is so developed that a baby will prefer soft flannel to coarse burlap.

Even babies—especially babies—know that. They revel in their senses and almost intuitively know what looks, tastes, feels, sounds and smells good. They love skin-to-skin touching, which can inhibit the release of stress hormones and heighten immune responses. They respond to their mothers' voices and can distinguish them (thanks to hearing her voice through the walls of the womb) from all others. They are fascinated by shapes and moving objects. And they definitely know what they like to eat. All of these talents reflect the fact that at birth a baby's sensory system is well developed, even though the neural pathways that underlie perception still need years of fine-tuning. In the first years of life neurons in the brain—the master sense organ—form circuits that will enable a child to distinguish the smell of lilacs from gasoline, the sight of cerulean from mauve, the sounds of her native tongue from all others.

A baby's journey through the realm of the senses begins in the womb. By the seventh month, nerves connecting the eye and the brain's visual cortex have begun to function in a rudimentary way, transmitting visual information in the form of electrical impulses (but not very efficiently). Nerves that relay touch perceptions appear on the skin of the fetus by about the 10th week. By the fourth month, the somatosensory cortex—the part of the brain that registers tactile perceptions—is coming online; a gentle massage of Mom's belly will likely stimulate fetal movement. By about 28 weeks, the fetus will respond to loud noises. Taste buds make an appearance at a remarkably early seven weeks.

And although the fetus doesn't smell in the conventional sense, it can absorb odors in the amniotic fluid by the 24th week of gestation.

Children fine-tune their sensory apparatus through the critical first years of life. "Infants and toddlers give their senses a tune up every time they are exposed to new stimuli," says pediatric neurologist Dr. Max Wiznitzer of Cleveland's Rainbow Babies & Children's Hospital. Each new stimulus sets off a cascade of brain events; in fact, in the first three months of life the regions of the brain with the highest metabolic rate are those processing sights, sounds and touches, as if the nascent circuits within the gray matter were burning the midnight oil to take in everything they could about their new world.

Sensory information doesn't just stop with perception; it also interacts with other functions and regions of the brain. In adults, the sense of smell can be a powerful trigger to memory (with the aroma of roses, perhaps, triggering memories of a long-ago romance), and such connections start to be forged in the first weeks of life. Right from birth a baby's ability to detect odors is well developed. That makes sense, since smell is processed in one of the most primitive and (evolutionarily) oldest parts

MAKING SENSE OF IT

Five Windows on the World

Although babies come into the world wired for vision, hearing, touch, smell and taste, their experiences in infancy and throughout childhood complete the neuronal circuitry.

Touch It's such a crucial sense that the area of the brain responsible for touch perceptions—the primary sensory cortex—can process tactile sensations by the fourth month of gestation. Skin nerves appear at week 10.

Vision It's the slowest sense to develop. Although the rudimentary visual cortex can receive signals from the fetus's eye at seven months' gestation, neurons in the vision pathway remain immature for months after birth. Much of the world looks fuzzy to babies.

Smell Even while in utero, babies perceive the smell of the amniotic fluid; at birth they can distinguish their mother's smell from all others. Olfaction seems to be tightly linked to memories and emotions.

PRIMARY SENSORY CORTEX

TASTE CORTEX

PRIMARY AUDITORY CORTEX

PRIMARY VISUAL CORTEX

OLFACTORY BULB

THE CEREBRAL CORTEX: This outermost layer of the brain processes signals from the peripheral nervous system

Taste Preferences are shaped so early that even newborns have definite likes and dislikes. The 10,000 or so taste buds on the tongue and soft palate begin to appear a mere seven weeks after conception. Each responds most strongly to salty, sour, sweet or bitter. In general, newborns prefer sweet. But the specific tastes that the fetus is exposed to before birth, through what Mom eats and through breast milk—whose taste also reflects Mom's previous meals— shape which ones he will prefer and which he will reject.

Hearing Just as prenatal exposure to tastes shapes a baby's preferences, so the sounds penetrating the womb leave a lasting effect. By 28 weeks' gestation, the brain's auditory cortex, which receives input from nerve cells in the inner ear, can perceive loud noises. At birth, a baby can usually distinguish her mother's voice, the one she has been hearing for the last 12 or so weeks of gestation, and prefers it to all others. Newborns can perceive every phoneme in the world's languages, an ability that's lost within the first year.

---

of the brain. A newborn can distinguish her mother's fragrance from all others and, since it is generally associated with pleasant things like food and comfort, comes to prefer it. When a baby smells his mother's skin, the olfactory signal reaching the brain triggers the formation of neuronal links between it and the brain's memory and emotion centers. As a result, the baby remembers Mom's smell and associates it with pleasant events.

LOOKIN' GOOD
The world looks fuzzy to newborns, but within 3 months they can track moving objects

As early as the second month, babies learn to distinguish between more types and intensities of aromas. Their repertoire continues expanding, with the result that toddlers form even more sophisticated

neuronal links between aromas and memories. Smelling a flower, for instance, sends signals to the brain's limbic system, a site of memory storage. Presto: emotion-laden memories—happy (if the toddler was having a lovely day with Mom when he picked the rose) or not (it was a prize-winning bloom, and plucking it led to a very, very long timeout).

Vision is the last sense to reach full capacity. At birth, the neurons of the visual cortex (which receive visual information from the eye) are still not "myelinated," or coated with the fatty substance that keeps nerve signals from leaking out like electricity from badly insulated transmission lines. As a result of the faulty lines, newborns see little more than light and shadow. They focus best on objects eight to 15 inches away—about the distance to the face of the person feeding them—and even with their fuzzy vision can tell circles from squares and prefer the former. They love to look at faces.

By 3 months a baby can track objects that move toward him, and soon after that

can follow moving objects smoothly. By 4 to 7 months a child develops full color vision; this is when brightly colored toys will capture his attention. By 6 months his depth and distance perception work reliably—convenient for a little being just starting to scoot around. By 2, most children have 20/60 vision, which will gradually improve over the next three years to 20/25. Vision will continue to sharpen until the age of 9 or so, when a child sees as clearly as a normal adult. But this progression is far from inevitable: visual stimulation is crucial to the developing child. When deprived of visual stimulation, the ocular columns in the brain's visual cortex fail to wire up correctly. That means those mobiles over the bed do more than just look pretty. They help your child focus and improve his vision (though everyday interactions and a caring environment are perfectly adequate to stimulate visual development).

Hearing depends on experience, too. Newborns have a well-developed auditory system, and can distinguish loud from quiet. But they can pick up higher-pitched sounds better than they can lower-frequency ones, which may be why they are entranced by the high-pitched coos and singsong of "parentese." Adults' practice of speaking to babies in a higher pitch therefore matches their auditory abilities. By 2 to 3 months a baby can distinguish the source of a sound, and follow it, which makes tracking the conversations around them possible.

FLAVOR CRAVER

Taste buds appear at seven weeks' gestation. Babies have an acute sense of taste, and prefer sweet.

Perhaps the most impressive aspect of newborns' auditory abilities is their enviable talent for hearing the phonemes of every language, from that odd (to an English speaker) French "eu" to the "r" and "l" that a Japanese adult can't distinguish. But by the age of 1, infants lose the ability to hear sounds not present in the language they hear every day, finds Patricia Kuhl, professor of speech and hearing at the University of Washington. A baby raised amid the sounds of English literally loses the ability to hear the sound of, say, a Swedish vowel; if auditory neurons that once had the ability to detect it are never exposed to it, they essentially give up and find a job detecting sounds that the baby *is* exposed to. The brain becomes deaf to other phonemes, which is why native Japanese speakers have trouble telling "l" from "r."

Even newborns revel in their senses; they seem to intuitively prefer sweet to bitter and high tones to low

---

At birth, the sense of touch is developed enough that a baby will prefer a soft piece of flannel to coarse burlap. There is growing evidence that touch is crucial to an infant's cognitive and physical development. Tiffany Field, director of the Touch Research Institutes at the University of Miami, has shown that premature infants massaged three times a day for 15 minutes gained weight 47 percent faster than preemies who were not massaged. She also finds that infants showed fewer signs of stress, such as grimacing or fist clenching, and had lower levels of stress hormones following a massage with oil.

Newborns' sense of taste is acute enough that some reject breast milk after Mom has eaten a heaping plate of broccoli. They can tell salty from sweet and bitter from acidic because amniotic fluid acts as a kind of "flavor bridge," says Julie Mennella, a biopsychologist at Philadelphia's Monell Chemical Senses Center. That bridge seems to lead babies to definite, and early, taste preferences. Earlier this year Mennella reported the findings of an experiment designed to trace the origins of babies' likes and dislikes. The old wives' tale about breast milk's influence on a child's taste preferences holds true, she found. When she gave 6-month-olds cereal prepared with either water or carrot juice, the infants who were exposed to carrot juice either prenatally or in breast milk strongly preferred the carrot-juice porridge to the water version. The other infants showed no preference, suggesting that if women eat a varied diet during pregnancy and while nursing, their babies are more likely to accept new foods. Scientists have confirmed another bit of folk wisdom: babies are born with a sweet tooth, probably because breast milk is sweet. In our drive to survive, we have a natural preference for the taste of that first food. (Formula manufacturers try to mimic the sweet taste of human breast milk.) A baby's sensory development starting in the months before birth is nothing short of extraordinary, says Field. "Children are little hedonists," she says. "That's how they learn about their world."

Kids, Start Your Engines

When it comes to those wonderful milestones of physical development, from rolling over to taking the first steps, 'normal' is a relative term. Children, remember, are individuals.

By Joan Raymond

FRANCESCA FABE WANTS TO make sure she really nails the flower-girl strut. Legs alternating perfectly, arms held delicately in front of her petite frame, Francesca, 2, is moving to an inner rhythm as she glides down the sidewalk of her suburban Cleveland home. "This is how you do it," she boasts, tossing imaginary blooms to her mother, Donna, her father, Guy, and her younger brother, Pete. Although Francesca lacks the smooth moves of a catwalk diva, she is nonetheless a picture of grace and toddler determination. Just last year, though, Donna was burning up the phone lines to Francesca's pediatrician, asking why her 13-month-old daughter wasn't walking. "I drove the doctor crazy," says Donna with a rueful smile. "But I just wanted to make sure everything was OK." It was. Francesca walked at 14 months, well within the average range. In the past year she has progressed to running, jumping, climbing, kicking and marching backward. "Francesca probably just wanted to get the walking thing right the first time," says Donna. Peter, on the

other hand, is walking at 12 months and has a damn-the-torpedoes approach to locomotion as he tries to elude Mom's clutches. "Pete," says Donna, "just kind of went for it."

64% of the parents of young children say they consulted books on parenting or the early childhood years before their firstborn arrived

---

Anxious parents of the world: take a timeout. When it comes to physical growth and development and those wonderful photo-op milestones, like sitting up or crawling, "normal" is a relative term. When next-door Johnny begins walking at 11 months but your own little Mary is still content with crawling at 15 months, a by-the-growth-chart parent can't help but wonder, *"What's wrong with my kid?"* An

explosion of research into the workings of the brain shows the answer may be… nothing. The development of the brain pathways that fire up nerve endings and muscle groups to perform specific tasks occurs at a pace as individual as a fingerprint. Although parents should be concerned if their child doesn't develop good head and neck control by 2 to 3 months, or if a baby's movements remain poor, with muscles stiff and rigid or floppy and uncontrolled, fretting over a week-long "delay" in when a child sits up is a waste of psychic energy.

A baby passes her first amazing milestone before the typical mother has even wiped off the sweat of labor. Full-term newborns, scientists established in 1996, recognize and prefer their mother's face to all others. (In the ingenious experiment, the scientists had babies suck a special pacifier that controlled a video screen. Depending on how the infant sucked, fast or slow, the image of Mom or another woman appeared; babies sucked so they'd see Mom.) From here on out, though, when a child reaches developmental milestones is only partly determined by biology; these events are also environmentally "sculpted," says neurodevelopmental pediatrician Dr. Alec Hoon of Baltimore's Kennedy Krieger Institute. Each time a child acquires new motor skills, such as lifting her head, she receives new environmental stimuli, like a view of the world from a new perspective. These new stimuli, even something as simple as a game of peekaboo, cement tentative brain circuits, which in turn prod and enable a child to take on more complex tasks. As these neuromotor connections mature, so does a child's sense of self. And in the seeming blink of an eye, the dependency of infancy gives way to the effervescent autonomy of toddlerhood. "Childhood," Hoon quotes his favorite bumper sticker, "is a journey, not a race."

HELLO, WORLD
From the very start, a baby is chalking up accomplishments

It is one that children start at birth, when they have virtually no motor control and only rudimentary reflexes. Physical milestones move from head to toe: brain regions that control the head and neck develop before those that direct the arms and legs. In six months a baby will progress from raising her head and chest when lying on her stomach, to sitting up as she develops better balance and her back and neck muscles strengthen. Rolling over takes major cortical power involving three brain structures: the motor cortex, which initiates movement; the basal ganglia, which both inhibits movement and stores "programs" for habitual movements, and the cerebellum, which excites motor nerves. Even the seemingly simple act of reaching for a cookie involves cementing connections between brain areas that register hunger, sight, smell and motivation with regions that control movement.

Whether a baby reaches developmental milestones on the early or late side of normal seems to bear little relation to either cognitive skills or future proficiency. A child who does not walk until 16 months is not fated to sit on the sidelines, the last one picked for a sport, once she reaches school, says Dr. Chris Johnson of the University of Texas Health Science Center, San Antonio. Similarly, having a child who walks at 9 months doesn't mean you've added a fu-

ture Marion Jones to your family tree. There is, therefore, no good reason for parents to push for early attainment of any major milestone. When parents ask Johnson whether to worry about a slowly developing toddler, she applies a "30 percent" rule: developing motor skills more than 30 percent later than average might warrant attention. Most children walk between 12 and 15 months, so a child who shows no interest in walking by nearly 17 months of age may benefit from a visit to the pediatrician. In rare cases, precocious motor-skill development warrants intervention. An infant who continually stands before mastering sitting could have muscle spasticity, indicative of numerous problems.

But underlying pathology or illness is the exception, not the rule. Some motor-skill delays may be easily explained by, for instance, the fact that "children need the opportunity to do things on their own," says Johnson. When one set of parents brought their son in because he wasn't rolling over, Johnson asked if they ever put the child on the floor. The answer was no. The child was always being held. Within a few days of being placed on the floor so he could see the world from a different perspective, he rolled over, and went on to develop just fine. "We all want to be good parents and do for our kids," says Johnson. "A child needs to do for himself."

SITTING UP
She now looks out at the world from a wider perspective

As common as developmental "delays" are a kind of developmental hiccup, in which children briefly lose a newly acquired skill. As a baby masters a new trick, finds kinesiologist Daniela Corbetta of Purdue University, the brain reorganizes itself. The result is a "temporary developmental step backward," she says. For instance, babies develop handedness—a preference for reaching or grasping with right rather than left, or vice versa—before they become proficient walkers. But walking requires such massive postural reorganization, balance and, initially, intense concentration that the brain apparently remaps itself to accomplish the task. One result is that many novice walkers regress to using both hands for reaching and holding, but return to using a preferred hand as

STEP BY LITTLE STEP
The nervous system develops from the head down, but gross motor skills can appear early, late or even out of sequence.

0–3 MONTHS
trusting

Babies begin to make simple associations: if he cries he gets picked up. Reflexive movements are **slowly replaced** with purposeful, voluntary ones.

4–7 MONTHS
moving

A baby rolls over, learns to sit without support and turns toward sounds. Most will **reach out** to grasp objects and may transfer them from one hand to the other.

7–12 MONTHS
crawling

The baby may show interest in other kids, though fear strangers, and start to **creep or crawl**. He will likely perfect crawling and standing before trying to walk.

12–18 MONTHS
walking

A baby will likely walk without support, **becoming stronger** and more coordinated. Most babies develop a preference for one hand over another.

19–23 MONTHS
running

Babies start running and climbing, even **kicking a ball**, without tripping. They often use hands to drink from cups and crayons to draw crude circles.

2–3 YEARS
exploring

Toddlers love to test their growing abilities by galloping, tumbling and hopping on one foot. They may **dance to music**, open jars and turn toy nuts and bolts.

their admissions policies, meaning it's no longer just the élite who can attend. With competition getting ever keener, kids have to do ever more to distinguish themselves.

Parents are also driven by something a lot more primal: old-fashioned guilt. Even as men take on more responsibility for rearing children, the lion's share of baby care is still handled by mothers. But in an era in which it often takes two incomes to meet the monthly nut, increasing numbers of moms can't spend nearly as much time with their kids as they'd like. In 1999, 62% of mothers worked outside the home. That figure was 54% in 1985 and just 44% in 1975. "Parents feel tremendous guilt because they feel they're spreading themselves too thin," says Dr. Joshua Sparrow of Children's Hospital in Boston. "When parents have time, they can wait for things to happen," adds Rachelle Tyler, an M.D. and professor of pediatrics at UCLA. "But when they're pressured, they feel they've got to see their children respond now."

Into this anxious mix have stepped hucksters and marketers who see worried parents as the most promising pigeons. Store shelves groan with new products purported to stimulate babies' brains in ways harried parents don't have time for. There are baby Mozart tapes said to enhance spatial reasoning and perhaps musical and artistic abilities too. There are black, white and red picture books, said to sharpen visual acuity. There are bilingual products said to train baby brains so they will be more receptive to multiple languages. The hard sell even follows kids to the one place you'd think they'd be allowed some peace—the womb—with handheld tummy speakers designed to pipe music and voices to the unborn baby, the better to stimulate the growing brain and get it ready for the work it will eventually have to do. Parents who don't avail themselves of these products do so at their children's peril: the brain, they are told, has very limited windows for learning certain skills. Let them close, and kids may be set back forever.

But is any of this true? Is it possible to turn an ordinary kid into an exceptional kid? Even if it is, is it worth it to try? Is it better to steer children gently through childhood, letting them make some mistakes and take some scrapes and accept the fact that some of them may not be marked for excellence? Or is it better to strive for a family of superkids, knowing that they are getting the most out of their potential if not out of their youth? Clearly, many parents are caught up in that quest, even if they quietly harbor doubts about its merits. "Parents

have, to a large extent, lost confidence in themselves and in their own good judgment," says Peter Gorski, a committee chair of the American Academy of Pediatrics.

The Myth

LISTENING TO MUSIC CAN BOOST CREATIVITY

Nope. The so-called Mozart effect doesn't enhance artistic skills but may improve spatial skills. The effect is just temporary, though, and seen only in adults.

The phenomenon of the driven child has been coming for a while, but it was in 1994 that the new breed was truly born. That was the year the Carnegie Corp. published a 134-page report describing a "quiet crisis" among U.S. children, who it argued were being ill served by their twin-career parents and their often failing school systems. The report's findings were worrisome enough, but buried in its pages were two disturbing paragraphs warning that schoolkids might not be the only ones suffering; babies could be too. Young brains are extremely sensitive to early influences, the report cautioned, and the right—or wrong—stimuli could have a significant impact on later development.

Those paragraphs went off like a grenade in the otherwise unremarkable study. The press ran alarming stories about blameless children being left behind. The White House called a conference on childhood development. Parents snapped up news of both, hoping it wasn't too late to undo whatever damage they had unwittingly done to their kids. "Every parent began to worry," says John Bruer, president of the McDonnell Foundation and author of the book *The Myth of the First Three Years*. "They thought, 'If I don't have the latest Mozart CD, my child is going to jail rather than Yale?'"

In order to make up for their feared lapses, parents indeed started buying the approved kinds of music—and a whole lot more. A study conducted by Zero to Three, a nonprofit research group, found that almost 80% of parents with a high school education or less were assiduously using flash cards, television and computer games to try to keep their babies' minds engaged.

Child-development experts, however, consider these sterile tools inferior to more

social and emotional activities such as talking with or reading to children. These specialists agree that the only thing shown to optimize children's intellectual potential is a secure, trusting relationship with their parents. Time spent cuddling, gazing and playing establishes a bond of security, trust and respect on which the entire child-development pyramid is based. "We have given social and emotional development a back seat," says UCLA's Tyler, "and that's doing a great disservice to kids and to our society."

Trying to pump up children's IQs in artificial ways may also lead to increased stress on the kids, as the parents' anxiety starts to rub off. By four or five years old, the brains of stressed kids can start to look an awful lot like the brains of stressed adults, with increased levels of adrenaline and cortisol, the twitchy chemicals that fuel the body's fight-or-flight response. Keep the brain on edge long enough, and the changes become long-lasting, making learning harder as kids get older.

But the fact is, the kids don't have to feel so pressured—and neither do their parents. It is true, as the marketers say, that a baby's brain is a fast-changing thing. Far from passively sponging up information, it is busy from birth laying complex webs of neurons that help it grow more sophisticated each day. It takes anywhere from a year to five years, depending on the part of the brain, for this initial explosion of connections to be made, after which many of them shut down and wither away, as the brain decides which it will keep, which new ones it will need and which it can do without. During this period, it's important that babies get the right kinds of stimulation so their brains can make the right decisions. The right kinds of stimulation, however, may not be the ones people think they are.

Asked in a recent study what skills children need in order to be prepared for school, parents of kindergartners routinely cited definable achievements such as knowing numbers, letters, colors and shapes. Teachers, however, disagree. Far more important, they say, are social skills, such as sharing, interacting with others and following instructions. Kids who come to school with a mastery of these less showy abilities stand a better chance of knocking off not only reading and writing when they are eventually presented but everything else that comes along as well. "Intelligence is based on emotional adequacy," says child-development expert T. Berry Brazelton. "The concept of emotional intelligence is at the base of all this."

A SMART TOY GUIDE (Parents Not Included)

Marketers are offering an explosion of new products to parents who think they can make their kids smarter by simply pressing PLAY. That's a myth, but some toys are better than others.

Birth to 1 Year
Babies are developing an attention span and motor control

1 to 3 Years
Toddlers are improving hand-eye coordination, developing the ability to count and to think symbolically

GOOD

Birth to 1 Year: Fisher-Price **Kick & Play Piano** ($25) attaches to the crib. Babies learning to kick and grasp are rewarded with songs, sounds and twinkling lights. Once babies learn to sit, at around seven months, the toy can be played on the floor like a piano.

1 to 3 Years: **Duplos,** the junior version of Legos, and other **building blocks** help strengthen sorting and fine-motor skills.

FAIR

Birth to 1 Year: ◄ **Black-white-and-red toys** attract babies' attention, but researchers say kids learn to track moving objects at their own pace with or without these bold patterns.

1 to 3 Years: ◄ LeapFrog's **Fun & Learn Phonics Bus** ($25) helps toddlers learn the alphabet, but teachers say that's what school is for. Best way to prepare kids for preschool: teach them how to share and follow directions.

HMMM...

Birth to 1 Year: ► **The Babbler** ($50) and **foreign-language videos** may introduce infants to a few sounds and words, but a language has to be spoken in the home for kids to become bilingual.

1 to 3 Years: The **Baby Genius** product line and other music videos and CDs may soothe and entertain but won't make your kid any smarter.

3 to 5 Years
Preschoolers are acting out fantasies and may become interested in playing an instrument

6 to 8 Years
Grade schoolers are learning to channel emotions, developing competitiveness

3 to 5 Years: ◄ **Crayons** help kids express themselves and use their imagination. **Dress-up clothes** encourage role playing.

6 to 8 Years: ► **Action figures** help kids express their feelings through a surrogate. **Monopoly** ($11) helps build strategic thinking.

3 to 5 Years: **LeapPad Pro** talking books ($65) "read" to preschoolers, who can interrupt the story by pointing a "magic pen" at a word to hear it pronounced or at a picture to hear a sound effect. It's better—and cheaper—for parents to do the tutoring.

6 to 8 Years: **Backyard Baseball CD-ROM** ($20) lets kids take a swing at managing a team. Of course, they also would benefit from actually playing ball.

3 to 5 Years: ► Golden Books' **The Poky Little Puppy CD-ROM** ($15) and other interactive stories don't improve much on the paper versions—and they keep kids tied to a computer.

6 to 8 Years: ► **Poo-Chi** ($20) outsold every toy last year except Hot Wheels cars. But the interactive dog restricts a child's imagination by programming play.

Compiled by Julie Rawe

Milestones in the Smart-Baby Industry

1984
Wimmer-Ferguson's **Stim-Mobile** hits stores, launching a trend of black-white-and-red baby gear.

1987
A study shows that preemies exposed to **music, massage and pictures** are more likely to develop normally.

1995
First video targeting infant audiences, **Babymugs!,** which consists of babies making faces, debuts. It launches a whole new video industry.

A study published on the **"Mozart effect"** leads to the belief that classical music makes kids smarter. Sales of pregaphones, which are headphones worn on an expectant mother's belly, boom.

1998
Georgia Governor **Zell Miller** allocates $105,000 in his budget proposal to give every newborn a classical CD or cassette; mompreneur Julie Aigner-Clark sells $1 million worth of her *Baby Mozart* and *Baby Einstein* videos.

1999
"Mozart effect" co-author reports that test scores improve when kids make music rather than just listen to it; companies begin cranking out **instruments** for infants and toddlers.

2001
American Academy of Pediatrics advises against letting kids under 2 watch **TV.** The group initiates the first studies on the effect of **computers** on young children. The findings won't be ready until next year.

It may not even be possible to prod children's intellectual growth. As babies' brains weave their neuronal connections, parents may be able to stimulate, say, the visual or musical ones by exposing kids to picture books or CDs, but it is doubtful that these fortify the brain in any meaningful way. "It's a myth that we can accelerate a child's developmental milestones," says Alan Woolf, a pediatrician at Children's Hospital. "Children are kind of preprogrammed to reach those points." Bruer puts it more bluntly: "The idea that you can provide more synapses by stimulating the child more has no basis in science."

One of the greatest sources of misunderstanding surrounds the so-called Mozart effect. For years researchers have found that playing background music can improve the spatial skills of listeners, causing many laymen to conclude that creative skills can be boosted too. Last year Harvard University released a study called Project Zero that analyzed 50 years of research on this idea. The studies showed that college students who had listened to music performed better on paper-and-pencil spatial tests, but the effect lasted no more than 15 minutes and then faded away. There was no evidence that the listening improved brain power or artistic skills, and certainly none that suggested babies could realize any benefit at all.

Many other misconceptions about brain potential can probably be traced to a series of studies in the 1970s showing that young rats raised with access to mazes and toys had more neural connections than those kept in barren cages. Similarly, studies indicate that children raised without sufficient nurturing often suffer from cognitive deficiencies. However, no evidence indicates that a lot of attention, in the form of early and constant stimulation, enhances a child's intellectual growth. According to the current scientific literature, the type and amount of stimulation needed for proper childhood development is already built into the normal life of an average baby. No whizbang tricks are necessary.

Parents might find it easier to believe all this if it weren't for the increasingly fashionable theory of windows of opportunity for learning—the idea that there are comparatively narrow periods when various parts of the brain can be taught various types of skills. What gives the theory special weight is that there is, in fact, a little truth to it—but only very little. When it comes to language—perhaps the most nuanced skill a person can master—the brain does appear to have fertile and less fertile periods. At birth, babies have the potential to learn any language with equal ease, but by six months, they have begun to focus on the one tongue they hear spoken most frequently. Parents can take advantage of this brain plasticity by introducing a second or even third language, but only if they intend to speak them all with equal frequency until the child is fluent. Merely buying the occasional bilingual toy or videotape will teach kids little, and it certainly will not make it easier for children to learn for real when they get to school.

When it comes to other skills, such as math or music, there is virtually no evidence for learning windows at all. Children grasp things at different rates, and parents whose child can read by age 3 may thus conclude that they somehow threaded the teaching needle perfectly, introducing letters and words at just the right time. But the reality is often that they simply got lucky and had a kid who took a shine early on to a particular skill. "People took the notion of a critical period and misunderstood it to apply to all learning," says Dr. Sparrow of Children's Hospital.

So if parents should be putting down the brain toys, what should they be picking up? For one thing, the kids themselves. If interpersonal skills are the true predictors of how well a child will do in school, parents are the best tutors. Experiments reveal that by the time babies are two months old, they are already fluent in the complex language of their parents' faces, and count on them for their sense of well-being. "Think about the human face," says Sparrow, "the wrinkles, the expressions in the eyes—and think about the infant brain being stimulated by that." To believe that even the best video game or toy could replace this kind of learning, Sparrow thinks, misses the point of just what it is babies are truly hungering to know.

Does this mean educational toys are useless? No. Babies are as engaged by pictures as adults are, and exposing them to books or flash cards early—especially black, white and red ones, which are indeed easier for them to perceive—helps them develop their ability to focus and follow, undeniably a form of learning. Babies are as soothed by music as their parents are, and a little Mozart may indeed hold their attention better than something less rich. Beyond that, however, there's a limit to what the products can do—and parents who follow their children's cues quickly learn that. "When our son was little, all he wanted to do was play with us," says Sharon Chantiles, a casting director and the mother of a four-year-old. "I decided to walk away from the fancy toys and invest in him as a child."

What's at stake for parents is far more than simply a child's school transcript or college options; it's a child's spirit. Recently, author David Brooks spent time on the campus of Princeton University getting to know the students, and he published what he learned in a searching article in the *Atlantic* magazine. The students were thoroughbred products of the American educational system—gifted, disciplined, driven to succeed, with a calm but consuming focus. And, Brooks found, they were curiously flattened too. There was no evidence of the wildfire energy of the college student, no evidence of much moral passion. More troublingly, there was no sign at all of the sweet and fleeting belief that they could try things and fail at them and try other things and discard them until they found something that truly touched and transformed them—and that they could do for the rest of their lives.

It's a high-stakes game letting kids roll the dice with their futures this way, and the risk—indeed the certainty—exists that at least a few of them will fail. But with their parents standing watchfully by, they need to be allowed to try. The more chances kids take, the greater the odds they will come up winners—and the chips they collect if they do can be priceless.

From *Time*, April 30, 2001, pp. 50-55. © 2001 by Time Inc. Reprinted by permission.

Evolution and Developmental Sex Differences

David C. Geary[1] Department of Psychology, University of Missouri at Columbia, Columbia, Missouri

Abstract

From an evolutionary perspective, childhood is the portion of the life span during which individuals practice and refine those competencies that facilitate survival and reproduction in adulthood. Although the skeletal structure of these competencies appears to be inherent, social interaction and play flesh them out during childhood so that they are adapted to local conditions. Darwin's principles of sexual selection, including male-male competition over mates and female choice of mating partners, successfully explain the acquisition and expression of reproduction competencies in hundreds of species. When this perspective is applied to humans, it predicts sex differences that are, in fact, found in the childhood activities of boys and girls and that reflect sex differences in reproductive strategies in adulthood. A few of these differences are described, along with cultural factors that modify their expression. The article closes with a brief discussion of the social and scientific implications.

Keywords

sex differences; sexual selection; development; childhood; culture

Sex differences are inherently interesting to the scientist and layperson alike. They always have been and always will be. Although the existence of such differences has been debated in the past, the scientific issue today concerns the source of these differences. The prevailing view in psychology is that most sex differences result from children's adoption of gender roles, roles that reflect society-wide differences in daily activities of men and women (Eagly, 1987). The goal here is not to provide a review or appraisal of this position, but rather to offer an alternative view of developmental sex differences, a view based on the principles of evolution (Darwin, 1871).

From an evolutionary perspective, cultural and ecological factors are expected to influence the expression of developmental sex differences, and a few of these influences are described in the final section. Before they are discussed, though, a basic evolutionary framework for understanding sex differences in general and developmental sex differences in particular is provided in the first section, and the second provides a few examples of the usefulness of this approach for understanding human developmental sex differences.

EVOLUTION AND DEVELOPMENT

Sexual Selection

One of Darwin's (1871) seminal contributions was the observation that evolutionary pressures often differ for males and females and that many of these differences center around the dynamics of reproduction. These pressures are termed sexual selection and typically result from males competing with one another for social status, resources, or territory—whatever is needed to attract mates—and from females' choice of mating partners (Andersson, 1994). Although the dynamics of male-male competition can vary across species and social and ecological conditions, one common result is the evolution of physical (see Fig. 1), cognitive, and behavioral sex differences. Females' choice of mates has been studied most extensively in birds, although it is also evident in insects, fish, reptiles, and mammals, including humans (Andersson, 1994; Buss, 1994). Females typically choose mates on the basis of indicators of physical, genetic, or behavioral fitness, that is, on the basis of traits that signal a benefit to them (e.g., provisioning) or their offspring (e.g., good genes). One example of the evo-

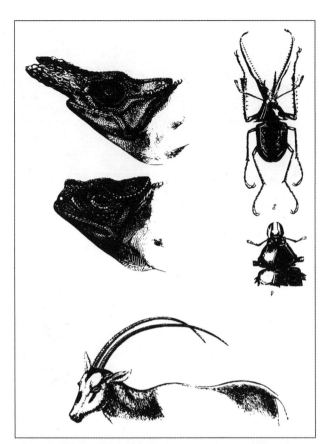

Fig. 1. Examples of sexually selected characteristics used in physical male-male competition. The pair in the upper left are the male (top) and female (bottom) of the *Chamaeleon bifurcus*; the pair in the upper right are the male and female of the beetle *Chiasognathus grantii*; at the bottom is a male *Oryx leucoryx*, a species of antelope (females do not have horns). From Darwin (1871, Vol. II, p. 35; Vol. I, p. 377; and Vol. II, p. 251, respectively). These exaggerated male characteristics are used in male-on-male aggression. For instance, two male *Oryx leucoryx* will compete by kneeling in front of each other, each then trying to maneuver the points of his horns under the body of his competitor. "If one succeeds in doing this, he suddenly springs up, throwing up his head at the same time, and can thus wound or perhaps even transfix his antagonist" (Darwin, 1871, Vol. II, pp. 251-252).

lutionary result of female choice is shown in Figure 2; the long and symmetric tail feathers of the male hummingbird are an indicator of his physical and genetic health.

Male-male competition and female choice are most evident in species in which males devote most of their reproductive energies to attracting mates, and females provide most or all of the parental care (Trivers, 1972), a pattern found in nearly 97% of mammalian species (Clutton-Brock, 1991). As is the case with other mammals, women throughout the world invest more time and resources in the well-being of their children than men do (Geary, 1998). Nonetheless, many men do provide some investment in the well-being of their children, unlike most other mammalian males. Paternal care, in turn, results in female-female competition and male choice of mates, along with male-male competition and female choice of mates.

The sex difference in the level of parental investment, along with other features (see Geary, 1998), results in dif-ferences in the nature of male-male versus female-female competition, and in the criteria used in mate choice (Geary, 1998). Throughout the world, men compete with one another for the control of culturally prized resources (e.g., status, money, or cows), and they often do so through physical contests (Keeley, 1996). Women compete with one another by means of relational aggression. They gossip, shun, and backbite their competitors (Crick, Casas, & Mosher, 1997). Both men and women want intelligent and cooperative spouses, but women more than men focus on the cultural success (e.g., control of money or cows) of suitors and men more than women focus on physical attractiveness (indicators of fertility; Buss, 1994).

Development

Biologists study development by documenting species' life history and by discerning the function of childhood. Life history refers to the typical ages associated with developmental milestones, such as age of weaning and length of childhood. The function of childhood is to refine the competencies that will be needed to survive and reproduce in adulthood (Mayr, 1974). It appears that many cognitive and behavioral systems are initially skeletal in structure—the basic framework is inborn—but are fleshed out as juveniles play, explore the environment, and interact socially (Gelman, 1990). Fleshing out these competencies results in the refinement of those skills needed to survive and reproduce in the local ecology and social group.

Developmental sex differences are expected to the degree that reproductive demands differ for male and females in adulthood. In species in which male-male competition is more intense than female-female competition, the juvenile period is longer for males than for females. Male satin bowerbirds (*Ptilonorhynchus violaceus*), for instance, mature many years after females have matured. Although there is some physical competition, males largely compete behaviorally, through the construction of complex stick structures called bowers. (Females make their mate choices, in part, on the basis of the complexity of these bowers.) During development, "young males spend a great deal of time observing older males at their bower, and practice bower building and display behaviors when the owner is absent from the bower site" (Collis & Borgia, 1992, p. 422). Young males also engage in play fighting, which provides the experience needed for dominance-related encounters in adulthood. Thus, delayed maturation and associated play allow for the refinement of those physical, cognitive, and behavioral skills associated with reproductive demands in adulthood.

HUMAN DEVELOPMENTAL SEX DIFFERENCES

Play Patterns

Play, in one form or another, is found in most mammalian species. "The consensus that emerges from the scores of definitions is that play incorporates many physical components of adult behavior patterns, such as those used in aggression, but without their immediate functional consequences" (Walters, 1987, p. 360). Play provides delayed benefits because the individual practices those behaviors that are important for survival and reproduction in adulthood, as described earlier. Sex differences in play patterns are found in many species and mirror sex differences found in adulthood.

Like juveniles of other mammalian species, boys and girls exhibit sex differences in their play patterns, and these differences in play are a reflection of sex differences found in adulthood (Geary, 1998). One of the most consistently found differences is in the frequency and nature of rough-and-tumble play. Beginning at about 3 years of age, groups of boys engage in various forms of play fighting, such as wrestling, three to six times more frequently than groups of girls do. Boys also engage in group-level competitive play (e.g., football) more frequently than girls do. These patterns are found in every culture in which play has been studied, are related to prenatal exposure to male hormones, and mirror the activities associated with primitive warfare (Keeley, 1996). The one-on-one and group-level play fighting of boys can be viewed as an evolved tendency to practice the competencies that were associated with male-male competition during human evolution (Geary, 1998).

Another sex difference, this one favoring girls, is in the frequency of play parenting (e.g., doll play): Play parenting is the norm in female primates and has been shown to significantly reduce the mortality rates of their first-born offspring. Again, this sex difference is found in all cultures in which play has been studied, is related to prenatal exposure to sex hormones, and mirrors the adult sex difference in investment in children. Play parenting can thus be understood as an evolved tendency to seek out activities that will enhance later parenting skills.

Social Development

Beginning in the preschool years and extending throughout the life span, girls and boys and women and men tend to segregate themselves into same-sex groups. One result is that boys and girls grow up in different social cultures. The tendency of boys to play fight and to organize themselves into competing groups is manifested in the context of the boys' culture. Social relationships among girls, in contrast, are more consistently communal: They manifest greater empathy; more concern for the well-being of other girls; and more nurturing, intimacy, and social and emotional support. In short, the social behavior of boys is focused on achieving status and dominance and developing coalitions for competing against groups of other boys. The social behavior of girls is focused on developing and maintaining a network of personal relationships and social support. Similar sex differences have been found in our closest relative,

Fig. 2. Female (left) and male (right) hummingbirds (*Spathura underwoodi*). From Darwin (1871, Vol. II, p. 77). The long and symmetric tail feathers of the male appear to signal to the female that he has immune-system genes that can confer resistance to local parasites (e.g., worms). If she mates with this male, then her offspring will also be resistant to local parasites.

the chimpanzee, suggesting that these are indeed evolved tendencies in humans (de Waal, 1993).

Nonetheless, girls and women can be quite competitive with one another. As noted earlier, this competition takes the form of relational aggression—attempting to disrupt the personal networks that are important to girls and women—and in adulthood, it is often associated with competition over resources (e.g., job promotion) and mates. As is the case with play fighting in boys, relational aggression emerges in the preschool years for girls and appears to be especially intense during early adolescence. It is likely, although not certain, that relational aggression has been shaped by sexual selection and in childhood is practice for later female-female competition.

CULTURAL AND ECOLOGICAL INFLUENCES

If the function of childhood is to adapt inherent skeletal competencies to local conditions, then cultural and ecological factors should influence the expression of developmental sex differences (Gelman, 1990; Mayr, 1974). Although research conducted within Western countries suggests that parents do not influence children's development as strongly as many people assume, cross-cultural studies suggest that there are important socialization influences on the expression (not creation) of developmental sex differences.

Although boys throughout the world engage in one-on-one and group-level competitive play, the nature and intensity of this play varies across cultures. The play fighting of boys tends to be rougher in societies where male-on-male physical aggression is common in adulthood than in other societies. For instance, intergroup aggression occurs frequently among the Yanomamö Indians of South America, and young Yanomamö boys often play fight with clubs or bows and arrows, practices that are typically discouraged in suburban America. In such societies, boys' play fighting often involves inflicting physical pain and sometimes injury, and there are often social rules that discourage boys from expressing this pain. In other words, boys' play fighting is encouraged and channeled to increase the aggressiveness and physical endurance of boys, and decrease their sensitivity to the distress of other people. These practices prepare boys for the life-and-death male-male competition that they will experience as adults. In other societies, such as our own, boys also play fight, but this behavior is relatively subdued and symbolic, as in competitive sports.

In a study of 93 cultures, Low (1989) found that the socialization of girls and boys was systematically related to the cultures' social structures (e.g., stratified vs. nonstratified societies) and marriage systems (i.e., polygynous vs. monogamous). In nonstratified polygynous societies—where men could improve their social status and thus increase the number of women they could marry—the socialization of boys focused on fortitude, aggression, and industriousness, traits that would influence their cultural and reproductive success in adulthood. For these societies, there was a strong linear relation between the socialization of competitiveness in boys and the maximum harem size allowed within the society. The larger the maximum harem size, the more the competitiveness of boys was emphasized in parental socialization.

For girls, there was a relation between the amount of economic and political power held by women in the society and socialization practices. In societies where women could inherit property and hold political office, girls were socialized to be less obedient, more aggressive, and more achievement oriented than were girls who lived in societies in which men had control over economic and political resources. On the basis of these and other patterns, Low (1989) concluded that "there is thus some evidence that patterns of child training across cultures vary in ways predictable from evolutionary theory, differing in specifiable ways between the sexes, and varying with group size, marriage system, and stratification" (p. 318).

CONCLUSION

From an evolutionary perspective, early biases in the ways in which boys and girls orient themselves to other people, in their play patterns, and in how they interact with and explore the wider ecology are expected, and, in fact, such biases are found (Geary, 1998). They lead girls and boys to create different cultures for themselves, and within these cultures to engage in activities that prepare them for the adult life of our ancestors. At the same time, a long childhood and the associated sensitivity to environmental influences ensure that the differences between boys and girls and men and women are not fixed, but rather are responsive to changing social and ecological conditions.

The combination of biological biases and sensitivity to early environmental conditions has important scientific and social implications. For instance, although boys and men are biologically destined to compete, this competition need not be deadly nor even physical, even if the evolutionary history of male-male competition was both physical and deadly (Keeley, 1996). One goal of psychological research, then, is to understand the social and ecological conditions that can push boys and men into deadly physical competition or to compete in ways that are socially beneficial (e.g., that lead to economic development). An evolutionary perspective on development highlights the importance of social and ecological factors in the expression of developmental sex differences and will provide an important theoretical framework for the study of the social and psychological aspects of these differences.

Recommended Reading

Buss, D.M. (1994). (See References)

Darwin, C. (1871). (See References)

Geary, D.C. (1998). (See References)

Morbeck, M.E., Galloway, A., & Zihlman, A.L. (Eds.). (1997). *The evolving female: A life-history perspective*. Princeton, NJ: Princeton University Press.

Note

1. Address correspondence to David C. Geary, Department of Psychology, 210 McAlester Hall, University of Missouri, Columbia, MO 65211-2500; e-mail: gearyd@missouri.edu.

References

Andersson, M. (1994). *Sexual selection*. Princeton, NJ: Princeton University Press.
Buss, D.M. (1994). *The evolution of desire: Strategies of human mating*. New York: Basic Books.
Clutton-Brock, T.H. (1991). *The evolution of parental care*. Princeton, NJ: Princeton University Press.
Collis, K., & Borgia, G. (1992). Age-related effects of testosterone, plumage, and experience on aggression and social dominance in juvenile male satin bowerbirds (*Ptilonorhynchus violaceus*). *Auk, 109*, 422–434.
Crick, N.R., Casas, J.F., & Mosher, M. (1997). Relational and overt aggression in preschool. *Developmental Psychology, 33*, 579–588.
Darwin, C. (1871). *The descent of man and selection in relation to sex* (2 vols.). London: J. Murray.

de Waal, F.B.M. (1993). Sex differences in chimpanzee (and human) behavior: A matter of social values? In M. Hechter, L. Nadel, & R.E. Michod (Eds.), *The origin of values* (pp. 285–303). New York: Aldine de Gruyter.

Eagly, A.H. (1987). *Sex differences in social behavior: A social-role interpretation.* Hillsdale, NJ: Erlbaum.

Geary, D.C. (1998). *Male, female: The evolution of human sex differences.* Washington, DC: American Psychological Association.

Gelman, R. (1990). First principles organize attention to and learning about relevant data: Number and animate-inanimate distinction as examples. *Cognitive Science, 14,* 79–106.

Keeley, L.H. (1996). *War before civilization: The myth of the peaceful savage.* New York: Oxford University Press.

Low, B.S. (1989). Cross-cultural patterns in the training of children: An evolutionary perspective. *Journal of Comparative Psychology, 103,* 311–319.

Mayr, E. (1974). Behavior programs and evolutionary strategies. *American Scientist, 62,* 650–659.

Trivers, R.L. (1972). Parental investment and sexual selection. In B. Campbell (Ed.), *Sexual selection and the descent of man 1871–1971* (pp. 136–179). Chicago: Aldine Publishing.

Walters, J.R. (1987). Transition to adulthood. In B.B. Smuts, D.L. Cheney, R.M. Seyfarth, R.W. Wrangham, & T.T. Struhsaker (Eds.), *Primate societies* (pp. 358–369). Chicago: University of Chicago Press.

Categories in Young Children's Thinking

Susan A. Gelman

The world is potentially a bewildering place for young children. Every day a child's senses are bombarded by countless different sights, sounds, tastes, and smells. Furthermore, all this variety is constantly changing, since the world is not a static place: people move, voices come and go, TV images flit across the screen, and new smells waft in as meals are served. In the nineteenth century William James (1890) suggested that infants and young children are overwhelmed by all this diversity, and they experience the world as a "blooming, buzzing confusion." Over the past few decades, however, researchers have discovered that even young children are able to make sense of the world by forming categories. A *category* is any grouping of things that are different in some way. Every time children use a word, put away a toy in the toy box, recognize a person's gender, or decide that a particular food is "yucky," they are using categories to organize their experience. Simple words like "doggie," "milk," or "ball" are among children's earliest categories of the world around them.

> **Researchers have consistently found that even newborns form sensible categories of simple sights, sounds, tastes, and smells. In some ways babies seem to be born knowing how to carve up the world into categories.**

This article will review some of the research on children's early categories. One of the most important findings from recent studies is that children can be quite sophisticated in how they group objects and think about those groupings. Children certainly do view the world somewhat differently from adults. However, the picture that emerges from recent research is that young children's categories are extremely important for guiding how they think about the world at large.

Early errors

Many past studies have shown that preschool children's categories differ from those of older children or adults. One primary difference is that the preschooler is more focused on superficial properties: how things look or where they can be found. We can see this with children's earliest words. Children younger than about age two-and-a-half typically "overextend" their words by applying them in overly broad ways, such as calling any round object a ball or any four-legged animal a dog (Clark 1973). These overextension errors have been documented in children learning a variety of languages across many different cultures.

Piaget's own observations suggest that throughout early childhood children form categories that seem immature from the standpoint of an adult (Inhelder & Piaget 1964). For example, if a five-year-old is asked to sort a set of plastic shapes, he might arrange them into a picture (such as putting a triangle on top of a square to form a house) rather than place together those of the same shape (such as separating all the triangles from all the squares). Likewise, preschool children often tend to put together items that go together in a scene rather than items that are alike in more fundamental ways. For instance, if a four-year-old is given pictures of a spider, a grasshopper, and a web and is asked to "put together the ones that go together," she typically will place the spider with the web (a *thematic* grouping) rather than with the grasshopper (a *taxonomic* grouping) (Smiley & Brown 1979). At this age, children also typically find it difficult to group together things in two different ways at the same time, such as realizing that someone can be *both* a boy *and* a brother (Piaget 1928; Markman 1989).

These kinds of difficulties are typical of preschool children and disappear as children get older. The same child who at age two is calling a tomato a ball will have no problem grouping it with other fruits and vegetables at age six, and may very well become a botanist as an adult! It is important to keep in mind, however, that the kinds of errors I've described above are not the only ways that young children classify. As described next, children are in

Early abilities

One way to observe early capabilities is to study infants. In the past 20 years, researchers have devised ingenious experimental methods for gauging what infants know. Researchers measure the very simple behaviors that infants can do, such as head-turns, sucking on a pacifier, gazing, facial expressions, and even heartbeats. Using these methods, researchers have consistently found that even newborns form sensible categories of simple sights, sounds, tastes, and smells (Mehler & Fox 1985). One-month-old babies group together speech sounds in much the same way as adults do, for example, perceiving that "bay" and "day" are different sounds. Before they are six months of age, infants categorize faces and emotional expressions (happy, sad, angry). They perceive colors, objects, even kinds of animals—all well before they can even speak (Quinn, Eimas, & Rosenkrantz 1993). It seems clear, then, that simple categories are not beyond the capacity of young children. In some ways babies seem to be born knowing how to carve up the world into categories.

> **Preschool children typically find it difficult to group together things in two different ways at the same time, such as realizing that someone can be both a boy and a brother.**

Perhaps even more impressive is the behavior of children who are "experts." Chi, Mervis, and their colleagues have studied young children who are exceptionally interested in a particular topic, such as dinosaurs, birds, or the game of chess. For example, one dinosaur expert who was studied at age four-and-a-half had been exposed to dinosaur information since turning three, and his parents read dinosaur books to him for an average of three hours per week (Chi & Koeske 1983). Another child became expert in identifying and naming birds and could identify 118 different kinds of birds by four years of age (Johnson & Mervis 1994). The general finding from this research is that when children know a great deal about a specialized domain, their categories look remarkably like the categories one would find with older children or even adults. Age seems to present few barriers for a child who has become an expert on a certain topic. Chi, Hutchinson, and Robin (1989) studied four-year-old children who were highly knowledgeable about the domain of dinosaurs

and found that their categories of dinosaurs were detailed, factually correct, and chock-full of information. These results tell us that even preschoolers can form mature categories.

We turn next to the question of how children use categories to think about information that is not immediately obvious.

Children younger than about age two-and-a-half typically "overextend" their words by applying them in overly broad ways, such as calling any round object a ball or any four-legged animal a dog.

Beyond the obvious

In *Beyond the Information Given*, Bruner (1973) points out that most of what we know about the world around us is not directly shown or visible. Instead, we make inferences from whatever information is available to go beyond what is most immediate. One can intuitively appreciate this point by considering a few familiar proverbs: "Don't judge a book by its cover," "Beauty is only skin deep," "Appearances can be deceiving." In real life, as in proverbs, how something looks can be misleading. Consider the trick-or-treater at Halloween who looks like a witch but is really the second-grader down the street; the apple that looks luscious on the outside but is full of worms inside; the animal that flies in the sky and looks like a bird but is really a bat.

Notice that these examples involve contrasting categories: witch versus girl, edible versus inedible, bird versus bat. Much of "going beyond the information given" involves forming categories that are based on information that's neither obvious nor visible.

I would like to turn now to the question of how and when children realize that categories go beyond the obvious. I will review three areas of research evidence with preschool children: the appearance-reality distinction, the power of words, and the thinking on biological growth. The theme that will emerge is that by four years of age preschool children clearly understand that categories include nonobvious information. In the summary, I bring out the positive—and negative—implications of this understanding for young children.

The appearance-reality distinction

When do children realize that appearances can be deceiving? Past research finds that, although three-year-olds have some difficulties holding in mind the distinction between appearance and reality, these difficulties greatly subside during the preschool years. For example, some years ago deVries (1969) examined children's reactions to a docile cat wearing a dog mask. Children first saw that the cat was harmless; then the cat briefly disappeared behind a screen, reappearing a moment later with the dog mask in place. Some of the three-year-olds become quite frightened after viewing the transformation and insisted that the cat had turned into a dog. However, by age six the children typically reported that the animal wasn't really a dog; it was only a cat wearing a mask.

> **When do children realize that appearances can be deceiving? Research finds that, although three-year-olds have some difficulties holding in mind the distinction between appearance and reality, these difficulties greatly subside during the preschool years.**
> **When appearance-reality distinctions (for example, you are still you even if you have on a mask) are complex or tricky, young children are still more likely than older children to get confused.**

Flavell (1986) found a marked shift between ages three and four in how children reason about appearance-reality conflicts. He presented children with deceptive objects, such as a glass of milk taken from plain view and placed

behind an orange filter. Even though children saw for themselves that the filter changed the appearance of the object, the three-year-olds typically insisted that appearance and reality were one and the same—for example, that the liquid looked orange and that it was "really and truly" orange juice. In contrast, the four-year-olds understood that even though the liquid looked orange, it was "really and truly" milk. Part of the difficulty for three-year-olds seems to be keeping both appearance and reality in mind at the same time.

These are all tigers, even though they are wearing and doing different things.

Other researchers have found some awareness of the appearance-reality distinction at even younger ages. When children are able to view a costume change directly, even three-year-olds realize that wearing a costume doesn't affect identity (Keil 1989). So, for example, a horse wearing a zebra costume is still a horse.

In fact, by four years of age, children realize that the "insides" of an animal or object may be even more important than its "outsides" for identifying what it is. In our own work Wellman and I asked children to show us which items had the same outsides and which had the same insides (Gelman & Wellman 1991). By age four, children could tell us that items that were alike on the outside were not necessarily alike on the inside. For example, a piggy bank and a real pig were judged to be alike on the outside but not the inside. Conversely, a real pig and a cow were judged to be alike on the inside but not the outside. Furthermore, when we asked children what would happen if a dog, say, didn't have its blood and bones, four- and five-year-olds told us that it would no longer be a dog and would no longer bark or eat dog food. However, when we asked them what would happen if a dog didn't have its fur, they reported that it still would be a dog and still could bark. Even though children can't see an object's insides, they understand that insides can be more important than outward appearances.

One final note about the appearance-reality distinction: Although four-year-olds *can* appreciate the distinction, this does not mean that they always *do*. When appearance-reality distinctions are complex or tricky, young children still are more likely than older children to get confused. For example, early elementary school children continue to err when asked whether superficial changes affect animal identity, often reporting that operations, ingestion of pills, or injections that result in physical appearance changes also can change what an animal actually is (Keil 1989).

The power of words

Young children place great weight on the names we give to things. Piaget (1929) suggested that children at first think that names are linked to the "essence" of a category: "In learning the names of things the child at this stage believes it is doing much more." He observed that children have some difficulty recognizing that the words we assign to objects are arbitrary, and instead they attach special significance to the name itself.

More recently, research has shown that children use category names (bird, dinosaur, squirrel) as a guide to extending their knowledge and making inferences. Children tend to assume that animals with the same category name are alike in important, nonobvious ways (Gelman & Markman 1986). For example, preschool children as young as two-and-a-half years typically assume that different kinds of birds all live in nests, feed their babies the same kinds of food, and have the same kinds of bones inside. Even when we teach children biological facts that they've never heard before, three- and four-year-olds generalize these facts to other animals with the same name.

We found also that children make use of new names that they learn in the context of the research study. For example, Coley and I showed two-and-a-half-year-old children pictures of unfamiliar animals such as a pterodactyl and a leaf-insect (Gelman & Coley 1990). One group of children learned no names for these animals and tended to assume incorrect labels for them (for example, that the pterodactyl was a bird and the leaf-insect a leaf). A second group of children learned the correct category names for these animals, for example, "dinosaur" for the pterodactyl and "bug" for the leaf-insect. We then asked children various questions about the animals: whether or not the pterodactyl lived in a nest, whether or not the leaf-insect grew on a tree, and so forth. The children who had

not learned the correct names typically answered the questions incorrectly, assuming that the pterodactyl lived in a nest (like other flying animals) or the leaf-insect grew on a tree. But the children who had learned the new category names made appropriate inferences based on the names. They said that the pterodactyl, like other dinosaurs, did not live in a nest, for example. Simply providing a name for the animal changed how children thought about the animal and what inferences they made.

Sample Generalizations Expressed in Spontaneous Talk

Some generalizations expressed by mothers

"Remember, I told you cats like balls of yarn?"
"That's a chipmunk. And they eat the acorns."
"Did you know when pigs get big, they're called hogs?"
"A wok is how people in China cook. Well, actually, a wok is how people in America cook like Chinese people."

Some generalizations expressed by children*

"That shirt's not for girls." (Ross, two years, seven months)

"Animals eat berries and they eat mushrooms." (Abe, two years, nine months)

"Indians live in Africa." (Adam, three years, three months)

"Bad guys have some guns." (Mark, three years, seven months)

*Bloom (1970), Brown (1973), Kuczaj (1976), Mac Whinney and Snow (1985, 1990), and Sachs (1983) have made their transcripts of adult-child interactions available through the Child Language Data Exchange System (CHILDES).

Preschool children pay close attention to the words we apply not just to categories of animals but also to categories of people. Hearing a child labeled "boy" or "girl" has vast implications for the kinds of inferences children form (Gelman, Collman, & Maccoby 1986). Preschoolers expect that a child's behaviors, preferences, goals, physical properties, and future identity can all be predicted based on whether the child is referred to as a boy or a girl. Children make such inferences even if they are thinking about a child whose appearance is atypical, such as a boy with long hair or a girl with very short hair. What is important in these cases is that an adult supplies the gender category label (boy, girl). If an adult doesn't say whether the child in question is a boy or a girl, children often have difficulty coming up with the correct classification on their own and tend instead to make inferences based on appearances. So when they meet a long-haired boy, many four-year-olds will assume that the child is a girl and

These are all pigs, even though they are wearing and doing different things.

plays with dolls. As soon as they hear he is a boy, however, their way of thinking about the child shifts.

Recently my colleagues and I have started to look at the kinds of generalizations children spontaneously express in their everyday talk and the kinds of generalizations that mothers express when talking with their children (Gelman et al. in press). Our focus was on statements and questions referring to an entire category rather than those referring to only a portion of a category. For example, we examined those times that children and mothers talked about mice (as a general category) rather than *some* mice, *my* mouse, or *those* mice. In other words, we wished to see when children and parents go beyond the specific context they are in to think about the category as an abstract whole. The box "Sample Generalizations Expressed in Spontaneous Talk," lists some examples.

Rodriguez and I are finding that children begin making broad generalizations about categories as early as two-and-a-half years of age, but that these generalizations increase rather dramatically between two-and-a-half and four years. This result suggests that children may become increasingly attentive to categories during this period. We are also finding that the sorts of generalizations that both children and parents express are especially frequent for categories of people and animals (for example, in the box these categories include cats, chipmunks, pigs, girls, animals, Indians, and bad guys). Both mothers and children make many fewer generalizations about categories of inert objects such as shoes, books, chairs.

Children sometimes maintain these generalizations even in the face of conflicting information. For example, consider the conversation that I recently had with my three-and-a-half-year-old son:

> *Adam*: Kids don't like coffee. Grown-ups do.
> *Me*: I don't like coffee.
> *Adam*: Yes you do! You're not a kid.

Similarly, many children express strong gender-stereotyped beliefs in the preschool years, reporting, for example, that mommies can't be doctors or that boys can't play with dolls (Liben & Signorella 1987). These category-based generalizations seem somewhat rigid and inflexible at the preschool age and are not easily overcome simply by giving the child counterevidence.

It is not yet clear whether or how the talk that children hear from others and other caregivers affects the kinds of generalizations they form. Do children who hear many generalizations tend to generalize more broadly than children who do not? Do the sorts of categories that parents and other caregivers talk about in this way affect how children think about these particular categories? For example, if a caregiver expresses many generalizations about gender categories, does this lead children to notice gender more or to make more inferences based on gender? These are important questions that await future research.

Thinking about biological growth

Caterpillars turn into butterflies, tadpoles turn into frogs, babies become adults, and acorns become oak trees. These examples of growth and metamorphosis provide an interesting arena for looking at how children understand categories because in every case the category member undergoes dramatic change and yet in some sense remains the same.

> **When children know a great deal about a specialized domain, their categories look remarkably like the categories one would find with older children or even adults.**

Long before they have any detailed knowledge of biological processes children come to understand several fundamental points about growth (Rosengren et al. 1991; Hickling & Gelman 1995). Four-year-olds understand that an individual animal can change shape, color, and size over the course of growth yet still keep the same name and identity. They understand that every kind of plant comes from a specialized kind of seed; for example, apple trees come from apple sees. They understand that the growth cycle is predictable and repeating: from seed to plant to fruit to seed to plant to fruit, and so on. They recognize that growth itself comes about due to natural processes (such as sunshine and rain) and not due to artificial processes (such as human activities).

> **Preschoolers expect that a child's behaviors, preferences, goals, physical properties, and future identity can all be predicted based on whether the child is referred to as a boy or a girl. Children sometimes maintain these generalizations even in the face of conflicting information. Many children express strong gender-stereotyped beliefs in the preschool years, reporting, for example, that mommies can't be doctors or that boys can't play with dolls.**

Four-year-olds also realize that nature can "win out" over nurture. For example, if four-year-old children hear about an animal that is adopted by another species and raised in this atypical environment (e.g., a cow raised by pigs), they predict that the animal will continue to grow and develop just like the birth parents (Gelman & Wellman 1991)—the cow will moo and have a straight tail when it grows up, even though it has been raised by pigs. Preschool children make similar predictions about nature-nurture conflicts with seeds (e.g., a lemon seed planted in a cornfield) or people (e.g., a baby whose birth parents and adoptive parents differ in skin color or personality traits) (Hirschfeld 1996; Springer 1996; Taylor 1996).

Taken altogether, these studies suggest that four-year-old children view growth and development as natural processes (Gelman & Kremer 1991) unfolding inside the animal or plant rather than resulting from outside influences. They expect that a great deal of how an animal or plant grows and develops is fixed at birth in the infant animal or the seed of the plant.

Children at age three know a great deal less about biological growth (Gelman & Wellman 1991; Rosengren et al. 1991; Hickling & Gelman 1995). It may be that early experiences are contributing to the changes between ages three and four. One study found that children who care for a pet goldfish at home are more knowledgeable about biology than children who do not (Inagaki 1990). However, at this point little is known about the kinds of experiences that children have with growth and metamorphosis in their preschools and at home and how these experiences affect children's understanding of growth.

Summary

Children have an impressive understanding of categories by age four—they grasp the distinction between appearance and reality, they use names as a guide for making inferences, and they realize that growth is an orderly, natural process. To some extent, even two-and-a-half and three-year-old children show some of these same early understandings. However, there are also developmental changes during the preschool period (especially between two-and-a-half and four years of age). The youngest children are apt to have more difficulties with the appearance-reality distinction, are less apt to form spontaneous generalizations using the categories that they have, and are easily confused about the growth process.

Altogether the lesson we have learned from studying children's early categories is that categories are tremendously important tools for young children and have implications for how they view the world. Like any tools, categories can be used in either useful or inappropriate ways. We have already seen some of the dangers in early categories: children sometimes take names more seriously than they should and draw overly broad generalizations based on the categories that they know. Overall, however, we view the effects of categories as mostly positive. Children make use of categories to expand their knowledge. By simply naming objects we can encourage children to notice how different items are similar and help children gain new information about the world. Furthermore, because children expect items in a category to be alike in nonobvious ways, they are able to learn about "scientific" properties (such as the insides of animals) well before kindergarten age. Both of these implications illustrate that categories are the foundation for later learning in school.

References

Bloom, L. 1970. Language development: Form and function in emerging grammars. Cambridge, MA: MIT Press.

Brown, R. W. 1973. A first language: The early stages. Cambridge, MA: Harvard University Press.

Bruner, J. S. 1973. *Beyond the information given: Studies in the psychology of knowing.* New York: Norton.

Chi, M., J. Hutchinson, & A. Robin. 1989. How inference about novel domain-related concepts can be constrained by structured knowledge. *Merrill-Palmer Quarterly* 35: 27–62.

Chi, M. T. H., & R. D. Koeske. 1983. Network representation of a child's dinosaur knowledge. *Developmental Psychology* 19: 29–39.

Clark, E. V. 1973. What's in a word? On the child's acquisition of semantics in his first language. In *Cognitive development and the acquisition of language*, ed. T. E. Moore. New York: Academic.

deVries, R. 1969. *Constancy of generic identity in the years three to six.* Monographs of the Society for Research in Child Development, vol. 34, no. 3, serial no. 127. Chicago: University of Chicago Press.

Flavell, J. H. 1986. The development of children's knowledge about the appearance-reality distinction. *American Psychologist* 41: 418–25.

Gelman, S. A., & J. D. Coley. 1990. The importance of knowing a dodo is a bird: Categories and inferences in 2-year-old children. *Developmental Psychology* 26: 796–804.

Gelman, S.A., J. D. Coley, K. Rosengren, E. Hartman, & T. Pappas. In press. *Beyond labeling: The role of maternal input in the acquisition of richly-structured categories.* Monographs of the Society for Research in Child Development. Chicago: University of Chicago Press.

Gelman, S. A., P. Collman, & E. E. Maccoby. 1986. Inferring properties from categories versus inferring categories from properties: The case of gender. *Child Development* 57: 396–404.

Gelman, S. A., & K. E. Kremer. 1991. Understanding natural causes: Children's explanations of how objects and their properties originate. *Child Development* 62: 396–414.

Gelman, S. A., & E. M. Markman. 1986. Categories and induction in young children. *Cognition* 23: 183–209.

Gelman, S. A., & H. M. Wellman. 1991. Insides and essences: Early understandings of the non-obvious. *Cognition* 38: 213–44.

Hickling, A. K., & S. A. Gelman. 1995. How does your garden grow? Early conceptualization of seeds and their place in plant growth cycle. *Child Development* 66: 856–76.

Hirschfeld, L. A. 1996. *Race in the making: Cognition, culture, and the child's construction of human kinds.* Cambridge, MA: MIT Press.

Inagaki, K. 1990. The effects of raising animals on children's biological knowledge. *British Journal of Developmental Psychology* 8: 119–29.

Inhelder, B., & J. Piaget. 1964. *The early growth of logic in the child.* New York: Norton.

James, W. 1890. *The principles of psychology.* New York: Dover.

Johnson, K. E., & C. B. Mervis. 1994. Microgenetic analysis of first steps in children's acquisition of expertise on shorebirds. *Developmental Psychology* 30: 418–35.

Keil, F. C. 1989. *Concepts, kinds, and cognitive development.* Cambridge, MA: MIT Press.

Kuczaj, S. 1976. -ing, -s, and -ed: A study of the acquisition of certain verb inflections. Ph.D. diss., University of Minnesota.

Liben, L. S., & M. L. Signorella, eds. 1987, *Children's gender schemata.* San Francisco: Jossey-Bass.

MacWhinney, B., & C. Snow. 1985. The Child Language Data Exchange System. *Journal of Child Language* 12: 271–95.

MacWhinney, B., & C. Snow. 1990. The Child Language Data Exchange System: An update. *Journal of Child Language* 17: 457–72.

Markman, E. M. 1989. *Categorization and naming in children: Problems of induction.* Cambridge, MA: MIT Press.

Mehler, J., & R. Fox, eds. 1985. *Neonate cognition: Beyond the blooming, buzzing confusion.* Hillsdale, NJ: Erlbaum.

Piaget, J. 1928. *Judgement and reasoning in the child.* London: Routledge & Kegan Paul.

Piaget, J. 1929. *The child's conception of the world.* London: Routledge & Kegan Paul.

Quinn, P. C., P. D. Eimas, & S. L. Rosenkrantz. 1993. Evidence for representations of perceptually similar natural categories by 3-month-old and 4-month-old infants. *Perception* 22: 463–75.

Rosengren, K. S., S. A. Gelman, C. W. Kalish, & M. McCormick, 1991. As time goes by: Children's early understanding of growth in animals. *Child Development* 62: 1302–20.

Sachs, J. 1983. Talking about the there and then: The emergence of displaced reference in parent-child discourse. In *Children's language, vol. 4,* ed. K. E. Nelson. Hillsdale, NJ: Erlbaum.

Smiley, S. S., & A. L. Brown. 1979. Conceptual preference for thematic or taxonomic relations: A nonmonotonic age trend from preschool to old age. *Journal of Experimental Child Psychology* 28: 249–57.

Springer, K. 1996. Young children's understanding of a biological basis for parent-offspring relations. *Child Development* 67: 2841–56.

Taylor, M. G. 1996. The development of children's beliefs about social and biological aspects of gender differences. *Child Development* 67: 1555–71.

Susan A. Gelman, Ph.D., is professor of psychology at the University of Michigan. She has received awards from the American Psychological Association, the J. S. Guggenheim Foundation, and the National Science Foundation for her research on concept and language learning in children.

*This is one of a regular series of Research in Review columns. The column in this issue was invited by Research in Review Editor, **Carol Seefeldt**, Ph.D., professor at the University of Maryland, College Park.*

Illustrations © by Patti Argoff.

From *Young Children*, January 1998, pp. 20–26. © 1998 by Susan A. Gelman, Reprinted by permission.

Do Young Children Understand What Others Feel, Want, and Know?

Angeline Lillard and Stephanie Curenton

Very young children can show surprising awareness of what other people feel, want, and know. By the time they are seven or eight months old, babies pay special attention to the emotional expressions of adults. By the second year of life, toddlers are beginning to know when others are feeling happy, angry, or sad. They may even try to comfort someone who is distressed. Toddlers also assume that others have desires and goals and may clutch a toy they are holding or try to hide it behind their backs when they see another child eyeing it.

From a very early age children appear to develop an intuitive or "folk" psychology in which they attribute wants and beliefs to others to account for people's actions. Young children, as well as adults, are very interested in what others are doing and feeling and why they do what they do.

Background

Learning to understand the feelings and intentions of other people is a critical part of becoming a functioning member of society. To get along well with others, interact cooperatively, and develop close social relationships, this learning must take place. The development of social understanding is so important to human development and it begins so early that psychologists are beginning to think of it as an innate potential, like the ability to learn language. This view differs from Piaget's theory that young children do not develop the ability to "take the perspective" of others and understand their feelings and intentions until at age six or seven they enter the "concrete operational" period of mental development.

People's understanding that others have mental states is a very interesting feat. When we see someone fall down and cry, we assume the person is *sad*, and *wants* comforting. When we see a child crouched over a piece of paper with a pencil in hand, sounding out letters, we guess that child is *trying* to write letters. An amazing aspect of these understandings is that mental states are usually not accompanied by any hard evidence of their existence. We have to make it up. It appears that even very young children, as early as 18 months of age, also make it up, inventing mental states in others (Meltzoff 1995).

Research suggests that humans are unique in this regard, since animals do not appear to invent mental states

(Povinelli & Eddy 1996). Animals simply respond to facial expressions, vocalizations, and body postures. People, on the other hand, attribute mental states with gusto, even applying them to cars and ovens and other entities in which they obviously do not belong.

> Many observant toddler and preschool teachers know how sensitive some of these very young children can be to the thoughts and feelings of others.

The study of how and when we acquire an understanding of other's minds has taken developmental psychology by storm, with a tenfold increase over the past decade in the number of publications discussing these issues. The reason for this attention is that knowledge about minds has consequences for so many areas of human functioning. Human interactions from the nursery onward are often about what we think others are thinking.

For example, when children learn the meaning of new words, they need to notice the focus of attention of the adult who is supplying the new word. Even by 18 months, children who are busy playing with a new toy will look to an adult's face when she sounds like she is supplying a new word label ("It's a cyclops! Look at the cyclops!"). Further, children will assume the new word refers to whatever the adult is looking at rather than simply assume it refers to their own toy (Baldwin 1991). This suggests that children have some perspective-taking ability even in Piaget's sensorimotor stage.

Another example of how understanding minds is fundamental to human interactions concerns intentions. Dodge and Price (1994) have shown that boys with very aggressive behavior attribute mean intentions to others, while nonaggressive boys who are in the same situation do not. Other research has shown that children with delinquency problems have trouble taking others' perspectives, and that training them in role-taking by discussing how others view the world is associated with reductions in their aggressive behavior (Chandler 1975).

Children with autism also show marked deficits on many tasks requiring an understanding of minds. Some researchers have even claimed that "mindblindness," the inability to understand others' mental states, is the fundamental deficit of autism (Baron-Cohen 1995). Talking about others' intentions and mental states helps very young children, even those who are not abnormally aggressive or delinquent, to understand mental states. For example, when parents talk more with their children at age two about others' emotions, the children by age four have a better understanding of others' minds.

What do young children know about minds, and when do they know it?

Studies of young children developing understanding of mental states have focused on four areas: children's understanding of (1) the relationship between information from the senses (perception) and what people know, (2) the emotions of others, (3) others' desires, and (4) others' beliefs.

Perception

Three-year-olds have some rudimentary understandings of how sensory experience is related to what people know. Even before three years of age, a child knows to behave differently toward his mother if she is out of the room when a coveted item is hidden (and therefore needs some clues about where to find it) than if she is in the room when the item is hidden (O'Neill 1996). By four or five years of age, children realize how they learned something.

In one study, two objects identical except for their color were shown to children. One of the objects was placed in a tunnel, and the children felt it but did not see it. When asked what color it was, children under five tended to positively assert that the object was one of the colors ("It's blue!"). When asked how they knew, children often responded with the impossible: "It felt blue!" (O'Neill, Astington, & Flavell 1992). By age five, most children realized they could not know an object's color by feeling it.

Emotions

Simple emotions are understood very early. Happiness is usually the first emotion children master, followed by anger and sadness (Borke 1971) and fear (Michalson & Lewis 1985). Repacholi and Gopnik (1997) had 18-month-olds observe a woman looking at broccoli, smiling at it, and saying, "Mmm! Broccoli!" Next she made an ugly face and said, "Yuck!" while looking at the children's preferred food, Goldfish crackers. When asked to give the experimenter some food, most toddlers chose to give her broccoli instead of the crackers. Fourteen-month-olds, in contrast, tried to give her the Goldfish crackers.

This study suggests that by 18 months of age children realize that others' desires might differ from their own and they can use emotional expressions to interpret those desires. Children also learn early how situations relate to emotions. For example, by age three most children assume that people are happy at birthday parties and sad when a dog bites them (Harris 1989).

> Now, new research validates what we see.

Although young children can understand emotions based on desires, they have difficulty understanding emotions, such as surprise, that are based on beliefs. Understanding surprise is difficult because the emotion is a mismatch between a person's beliefs and reality. Most children do not understand surprise until they have mastered belief, which occurs usually at age five (Hadwin & Perner 1991). They also find it hard to understand the notion that emotional expressions might not represent true feelings. For example, until age five or six, children do not seem to realize that one might smile upon receiving a gift even if one does not like the gift (Saarni 1984). Preschoolers also have difficulty understanding ambivalent feelings, such as being happy about getting a new bicycle but disappointed because it is the wrong color (Kestenbaum & Gelman 1995).

Desires

Children's earliest understanding of the mental states of others has been described as desire psychology (Wellman 1990), because they interpret someone's actions in terms of what that person might want. By age three children understand that desires are positive attitudes toward something outside of themselves. They can also understand the differences between what is wanted and what is reality. For example, when talking about ice cream, one young child said, "I don't want it cold. I wanted it warm" (Bartsch & Wellman 1995, 71).

Similarly, children realize that although one person might like something, another might not. They also have a grasp of how desires relate to actions. Three-year-olds predict that if someone wants something and does not succeed in finding it, the person will keep looking. Furthermore, they understand the link between desires and emotions: that if someone gets what she wants, she will be happy, and if someone does not get what she wants, she will be sad (Wellman & Woolley 1990).

Beliefs

A major development of the preschool years is an understanding that others have beliefs about the world that affect what they do. Until about age four, children have a tendency to act as if everyone knows and believes what they themselves know to be true. If a child falls down at school, she expects her mother to know about the event because she herself knows about it. If a child knows that the ladder on the slide has a broken rung, he believes that his friend knows it too (and will be careful without being told).

One way psychologists have studied children's understanding of belief has been by using *false-belief tasks*. In one such task, children are shown a doll and told that the doll has left a treasured candy bar in a drawer and gone out to play. Children see the doll's mother move the candy to a cupboard. The doll returns, and children are asked where the doll will look for his candy. Until they are four or five years old, children usually predict that the doll will go straight to the cupboard to retrieve the candy bar (Wimmer & Perner 1983). Older children usually understand that the doll would falsely believe the candy was in the drawer.

This error holds even in greatly simplified circumstances and even when the child herself is the actor. For example, in another type of false-belief task, children first are shown a cracker box and asked what is inside. Most respond, "Crackers!" Then the children are shown that the box actually contains leaves, not crackers, and they now are asked what they had thought was inside. Although the task is very simple and other children are asked about their own mental states rather than someone else's, until age four or five a child will usually respond, "Leaves!" (Gopnik & Astington 1988).

This outcome is not due to a problem with the word *think*, because the same error applies when the word *say* is used. It is not due to embarrassment, because the error holds if children are asked what a friend or parent would think. It is not due to misunderstanding the temporal aspect of the question, because when asked what someone else would think was inside if they were seeing the closed-up box for the first time, three-year-olds still usually say, "Leaves!"

It seems that until children are about four years old (perhaps a year later in children from families with low incomes ([Holmes, Black, & Miller 1996]), they have difficulty with the notion that our beliefs about the world are sometimes false. What appears to underlie this error is a failure to understand that our minds represent a version of the world, like a photograph represents some state of affairs at the time it was taken. Perhaps children view minds more like photographs that are updated to match reality.

Most young children act as if there is only one way to represent the world, an object, or a situation, and other lines of research support this. In *appearance-reality tasks*, for example, children are shown fake objects, like a candle that looks just like an apple. After discussing its appearance and reality, children are asked both what it is (really and truly) and what it looks like "to your eyes right now." Children older than four will give two answers: it is really a candle, but it looks like an apple. Younger children, however, give just one answer, usually claiming that the object looks like what it really is: a candle (Flavell, Green, & Flavell 1986).

Children do not understand that one reality can be represented in two different ways. This misconception about minds presumably has important effects. For example, children's lies before age four may be told only to influence behavior rather than with full understanding of the consequences for belief.

Psychologists' studies have suggested ages at which most children acquire certain understandings about minds. The fact is that even a two-year-old might make a comment that reflects a grasp of false belief. At age two, after answering the phone, one author's elder daughter announced, "I thought it was going to be Dad, but it was Sally!" What this suggests is that under highly supportive conditions children might occasionally evidence early insight about some concept, like mental representation, but mastery of that concept might be years off. Development is rarely all or none (Siegler 1998). Most children appear to have a pretty solid understanding of mental representation around age four or five.

How parents and teachers can support the development of children's understanding of others, and how culture might be important

When children have developed a *theory of mind*—an understanding that others have feelings and desires and beliefs—they are likely to engage in more positive interactions with others (Leekam 1993; Lalonde & Chandler 1995; Happe & Frith 1996). Since an ability to understand other minds is related to positive social relations, a major goal in both home and school settings becomes supporting this development. Researchers believe that to some degree the capacity for understanding other minds comes with biological maturation and accompanying increases in cognitive ability. In addition, studies suggest that engaging in pretend play (Youngblade & Dunn 1995) and having conversations about mental states (Dunn, Brown, & Beardsall 1991) may support the development of children's social understanding.

Encouraging pretend play

One reason that pretending may help children understand the mental states of others is that in social pretense the child must negotiate the pretend world and come face-to-face with others' representations of it. Piaget would endorse such a view, in which intense peer interaction promotes social understanding. Another aspect is that, in pretending to be other people, the child takes on others' views of the world. Regardless of why pretend play appears to help, it does seem that facilitating social pretense in children close to age four could helpfully boost them over the edge to understanding that people mentally represent their worlds.

Talking to children about minds

A second way of helping young children understand others' minds is by talking to them about minds and mental states. Dunn has found that talking more about emotional states in natural contexts to children at 33 months is associated with better performance on false-belief tasks at 40 months (Dunn, Brown, & Beardsall 1991).

Many children's books center on changes in feelings, and reading such books and discussing the feelings may also assist children's understanding that minds represent the world. Additionally, reading such books and discussing the feelings may also aid children's understanding of how other people think and feel.

Researchers have also found that younger siblings understand false beliefs earlier than do older siblings (Lewis et al. 1996). Perhaps this is because the more siblings a child has, the more feelings there are to talk about, and younger siblings might be particularly influenced by such talk.

There is evidence that children who are deaf, whose parents do not use sign language, are delayed in passing false-belief tasks, whereas those children whose parents do sign pass tasks at the usual age. This finding further supports the role of conversation in developing social understanding.

Finally, although we may balk at the idea of organized lessons around mental states, some researchers have found that both explaining thoughts by using cartoon-type "thought bubbles" and discussing false beliefs with children after watching carefully constructed false-belief videotapes assists them in understanding false beliefs. Such methods are not being used to help children with autism.

The role of culture

Another powerful influence on children's growing understanding of others' minds is most likely culture, but research on this topic is relatively scarce. Most psychologists who have studied children's theories of mind have been guided by mainstream cognitive development approaches that pay little attention to the impact of culture. It has been generally assumed that certain basic understandings occur in children at about the same age everywhere in the world with only minor variations due to cultural practices. One study did find that children of Baka pygmies of Cameroon passed false-belief tasks at about the same age as did most of their European and American peers (Avis & Harris 1991).

Until about age four children have a tendency to act as if everyone knows and believes what they themselves know to be true. A major development of the preschool years is an understanding that others have beliefs about the world that affect what they do.

Yet different cultures do have different ways of understanding minds (Lillard 1998), and cultural understandings may well influence children. One prominent difference is how much attention is paid to minds. Although Northern Europeans and Americans (at least middle-class, more highly educated families) tend to focus a lot of attention on how minds and mental states cause behaviors, people from Asian cultures pay more attention to how the situations people are in dictate behavior.

Perhaps a subtle difference in the concept of the person underlies this distinction, some viewing the person as an autonomous unit seeking to fill her own desires and others considering the person as part of a larger social whole whose actions are dictated by the needs of the group, not the self. Such concept differences appear within the United States as well, with rural American children (whose parents most likely have no more than a high school education and a working-class income) resembling Asian children in that they refer more to context-based reasons for behaviors than to mental-state reasons (Lillard, Zeljo, & Harlan 1998; Lillard in press).

Cultures also differ in their attention to certain types of mental states. One study suggests that African American children engage in more emotion talk than do European American children (Blake 1994). Japanese families also talk more to their children about emotions, engaging in what could be seen as intensive empathy training (Azuma 1994). As one example, instead of telling children to eat their dinner so they will grow or because they are lucky not to be starving like children in some other part of the world, Japanese parents are apt to emphasize that a poor farmer worked hard to grow the food and that the children will hurt his feelings if they do not eat it. When a single sock was found in a classroom during a visit one author made to a Japanese preschool, the teacher said to the class, "This poor sock has no partner. Poor sock. Can we help the sock?"

Such cultural practices train children to respond with feeling to those around them as behooves one in Japanese society. Indeed, Japanese adults are not supposed to talk about mental states. References to mental state are taboo, because a truly sensitive person should know others' mental states without being told about them. These adult conventions may necessitate a great deal of talk about mental state with children, so they learn to be very good at making inferences about mental states before they become taboo topics.

Another apparent cultural difference related to how we understand minds is the extent to which children are allowed to live in mentally constructed worlds as opposed to a single-objective world. Middle-class European American parents appear to socialize children to see the priority of personal views over reality. One recent study reports that middle-class European American parents even accept their children's false statements, apparently to protect their children's self-esteem (Wiley et al. 1998). For example, when a child asserted that Santa Claus comes at Easter, her mother yielded, "Oh, I'm confused," rather than correcting her. Working-class European American parents, in contrast, tended to correct their children, expecting them to get the story right.

Such cultural differences probably lead children to think differently about minds and behaviors. Indeed, researchers have found that children from working-class rural homes tend to explain behaviors as being mandated by circumstances, while children from middle-class urban homes tend to explain them as arising from desires and emotions (Lillard, Zeljo, & Harlan 1998). If reality can be any way that you imagine it, minds become more important. Such views have implications for classroom behavior. In Mexican culture the teacher is revered, and children are expected to learn the teacher's way as the one right way (Delgado-Gaitan 1994); Asian culture is purportedly similar. In contrast, European American children are expected to learn to think critically and challenge the teacher, imposing their own reality on the topic.

Summary

Generally, research suggests that children who understand others' minds at an early age may be more able to get along well with others and that parents and teachers can support the development of this understanding by encouraging pretend play and discussing mental states with them from storybooks or real-life encounters. It is probably not worth discussing the concept of thoughts with toddlers because it may be beyond their understanding. However, some research suggests that by age three, discussions of what other people are thinking may be helpful.

The fact that discussion leads to understanding aspects of the mind, coupled with different approaches to minds across cultures, suggests that we need to be sensitive about minds and behavior. Every child develops ideas about minds and behaviors, but the ideas individual children have may be different depending on their cultural milieu.

References

Avis, J., & P. L. Harris, 1991. Belief-desire reasoning among Baka children: Evidence for a universal conception of mind. *Child Development* 62: 460–67.

Azuma, H. 1994. Two modes of cognitive socialization in Japan and the United States. In *Cross-cultural roots of minority child development*, eds. P. M. Greenfield & R. R. Cocking, 275–84. Hillsdale, NJ: Erlbaum.

Baldwin, D. A. 1991. Infants' contribution to the achievement of joint reference. *Child Development* 62: 875–90.

Baron-Cohen, S. 1995. *Mindblindness: An essay on autism and theory of mind*. London: MIT Press.

Bartsch, K., & H. M. Wellman. 1995. *Children talk about the mind.* Oxford: Oxford University Press.

Blake, I. K. 1994. Language development and socialization in young African-American children. In *Cross-cultural roots of minority child development*, eds. P. M. Greenfield & R. R. Cocking, 147–66. Hillsdale, NJ: Erlbaum.

Borke, H. 1971. Interpersonal perception of young children: Egocentrism or empathy? *Developmental Psychology* 5: 263–69.

Chandler, M. J. 1975. Egocentrism and anti-social behavior: The assessment and training of social perspective-taking skills. *Developmental Psychology* 9: 326–32.

Delgado-Gaitan, C. 1994. Socializing young children in Mexican-American families: An intergenerational perspective. In *Cross-cultural roots of minority child development*, eds. P. M. Greenfield & R. R. Cocking, 55–86. Hillsdale, NJ: Erlbaum.

Dodge, K. A., & J. M. Price. 1994. On the relation between social information processing and socially competent behavior in early school-aged children. *Child Development* 65: 1385–97.

Dunn, J., J. Brown, & L. Beardsall. 1991. Family talk about feeling states and children's later understanding of others' emotions. *Developmental Psychology* 27: 448–55.

Flavell, J. H., F. L. Green, & E. R. Flavell. 1986. *Development of knowledge about the appearance-reality distinction.* Monographs of the Society for Research in Child Development, vol. 51, no. 1, serial no. 212.

Gopnik, A., & J. W. Astington, 1988. Children's understanding of representational change and its relation to the understanding of false belief and the appearance-reality distinction. *Child Development* 59: 26–37.

Hadwin, J., & J. Perner. 1991. Pleased and surprised: Children's cognitive theory of emotion. *British Journal of Developmental Psychology* 9: 215–34.

Happe, F., & U. Frith. 1996. Theory of mind and social impairment in children with conduct disorder. *British Journal of Developmental Psychology* 14: 385–98.

Harris, P. L. 1989. *Children and emotion.* Oxford: Basil Blackwell.

Holmes, H., C. Black, & S. Miller. 1996. A cross-task comparison of false belief understanding in a Head Start population. *Journal of Experimental Child Psychology* 63: 263–85.

Kestenbaum, R., & S. A. Gelman. 1995. Preschool children's identification and understanding of mixed emotions. *Cognitive Development* 10: 443–58.

Lalonde, C. E., & M. J. Chandler. 1995. False belief understanding goes to school: On the social-emotional consequences of coming early or late to a first theory of mind. *Cognition and Emotion* 9: 167–85.

Leekam, S. 1993. Children's understanding of mind. In *The development of social cognition: The child as psychologist,* ed. M. Bennett, 26–61. New York: Guilford.

Lewis, C., N. Freeman, C. Kyriakidou, K. Maridaki-Kassotaki, & D. Berridge. 1996. Social influences on false belief access: Specific sibling influences or general apprenticeship? *Child Development* 67: 2930–47.

Lillard, A. S. 1998. Ethnopsychologies: Cultural variations in theory of mind. *Psychological Bulletin* 123: 3–33.

Lillard, A. S. In press. Developing a cultural theory of mind: The CIAO approach. *Current Directions in Psychological Science.*

Lillard, A. S., A. Zeljo, & D. Harlan. 1998. Developing cultural schemas: Behavior explanation in Taipei, the rural U.S., and the urban U.S. University of Virginia. Typescript paper.

Meltzoff, A. 1995. Understanding the intentions of others: Re-enactment of intended acts by 18-month-old children. *Child Development* 31: 838–50.

Michalson, L., & M. Lewis. 1985. What do children know about emotions and when do they know it? In *The socialization of emotions,* eds. M. Lewis & C. Saarni, 117–39. New York: Plenum.

O'Neill, D. K. 1996. Two-year-old children's sensitivity to a parent's knowledge state when making requests. *Child Development* 67: 659–77.

O'Neill, D. K., J. Astington, & J. H. Flavell. 1992. Young children's understanding of the role that sensory experiences play in knowledge acquisition. *Child Development* 63: 474–90.

Povinelli, D. J., & T. J. Eddy. 1996. *What young chimpanzees know about seeing.* Monographs of the Society for Research in Child Development, vol. 61, no. 3, serial no. 247.

Repacholi, B. M., & A. Gopnik. 1997. Early reasoning about desires: Evidence from 14- and 18-month-olds. *Developmental Psychology* 33: 12–21.

Saarni, C. 1984. An observational study of children's attempts to monitor their expressive behavior. *Child Development* 55: 1504–13.

Siegler, R. S. 1998. *Children's thinking.* Upper Saddle River, NJ: Prentice-Hall.

Wellman, H. M. 1990. *The child's theory of mind.* Cambridge, MA: Bradford Books/MIT Press.

Wellman, H. M., & J. D. Woolley. 1990. From simple desires to ordinary beliefs: The early development of everyday psychology. *Cognition* 35: 245–275.

Wiley, A. R., A. J. Rose, L. K. Burger, & P. J. Miller. 1998. Constructing autonomous selves through narrative practices: A comparative study of working-class and middle-class families. *Child Development* 69: 833–47.

Wimmer, H., & J. Perner. 1983. Beliefs about beliefs: Representation and constraining function of wrong beliefs in young children's understanding of deception. *Cognition* 13: 103–28.

Youngblade, L. M., & J. Dunn. 1995. Individual differences in young children's pretend play with mother and sibling: Links to relationships and understanding of other people's feelings and beliefs. *Child Development* 66: 1472–92.

For further reading and information

Berk, L. E. 1994. Research in Review. Vygotsky's theory: The importance of make-believe play. *Young Children* 50 (1): 30–39.

Curry, N. E., & S. H. Arnaud. 1995. Personality difficulties in preschool children as revealed through play themes and styles. *Young Children* 50 (4): 4–9.

Dyson, A. H. 1990. Research in Review. Symbol makers, symbol weavers: How children link play, pictures, and print. *Young Children* 45 (2): 50–57.

Gowen, J. W. 1995. Research in Review. The early development of symbolic play. *Young Children* 50 (3): 75–83.

Katz, L. G., & D. E. McClellan. 1997. *Fostering children's social competence: The teacher's role.* Washington, DC: NAEYC.

Nourot, P. M., & J. L. Van Hoorn. 1991. Research in Review. Symbolic play in preschool and primary settings. *Young Children* 46 (6): 40–50.

Sawyers, J. K., & C. S. Rogers. 1988. *Helping young children develop through play: A practical guide for parents, caregivers, and teachers.* Washington, DC: NAEYC.

Slaby, R. G., W. C. Roedell, D. Arezzo, & K. Hendrix. 1995. *Early violence prevention: Tools for teachers of young children.* Washington, DC: NAEYC.

Stark County (Ohio) School District; North Central Regional Educational Laboratory; Iowa, Nebraska, and Ohio Departments of Education: Jennings Foundation; & NAEYC. 1996. *Play—The seed of learning.* The Early Childhood Program series. 30 min. Distributed by NAEYC, Washington, D.C. Videocassette.

Stone, J. G. 1990. *Teaching preschoolers: It looks like this… In pictures.* Washington, DC: NAEYC.

Zavitkovsky, D., K. R. Baker, J. R. Berlfein, & M. Almy. 1986. *Listen to the children.* Washington, DC: NAEYC.

Angeline Lillard, Ph.D., is assistant professor of psychology at the University of Virginia in Charlottesville. She has conducted many studies on children's theories of mind and was recently awarded the American Psychological Association's (Division 7) Boyd McCandless Young Scientist Award for distinguished contribution to developmental psychology.

Stephanie M. Curenton, *M.A., is a graduate student at the University of Virginia. Her research interests include the development of theory of mind in low-income and ethnic minority populations.*

This is one of a regular series of Research in Review columns. The column in this issue was edited by ***Martha B. Bronson,*** *Ph.D., professor of early childhood education at Boston College.*

Giftedness: Current Theory and Research

Ellen Winner[1]

Abstract

Gifted children, those with unusually high ability in one or more domains, not only develop more rapidly than typical children, but also appear to be qualitatively different. They have an intense drive to master, require little explicit tuition, and, if intellectually gifted, often pose deep philosophical questions. Although some psychologists have tried to account for the achievements of gifted individuals solely in terms of drive or "deliberate practice," no evidence allows us to rule out innate differences in talent. Profiles of gifted individuals are often uneven: Extremely high ability in one area can coexist with ordinary or even subnormal ability in another area. Scientific investigation of the gifted reveals the importance of drive and hard work in achievement of any kind, and the lack of necessary correlation among abilities in different areas.

Keywords

gifted; drive; innate; talent; savant

While mainstream psychology has sought to understand the universal in human mental processes, a respectable complementary tradition has investigated individual differences and the atypical. Like the study of retardation, psychopathology, and emotional disorders, research on the gifted belongs to the latter tradition. Psychologists have studied such populations not only in order to understand them on their own terms, but also in the hope that an understanding of the atypical may shed light on the typical.

Systematic study of the gifted began in the 1920s with Terman's (1925) longitudinal study of 1,528 children with IQs averaging 151. These children were surprisingly well rounded and socially well adjusted, and grew up to be successful professionals. However, none made widely recognized intellectual breakthroughs. Thus, even extraordinarily high IQs do not by themselves lead to creative eminence. Whether such IQs predict even professional success could not be determined because Terman did not control for possible effects of socioeconomic background.

Since Terman's time, there has developed a consensus that giftedness is often not captured by the unidimensional measure of IQ. Some researchers have differentiated mathematical and verbal giftedness and have shown how domain-specific tests (math and verbal Scholastic Assessment Tests) are more accurate than IQ tests in distinguishing such gifts (Stanley, 1973). Some have broadened giftedness to include high ability in any areas, including music, spatial reasoning, and interpersonal understanding (Gardner, 1993). The case has also been made that intellectual giftedness is more than high ability, and should include creativity and motivation (Renzulli, 1978). One understanding of giftedness is most likely to advance if we define giftedness simply as unusually high ability in any area (including domain-specific ability as well as high global IQ), and then proceed to investigate the correlates (e.g., drive, creativity) and developmental path of each type of high ability.

ARE GIFTED INDIVIDUALS QUALITATIVELY OR QUANTITATIVELY DIFFERENT?

Perhaps the most basic question about giftedness is its relationship to the typical. Do gifted individuals stand out chiefly in terms of the speed with which their abilities develop and with which they process information? Or do they develop and process information in a way that is qualitatively different from normal?

Strong claims have been made about qualitatively different modes of thinking in high-IQ children, but the evidence remains anecdotal. According to clinical observations, high-IQ children consider many possible interpretations of a question, grasp the essential elements of a complex problem, and often pose deep philosophical questions (Lovecky, 1994). Controlled studies are required to determine whether these observations are true of gifted children in general, only those with high IQs, or perhaps only a subset of IQ-gifted children (e.g., only those above a certain level of IQ, verbally but not mathematically gifted). These studies must compare gifted children with peers matched for mental age so that the effects of ability level and giftedness can be disentangled.

Gifted children also appear to be qualitatively different from ordinary children in motivation, but again the evidence remains anecdotal. The gifted children who come to the attention of teachers and parents display an intense drive, or "rage to master." They work for hours with no parental prodding or external reinforcement. As they work, they pose challenges for themselves. Such children also differ from ordinary children in the way they learn. They make discoveries on their own, and much of the time they appear to teach themselves. But we do not know how many children have high ability but low motivation to demonstrate that ability (or high motivation in an area in which they do not have high ability) and who thus do not come to our attention as gifted. Again, controlled studies are needed to compare gifted children with older children who have similar levels (but in their case, age-typical levels) of ability.

The strong drive that accompanies giftedness, the posing of challenges, the mastery orientation, and the ability to make discoveries independently together suggest that gifted children do not just develop more rapidly than others, but develop and think differently from others. But there is a clear need for systematic research so that we can move beyond anecdotal evidence and determine whether high ability is always accompanied by such qualitative cognitive and motivational differences.

THE ROLE OF INNATE TALENT

Giftedness provides an ideal arena in which to investigate the relation between inborn talent and learning (Simonton, 1999). According to the layperson's view, gifted children are endowed with innate talents that make themselves known from a very early age, a view echoed by researchers whose focus is giftedness, and who publish in journals devoted to the study of gifted children (typically IQ-gifted children). A contrasting environmental view has emerged among psychologists who identify their focus as the study of talent or expertise.

The evidence for the nurture position rests on retrospective studies of eminent individuals. An early study revealed the importance of drive as separate from ability. Roe (1952) showed that scientists who achieve the highest levels differ from their less eminent colleagues not in intellectual ability but in capacity for concentration and hard work. However, because all of Roe's scientists had high ability, this study tells us nothing about what one can accomplish with low inborn ability along with a strong drive to work.

The importance of a supportive environment and intensive training was demonstrated by Bloom (1985), who found that individuals of world-class status in the arts, mathematics, science, or athletics all reported strong family support and years of training. However, such a finding hardly rules out innate talent: Bloom's subjects also recalled signs of high ability at a very young age, prior to or at the very start of formal training. These memories of early signs of high ability are consistent with parental accounts of child prodigies whose extraordinary abilities seem to emerge from nowhere.

Most recently, studies have revealed the necessity of "deliberate practice"—effortful work designed to improve performance. Ericsson, Krampe, and Tesch-Romer (1993) demonstrated that level of achievement in piano, violin, ballet, chess, bridge, and athletics is predicted by sheer amount of deliberate practice. For example, the best musicians in this study had engaged in twice as many

hours of deliberate practice over their lives as had the least successful ones. However, children who work the earliest and hardest may well be those with the highest levels of talent. Most children cannot be cajoled to play music or think about math problems for hours on end, but highly gifted children often cannot be cajoled away from such activities. Amount of deliberate practice is thus likely to be a function of drive and interest, temperamental factors associated with talent. That is, children with high ability in a given area are likely to have a high drive to master that area.

As pointed-out by Schneider (in press), Ericsson and his colleagues never measured ability levels, and thus there is no way to rule out ability differences among individuals of unequal levels of eminence. Independent assessments of the predictive power of ability and deliberate practice have shown that both are important (Schneider, in press). Simonton (1991) showed that the most eminent classical composers began to compose and made lasting contributions after fewer years of formal training than their less eminent peers. The fact that they achieved greater heights with less practice suggests that their success reflected another ingredient besides practice—and a likely candidate is a higher level of inborn musical talent.

Despite attempts to account for giftedness in terms of nurture, no evidence allows us to rule out the necessity of an innate component. Simonton (1999) proposed a model of innate talent that is multidimensional and dynamic. He argued that achievement in any domain requires various innate components, with some domains requiring far more than others; components develop independently over time; level of ability is determined by a multiplicative composite of these components; and giftedness is emergenic (i.e., it manifests itself only when all of the required components are inherited). This model can account for many of the complexities of giftedness, including the rarity of giftedness particularly in complex domains (because if only one component skill in a domain is assigned a weight of zero, the individual cannot be gifted in that domain). Of course, granting a role to nature does not rule out nurture. Whether nature or nurture accounts for more of the variance in giftedness remains to be determined, and the answer to this question is likely to differ across different domains of giftedness (Simonton, 1999).

HOW UNEVEN ARE THE COGNITIVE PROFILES OF GIFTED INDIVIDUALS?

If the components of giftedness within a given domain develop independently of one another, the profiles of individuals gifted in that domain should be uneven. There is some evidence for this. Adults with high IQs show lower correlations among subtests of the IQ than do those with ordinary IQs (Detterman & Daniel, 1989). In addition, the cognitive profiles of academically gifted children are often quite uneven, with mathematical ability far outstripping verbal ability, or the reverse (Benbow & Minor, 1990). Research is needed to determine how common such uneven profiles are among the gifted, and how common it is to have gifts accompanied by absolute rather than relative weaknesses.

Just as uneven profiles often characterize the abilities of high-IQ individuals, uneven profiles also characterize individuals gifted in music or art, who may have a strong gift in the presence of an unremarkable IQ. For example, Simonton (1999) noted that Beethoven had almost no mathematical ability; nor was he particularly strong verbally. And Csikszentmihalyi, Rathunde, and Whalen (1993) found that the artistically gifted adolescents they studied had poor academic skills.

In the case of savants, who present the most striking cases of unevenness, an extreme ability coexists with a subnormal IQ. Savants are retarded, autistic, or both, yet exhibit a strong gift in a particular domain (typically music, visual art, or numerical calculation). They have often been dismissed as mere imitators whose abilities are irrelevant to an understanding of giftedness in nonsavants. However, savants show an implicit understanding of the rules of their domain, revealing that they are not rote imitators. In addition, the drawings and musical works they produce can be expressive and have artistic merit. Because savant gifts are similar to nonsavant gifts in important respects, savants provide strong evidence that general intelligence, or what psychologists often call *g*, is unrelated to high levels of achievement in some domains.

UNANSWERED QUESTIONS

An understanding of what constitutes giftedness shows the importance of drive and hard work in achievement of any kind, and reveals that high abilities in some domains do not require a high IQ. A fundamental question not yet resolved is whether gifted children differ from average ones only in a quantitative way, or whether they differ qualitatively, in which case new principles are required to account for their performance. Several other perplexing questions that open the door to intriguing new lines of research include whether the heritability of gifts differs across domains, whether the role of practice and its interaction with innate talent differ across domains, what forms of early prodigiousness do and do not predict creative eminence in adulthood, and whether brain imaging can demonstrate similarities in the brain organization and functioning of savant and nonsavant gifted individuals working in the same domain.

Answers to some of these questions also have educational implications. The question of how gifted children should be educated (most often asked about the intellectually gifted) is of enormous practical importance. These children benefit cognitively and socially from ability grouping and acceleration (including early entrance to college programs; Janos, Robinson, & Lunneborg, 1989). Research on the long-term cognitive and social outcomes of these methods should continue, and policy should follow from research findings rather than ideological positions.

Recommended Reading

Heller, K. A., Monks, F. J., Sternberg, R. J., & Subotnik, R. F. (Eds.). (in press) *International handbook of research and development of giftedness and talent* (2nd ed.). London: Elsevier.

Miller, L. K. (1999). The savant syndrome. Intellectual impairment and exceptional skill. *Psychological Bulletin, 125*, 31–46.

Simonton, D. K. (1994). *Greatness: Who makes history and why*. New York: Guilford Press.

Sternberg, R. J., & Davidson, J. E. (1986). *Conceptions of giftedness*. New York: Cambridge University Press.

Winner, E. (1996). *Gifted children: Myths and realities*. New York: Basic Books.

Acknowledgments—I thank Howard Gardner, Deirdre Lovecky, Nancy Robinson, and Catya von Karolyi for helpful comments on an earlier draft of this article.

Note

1. Address correspondence to Ellen Winner, Department of Psychology, McGuinn Hall, Boston College, Chestnut Hill, MA 02467; e-mail: ewinner@ mediaone.net.

References

Benbow, C. P., & Minor, L. L. (1990). Cognitive profiles of verbally and mathematically precocious students: Implications for identification of the gifted. *Gifted Child Quarterly, 34*, 21–26.

Bloom, B. S. (Ed.), (1985). *Developing talent in young people*. New York: Ballantine Books.

Csikszentmihalyi, M., Rathunde, K., & Whalen, S. (1993). *Talented teenagers: The roots of success and failure*. New York: Cambridge University Press.

Detterman, D. K., & Daniel, M. H. (1989). Correlations of mental tests with each other and with cognitive variables are highest for low IQ groups. *Intelligence, 15*, 349–359.

Ericsson, K. A., Krampe, R., & Tesch-Romer, C. (1993). The role of deliberate practice in the acquisition of expert performance. *Psychological Review, 199*, 363–406.

Gardner, H. (1993). *Multiple intelligences: The theory in practice*. New York: Basic Books.

Janos, P. M., Robinson, N. M., & Lunneborg, C. E. (1989). Markedly early entrance to college. *Journal of Higher Education, 60*, 494–518.

Lovecky, D. V. (1994). Exceptionally gifted children: Different minds. *Roeper Review, 17*, 116–120.

Renzulli, J. (1978). What makes giftedness? Reexamining a definition. *Phi Delta Kappan, 60*, 180–184.

Roe, A. (1952). *The making of a scientist*. New York: Dodd, Mead.

Schneider, W. (in press). Giftedness, expertise, and (exceptional) performance: A developmental perspective. In K. A. Heller,

F. J. Monks, R. J. Sternberg & R. F. Subotnik (Eds.), *International handbook of research and development of giftedness and talent* (2nd ed.). London: Elsevier.

Simonton, D. K. (1991). Emergence and realization of genius: The lives and works of 120 classical composers. *Journal of Personality and Social Psychology, 61*, 829–840.

Simonton, D. K. (1999). Talent and its development: An emergenic and epigenetic model. *Psychological Review, 106,* 435–437.

Stanley, J. C. (1973). Accelerating the educational progress of intellectually gifted youths. *Educational Psychologist, 10*, 133–146.

Terman, L. M. (1925). *Genetic studies of genius: Vol. 1. Mental and physical traits of a thousand gifted children.* Stanford, CA: Stanford University Press.

Department of Psychology, Boston College, Chestnut Hill, Massachusetts, and Project Zero, Harvard Graduate School of Education, Cambridge, Massachusetts

The First Seven...
and the Eighth

A Conversation with Howard Gardner

Human intelligence continues to intrigue psychologists, neurologists, and educators. What is it? Can we measure it? How do we nurture it?

Kathy Checkley

Howard Gardner's theory of multiple intelligences, described in Frames of Mind *(1985), sparked a revolution of sorts in classrooms around the world, a mutiny against the notion that human beings have a single, fixed intelligence. The fervor with which educators embraced his premise that we have multiple intelligences surprised Gardner himself. "It obviously spoke to some sense that people had that kids weren't all the same and that the tests we had only skimmed the surface about the differences among kids," Gardner said.*

Here Gardner brings us up-to-date on his current thinking on intelligence, how children learn, and how they should be taught.

How do you define intelligence?

Intelligence refers to the human ability to solve problems or to make something that is valued in one or more cultures. As long as we can find a culture that values an ability to solve a problem or create a product in a particular way, then I would strongly consider whether that ability should be considered an intelligence.

First, though, that ability must meet other criteria: Is there a particular representation in the brain for the ability? Are there populations that are especially good or especially impaired in an intelligence? And, can an evolutionary history of the intelligence be seen in animals other than human beings?

I defined seven intelligences (see box) in the early 1980s because those intelligences all fit the criteria. A decade later when I revisited the task, I found at least one more ability that clearly deserved to be called an intelligence.

That would be the naturalist intelligence. What led you to consider adding this to our collection of intelligences?

Somebody asked me to explain the achievements of the great biologists, the ones who had a real mastery of taxonomy, who understood about different species, who could recognize patterns in nature and classify objects. I realized that to explain that kind of ability, I would have to manipulate the other intelligences in ways that weren't appropriate.

So I began to think about whether the capacity to classify nature might be a separate intelligence. The naturalist ability passed with flying colors. Here are a couple of reasons: First, it's an ability we need to survive as human beings. We need, for example, to know which animals to hunt and which to run away from. Second, this ability isn't restricted to human beings. Other animals need to have a naturalist intelligence to survive. Finally, the big selling point is that brain evidence supports the existence of the naturalist intelligence. There are certain parts of the brain particularly dedicated to the recognition and the naming of what are called "natural" things.

How do you describe the naturalist intelligence to those of us who aren't psychologists?

The naturalist intelligence refers to the ability to recognize and classify plants, minerals, and animals, including rocks and grass and all variety of flora and fauna. The ability to recognize cultural artifacts like cars or sneakers may also depend on the naturalist intelligence.

Now, everybody can do this to a certain extent—we can all recognize dogs, cats, trees. But, some people from an early age are extremely good at recognizing and classifying artifacts. For example, we all know kids who, at age

3 or 4, are better at recognizing dinosaurs than most adults.

Darwin is probably the most famous example of a naturalist because he saw so deeply into the nature of living things.

Are there any other abilities you're considering calling intelligences?

Well, there may be an existential intelligence that refers to the human inclination to ask very basic questions about existence. Who are we? Where do we come from? What's it all about? Why do we die? We might say that existential intelligence allows us to know the invisible, outside world. The only reason I haven't given a seal of approval to the existential intelligence is that I don't think we have good brain evidence yet on its existence in the nervous system—one of the criteria for an intelligence.

© Susie Fitzhugh

You have said that the theory of multiple intelligences may be best understood when we know what it critiques. What do you mean?

The standard view of intelligence is that intelligence is something you are born with; you have only a certain amount of it; you cannot do much about how much of that intelligence you have; and tests exist that can tell you how smart you are. The theory of multiple intelligences challenges that view. It asks, instead, "Given what we know about the brain, evolution, and the differences in cultures, what are the sets of human abilities we all share?"

My analysis suggested that rather than one or two intelligences, all human beings have several (eight) intelligences. What makes life interesting, however, is that we don't have the same strength in each intelligence area, and we don't have the same amalgam of intelligences. Just as we look different from one another and have different kinds of personalities, we also have different kinds of minds.

This premise has very serious educational implications. If we treat everybody as if they are the same, we're catering to one profile of intelligence, the language-logic profile. It's great if you have that profile, but it's not great for the vast majority of human beings who do not have that particular profile of intelligence.

School matters, but only insofar as it yields something that can be used once students leave school.

Can you explain more fully how the theory of multiple intelligences challenges what has become known as IQ?

The theory challenges the entire notion of IQ. The IQ test was developed about a century ago as a way to determine who would have trouble in school. The test measures linguistic ability, logical-mathematical ability, and, occasionally, spatial ability.

What the intelligence test does not do is inform us about our other intelligences; it also doesn't look at other virtues like creativity or civic mindedness, or whether a person is moral or ethical.

We don't do much IQ testing anymore, but the shadow of IQ tests is still with us because the SAT—arguably the most potent examination in the world—is basically the same kind of disembodied language-logic instrument.

The truth is, I don't believe there is such a general thing as scholastic aptitude. Even so, I don't think that the SAT will fade until colleges indicate that they'd rather have students who know how to use their minds well—students who may or may not be good test takers, but who are serious, inquisitive, and know how to probe and problem-solve. That is really what college professors want, I believe.

Can we strengthen our intelligences? If so, how?

We can all get better at each of the intelligences, although some people will improve in an intelligence area more readily than others, either because biology gave them a better brain for that intelligence or because their culture gave them a better teacher.

Teachers have to help students use their combination of intelligences to be successful in school, to help them learn whatever it is they want to learn, as well as what the teachers and society believe they have to learn.

Now, I'm not arguing that kids shouldn't learn the literacies. Of course they should learn the literacies. Nor am I arguing that kids shouldn't learn the disciplines. I'm a tremendous champion of the disciplines. What I argue against is the notion that there's only one way to learn how to read, only one way to learn how to compute, only one way to learn about biology. I think that such contentions are nonsense.

It's equally nonsensical to say that everything should be taught seven or eight ways. That's not the point of the MI theory. The point is to realize that any topic of importance, from any discipline, can be taught in more than one way. There are things people need to know, and educators have to be extraordinarily imaginative and persistent in helping students understand things better.

A popular activity among those who are first exploring multiple intelligences is to construct their own intellectual profile. It's thought that when teachers go through the process of creating such a profile, they're more likely to recognize and appreciate the intellectual strengths of their students. What is your view on this kind of activity?

My own studies have shown that people love to do this. Kids like to do it, adults like to do it. And, as an activity, I think it's perfectly harmless.

I get concerned, though, when people think that determining your intellectual profile—or that of someone else—is an end in itself.

You have to use the profile to understand the ways in which you seem to learn easily. And, from there, determine how to use those strengths to help you become more successful in other endeavors. Then, the profile becomes a way for you to understand yourself better, and you can use that understanding to catapult yourself to a better level of understanding or to a higher level of skill.

How has your understanding of the multiple intelligences influenced how you teach?

My own teaching has changed slowly as a result of multiple intelligences because I'm teaching graduate students psychological theory and there are only so many ways I can do that. I am more open to group work and to student projects of various sorts, but even if I wanted to be an "MI professor" of graduate students, I still have a certain moral obligation to prepare them for a world in which they will have to write scholarly articles and prepare theses.

As long as you can lose one ability while others are spared, you cannot just have a single intelligence.

Where I've changed much more, I believe, is at the workplace. I direct research projects and work with all kinds of people. Probably 10 to 15 years ago, I would have tried to find people who were just like me to work with me on these projects.

I've really changed my attitude a lot on that score. Now I think much more in terms of what people are good at and in putting together teams of people whose varying strengths complement one another.

How should thoughtful educators implement the theory of multiple intelligences?

Although there is no single MI route, it's very important that a teacher take individual differences among kinds very seriously. You cannot be a good MI teacher if you don't want to know each child and try to gear how you teach and how you evaluate to that particular child. The bottom line is a deep interest in children and how their minds are different from one another, and in helping them use their minds well.

Now, kids can be great informants for teachers. For example, a teacher might say, "Look, Benjamin, this obviously isn't working. Should we try using a picture?" If Benjamin gets excited about that approach, that's a pretty good clue to the teacher about what could work.

The theory of multiple intelligences, in and of itself, is not going to solve anything in our society, but linking the multiple intelligences with a curriculum focused on understanding is an extremely powerful intellectual undertaking.

When I talk about understanding, I mean that students can take ideas they learn in school, or anywhere for that matter, and apply those appropriately in new situations. We know people truly understand something when they can represent the knowledge in more than one way. We have to put understanding up front in school. Once we have that goal, multiple intelligences can be a terrific handmaiden because understandings involve a mix of mental representations, entailing different intelligences.

People often say that what they remember most about school are those learning experiences that were linked to real life. How does the theory of multiple intelligences help connect learning to the world outside the classroom?

The theory of multiple intelligences wasn't based on school work or on tests. Instead, what I did was look at the world and ask, What are the things that people do in the world? What does it mean to be a surgeon? What does it mean to be a politician? What does it mean to be an artist or a sculptor? What abilities do you need to do those things? My theory, then, came from the things that are valued in the world.

So when a school values multiple intelligences, the relationship to what's valued in the world is patent. If you cannot easily relate this activity to something that's valued in the world, the school has probably lost the core idea of multiple intelligences, which is that these intelligences evolved to help people do things that matter in the real world.

School matters, but only insofar as it yields something that can be used once students leave school.

The Intelligences, in Gardner's Words

• Linguistic intelligence is the capacity to use language, your native language, and perhaps other languages, to express what's on your mind and to understand other people. Poets really specialize in linguistic intelligence, but any kind of writer, orator, speaker, lawyer, or a person for whom language is an important stock in trade highlights linguistic intelligence.

• People with a highly developed logical-mathematical intelligence understand the underlying principles of some kind of a causal system, the way a scientist or a logician does; or can manipulate numbers, quantities, and operations, the way a mathematician does.

• Spatial intelligence refers to the ability to represent the spatial world internally in your mind—the way a sailor or airplane pilot navigates the large spatial world, or the way a chess player or sculptor represents a more circumscribed spatial world. Spatial intelligence can be used in the arts or in the sciences. If you are spatially intelligent and oriented toward the arts, you are more likely to become a painter or a sculptor or an architect than, say, a musician or a writer. Similarly, certain sciences like anatomy or topology emphasize spatial intelligence.

• Bodily kinesthetic intelligence is the capacity to use your whole body or parts of your body—your hand, your fingers, your arms—to solve a problem, make something, or put on some kind of a production. The most evident examples are people in athletics or the performing arts, particularly dance or acting.

• Musical intelligence is the capacity to think in music, to be able to hear patterns, recognize them, remember them, and perhaps manipulate them. People who have a strong musical intelligence don't just remember music easily—they can't get it out of their minds, it's so omnipresent. Now, some people will say, "Yes, music is important, but it's a talent, not an intelligence." And I say, "Fine, let's call it a talent." But, then we have to leave the word *intelligent* out of *all* discussions of human abilities. You know, Mozart was damned smart!

• Interpersonal intelligence is understanding other people. It's an ability we all need, but is at a premium if you are a teacher, clinician, salesperson, or politician. Anybody who deals with other people has to be skilled in the interpersonal sphere.

• Intrapersonal intelligence refers to having an understanding of yourself, of knowing who you are, what you can do, what you want to do, how you react to things, which things to avoid, and which things to gravitate toward. We are drawn to people who have a good understanding of themselves because those people tend not to screw up. They tend to know what they can do. They tend to know what they can't do. And they tend to know where to go if they need help.

• Naturalist intelligence designates the human ability to discriminate among living things (plants, animals) as well as sensitivity to other features of the natural world (clouds, rock configurations). This ability was clearly of value in our evolutionary past as hunters, gatherers, and farmers; it continues to be central in such roles as botanist or chef. I also speculate that much of our consumer society exploits the naturalist intelligences, which can be mobilized in the discrimination among cars, sneakers, kinds of makeup, and the like. The kind of pattern recognition valued in certain of the sciences may also draw upon naturalist intelligence.

How can teachers be guided by multiple intelligences when creating assessment tools?

We need to develop assessments that are much more representative of what human beings are going to have to do to survive in this society. For example, I value literacy, but my measure of literacy should not be whether you can answer a multiple-choice question that asks you to select the best meaning of a paragraph. Instead, I'd rather have you read the paragraph and list four questions you have about the paragraph and figure out how you would answer those questions. Or, if I want to know how you can write, let me give you a stem and see whether you can write about that topic, or let me ask you to write an editorial in response to something you read in the newspaper or observed on the street.

The current emphasis on performance assessment is well supported by the theory of multiple intelligences. Indeed, you could not really be an advocate of multiple intelligences if you didn't have some dissatisfaction with the current testing because it's so focused on short-answer, linguistic, or logical kinds of items.

MI theory is very congenial to an approach that says: one, let's not look at things through the filter of a short-answer test. Let's look directly at the performance that we value, whether it's a linguistic, logical, aesthetic, or social performance; and, two, let's never pin our assessment of understanding on just one particular measure, but let's always allow students to show their understanding in a variety of ways.

You have identified several myths about the theory of multiple intelligences. Can you describe some of those myths?

One myth that I personally find irritating is that an intelligence is the same as a learning style. Learning styles are claims about ways in which individuals purportedly approach everything they do. If you are planful, you are supposed to be planful about everything. If you are logical-sequential, you are supposed to be logical-sequential about everything. My own research and observations suggest that that's a dubious assumption. But whether or not that's true, learning styles are very different from multiple intelligences.

© Susie Fitzhugh

Multiple intelligences claims that we respond, individually, in different ways to different kinds of content, such as language or music or other people. This is very different from the notion of learning style.

You can say that a child is a visual learner, but that's not a multiple intelligences way of talking about things. What I would say is, "Here is a child who very easily represents things spatially, and we can draw upon that strength if need be when we want to teach the child something new."

Another widely believed myth is that, because we have seven or eight intelligences, we should create seven or eight tests to measure students' strengths in each of those areas. That is a perversion of the theory. It's re-creating the sin of the single intelligence quotient and just multiplying it by a larger number. I'm personally against assessment of intelligences unless such a measurement is used for a very specific learning purpose—we want to help a child understand her history or his mathematics better and, therefore, want to see what might be good entry points for that particular child.

What experiences led you to the study of human intelligence?

It's hard for me to pick out a single moment, but I can see a couple of snapshots. When I was in high school, my uncle gave me a textbook in psychology. I'd never actually heard of psychology before. This textbook helped me understand color blindness. I'm color blind, and I became fascinated by the existence of plates that illustrated what color blindness was. I could actually explain why I couldn't see colors.

Another time when I was studying the Reformation, I read a book by Erik Erikson called *Young Man Luther* (1958).[1] I was fascinated by the psychological motivation of Luther to attack the Catholic Church. That fascination influenced my decision to go into psychology.

The most important influence was actually learning about brain damage and what could happen to people when they had strokes. When a person has a stroke, a certain part of the brain gets injured, and that injury can tell you what that part of the brain does. Individuals who lose their musical abilities can still talk. People who lose their linguistic ability still might be able to sing. That understanding not only brought me into the whole world of brain study, but it was really the seed that led ultimately to the theory of multiple intelligences. As long as you can lose one ability while others are spared, you cannot just have a single intelligence. You have to have several intelligences.

Note

1. See Erik Erikson, *Young Man Luther* (New York: W. W. Norton, 1958).

Howard Gardner is Professor of Education at Harvard Graduate School of Education and author of, among other books, *The Unschooled Mind: How Children Think and How Schools Should Teach* (1991). He can be reached at Roy B. Larsen Hall, 2nd Floor, Appian Way, Harvard Graduate School of Education, Cambridge, MA 02138. **Kathy Checkley** is a staff writer for *Update* and has assisted in the development of ASCD's new CD-ROM, *Exploring Our Multiple Intelligences*, pilot online project on multiple intelligences.

From *Educational Leadership,* September 1997, pp. 8–13. © 1997 by the Association for Supervision and Curriculum Development. All rights reserved. Reprinted by permission

Parental Engagement That Makes a Difference

Parental involvement in schooling can lead to real academic benefits for children—but some parent behaviors are more effective than others.

Jeremy D. Finn

Home-school partnerships command a lot of attention these days. Well-intentioned educators are recommending an infusion of energy toward increasing parental participation in schools. The federal government has issued documents to help schools organize parent participation programs (for example, Rutherford et al. 1997). Major reform efforts and educational interventions list parental involvement as an important ingredient. Scholarly writing on the topic abounds, and various publications offer guidance to schools or describe exemplary programs.

It is important to understand how, and to what extent, "parental engagement behaviors" bolster student learning.

What does research say about the role of parental involvement—at home and in school—in supporting youngsters' academic achievement? Unfortunately, the mountain of material about parent-school partnerships yields few if any empirical data about the impact of parental involvement on students' academic achievement. But a different set of research studies provides much information that educators should consider. Empirical data show that *specific parenting practices* are related to students' academic achievement. It is important to understand how, and to what extent, "parental engagement behaviors" bolster student learning.

The Importance of the Home Environment

Until the early 1960s, sociologists believed that school performance and intelligence were immutably connected with socio-economic status and family structure. However, building on the ideas of Benjamin Bloom, Dave (1963) and Wolf (1964) demonstrated that differences in children's performance could be explained instead by specific conditions and parental behaviors, including parents' roles as language models, parents' press for achievement, and provisions for general learning.

Clark (1983) added significantly to our understanding through an intensive study of 10 African-American students from poor homes, half of whom were successful academically and half of whom were not. The researchers discovered that parents of high-achieving students had distinct styles of interacting with their children. They created emotionally supportive home environments and provided reassurance when the young students encountered failure. They viewed school performance as being accomplished through regular practice and work. They accepted responsibility for assisting their children to acquire learning strategies as well as a general fund of knowledge.

Research reveals that parental *engagement at home* and *engagement at school* are not equally important to children's learning. At the same time, extensive research reviews find that the home environment is among the most important influences on academic performance (Wang et al. 1993).

Parental Engagement at Home

Researchers have identified three types of parental engagement at home that are consistently associated with school performance:

- actively organizing and monitoring the child's time;

- helping with homework; and

- discussing school matters with the child.

A fourth set of activities that is germane, particularly for younger children, consists of parents reading to and being read to by their children.

©Susie Fitzhugh

The exact form that each of these takes may differ from one family to another, but research shows that each is important. In fact, studies of student resilience indicate that many of these same behaviors explain why some students succeed academically despite the adversities posed by poverty, minority status, or native language (Finn 1993, Masten 1994, Peng and Lee 1992).

Managing and organizing time. Clark's original study found that parents of successful students actively helped them organize their daily and weekly schedules and checked regularly to see whether they were following the routines. Other studies have shown that children who are involved in regular routines at home tend to have better school performance (for example, Astone and McLanahan 1991, Taylor 1996).

Monitoring children's use of time is identified as important in all studies of parental engagement (for example, Astone and McLanahan 1991; Ho and Willms 1996; Crouter et al. 1990; Lamborn et al. 1992). Research shows that parents of academically successful students make sure they are informed about the youngsters' activities in school, their school performance, and whether or not they have been assigned homework; and they make certain that a place and time are allocated for homework. In addition, school performance is better among students whose parents know where they are, who they are with, and when they plan to come home. These parents also exercise reasonable control over nonschool activities—television viewing, in particular.

Involvement with homework. Homework offers an opportunity for parents to show an interest and to take a direct role in their youngsters' schooling. Making certain that homework is completed, discussing the specifics of assignments and papers, explaining the assignments, checking accuracy, and actively helping children complete assignments have all been found to be related to children's academic performance (Ho and Willms 1996, Clark 1983, Finn 1993, Lamborn et al. 1992). If a parent is not familiar with the content of the schoolwork, the acts of asking questions about an assignment and examining completed work still underscore the importance attached to skill development.

In some instances, parents may serve as tutors to their children. Peterson (1989) notes that the familiarity of the home environment, in contrast to the structure of the classroom, can become a comfortable setting for tutoring. In a survey of parents of elementary schoolchildren, Epstein (1983) found that more that 85 percent spent at least 15 minutes daily tutoring their children when the teacher requested it. Of course, tutoring requires some degree of subject-matter knowledge and some knowledge of teaching strategies.

Discussing school matters. Children whose parents converse regularly with them about school experiences perform better academically than children who rarely discuss school with their parents (Astone and McLanahan 1991, Ho and Willms 1996, Finn 1993). Other research suggests that the *nature* of parent-child discussions is also important. Parents should be willing to hear about difficulties, as well as successes, and play a supportive role, encouraging persistence when schoolwork or relationships at school are problematic (Clark 1983, Lamborn et al. 1992, Steinberg 1996). Research supports joint parent-student decision making when the situation permits, such as choosing what project to undertake or, in later grades, what courses to take (for example, Lamborn et al. 1992, Taylor 1996). This level of interest is associated with higher student engagement, as well as academic achievement.

Literacy and reading at home. Studies from Wolf and Dave to the present have shown a positive relationship between a literacy-laden home and students' school performance. The presence of newspapers, magazines, books, a dictionary, and a computer or word processor helps to create a positive home setting. Even when these resources are in short supply, reading to a child and asking a child to read to the parent are crucial activities for the development of literacy. A great deal of research confirms a strong relationship between parents reading to their children and the development of reading proficiency (see Anderson et al. 1985 for a summary). Further, there is an important connection between children's reading to their parents and reading achievement—especially if the parents guide and correct the young readers (Tracey 1995).

Unfortunately, many households, especially low-income or minority homes, have few books in total and even fewer that are appropriate and interesting to children (Edwards 1992; Barker et al. 1997). Children from these homes arrive at school with surprisingly little experience with books. At the same time, many parents feel that they lack, or actually do lack, the skills to guide their children's reading or schoolwork (Edwards 1995; Hoover-Dempsey et al. 1995). Some parents who do attempt to read with their youngsters make beginner's mistakes, such as reading an entire story just to get through it when part of a story would suffice; focusing so much on mechanics that their child's motivation is diminished; and taking a punitive attitude when the child makes errors.

The most efficient time to set a child on a positive path is at a young age.

School-sponsored programs, although not universally available, have been highly successful in improving these situations. At least one program provided books for children to take home twice a week (Toomey 1992). A large number of school-parent reading programs have been reviewed by Topping (1986), Edwards (1992), and Tracey (1995). Better programs have proactive components to recruit parents, improve their literacy skills, help them develop a regular structure for home-based literacy, help them overcome obstacles to literacy activities in the home, and convince them that their children can become successful readers.

Most research on parental engagement at home, with the exception of studies of parent-child reading, has involved students at the junior high level. There are good reasons to believe that the same parental engagement behaviors are important for younger children. Psychologists and educators agree on the importance of setting habits early on that persevere throughout childhood and beyond. Early behavior that is dysfunctional tends to be sustained and to increase over the years (see Finn 1993); the most efficient time to set a child on a positive path is at a young age.

Parental Engagement in School

The opportunity for parents to stay intensively involved in school diminishes as students become increasingly independent and as peers come to have greater influence (Epstein 1984, Steinberg 1996). At the same time, parents can continue to be in-school participants by visiting the school; attending school events, performances, and athletics; and initiating contact with teachers and administrators.

It may be surprising that research has *not* consistently documented links between parents' in-school engagement and student achievement. Steinberg (1996) found a small but statistically significant correlation of achievement with parents' attendance at school programs, conferences, and extracurricular activities. The author noted that teachers may pay more attention to students whose parents are involved in the school, which may in turn explain the relationship. But others (for example, Finn 1993, Ho and Willms 1996, Taylor 1996) found little or no relationship between grades or achievement scores and parental

visits to school, volunteer work, attendance at school events, and so on. Interestingly, several studies found that the relationship between parent-teacher contacts and academic achievement is negative; obviously, contacts increase when a student experiences academic or behavior problems (Milne et al. 1986; Ho and Willms 1996).

Given this research base, it is natural to ask why there is so much pressure to increase parent-school partnerships. Much has been written about different ways in which parents and schools can work together to facilitate academic outcomes. For example, Epstein and Dauber (1991) list basic health and safety responsibilities of parents and of schools; volunteering and attending school functions; parental involvement in learning at home, as recommended and supported by school staff; parental involvement in decision making; and encouraging parents and schools to become involved in community organizations that can support families and children's learning. Like other research, the data presented by Epstein and Dauber show that parents who are involved in some of these activities tend also to be involved in others, but not that these activities are related to children's school performance. These types of activities require real time commitments—time not always available to a single or working parent (Moles 1987). A parent who does not have the time for in-school involvement may, out of frustration, not consider more helpful activities that can take place at home.

For these reasons, we must ask whether it is prudent to emphasize increased parent-school connections at this time. Although there can certainly be no harm in promoting parental involvement, and although parents who exhibit one sort of engagement are likely to practice others, the only answer research provides about the unique benefits of engagement in school is "the jury is still out."

What of the Disengaged?

In his work on child-rearing practices, Steinberg (1996) described parents who are "disengaged"—that is, who are authoritarian in their interactions with their children, who fail to provide guidance or structure in the family setting, and who fail to provide the emotional support needed when the child encounters problems. Steinberg found that children whose parents are disengaged have the *poorest developmental patterns*, lacking psychological maturity, social competence, and self-esteem. The problems encountered by these youngsters, in school and out, multiply throughout the school years.

The research reviewed here points to specific attitudes and behaviors that, if implemented by parents, are associated with improved academic performance. These practices have been classified by Hoover-Dempsey and others (1995) as (1) providing structure—structuring routines at home, and coordinating with school when problems arise; and (2) active involvement—monitoring the youngster's expenditure of time, teaching and explaining concepts, reviewing homework, and providing support when the child experiences difficulties. These authors and others give guidelines for parents who wish to increase their support for their children's academic work, and many effective programs are available for parents who would like assistance. Although the research evidence on participation in school is mixed, the evidence about parental engagement at home is persuasive. Disengagement is incapacitating.

Studies reviewed here (Epstein 1983, Toomey 1992) indicate that schools can foster the specific behaviors at home that promote student performance. In view of this, educators should pay particular attention to one ingredient of home-school partnerships. Most programs include an "outreach" effort to encourage parental involvement, both at home and at school. Educators should encourage this function, at least, of parent-school partnerships.

References

Anderson, R.C., E.H. Hiebert, J.A. Scott, and I.A.G. Wilkinson. (1985). *Becoming a Nation of Readers: The Report of the Commission on Reading*. Washington, D.C.: National Institute of Education.

Astone, N.M., and S.S. McLanahan. (1991). "Family Structure, Parental Practices and High School Completion." *American Sociological Review* 56, 3: 309–320.

Baker, L., D. Scher, and K. Mackler. (1997). "Home and Family Influences on Motivations for Reading." *Educational Psychologist* 32, 2: 69–82.

Clark, R.M. (1983). *Family Life and School Achievement*. Chicago: University of Chicago Press.

Crouter, A.C., S.M. MacDermid, S.M. McHale, and M. Perry-Jenkins. (1990). "Parental Monitoring and Perceptions of Children's School Performance and Conduct in Dual- and Single-Earner Families." *Developmental Psychology* 26, 4: 649–657.

Dave, R.H. (1963). "The Identification and Measurement of Environmental Process Variables That Are Related to Educational Achievement." Unpublished doctoral diss., University of Chicago.

Edwards, P.A. (1992). "Involving Parents in Building Reading Instruction for African-American Children." *Theory into Practice* 31, 4: 350–359.

Edwards, P.A. (1995). "Combining Parents' and Teachers' Thoughts About Storybook Reading at Home and School." In *Family Literacy: Connections in Schools and Communities*, edited by L.M. Morrow. College Park, Md.: International Reading Association.

Epstein, J.L. (1983). *Study of Teacher Practices of Parent Involvement: Results from Surveys of Teachers and Parents*. Baltimore: Johns Hopkins University, Center for Social Organization of Schools.

Epstein, J.L. (1984). *Effects on Parents of Teacher Practices in Parental Involvement*. Baltimore: Johns Hopkins University, Center for Social Organization of Schools.

Epstein, J.L., and S.L. Dauber. (1991). "School Programs and Teacher Practices of Parent Involvement in Inner City Elementary and Middle Schools." *The Elementary School Journal* 91, 3: 289–305.

Finn, J.D. (1993). *School Engagement and Students at Risk*. Washington, D.C.: National Center for Education Statistics.

Ho, E.S., and J.D. Willms. (1996). "Effects of Parental Involvement on Eighth-Grade Achievement." *Sociology of Education* 69, 2: 126–141.

Hoover-Dempsey, K.V., O.C. Bassler, and R. Burow. (1995). "Parents' Reported Involvement in Students' Homework: Strategies and Practices." *The Elementary School Journal* 95, 5: 435–450.

Lamborn, S.D., B.B. Brown, N.S. Mounts, and L. Steinberg. (1992). "Putting School in Perspective: The Influence of Family, Peers, Extracurricular Participation, and Part-time Work on Academic Engagement." In *Student Engagement and Achievement in American Secondary Schools*, edited by F.M. Newmann. New York: Teachers College Press.

Masten, A. (1994). "Resilience in Individual Development: Successful Adaptation Despite Risk and Adversity." In *Educational Resilience in Inner-city America*, edited by M.C. Wang and E.W. Gordon. Hillsdale, N.J.: Erlbaum.

Milne, A.M., D.E. Myers, A.S. Rosenthal, and A. Ginsburg. (1986). "Single Parents, Working Mothers, and the Educational Achievement of School Children." *Sociology of Education* 59, 3: 125–139.

Moles, O.C. (1987). "Who Wants Parent Involvement? Interests, Skills, and Opportunities Among Parents and Educators." *Education and Urban Society* 19, 2: 137–145.

Peng, S.S., and R.M. Lee. (April 1992). "Home Variables, Parent-Child Activities, and Academic Achievement. A Study of 1988 Eighth Graders." Paper presented at the annual meeting of the American Educational Research Association, San Francisco.

Peterson, D. (1989). *Parent Involvement in the Educational Process*. (Eric Digest Series No. EA 43). Eugene, Ore.: Eric Clearinghouse on Educational Management. Eric Document Reproduction Service No. ED 312 776.

Rutherford, B., B. Anderson, and S. Billig. (1997). *Parent and Community Involvement in Education*. Washington, D.C.: U.S. Department of Education, Office of Educational Research and Improvement.

Steinberg, L. (1996). *Beyond the Classroom*. New York: Simon and Schuster.

Taylor, R.D. (1996). "Adolescents' Perceptions of Kinship Support and Family Management Practices: Association with Adolescent Adjustment in African-American Families." *Child Development* 32, 4: 687–695.

Toomey, D. (April 1992). "Short and Medium Run Effects of Parents Reading to Pre-School Children in a Disadvantaged Locality." Paper presented at the annual meeting of the American Educational Research Association, San Francisco. Eric Document Reproduction Service No. ED 346 439.

Topping, K.J. (1986). *Parents as Educators*. London: Croom Helm.

Tracey, D.H. (1995). "Children Practicing Reading at Home: What We Know About How Parents Help." In *Family Literacy: Connections in Schools and Communities*, edited by L.M. Morrow. College Park, Md.: International Reading Association.

Wang, M.C., G.D. Haertel, and H.J. Walberg. (1993). "Toward a Knowledge Base for School Learning." *Review of Educational Research* 63, 3: 249–294.

Wolf, R.M. (1964). "The Measurement of Environments." In *Invitational Conference on Testing Problems*, edited by A. Anastasi. Princeton, N.J.: Educational Testing Service.

Jeremy D. Finn, Professor of Education at State University of New York at Buffalo, is Visiting Scholar at the Center for Research in Human Development and Education during the 1997–98 academic year. He may be reached at Temple University, Center for Research in Human Development and Education, 915 Ritter Hall Annex, Philadelphia, PA 19122-6091 (e-mail: jfinn@nimbus.temple.edu).

Where the Boys Are

Is America shortchanging male children?

By Cathy Young

One day last September, there were two back-to-back events in adjacent rooms at the National Press Club in Washington, D.C. "Beyond the 'Gender Wars,'" a symposium organized by the American Association of University Women (AAUW), was followed by a rejoinder from the Independent Women's Forum (IWF), "The XY Files: The Truth Is Out There… About the Differences Between Boys and Girls." Each event largely followed a predictable script. On the AAUW side, there was verbiage about "gender, race, and class" and hand-wringing about the "conservative backlash"; despite an occasional nod to innate sex differences, "gender equity" was pointedly defined as "equal outcomes." On the IWF side, there were affirmations of *vive la différence* and warnings about the perils of trying to engineer androgyny; despite some acknowledgment that there are not only differences between the sexes but much overlap, the old-fashioned wisdom about men and women was treated as timeless truth. And yet both discussions shared one major theme: the suddenly hot issue of boys—to be more specific, boys as the victimized sex in American education and culture.

Just a few years ago, of course, girls were the ones whose victimization by sexist schools and a male-dominated society was proclaimed on the front pages of newspapers and lamented in editorials, thanks largely to widely publicized reports released by the AAUW in the early 1990s. It was probably only a matter of time before somebody asked, "But what about boys?" By the end of the decade, headlines like "How Boys Lost Out to Girl Power" began to crop up in the media, and boys-in-crisis books began to hit the shelves.

But as the two National Press Club panels underscored, two contrasting arguments are being made on behalf of boys. In one room, there was sympathy for boys who yearn to be gentle, nurturing, and openly emotional but live in a society that labels such qualities "sissy"; in the other, there was sympathy for boys who want only to be boys but live in a society that labels their natural qualities aggressive and patriarchal. Harvard psychiatrist William Pollack, author of the 1999 bestseller *Real Boys: Rescuing Our Sons From the Myths of Boyhood*, believes boys are suffering because our culture traps them in the rigid codes of traditional manhood. American Enterprise Institute scholar Christina Hoff Sommers, author of the controversial new volume *The War Against Boys: How Misguided Feminism Is Harming Our Young Men*, believes boys are suffering because our culture seeks to "feminize" them and devalues manhood. (Guess which of them spoke on which panel.) One camp wants to reform masculinity, the other to restore it; one seeks to rescue boys from patriarchy, the other from feminism.

Both sides, however, agree that something is rotten in the state of boyhood. *Real Boys* opens with the assertion that boys, including many who seem to be doing fine, are "in serious trouble" and "in a desperate crisis." Pollack and other gender reformers paint the typical American boy as an emotional cripple, if not a walking time bomb ready to explode into a school massacre. The shooters of Littleton and Jonesboro, Pollack has said, are merely "the tip of the iceberg."

In *The War Against Boys*, Sommers persuasively challenges this hysteria, noting that it's ludicrous to generalize from a few sociopaths to "millions of healthy male children" who manage to get through high school without gunning down a single person. (She fails to mention that some people in the pro-manhood camp have been just as eager to use homicidal boys as symbols of a male crisis: A couple of years ago in *Commentary*, Midge Decter wrote that "raging schoolyard murder" is what happens when boys are deprived of "manly instruction" and honorable ways to assert their masculinity.) Sommers argues that most children, male and female, are in fairly good psychological health and in no need of "fixing."

Yet Sommers herself refers to boys as "the gender at risk," and her book is hardly free of alarmism, from the title to an opening that rivals Pollack's: "It's a bad time to be a boy in America."

Gender Gap

The most tangible and effectively documented cause of concern is male academic underachievement:

• Girls make up 57 percent of straight-A students; boys make up 57 percent of high school dropouts.

• In 1998, 48 percent of girls but only 40 percent of boys graduating from high school had completed the courses in English, social studies, science, math, and foreign languages recommended as a minimum by the National Commission on Excellence in Education. (In 1987 there was no such gender gap, though only 18 percent of students met these requirements.) According to the National Center for Education Statistics, high school girls now outnumber boys in upper-level courses in algebra, chemistry, and biology; physics is the only subject in which males are still a majority.

• On the National Assessment of Educational Progress (NAEP) tests in 1996, 17-year-old girls, on average, outscored boys by 14 points in reading and 17 points in writing (on a scale of 0 to 500). While boys did better on the math and science tests, it was by margins of five and eight points, respectively.

• Women account for 56 percent of college enrollment in America. This is not due simply, as some feminists claim, to older women going back to school; among 1997 high school graduates, 64 percent of boys and 70 percent of girls went on to college. Female college freshmen are also more likely than men to get a degree in four years.

These differences do not cut across all racial and social lines. The gender gap in higher education has reached truly startling proportions among blacks. From 1977 to 1997, the number of bachelor's degrees awarded annually rose by 30 percent for black men but by 77 percent for black women; among 1996–97 college graduates, black women outnumbered men almost 2 to 1. The "man shortage" among college-educated blacks, which has contributed to tensions over interracial dating, is singled out as a "cause for concern" in the Urban League's recent report *The State of Black America 1999*.

Among non-Hispanic whites, women now receive 55 percent of bachelor's degrees. Feminists are correct when they say this imbalance is partly due to older women going back to school after growing up in an era when girls were expected to pursue the "MRS degree." In 1998, according to the Census Bureau, 48 percent of white college students under 35 were male. But for blacks and Hispanics, a female-to-male ratio of about 3 to 2 persists even when older students are excluded.

For middle-class girls and boys, college is now as much of a given as a high school diploma. Girls from working-class and poor families, on the other hand, are significantly more likely to go to college than boys. There are complex reasons for this. About one-tenth of women in college are training for the health professions, "feminine" jobs similar in status to predominantly male skilled trades that don't require college studies. (Interestingly, female registered nurses and therapists now outearn male mechanics and construction workers.) There is also a theory that, in the new economy, a certificate from a high-tech company's training program may be worth more than a college degree, and that it's mostly young men who skip college to pursue such options. But this explanation, appealing to many feminists, remains speculative. No one knows how many people actually do this; generally, for men or women, the lack of a college degree is still a serious handicap in the marketplace.

In many cases, the "college gap" indisputably reflects a trend toward more upward mobility for women. In a 1999 Rutgers Marriage Project study of sex and relationships among noncollege men and women under 30, David Popenoe and Barbara Dafoe Whitehead report that the women in their focus groups came across as more confident and responsible, with "clear and generally realistic plans for moving up the career ladder," including plans for going back to school. The men seemed less focused and mature; when they talked about their plans for getting ahead, it was often in terms of such "goals" as winning the lottery.

Girls Rule

Perhaps the social changes of the past three decades have made young women more self-assured and eager to use their new opportunities, while leaving many men unnerved and confused about what's expected of them. It may also be that boys, particularly those from low-income families, often become alienated from school early—both because their slower developmental timetable causes them to fall behind girls and because school is a "feminized" environment with mostly female authority figures and boy-unfriendly rules that emphasize being quiet and sitting still.

Some teachers may be prejudiced against boys, regarding them as little brutes or rascals. In a 1990 survey commissioned by the AAUW, children were asked whom teachers considered smarter and liked better; the vast majority of boys and girls alike said "girls." Journalist Kathleen Parker recalls that her son, now a teenager, had a grade school teacher who openly said she liked girls more and singled out boys for verbal abuse—such as telling a student who had his feet up on the desk, "Put your feet down; I don't want to look at your genitalia."

Traditional schoolmarmish distaste for unruly young males may be amplified by modern gender politics. Some educators clearly see boys as budding sexists and predators in need of re-education. Some classrooms become forums for diatribes about the sins of white males, and some boys may be hit with absurd charges of misconduct—such as Jonathan Prevette, the Lexington, North Carolina, first-grader punished with a one-day suspension in 1996 for kissing a girl on the cheek.

"If you listen to 10- or 11-year-old boys, you will hear that school is not a very happy place for them," says Bret Burkholder, a counselor at Pierce College in Puyallup, Washington, who also works with younger boys as a baseball coach. "It's a place where they're consistently made to feel stupid, where girls can walk around in T-shirts that say 'Girls rule, boys drool,' but if a boy makes a negative comment about girls he'll have the book thrown at him."

Even apart from feminism, some "progressive" trends in education may have been detrimental to boys. For example, British researchers have found that "whole language" reading instruction, based on word recognition by shapes, pictures, and contextual clues rather than knowledge of letters, is particularly ineffective with male students.

Early "school turnoff" may cause many boys to develop an anti-learning mindset the British have labeled "laddism"—a mirror image of the prefeminist notion that it isn't cool for a girl to be too bright. "The boys become oppositional and band together in the belief that manly culture doesn't include grade grubbing," observes University of Alaska psychologist Judith Kleinfeld. For black boys, this attitude may be exacerbated by the notion that learning is a "white thing."

Sommers convincingly argues that boys' academic shortcomings have not received proper attention because the discussion of gender and education has been hijacked by "girl partisans." In the 1992 report *How Schools Shortchange Girls*, the AAUW brushed aside boys' disadvantages and explicitly warned against targeted efforts to remedy their deficits in literacy. A few years later, it effectively hushed up a study it had commissioned—*The Influence of School Climate on Gender Differences in the Achievement and Engagement of Young Adolescents*, by University of Michigan psychologist Valerie Lee and her associates—when the findings failed to support the shortchanged-girls premise.

These days, feminists are more willing to admit the good news about girls. The AAUW's new leitmotif, evident at the "Beyond the Gender Wars" symposium, is

that we should stop pitting girls against boys in a victimhood contest and work to make the schools better for everyone—which sounds fine, except that it's a little disingenuous to trumpet girls' victimization and then shout, "Let's not play victim!" as soon as boys' problems are mentioned. What's more, the "gender equity" crowd still grasps for any excuse to discount young men's problems. If more women go to college, said some AAUW panelists, that's because they need it just to break even with men who finish high school. In fact, while female college graduates over 25 earn only 15 percent more than male high school graduates, that group includes older women who went to college with no plans for a career and were out of the labor force for years as well as women who went back to school after raising a family and have limited work experience. This hardly means that young women who are going to college today will do only slightly better financially than young men who are not.

Clash of the Stereotypes

"Boy partisans" can exaggerate too. In his remarks at the IWF's National Press Club event, Rutgers University anthropologist Lionel Tiger inflated the 2-to-1 female-to-male ratio among black college graduates to 5 to 1. (When pressed afterward, he could not recall the source for this surprising figure.) In *The War Against Boys*, Sommers asserts that recent data on high school and college students clearly lead to "the conclusion that girls and young women are thriving, while boys and young men are languishing." Yet this dramatic statement is contradicted further down the page by her own summary of Valerie Lee's study of gender and achievement, which she lauds as "responsible and objective." Lee reports that sex differences in school performance are "small to moderate" and "inconsistent in direction"—boys fare better in some areas, girls in others.

More boys flounder in school (and, as Sommers acknowledges, more of them reach the highest levels of excellence, from the best test scores to top rankings in prestigious law schools). But it's important to put things in perspective. Boys are twice as likely as girls to be shunted into special education with labels that may involve a high degree of subjectivity or even bias, but we are talking about a fairly small proportion of all children. About 7 percent of boys and 3 percent of girls are classified as learning disabled, 1.5 percent of boys and 1.1 percent of girls as mentally retarded; just over 1 percent of boys and fewer than half as many girls are diagnosed with severe emotional disturbances.

Clearly, many boys are doing well; just as clearly, it's an overstatement to say that girls in general are "thriving," since all too often the educational system serves no one well. Twelfth-grade girls may do better than boys on reading and writing tests, but their average scores still fall short of the level that indicates real competence—the ability to understand and convey complicated information.

There's quite a bit of exaggeration, too, in the notion of schools as a hostile environment for boys. Few would dispute that boys tend to be more physically active and less patient than girls; but these differences are far less stark than the clichés deployed in the "boy wars." In a 1998 Department of Education study, 65 percent of boys and 78 percent of girls in kindergarten were described by teachers as usually persistent at their tasks, and 58 percent of boys and 74 percent of girls as usually attentive—a clear yet far from interplanetary gap.

Still smaller are the differences between boys' and girls' views of the school climate. Surprisingly, in a 1995 survey by the Institute for Social Research at the University of Michigan, virtually the same percentages of female and male high school seniors said they liked school. When the question "Whom do teachers like more?" is posed in such a way that they must select one favored sex, kids are likely to answer "girls." Yet when asked about their own experiences, boys are only slightly less likely than girls to say that teachers listen to them, that they call on them often and encourage them, and that discipline and grading at their school are fair.

"We used to think that the schools shortchanged girls; now the news is that schools are waging a war against boys," says psychologist Judith Kleinfeld. "Neither view is right."

Even the image of sexual harassment policies as a wholesale anti-boy witch hunt is too simplistic. For one thing, girls also get caught in the net; last fall, two eighth-grade girls in Euless, Texas, were punished for hugging in the hallway. The bizarre overreactions (which even the Department of Education cautions against) reflect not only gender warfare but the zero tolerance lunacy that has also caused children to be suspended under anti-drug policies for giving an aspirin to a friend. Moreover, these stories coexist with cases in which real sexual assaults are ignored or covered up by school officials.

Some critics of girls-as-victims mythology are uncomfortable with sweeping claims about the plight of boys. "All this haggling about who's the *real* victim is absurd—and unseemly, coming from Americans and describing what must be the most fortunate generation of young people ever to inhabit the planet," says Daphne Patai, a comparative literature scholar at the University of Massachusetts at Amherst and author of *Heterophobia: Sexual Harassment and the Future of Feminism*.

Judith Kleinfeld, who authored the 1996 paper "The Myth That Schools Shortchange Girls," published by the Washington, D.C.-based Women's Freedom Network (of which I am vice president), credits Sommers with drawing attention to an often-ignored problem but wishes her argument had been more nuanced. "We used to think that the schools shortchanged girls; now the news is that schools are waging a war against boys, that girls are on top and boys have become the second sex," says Kleinfeld. "Neither view is right. We should be sending a dual message: one, boys and girls do have characteristic problems, and we need to be aware of what they are; two, boys and girls are also individuals. Unfortunately, there's a lot of exaggeration going on, and a lot of destructive stereotyping by both sides."

Monolithic Manhood

Stereotypes and exaggerations fly just as freely when it comes to the larger debate about how boys should be raised in an age of sexual equality. Gender reformers like Pollack and his Harvard colleague Carol Gilligan, the psychologist and professor of gender studies who pioneered the notion of girls' failing self-esteem in the 1980s before turning her attention to boys, lament that patriarchal norms force boys to separate prematurely from their families, especially their mothers, and to deny their pain, sadness, vulnerability, and fear. As a result, Pollack argues, boys disconnect from their true selves and go into a kind of emotional deep freeze, or even become bullies to prove their manhood.

Real Boys is full of "gender straitjacket" horror stories in which boys barely out of diapers are called "wimps" and told to "act like a man" (usually by fathers) when they are scared or upset. Pollack's dismay is understandable, but how many American fathers really act out such John Wayne parodies? The generalizations are especially shaky since most of Pollack's conclusions seem to be based on troubled boys in his clinical practice. While he occasionally tempers his melodramatic claims, observing that "many, if not most, boys maintain an inner wellspring of emotional connectedness," this does little to change the bleak overall picture.

Mark Kiselica, a psychologist at the College of New Jersey and past president of the American Psychological Association's Society for the Psychological Study of Men and Masculinity, bristles at the notion of boys as "emotional mummies" cut off from relationships. In fact, recent studies by psychologist Susan Harter and her colleagues at the University of Denver, which refute Gilligan's theory that girls lose self-confidence as teenagers, also suggest that adolescent boys are only slightly less open about their thoughts and feelings with parents and friends than are girls. In a 1997 survey by Louis Harris and Associates for the Commonwealth Fund, only one in five teenage boys (and one in seven girls) said they talked to no one when they felt stressed or depressed.

If there's a truth in the arguments of would-be reformers of masculinity, it is that in the past 30 years "gender rules" have been loosened for women more than for men: A boy taking ballet classes raises more eyebrows than a girl playing hockey. But these issues shouldn't and won't be resolved by a bureaucracy of social engineers. The reformers, in any case, vastly overestimate the rigidity and the power of traditional male norms, depicting masculinity as far more monolithic than it has ever been. Most parents don't need Pollack to remind them that, when talking to sons about male family members or friends, they should praise these men's warm and nurturing qualities.

If the "save the males" crowd inflates the harm hypermasculine cultural values can do to American boys at the turn of the millennium, many conservatives probably underestimate it—and, in turn, inflate the perils of creeping androgyny. To be sure, there are educators eager to impose their egalitarian vision on other people's children by banning toy guns from preschools, prohibiting "segregated" play at recess, or herding boys into quilting groups and prodding them to talk about how they feel. It's difficult to tell how widespread this is outside the elite Eastern private schools from which Sommers gets several of her examples, where parents not only choose but pay big money to send their offspring. On the other hand, in many communities, boys still face strong pressure to be jocks—and the jock culture probably is more damaging to boys' learning than the occasional quilting circle.

Would conservative champions of boyhood also praise traditionally masculine fathers who came to honor and cherish their sons' "soft" qualities, even when those sons chose to become hairdressers?

Not unlike the feminists, many conservatives have a vision of a monolithic, virtually unchanging "culture of manhood" that boys must join. Yet one does not have to believe that gender is only a "social construct" to know that standards of male behavior and beliefs about male nature in different times and places have varied as greatly as male dress. Two hundred years ago, it wasn't unusual or inappropriate for men to weep at sentimental plays and for male friends to exchange letters with gushy expressions of affection.

The truth is, both efforts to produce "unisex" children and efforts to enforce traditional masculine or feminine norms are likely to warp children's individuality. Kleinfeld had a chance to observe this when raising her own children: a girl who liked mechanical tools and had an aptitude for science, yet resisted efforts to get her interested in a scientific career and chose humanitarian work instead, and a quiet, gentle boy who was an avid reader. "We tried to get him active in sports, but we were fighting his individual nature," says Kleinfeld. "The one time he made a touchdown in football, he was running the wrong way."

In *The War Against Boys*, Sommers praises feminists who came to honor and cherish their sons' masculine qualities, among them a pacifist-liberal writer whose son chose a military career. But would conservative champions of boyhood also praise traditionally masculine fathers who came to honor and cherish their sons' "soft" qualities, even when those sons chose to become elementary school teachers or hairdressers?

Male Achievement Initiatives

While boys may not be a "second sex," there are clearly distinct educational problems that disproportionately affect male students. Surely it makes sense to look at these problems and consider some gender-specific solutions. Yet such efforts have been virtually nonexistent, largely, no doubt, because they are seen as politically incorrect. In November 1999, Goucher College in Baltimore held a conference called "Fewer Men on Campus: A Puzzle for Liberal-Arts Colleges and Universities." While the event was ostensibly free of any anti-feminist stridency, it drew hostile barbs from the AAUW and warnings about a "backlash" against women's gains from the American Council on Education's Office of Women in Higher Education. (ACE has no special office addressing the issues of men, the new minority on college campuses.) Government efforts to advance "gender equity" in education remain focused solely on inequities allegedly holding back girls and women.

While programs to remedy girls' underachievement in math, science, and computers have proliferated in recent years, funded by the government and by private groups such as the National Science Foundation, there are no programs targeting boys' deficits in reading and writing. (Such programs seem to be working well in England.) Literacy is a popular issue for politicians of both parties, and this year the U.S. Department of Education has given nearly $200 million in grants to state initiatives aimed at improving reading skills in elementary school as part of the Reading Excellence Program. But when I asked project coordinators in Pennsylvania, Illinois, and the District of Columbia if any of these programs would address the gender gap in literacy, it was obvious that the question took them by surprise.

Efforts to help boys can be regarded as suspect even if they target black boys, who have an acknowledged place in the pantheon of the oppressed. In 1996, acting on a complaint from a female student's mother, the Department of Education's Office of Civil Rights ruled that the Black Male Achievement Initiative, a mentoring network in the predominantly black schools of Prince George's County, Maryland, that matched boys with successful professional men, had to be opened to girls. Zack Berry, a staffer in the school district's Office of Youth Development, has no doubt that boys suffered as a result: "Once the program went coed, we found we were doing very well by the young ladies but we were losing our boys left and right, especially in high school." In a few schools, he says, male participation dwindled to less than one-fifth of the total.

This bias against male-only services may be waning. Even the story of Black Male Achievement Initiative has something of a happy ending. In 1999, after the school district collected data showing that boys did not fare as well as girls and presented them to the Office of Civil Rights, the OCR reversed itself and gave a green light to single-sex mentoring programs and activities. Another all-male program that has chapters in several mostly black public schools in Maryland, BROTHERS (Brothers Reaching Out To Help Each Reach Success), has met with no objections so far. "Faculty and adults have rallied around BROTHERS because it has helped a group of kids who just weren't buying into school," says Mike Durso, the principal of Springbrook High School in Silver Spring. The group, which arranges for teens to mentor and tutor younger boys, has been credited with improving discipline, graduation rates, and college enrollment.

Single-sex education, whose popularity for girls surged after the girl crisis hysteria of the early 1990s—leading to the somewhat controversial opening of an all-girl public charter school in New York in 1996 and a sister school in Chicago last fall—deserves more consideration for boys as well. True, there are few reliable data on how children fare in single-sex vs. coed classrooms; if single-sex schools often do better, it may be because they are the product of a conscious effort to create a more academically oriented, more orderly, more individually focused learning environment.

> ## If there's an answer to the "boy question," it lies in getting away from a one-size-fits-all model and making sure that parents and children have as many choices as possible.

Nonetheless, single-sex schooling may be the best option for some boys and girls, not necessarily because the sexes are so radically different but because some teenagers learn best without the distracting presence of the other sex. Susan Harter and other researchers have found that the fear of looking stupid in front of opposite-sex classmates is a major deterrent to speaking in class for boys and girls alike. Boys in particular may try to impress girls by acting "cool" or goofy. Counterintuitively, many education experts believe that all-boy classrooms may also al-

low boys to show their gentle side—pursue interests in art or poetry, discuss the emotions of literary characters—without the fear of appearing "girly."

As for coeducational schools, it goes without saying that they should not be places where children are insulted because of their sex or turned into lab rats for social engineers bent on reinventing gender. Fortunately, unlike the parents of college students, people with children in primary or secondary schools usually have some idea of what's happening in classrooms, and they can help keep the gender warriors in check. Several years ago, a particularly noxious sexual harassment prevention curriculum introduced in Minnesota, which would have had 7-year-olds reciting a solemn pledge to combat harassment, was shelved because of parental opposition and adverse publicity.

Many of the "unmanly" educational fads conservatives deplore are bad for reasons that have little to do with gender. "Cooperative" teaching can turn off bright girls as well as competitive boys. Nor is touchy-feely pedagogy, such as writing assignments requiring students to explore intimate issues, necessarily "female-friendly." Girls who like sharing confidences with each other may balk at "sharing" with teachers. A 1994 *Los Angeles Times* story described reactions to a controversial statewide exam with essay questions about conflicts with parents and regrets about the past. Most of the students who were quoted as complaining about invasive questions were girls.

On the other hand, it's doubtful that many people will worry that their sons will be emasculated by making quilts at school, or by adopting the persona of a famous woman in a class presentation. It would be interesting, though, to see a feminist teacher's reaction if a boy chose Margaret Thatcher as his heroine instead of Anita Hill.

Answering the 'Boy Question'

If there's an answer to the "boy question," it lies in getting away from a one-size-fits-all model, whether feminist or traditionalist, and making sure that parents and children have as many choices as possible. Right now, parents with sexually egalitarian values can generally rely on free government schools to transmit these values to their children, while those who want their children's education to instill traditional beliefs about sex roles have to pay tuition at a private school (as well as taxes to help finance the public schools). Parents who want single-sex schooling for their children are also left with fewer and more expensive options than those satisfied with coeducation. This is one problem that school vouchers could address.

The more diversity there is in education, the more it can be tailored to each child's individuality. Even those who agree that boys have specific needs based on sex-linked traits may define these needs quite differently. Sommers stresses strict discipline in a teacher-led, structured classroom; Kleinfeld suggests that active and non-conformist children, who are disproportionately male, would do well in "open classrooms where children move around a lot," with "teachers who enjoy wiseacres." Each prescription is undoubtedly right for some boys. And there are still other boys who, defying averages, do not thrive on competition and do better in cooperative settings.

We are still far away from a truly diverse educational system. But we have come a long way toward a diverse society that respects both the maleness and the individuality of boys and young men. This diversity will always have room for conservative subcultures that uphold traditional ideals of manhood, as well as for feminist-pacifist communes in which a little boy who uses a stick as a toy sword immediately has the weapon confiscated. But I'd like to think that the future belongs to the feminist who can respect her son the career soldier and to the career soldier who can respect his son the hairdresser.

Contributing Editor Cathy Young (CathyYoung2@cs.com) is the author of Ceasefire: Why Women and Men Must Join Forces to Achieve True Equality (*The Free Press*).

UNIT 3

Social and Emotional Development

Unit Selections

Key Points to Consider

- Not all babies seem to be created from the same cloth in terms of personality. If your child has a difficult temperament, are you doomed to trying to help this child cope effectively? Why or why not? Based on "A Sense of Self," can the things that parents do help the child to adjust to his or her environment? Give some examples of how you as a parent might help a hypersensitive child, an extremely withdrawn child, or an extremely sociable child. Do you think that the birth order of children plays a significant role in their personality? Why or why not? Describe the research evidence that bears on this issue.

- Since the publication of Daniel Goleman's seminal book on emotional intelligence, or EQ, a whole host of researchers and writers have jumped on the EQ bandwagon. What is your best summary of the research on EQ? Do you think EQ is a better predictor of life success than IQ? Why or why not? Do you think emotional intelligence is something that can be learned or is inborn? Should schools be charged with increasing students' EQ? Why or why not?

- When you were a child, did you experience gender segregation—boys playing with boys, girls with girls? How might this have influenced your social and emotional development? Did your teachers encourage or discourage segregation between the sexes? What could a teacher or parents do to influence gender segregation? Recently, there is growing interest in schooling boys and girls in completely separate schools. What advantages or disadvantages might this have for boys and girls educated separately?

- Many people now in America started off as an immigrant. While immigrant children often do have to make a number of adjustments to life in America, the research seems to indicate that children of immigrants actually may do better than native-born children in some areas; for example, they are less likely to have engaged in delinquent or violent behavior or to have used drugs. Why do you think this is the case and what does it say for our American culture? Do you think children from immigrant families ought to develop a more Americanized cultural identity rather than hold to their culture of origin? Why or why not?

 **Links: www.dushkin.com/online/**
These sites are annotated in the World Wide Web pages.

One of the truisms about our species is that we are social animals. From birth, each person's life is a constellation of relationships, from family at home to friends in the neighborhood and school. This unit addresses how children's social and emotional development is influenced by important relationships with parents, peers, and teachers.

When John Donne in 1623 wrote, "No man is an island... every man is... a part of the main," he implied that all humans are connected to each other and that these connections make us who we are. Early in this century, sociologist C. H. Cooley highlighted the importance of relationships with the phrase "looking-glass self" to describe how people tend to see themselves as a function of how others perceive them. Personality theorist Alfred Adler, also writing in the early twentieth century, claimed that personal strength derived from the quality of one's connectedness to others: The stronger the relationships, the stronger the person. The notion that a person's self-concept arises from relations with others also has roots in de-

velopmental psychology. As Jean Piaget once wrote, "There is no such thing as isolated individuals; there are only relations." The articles in this unit respect these traditions by emphasizing the theme that a child's development occurs within the context of relationships.

In "A Sense of Self," author Thomas Hayden discusses the research on children's inborn personality traits and provides parents with a view on how changing one's parenting behaviors can have a profound influence on a child's initial temperament. Since the celebrated publication of Daniel Goleman's book on emotional intelligence, scores of programs and research in the area have emerged. In "Emotional Intelligence: What the Research Says," authors Casey Cobb and John Mayer caution against unbridled, wholesale untested acceptance of the concept. Instead, they argue for a more careful analysis of two models regarding the concept of emotional intelligence when implementing programs in the schools.

Another major influence in the landscape of childhood is friendship. When do childhood friendships begin? Friends become increasingly important during the elementary school years. If forming strong, secure attachments with family mem-

bers is an important task of early childhood, then one of the major psychological achievements of middle childhood is a move toward the peer group. Across the elementary school years, children spend ever-increasing time with peers in the neighborhood and at school. The authors of "What Ever Happened to Play?" lament the loss of free, unscheduled playtime for children as parents continue to feel pressure to enroll their children in a whole host of scheduled after-school activities and lessons. Some child experts warn that this trend may have negative consequences for children. Noted researcher Willard Hartup's research in "The Company They Keep: Friendships and Their Developmental Significance," distinguishes among having friends, the identity of one's friends, and friendship quality as having important developmental outcomes for children. He asserts that friends differ from nonfriends in a variety of important ways.

A dramatic rise in immigration to the United States has resulted in growing numbers of children with foreign-born parents. "The Adjustment of Children From Immigrant Families" describes and summarizes the roles of socioeconomic, psychosocial, and cultural factors that predict adjustment of immigrant children.

A Sense of Self

Children seem to have well-defined personalities from birth. But how their parents and others treat them will shape their characters.

By Thomas Hayden

SOME OF US TEND TO GREET A NEW DAY with a smile, others with a frown, even if it happens to be our very first day. Take Samanta and Neil. Fraternal twins, they were born within minutes of each other two and a half years ago in Panama, and right from the start they each just seemed to have a different way of looking at the world. Neil was the feisty one, screaming and fidgety. His sister was patient, a quiet and curious observer. And it probably wasn't just because she was the one born with a lovely head of hair while her brother had to face his first year as a cue ball.

Any parent knows that personality is not something that comes on gradually with age, but instead seems to be present from birth. And it takes only two kids—even twins—for you to be surprised by just how *different* your little darlings' personalities can be. But what accounts for that difference? Is Neil more aggressive than Samanta because he's a boy? Is Sam more willing to compromise because she's the girl, or because she was born a few minutes later? Or did they just get different mixes of "personality genes," if such things exist? And how much of the personality a child eventually develops has to do not with genetics or biology but with how Mom and Dad respond to each of them, or how they treat each other? Despite the complexity of human behavior, researchers in fields as diverse as genetics, neurobiology, psychology and sociology are starting to get some reliable answers as they poke and prod at the human condition,

trying to figure out what makes us behave, respond and feel the way we do. Is it nature? Is it nurture? Are we controlled by our genes—and do parents even matter? The scientists have a long way to go, but the answers are starting to roll in, and so far it looks like they're yes, yes and yes.

> **43%** of the parents think most of a child's personality and ability is genetic;
>
> **34%** believe personality differences between boys and girls are inborn

Let's start with genes. The story of the '90s was that scientists were discovering "genes for" all sorts of personality traits—happiness, aggressiveness, neuroticism, sexual orientation, risk taking and so on. Virtually all those findings, or their significance, have been disputed in the scientific community, but for a moment it looked as

if we might indeed turn out to be a little more than a product of our DNA, the master molecule of heredity that lies coiled within virtually every one of our cells. Proponents of the power of nature, like geneticist Dean Hamer of the National Institutes of Health, were quick to proclaim that "we come in large part ready-made from the factory." But genes do not act in a vacuum. The information they carry, according to the rigorous studies now emerging, can be quieted or amplified depending on what environment a child lives in—and for infants, "environment" means to a large extent the adults they depend on.

Early life events can teach children to take things in stride

The child's genes often set the tone of parenting. "Parents' behavior reflects genetic differences in their children," says geneticist Robert Plomin of the Institute of Psychiatry in London. Drawing on their 12-year study of adolescents in 720 families, described this year in the book "The Relationship Code," Plomin and his American colleagues conclude that "genetically related kids adopted apart are just as similar" as brothers and sisters who are raised together. That's not because being raised by different parents doesn't matter.

It reflects instead the fact that children who share many genes (as siblings do) and hence personality traits tend to elicit the same reactions from whoever their parents might be. "Basically," says Plomin, "if you've got an antisocial, pain-in-the-ass kid, you reflect that back in your parenting." Genes make the kid a pain, *and* they make the parent a frustrated, anxious wreck. Nervous, short-tempered parenting reinforces the child's natural pain-inducing tendencies, just as more angelic offspring encourage more relaxed, nurturing parenting.

That is not to say that a different parenting style would not produce a different kind of child. Therapists at the Oregon Social Learning Center taught parents of overly aggressive children to break the reinforcement loop by "parenting against type"—talking and listening to their children after explosive outbursts, rather than getting angry or punishing the little powder kegs. Allowing a child to vent her anger and then talk about what caused it in the first place helped prevent future tantrums, the researchers found, and the children became less impulsive and did better in school than aggressive kids whose parents who didn't learn the technique. Parents, whether or not they reinforce a child's innate tendencies, matter.

Biology can make kids a pain and it can make their parents wrecks

One of the very first traits that researchers inferred was strongly influenced by genes—shyness—also turns out to be highly subject to parenting style. Developmental psychologist Jerome Kagan of Harvard University reported as long ago as the late 1970s that shyness has a strong genetic component. He has been following 500 children for some two decades now, and by their 1st or 2nd birthday, Kagan finds, "15 to 20 percent of children are shy and cautious with newness." As infants, they thrash their legs and cry when they hear unfamiliar voices and when they are confronted by bright, colorful toys. "They inherit a neurochemistry [that gives them] a low threshold for unfamiliar things," says Kagan. By the same age, an additional 25 to 30 percent of children in his study are bold, outgoing and not fearful, he says, "like a young Bill Clinton." By the time the children reach the tender age of 4 months, Kagan can predict "better than chance" whether a child has inherited a tendency to by shy ("inhibited") or outgoing ("low reactive").

But does that mean that kids are locked into a genetic personality destiny right from conception? It might be nice to think so—it would let Mom and Dad off the hook for supermarket temper tantrums, anyway—but that would be just a bit too easy. According to a new report on early-childhood development from the National Academy of Sciences, early experiences help children learn how to "self-regulate" their behavior, basically the ability to take things in stride. Manageable challenges—like a short wait between hunger and feeding—can help kids learn to handle stress, according to the report, while overwhelm-

---

FAMILY DYNAMICS

Is Birth Order Destiny?

When kids arrive may affect who they'll become

Charles darwin may have grown up to be a scientific genius, but this family thought the young lad was a troublemaker. His father heartily disapproved of Charles's fascination with plants and animals, and his oldest sister regularly scolded Charles with the zeal of a schoolmarm. Darwin resented his sister's rules: "I made myself dogged so as not to care what she might say," he later wrote. That the boy grew into a rebel, authoring one of the most revolutionary science theories in history, was no mere coincidence, claim some researchers: being the fourth of six children shaped his character and his future.

Younger siblings often grow into defiant adults, argues psychologist Frank Sulloway, a leading exponent of the "birth order" hypothesis. Parents treat firstborns differently from later-borns, and siblings have different childhood experiences depending on which order they arrive in. While firstborns enjoy parents' undivided attention, later-borns must compete for it from birth. Firstborns typically imitate their parents and grow into adults who are more assertive, socially dominant and ambitious. Later-borns, like Darwin, Copernicus, Voltaire and Henry VIII must find other ways to win parental approval, so they're more likely to experiment and defy authority. "Later-borns are more unconventional, more likely to take risks," says Sulloway. In his 1996 book, "Born to Rebel," he concludes form his study of historical figures who championed or opposed revolutions that later-borns are more likely than firstborns to support radical theories.

The birth-order idea remains controversial, however. Many studies supporting it are flawed because their findings are equally explicable by social class or family size rather than birth order. (Youngest siblings were long thought to be less intelligent than firstborns, for instance, until sociologists realized that less-educated parents frequently have larger families.) And a rebel in one situation may be a conformist in another. Judith Harris, author of the 1998 book "The Nurture Assumption," argues that children adopt one set of tactics for dealing with family members and another for the outside world. An oldest child who beats up her younger siblings can't necessarily batter kids at school. So while birth order may be one factor that shapes a child's temperament, influences like gender and genes seem to mold it more strongly. Even if Darwin had been born first, he might still have discovered how evolution works.

ERIKA CHECK

ing challenges, such as chronic abuse, can lead to serious behavioral problems. Kagan finds, for example, that if parents provide extra nurturing and a gentle but firm guiding hand in new or upsetting situations, by the age of 4 most previously inhibited children overcome their "innate" shyness.

To help work out the details of how genes shape personality, researchers have turned to lab animals. Stephen Suomi of the National Institute of Child Health and Human Development has found that some 20 percent of the baby rhesus monkeys he studies not only act like Kagan's shy kids but also share the elevated heart rates and other metabolic traits that set the genetically timid apart from their more outgoing peers. In an experiment similar to matchmaking all the wallflowers at a dance, Suomi and his team have selectively bred monkeys to be shy, proof positive of a genetic basis for the trait. Another group of Suomi's monkey babies, about 5 to 10 percent of them, are overly impulsive, and tend to get into trouble by confronting dominant males or attempting stunts, such as leaping to a distant branch, that are beyond their abilities. Suomi's team found that in the impulsive monkeys, metabolism of the brain chemical serotonin is lower

than average. Serotonin inhibits impulsiveness in both monkeys and humans; if its metabolism is low, the individual is much more likely to take foolish risks and give in to bursts of rage. A recently identified variation in a serotonin-transporter gene—also present in humans—seems to be the cause. Monkeys with a longer version of the gene, which helps regulate how much serotonin gets to the cells that use it, tend to be calm and rational. A shorter version of the gene, says Suomi, "is associated with impaired serotonin metabolism, aggressiveness and a tendency to overconsume alcohol."

Genes that mold personality can be quieted or amplified by the experiences a child has and how she is raised

But not even rhesus monkeys are slaves to their DNA, fated to a lifetime of good sense and happiness or impulsive, self-destructive despair, depending on which form of the gene they inherit from their parents. Short gene or no, says Suomi, a life of "social stupidity" depends very much on how things work out with Mom. When newborn monkeys with the short form of the gene are raised by an average mother—either their own or a foster mom—they tend to grow up poorly adjusted, landing near the bottom of the colony's social ladder. But when the researchers recruit a mother with a history of being extranurturing to raise the anxious little things, everything changes. "They learn to avoid stressful situations," says Suomi, "or get help dealing with them, and as a result often end up at the top of the hierarchy." And it's not just that the youngsters have learned to cover up their natural personality. The extra nurturing actually changes their physiology, bringing their serotonin metabolism into the normal range. "Just because it's biology, and even if it's highly heritable, doesn't mean it's destiny," says Suomi. "Virtually all of the outcomes can be altered substantially by early experiences. Biology just provides a different set of probabilities."

PERSONALITY TRAITS

Lending a Helping Hand

How mothers and fathers treat hypersensitive children, risk takers and other 'problem' kids makes a difference

SCIENTISTS HAVE IDENTIFIED SEVERAL personality patterns that seem to be largely inherited. Most are just part of the intriguing differences between children, but some may signal underlying problems and require parental intervention. Here are some common infant personalities, and how parents can respond.

Hypersensitive, fearful children seem to feel the world more intensely than the rest of us. To these sensitive souls, "a cat's meow sounds like a lion's roar," says child psychiatrist Stanley Greenspan. Extra soothing helps keep them from being overwhelmed; gentle but firm challenges can help them learn to be assertive and confident by the age of 2.

Risk takers are always in motion, pulling and pushing and making a racket. These toddlers are at risk for developing aggressive, antisocial behavior. Parents can help them control impulses by playing games that teach how to regulate actions, like hitting a toy drum hard, then soft, and setting rules for what's acceptable (play wrestling with Dad) and what's not (biting).

Underreactive kids tend to show little interest in the outside world. They rarely complain, so parents may pay more attention to fussier siblings. To avoid self-absorption and poor social abilities, woo them into interacting more. They often be-

come creative problem solvers because they like to work things out in their heads.

Inattentive children may simply be unable to sequence events in time. Setting up obstacle courses for 2-year-olds, with a prize at each step of the way, can help them learn to follow directions. As sequencing ability improves, so will attention span.

Stubborn, defiant kids are trying to control their world, so parents should replace power struggles with negotiation, and hold firm on important issues like bedtime. Your budding tyrant may become a great little debater.

T.H.

Genes do influence personality, but rather than setting an absolute fate, they describe a range of starting places and possibilities. We may indeed come "ready-made from the factory," like, say, a television set. But many of our genes, especially those that work together to influence personality, seem to operate like volume controls. The TV may be set at a nice midrange volume, but you can turn it up or down, within limits. Likewise, we tend to enter the world with our personality "volumes" set to different pitches, but where we end up along the spectrum from grumpy to cheerful or shy to aggressive depends at least in part on our early environment. There's complete interaction between genes and rearing condition," says Suomi. "Very few traits seem to be pure gene and pure environment, but there are oodles and oodles of gene-environment interactions." According to the new NAS report, early gene-environment interactions can set the tone for how a child adapts to challenges throughout life, but, write the report's authors, "this early trajectory is by no means chiseled in stone."

Some scientists have estimated that as much as 50 percent of a child's personality is determined by her genes, but it has proved difficult to parse out exactly how much of a given personality trait is genetic. As with shyness, significant genetic influence has been found for traits such as novelty seeking, a violent temper and a predisposition toward addiction. In some cases, scientists have identified specific genetic differences that seem to be involved, and in many others, researchers are busily using the newly available Human Genome Project data to speed their searches. It seems that different forms of a molecule that ferries the neurochemical dopamine around the brain, for instance, influence whether people are likely to seek out new experiences and take risks, or to be well organized and precise and much happier with routine than with change. But deciphering the importance of specific genes in controlling personality is complicated not just by environmental influences but also by interactions between the estimated 80,000 human genes. For complex traits like shyness or risk taking, says Suomi, "it's very unlikely that it's a single gene."

The world surely has room for quiet, thoughtful but adventuresome sweethearts like Samanta *and* for affectionate but more highly strung guys like Neil. "Each personality has advantages and disadvantages," says Kagan. "The best thing to do is relax and accept it. That could be the positive dividend of genetic research." After all, nothing any scientist has turned up denies that your kids are what kids have always been—their own little people with all sorts of unique and wonderful potential.

Emotional Intelligence: What the Research Says

When integrating the concept of emotional intelligence into curriculum practice, educators need to understand the models, rely on solid research, and—as always—tread carefully.

Casey D. Cobb and John D. Mayer

Emotional intelligence was popularized by Daniel Goleman's 1995 best-selling book, *Emotional Intelligence*. The book described emotional intelligence as a mix of skills, such as awareness of emotions; traits, such as persistence and zeal; and good behavior. Goleman (1995) summarized the collection of emotional intelligence qualities as "character."

The public received the idea of emotional intelligence enthusiastically. To some, it de-emphasized the importance of general IQ and promised to level the playing field for those whose cognitive abilities might be wanting. To others, it offered the potential to integrate the reasoning of a person's head and heart. Goleman made strong claims: Emotional intelligence was "as powerful," "at times more powerful," and even "twice as powerful" as IQ (Goleman, 1995, p. 34; Goleman, 1998, p. 94). On its cover, *Time* magazine declared that emotional IQ "may be the best predictor of success in life, redefining what it means to be smart" (Gibbs, 1995). Goleman's book became a *New York Times*—and international—best-seller.

The claims of this science journalism extended easily to the schools. *Emotional Intelligence* concluded that developing students' emotional competencies would result in a "caring community," a place where students feel respected, cared about, and bonded to classmates" (Goleman, 1995, p. 280). A leader of the social and emotional learning movement referred to emotional intelligence as "the integrative concept" underlying a curriculum for emotional intelligence (Elias et al., 1997, pp. 27, 29). And the May 1997 issue of *Educational Leadership* extensively covered the topic of emotional intelligence.

Two Models

This popular model of emotional intelligence was based on, and added to, a 1990 academic theory and subsequent publications now referred to as the *ability* approach to emotional intelligence. The logic behind the ability model was that emotions are signals about relationships. For example, sadness signals loss. We must process emotion—perceive, understand, manage, and use it—to benefit from it; thus, emotional processing—or emotional intelligence—has great importance (Mayer & Salovey, 1997; Salovey & Mayer, 1990).

The concept of emotional intelligence legitimates the discussion of emotions in school.

The ability model argued for an emotional intelligence that involves perceiving and reasoning abstractly with information that emerges from feelings. This argument drew on research findings from areas of nonverbal perception, empathy, artificial intelligence, and brain research. Recent empirical demonstrations have further bolstered the case (Mayer, Caruso, & Salovey, 1999; Mayer, DiPaolo, & Salovey, 1990; Mayer & Salovey, 1993; Salovey & Mayer, 1990).

The ability model made no particular claims about the potential predictive value of emotional intelligence. In fact, even several years after the publication of Goleman's book, psychologists view the popular claims about predicting success as ill-defined, unsupported, and implausible

(Davies, Stankov, & Roberts, 1998; Epstein, 1998). Rather, the ability version emphasizes that emotional intelligence exists. If emotional intelligence exists and qualifies as a traditional or standard intelligence (like general IQ), people who are labeled *bleeding hearts* or *hopeless romantics* might be actually engaged in sophisticated information processing. Moreover, the concept of emotional intelligence legitimates the discussion of emotions in schools and other organizations because emotions reflect crucial information about relationships.

Educational practices involving emotional intelligence should be based on solid research, not on sensationalistic claims.

Two models of emotional intelligence thus developed. The first, the ability model, defines emotional intelligence as a set of abilities and makes claims about the importance of emotional information and the potential uses of reasoning well with that information. The second, which we will refer to as the mixed model, is more popularly oriented. It mixes emotional intelligence as an ability with social competencies, traits, and behaviors, and makes wondrous claims about the success this intelligence leads to.

Educational leaders have experimented with incorporating emotional learning in schools. For the most part, emotional intelligence is finding its way into schools in small doses, through socioemotional learning and character education programs. But examples of grander plans are evolving, with a few schools organizing their entire curriculums around emotional intelligence. One state even attempted to integrate emotional learning into all its social, health, and education programs (Elias et al., 19978; Rhode Island Emotional Competency Partnership, 1998).

The problem is that some educators have implemented emotional intelligence programs and policies without much sensitivity to the idea that there is more than one emotional intelligence model. We have expressed concern that school practices and policies on emotional intelligence relied on popularizations that were, in some instances, far ahead of the science on which they were presumably based (Mayer & Cobb, 2000). The early claims of the benefits of emotional intelligence to students, schools, and beyond were made without much empirical justification.

We hope that emotional intelligence is predictive of life success or that it leads to good behavior, but we recognize that it is fairly early in the game. We are also wary of the sometimes faddish nature of school reform and the grave fate of other hastily implemented curricular innovations. Consider the rush by California to implement self-esteem programs into its schools in the late 1980s (Joachim, 1996). Substantial resources were exhausted for years before that movement was deemed a failure. The construct of

emotional intelligence comes at a time when educators are eager to find answers to problems of poor conduct, interpersonal conflict, and violence plaguing schools; however, educational practices involving emotional intelligence should be based on solid research, not on sensationalistic claims. So, what *does* the research say?

Measuring Emotional Intelligence

Emotional intelligence, whether academically or popularly conceived, must meet certain criteria before it can be labeled a psychological entity. One criterion for an intelligence is that it can be operationalized as a set of abilities. Ability measures—measures that ask people to solve problems with an eye to whether their answers are right or wrong—are the sine qua non of assessing an intelligence. If you measure intelligence with actual problems (such as, What does the word *season* mean?), you can assess how well a person can think. If you simply ask a student how smart she is (for example, How well do you solve problems?)—a so-called self-report—you cannot be certain that you are getting an authentic or genuine answer. In fact, the correlation between a person's score on an intelligence test and self-reported intelligence is almost negligible. Early evidence suggests that self-reported emotional intelligence is fairly unrelated to actual ability (Mayer, Salovey, & Caruso, 2000).

Ability-based testing of emotional intelligence has centered on the Mayer-Salovey-Caruso Emotional Intelligence Test (MSCEIT) and its precursor, the Multifactor Emotional Intelligence Scale (MEIS). Both tests measure the four areas of emotional intelligence: perception, facilitation of thought, understanding, and management (Mayer, Caruso, & Solovey, 1999). For example, look at the pictures of the faces on this page. Is the person happy? Sad? Are other emotions expressed? Identifying emotions in faces, pictorial designs, music, and stories are typical tasks for assessing the area of emotional intelligence called emotional perception.

What may work better, at least for some students, is helping them develop the capacity to make decisions on their own in their own contexts.

Another type of MSCEIT question asks, When you are feeling slow and sour, which of the following emotions does this most closely resemble: (A) frustration, (B) jealousy, (C) happiness, or (D) joy? Most people would probably choose *frustration* because people become frustrated when they move too slowly and are disappointed (or sour) that things aren't going as planned. This kind of question measures the second area of emotional intelligence: emotional facilitation of thought.

A third type of MSCEIT question tests individuals' knowledge about emotions: Contempt is closer to which combination of emotions: *anger and fear* or *disgust and anger?* Such a question assesses emotional understanding.

The final type of MSCEIT questions measures emotional management. These questions describe a hypothetical situation that stirs the emotions (such as the unexpected break-up of a long-term relationship) and then ask how a person should respond to obtain a given outcome (for example, staying calm).

One crucial aspect of assessing emotional intelligence lies in the method by which answers are scored. Scoring a standard IQ test is fairly straightforward, with clear-cut, defensible answers for every item. The responses on a test of emotional intelligence are better thought of as *fuzzy sets*—certain answers are more right or plausible than others, and only some answers are absolutely wrong all the time. To assess the relative correctness of an answer, we can use consensus, expertise, or target criteria (or some combination). A correct response by way of the consensus approach is simply the answer most frequently selected by test-takers. Answers can also be deemed correct by such experts as psychologists or other trained professionals. Finally, correct responses can be validated using a target criterion. For instance, the actual emotional reaction of an anonymously depicted spouse facing a difficult decision could serve as the targeted response in a test item that described his or her situation.

The MSCEIT and MEIS are undergoing considerable scrutiny from the scientific community. Although not everyone is convinced yet of their validity, the tests do provide the most dramatic evidence thus far for the existence of an emotional intelligence. Early findings provide strong evidence that emotional intelligence looks and behaves like other intelligences, such as verbal intelligence, but remains distinct enough to stand alone as a separate mental ability. Like other intelligences, emotional intelligence appears to develop with age (Mayer, Caruso, & Solovey, 1999).

Predictive Value

The first emotional intelligence tests were used two years *after* the popular claims of 1995, so the actual findings lag behind the popular perception of a well-established area of research. One important pattern is emerging, however. Preliminary research (primarily from unpublished studies and dissertations) from the MEIS suggests a modest relationship between emotional intelligence and lower levels of "bad" behaviors.

In one study, high scores in emotional intelligence moderately predicted the absence of adult bad behavior, such as getting into fights and arguments, drinking, smoking, and owning firearms (Mayer, Caruso, Salovey, Formica, & Woolery, 2000). In a dissertation study, the MEIS-A measured the emotional intelligence of fifty-two 7th and 8th graders in an urban school district (Rubin,

1999). Analyses indicated that higher emotional intelligence was inversely related to teacher and peer ratings of aggression among students. In another study, researchers reported that higher MEIS-A scores among 200 high school students were associated with lower admissions of smoking, intentions to smoke, and alcohol consumption (Trinidad & Johnson, 2000). The conclusion suggested by such research is that higher emotional intelligence predicts lower incidences of "bad" behavior. As for the claims about success in life—those studies have yet to be done.

What Can Schools Do?

Educators interested in emotional intelligence of either the ability or mixed type are typically directed to programs in social and emotional learning (Goleman, 1995; Goleman, 1996; Mayer & Salovey, 1997). These programs had been around for years before the introduction of the emotional intelligence concept. Some aspects of the programs overlap with the ability approach to emotional intelligence. This overlap occurs when programs ask early elementary children to "appropriately express and manage" various emotions and "differentiate and label negative and positive emotions in self and others," or call for students to integrate "feeling and thinking with language" and learn "strategies for coping with, communicating about, and managing strong feelings" (Elias et al., 1997, p. 133–134). Other aspects of these programs are specifically more consistent with the mixed (or popular) models than the ability approach in that they include distinct behavioral objectives, such as "becoming assertive, self-calming, cooperative," and "understanding responsible behavior at social events" (p. 135). There is also an emphasis on such values as honesty, consideration, and caring.

Correctly perceiving emotional information is part of the way that children make sense of things.

What would a curriculum based on an ability model look like? Basically, it would drop the behavioral objectives and values and focus on emotional reasoning.

Choosing Approaches

The emotional intelligence curriculum (or ability model) and the social and emotional learning curriculum (or mixed model) both overlap and diverge. The emotional ability approach focuses only on teaching emotional reasoning. The social and emotional learning curriculum mixes emotional skills, social values, and behaviors. In the case of these two approaches, less—that is, the pure ability model—may be better. What troubles us about the broader social and emotional learning approach is that the emphasis on students getting along with one another could stifle creativity, healthy skepticism, or spontaneity—all valued outcomes in their own right. Teaching people to be tactful or compassionate as full-time general virtues runs counter to the "smart" part of emotional intelligence, which requires knowing when to be tactful or compassionate and when to be blunt or even cold and hard.

Moreover, a social and emotional approach that emphasizes positive behavior and attitudes can be a real turn-off for a negative thinker—often the very student that the teacher is trying to reach. Research supports this concern. Positive messages appear less believable and less sensible to unhappy people than sad messages do (Forgas, 1995). We suspect that troubled students will be alienated by insistent positivity. There may be nothing wrong with trying such approaches, but they may not work.

What may work better, at least for some students, is helping them develop the capacity to make decisions on their own in their own contexts. This type of education is knowledge-based and is more aligned with an ability model of emotional intelligence. It involves teaching students emotional knowledge and emotional reasoning, with the hope that this combination would lead children to find their own way toward making good decisions.

Most children will require gentle guidance toward the good. We wonder, however, whether we can achieve this goal better by example and indirect teaching than by the direct, uniform endorsement of selected values in the curriculum.

How Might the Ability Curriculum Work?

The teaching of emotional knowledge has been a facet of some curriculums for years. For example, educators can help children perceive emotions in several ways. Elementary teachers could ask the class to name the feelings that they are aware of and then show what they look or feel like (for example, Show me sad). Similarly, teachers could ask students to identify the emotions depicted by various pictures of faces. Children can also learn to read more subtle cues, such as the speed and intonation of voice, body posture, and physical gestures.

Correctly perceiving emotional information is one way children make sense of things. The ability to perceive emotions can be further fine-tuned as a student ages. Consider the level of sophistication required for an actor to put on a convincing expression of fear—and for the audience to recognize it as such.

Students can also learn to use emotions to create new ideas. For instance, asking students in English class to write about trees as if they were angry or delighted facilitates a deeper understanding of these emotions.

Understanding emotions should also be a goal of the curriculum. For example, social studies expert Fred Newmann (1987) has suggested that higher-order thinking can be enhanced through empathic teaching. A social studies teacher could show images of the Trail of Tears, the forced exodus of the Cherokee from their homeland, and

have students discuss the feelings involved. This could help students vicariously experience what those perilous conditions were like. In literature courses, teachers who point out the feelings of a story character, such as a triumphant figure skater or a despairing widow, can teach a great deal about what emotions tell us about relationships. Because the ability version of emotional intelligence legitimizes discussing emotions by considering them to convey information, it also supports emotionally evocative activities—such as theater, art, and interscholastic events—that help kids understand and learn from personal performance.

Identifying emotions in faces, pictorial designs, music, and stories are typical tasks for assessing the area of emotional intelligence called emotional perception.

Identifying emotions in faces, pictorial designs, music, and stories are typical tasks for assessing the emotional perception area of emotional intelligence.

Emotional Intelligence in Schools

Educators looking to incorporate emotional intelligence into their schools should be aware that the two different models of emotional intelligence suggest two somewhat different curricular approaches. The model of emotional intelligence that makes its way into schools should be empirically defensible, measurable, and clear enough to serve as a basis for curriculum development. We believe that an ability-based curriculum, which emphasizes emotional knowledge and reasoning, may have advantages because it reaches more students.

References

Davies, M., Stankov, L., & Roberts, R. D. (1998). Emotional intelligence: In search of an elusive construct. *Journal of Personality & Social Psychology, 75,* 989–1015.

Elias, M. J., Zins, J. E., Weissberg, R. P., Frey, K. S., Greenberg, M. T., Haynes, N. M., Kessler, R., Schwab-Stone, M. E., & Schriver, T. P. (1997). *Promoting social and emotional learning: Guidelines for educators.* Alexandria, VA: ASCD.

Epstein, S. (1998). *Constructive thinking: The key to emotional intelligence.* Westport, CT: Praeger.

Forgas, J. P. (1995). Mood and judgement: The affect infusion model (AIM). *Psychological Bulletin, 117*(1), 39–66.

Gibbs, N. (1995, October 2). The EQ factor. *Time, 146*(14), 60–68.

Goleman, D. (1995). *Emotional intelligence.* New York: Bantam.

Goleman, D. (1996). *Emotional intelligence: A new vision for educators* [Videotape]. Port Chester, NY: National Professional Resources.

Goleman, D. (1998, November/December). What makes a leader? *Harvard Business Review, 76,* 93–102.

Joachim, K. (1996). The politics of self-esteem. *American Educational Research Journal, 33,* 3–22.

Mayer, J. D., Caruso, D. R., & Salovey, P. (1999). Emotional intelligence meets standards for a traditional intelligence. *Intelligence, 27,* 267–298.

Mayer, J. D., Caruso, D. R., Salovey, P., Formica, S., & Woolery, A. (2000). Unpublished raw data.

Mayer, J. D., & Cobb, D. C. (2000). Educational policy on emotional intelligence: Does it make sense? *Educational Psychology Review, 12*(2), 163–183.

Mayer, J. D., DiPaolo, M. T., & Salovey, P. (1990). Perceiving affective content in ambiguous visual stimuli: A component of emotional intelligence. *Journal of Personality Assessment, 54,* 772–781.

Mayer, J. D., & Salovey, P. (1993). The intelligence of emotional intelligence. *Intelligence, 17*(4), 433–443.

Mayer, J. D., & Salovey, P. (1997). What is emotional intelligence? In P. Salovey & D. Sluyter (Eds.), *Emotional development and emotional intelligence: Implications for educators* (pp. 3–31). New York: BasicBooks.

Mayer, J. D., Salovey, P., & Caruso, D. R. (2000). Models of emotional intelligence. In R. J. Sternberg (Ed.), *Handbook of intelligence* (pp. 396–420). Cambridge: Cambridge University Press.

Newmann, F. M. (1987). *Higher order thinking in the teaching of social studies: Connections between theory and practice.* Madison, WI: National Center on Effective Secondary Schools. (ERIC Document Reproduction Service No. 332 880)

Rhode Island Emotional Competency Partnership. (1998). *Update on emotional competency.* Providence, RI: Rhode Island Partners.

Rubin, M. M. (1999). *Emotional intelligence and its role in mitigating aggression: A correlational study of the relationship between emotional intelligence and aggression in urban adolescents.* Unpublished manuscript, Immaculata College, Immaculata, PA.

Salovey, P., & Mayer, J. D. (1990). Emotional intelligence. *Imagination, Cognition, & Personality, 9*(3), 185–211.

Trinidad, D. R., & Johnson, A. (2000). *The association between emotional intelligence and early adolescent tobacco and alcohol use.* Unpublished manuscript, University of Southern California, Los Angeles, CA.

Casey D. Cobb (casey.cobb@unh.edu) is Assistant Professor of Education and **John D. Mayer** is Professor of Psychology at the University of New Hampshire, 62 College Rd., Durham, NH 03824.

Everybody knows a kid needs love. Now neuroscience is closing in on just how TLC shapes a child's brain and behavior.

BABIES, BONDS, AND BRAINS

BY KAREN WRIGHT

IN TERMS OF BEHAVIORAL DEVELopment, I was something of a late bloomer. My mother reports that I slept away most of my infancy and toddlerhood, and even my adolescence was unremarkable. I didn't enter my angst-and-experimentation phase until my mid-20s, when, like a tortured teen, I blamed my parents for everything. Several years and several thousand dollars of psychotherapy later, I let my parents off the hook. I realized it couldn't all be their doing—my faults, my fears, my penchant for salty, cheese-flavored snack foods. I am not, after all, the simple product of my upbringing.

This healthy outlook threatened to come undone one recent afternoon as I stood outside the cages at the National Institutes of Health Animal Center in Poolesville, Maryland, watching Stephen Suomi's monkeys. Suomi, a primatologist at the National Institute of Child Health and Human Development, studies the effects of rearing environments on the behavior of young rhesus macaques. Fifty graduates of his program live in the center's five-acre enclosure; at the moment,

they are gathered in a large chain-link cell with sawdust on the floor and monkey toys dangling from the ceiling. The arrival of human visitors stirs this cohort like dry leaves in a whirlwind, and its members quickly segregate into three factions. The boldest rush to get a cage-front view of the newcomers; a second phalanx hovers behind them, cautious but curious; and at the far end of the cage a third group forms a simian huddle of abject fear.

These monkeys are most definitely the products of their respective upbringings. The three groups were raised in three distinct settings. The bold monkeys spent the first six months of life being shuttled between monkey play groups and individual cages (and so were used to human handling); the sensibly cautious ones were reared by their natural families, with mothers, fathers, and siblings; and the fearful monkeys grew up parentless among same-age peers, to whom they retain an abnormally strong attachment.

Suomi is keenly interested in the spectrum of behavior among his macaques— from bold and aggressive to anxious and

withdrawn—for it parallels the human trait known as temperament, the fundamental cast of personality that governs our propensity for hobnobbing, taking risks, or seeking thrills. He and other researchers have found that temperament is reflected in biology as well as behavior: heart rate, immune response, stress-hormone levels, and other physiological measures can be correlated with temperamental styles in humans and monkeys alike. And despite some investigators' assertions to the contrary, Suomi's experiments imply that temperament may be largely the result of a young monkey's home life.

"The patterns have some genetic heritability," says Suomi, jangling his car keys in front of the cage to get an even more exaggerated response. "But our work shows that you can modify these tendencies quite dramatically with certain types of early experiences."

Suomi belongs to the league of scientists who are studying the role that early childhood environment plays in determining adult behavior. He and his colleagues are working a bit beyond the pale, as late-twentieth-century science seems to savor the notion of genetic determinism. But the effects of childhood environment—specifically, the "environment" supplied by parenting—are coming under renewed scrutiny now, in large part because recent neurological studies have revealed that the structure of a child's brain remains surprisingly malleable months and even years after birth. The number of connections between nerve cells in an infant's brain grow more than 20-fold in the first few months of life, for example; a two-year-old's brain contains twice as many of these connections, called synapses, as an adult's brain. Throughout early childhood, synapses multiply and are pruned away at a furious pace. Something directs this dynamic rewiring, and researchers have concluded that that something is experience.

Of course, "experience" can come in all shapes and sizes. Childhood illness and diet, for example, count as experiences, too. But there's reason to believe that a child's experience of his parents is an especially potent sculptor of the parts of the brain involved in emotion, personality, and behavior. Some studies indicate that the strength of a child's bonding with his caregivers may increase his ability to learn and to cope with stress. Others show that childhood abuse and neglect can prime the brain for a lifetime of inappropriate aggression and scattered attention.

As THE TWENTIETH CENTURY draws to a close, more than half of America's one-year-olds are spending their days with someone other than their mothers. This historic surge in day care has coincided with a rush of reports showing that early experiences may be more critical to brain development than anyone had previously imagined. Naturally, each new bulletin tweaks the guilty fears of working parents. So far, however, the news about kids and day care is pretty good. Children in day care appear to do just fine—provided the quality of the interactions between caregiver and child is high—and good day care may even enhance their social skills and performance in school. Low-quality day care, on the other hand, may compromise a child's adjustment and academic performance.

These results are not surprising to behavioral researchers, who have long appreciated the importance of bonds between caregivers and children. "We know that little kids don't hop up and run away from lions—they don't deal directly with the world much," says Megan Gunnar, a developmental psychologist at the University of Minnesota in Minneapolis. "Their survival depends on their relationships." Hence, children are keenly attuned to the cues they receive from parents, says Gunnar, and they are especially sensitive to signs of indifference. Responsive, sensitive parents inspire trust in their children, giving rise to what behavioral scientists call secure attachment; insensitive or withdrawn parents can foster insecure attachment.

Nearly four decades of behavioral research has painted a dramatic picture of how important this attachment is to a child's emotional health. University of Wisconsin psychologist Harry Harlow's pioneering studies in the late fifties and early sixties found that monkeys reared in total isolation developed aberrant feeding, mating, parenting, and socializing behaviors. Developmental psychologists now believe that bonding with a parent or other caregiver is as essential to a normal childhood as learning to walk and talk. In the absence of a "good mother," children will attach as best they can to whatever figure presents itself—just as Harlow's infant monkeys became virtually inseparable from the cloth-and-wire surrogates in their cages.

"It's not just what happens to you that counts—it's what you think happens to you. And it's difficult to figure out what a child is thinking."

Stephan Suomi's simian charges are another example of how behavior can be warped by bonding with a maladroit mom. The timid peer-reared monkeys at the NIH center are the victims of insecure attachment; their peers didn't provide the stability and sensitivity that make for a secure bond. (Imagine what a wreck you'd be if you were raised by a twin sister.) These monkeys are anxious and inhibited, and their temperaments are reflected in their reluctance to explore strange objects, their shyness with unfamiliar peers, their low status in monkey communities, and their distress on being separated from their companions. Some peer-reared monkeys, mostly males, also have self-destructive tendencies toward impulsive behavior and aggression. They're the playground bul-

lies, and they're often shunned by, or even kicked out of, their play groups.

Clearly, peer-rearing has unhappy consequences for an individual's social skills and ability to cope with stress. It has at least one other embarrassing side effect as well. "Every animal that's reared without a mother, no matter what its other social experience may be, turns out to be hyper-oral," says Suomi. "They all suck their thumbs a lot."

Peer-rearing also leaves a distinctive stamp on the monkey's physiology. Samples of cerebrospinal fluid from Suomi's impulsive monkeys show that they grow up with lower levels of serotonin, a mood-regulating biochemical that has been linked with aggression, antisocial behavior, and depression in human beings. At the same time, turnover of norepinephrine, a chemical messenger associated with fearfulness, is unusually rapid in peer-reared monkeys. The monkeys' immune systems tend to be suppressed, while their levels of stress hormones are higher and their heart rates faster than those of mother-reared monkeys. Might these be the fruits of insecure attachment?

Megan Gunnar thinks so. Gunnar studies the relationship between attachment security and reactions to stress in human infants and toddlers. She's found that stressful circumstances such as vacinations, the presence of strangers, and separation from mom produce elevations of the stress hormone cortisol in infants. By age two, however, children with secure attachments to their mothers don't get these cortisol rushes, even when they act stressed out. Children with insecure attachment, on the other hand, continue to show elevations of cortisol. It's as if secure attachment comforts the body more than the mind.

"In the animal literature, the contact with adult conspecifics—it doesn't have to be the mom, but it needs to be somebody who acts like a mom and that the baby is familiar with—has powerful effects at blocking the activity of stress-response systems," says Gunnar. "If the attachment figure is present, and the relationship has been reliable, then some aspect of the stress response just doesn't happen."

That's a good thing, says Gunnar, because a hyperactive stress-response system can wreak havoc on the body. The racing heartbeats and suppressed immune systems that Suomi sees in peer-rearing monkeys, for example, are responses that would normally occur to help the young animal cope with a transient stress—such as being left alone while mom goes out and mates. But in peer-reared monkeys, the stress response is cranked up day in, day out, and that super-responsiveness persists into adolescence—long past the age of primate attachment. Gunnar proposes that such a skewed stress-response system can promote lasting behavioral changes by interfering with brain development. In rat pups, she points out, chronic stress is known to disturb the development of the limbic system, frontal lobes, and hippocampus, parts of the brain that are involved in fearfulness and vigilance, attention focusing, learning, and memory. Gunnar suggests that secure attachment serves as a buffer against these disturbances, while insecure attachment leaves the brain open to insults that can result in lifelong anxiety, timidity, and learning difficulties.

OF COURSE, ANXIOUS, INHIBITED, or impulsive behavior isn't necessarily the result of early attachment problems. The extensive work of Harvard psychologist Jerome Kagan certainly suggests that such traits can be inborn. Kagan finds that 20 percent of human infants have the behavioral and physiological signs of an inhibited temperament at just four months of age—presumably, in Kagan's view, before a child's environment would have exerted its effects. He has also found that up to 40 percent of four-month-olds have signs of a bold or fearless nature. These tendencies often mellow with time, however, so that by age four only 10 percent of children are either fearful or reckless.

Suomi finds virtually the same proportions of bold and fearful monkeys in his mother-reared troops—a fact that seems to argue for the genetic conservation of temperament. But Kagan contends that the rich inner life of the child may limit the relevance of animal studies, despite the seeming parallels in primate personalities. "It's not just what happens to you that counts—it's what you *think* happens to you," says Kagan. "And it is inordinately difficult to figure out what a child is thinking. Until we devise ways to measure what is in a child's head, we're not going to understand the child's environment."

The inner life of the child may help explain the phenomenon of so-called resilient children, those who somehow manage to rise above difficult home environments and live normal, even accomplished, lives. But these children are exceptional; it's clear that abusive or negligent parenting can have devastating effects on a child's emotional development. All the evidence

suggests that physical abuse in childhood, for example, leads to a higher risk of drug use, mood disorders, violence, and criminality in adulthood. Girls who are sexually abused are more prone to depression, panic attacks, eating disorders, drug use, and suicide. And children reared in orphanages, without any parenting at all, often develop a disturbing array of social and behavioral problems. Researchers are beginning to explore the biological mechanisms for these associations, but it's not hard to imagine the psychological ones.

"I think there are people who, for genetic reasons, are more susceptible to certain kinds of stressful stimulation," says Bruce Perry, who studies the physiology of abused and neglected children at the Baylor College of Medicine in Houston. "But even with the optimum genetic organization, trauma will create the problems we're talking about."

Growing up in even a mildly bad environment appears to affect your biology. The question is whether those changes can be reversed.

Many of the kids Perry sees have been exposed to domestic violence, and their unpredictable and threatening home lives, he says, can be read in both their physiology and their behavior. They seem to be in a perpetual state of arousal: their "fight or flight" response has somehow been permanently activated, and they have tense muscles, rapid heart rates, and trouble sleeping. Their stress-response systems may be irreparably altered. "These kids grow up with a neurophysiology that is perfectly adapted to survive in a chaotic, distressing environment," says Perry. "They develop this extreme hypervigilance because they never know what is going to happen next."

But the children of domestic violence are poorly adapted to life in a nonviolent world. Their vigilance can lead them to misinterpret other people's behavior and intentions, says Perry. Boys, for example, will perceive hostility and aggression in a look or an offhand remark and respond too readily in kind (think Robert DeNiro in *Taxi Driver*). Girls are more likely to shut down or withdraw completely from even mildly threatening circumstances. In school, both boys and girls tend to tune out verbal information and become hypersen-

sitive to nonverbal cues. They might focus more on a teacher's hand gestures, for example, than the subject he's lecturing on.

Perhaps it's not surprising that severe stress in childhood leaves both biological and behavioral scars. But researchers are learning that even less extreme emotional stressors, such as parental conflict or depression, can also have an impact on kids' behavior and biology. The children of depressed mothers, for example, are at increased risk for depression themselves, and most psychologists think the risk cannot be ascribed entirely to genetics. EEG studies by psychologist Geraldine Dawson of the University of Washington in Seattle show that babies whose mothers are depressed have reduced activity in the left frontal region of the brain—the area implicated in joy, interest, and other positive emotions.

Growing up in even a mildly bad environment appears to affect your biology. The question, of course, is whether those changes can be reversed. Several lines of research suggest that they can be. Suomi, for example, has shown that even monkeys who *are born* anxious and inhibited can overcome their temperamental handicap—and even rise to the top of the dominance hierarchy in their troop—if they are raised by ultranurturing supermoms. Kagan's work confirms that mothering can alter the course of an inhibited child's development. A pioneering day-care program at the University of North Carolina at Chapel Hill has cut the incidence of mental retardation by as much as 80 percent among kids whose unstimulating home environment put them at high risk for low IQ. Dawson, too, has found that psychologically depressed mothers who manage to stay positive and engaged in caregiving can minimize the impact of their depression on their babies' brain waves. And her follow-up work revealed that, at age three, children's EEGs will return to normal if their mothers' depression lifts.

"So I wonder, how plastic is the brain?" says Dawson. "At what point in development do we start to see enduring effects as opposed to transient effects?"

The answer may be never. The new model of neural development holds that the primitive areas of the brain mature first: in the first three years of life, the regions in the cortex that govern our sensory and motor skills undergo the most dramatic restructuring, and these perceptual centers, along with instinctual ones such as the limbic system, will be strongly affected by early childhood experiences. This vulnerability is nothing to scoff at, says Robert Thatcher, a neuroscientist at the University of South Florida College of Medicine in Tampa. "The limbic system is where we live, and the cortex is basically a slave to that," he explains.

But the frontal cortex, which governs planning and decision making, and the cerebellum, a center for motor skills, are also involved in emotional development. And those parts of the brain don't get rewired until a person is five to seven years old. What's more, another major restructuring of the brain occurs between ages nine and eleven, says Thatcher. Suddenly, the brain is looking less like a sculpture in stone and more like a work in progress.

In fact, Thatcher's reading of the EEGs of adolescents and adults have revealed that some reorganization of the brain may occur about every two years from birth to death. He proposes that these reorganizations happen in response to waves of nerve growth factor that sweep across the cerebral hemispheres in two-year cycles, revamping up to one-fifth of the brain's synaptic connections at the leading edge of the wave. The idea of the traveling waves is just a theory now—but it's a theory that's making more sense to more scientists.

"The brain doesn't stop changing after three years," says Megan Gunnar. "For some things, the windows of influence are only beginning to close at that age, and for others they're only beginning to open." If Thatcher is right, the brain is, in fact, under lifelong renovation. Long-term studies are just now beginning to demonstrate that experiences later in life can redirect emotional and behavioral development, even in adulthood. Some of us—and our parents—are greatly relieved by the news.

What Ever Happened To PLAY?

Kids are spending less time frolicking freely, though fun is one of the best things for them

By WALTER KIRN with WENDY COLE

Theresa Collins lives next to a park, but her kids don't play there all that often. For one thing, all three of her children lead busy lives, what with school, piano lessons, soccer practice and the constant distraction of the home computer. What's more, she fears that the park is dangerous. "I've heard of people exposing themselves there," says Theresa, a 42-year-old special-education teacher in Sarasota, Fla. And while she's not sure if the scary stories are true, she would rather be safe than sorry, like so many other contemporary parents. Her daughter Erica, 9, isn't allowed to visit the park without her brother Christopher, 11, who wasn't permitted to play alone there until about a month ago. As for Matthew, 16, who might have supervised Christopher, he avoids the park by choice. He favors video games. "It's a shame," says Theresa. So why doesn't she take the kids to the park? "It's boring. And I don't have time," she says.

"When I'm home, I have a lot to do here."

No wonder America's swing sets are feeling lonely. With so many roving flashers to elude, so many high-tech skills to master, so many crucial tests to pass and so many anxious parents to reassure, children seem to be playing less and less these days. Even hassled grown-ups are starting to notice. "We're taking away childhood," says Dorothy Sluss, a professor of early-childhood education at East Tennessee State University. "We don't value play in our society. It has become a four-letter word."

Statistics back her up. In 1981, according to University of Michigan researchers, the average school-age child had 40% of the day for free time—meaning hours left over after sleeping, eating, studying and engaging in organized activities. By 1997, the figure was down to 25%.

The very existence of research studies on play suggests that ours is a serious society that can take the fun out of almost anything, including the issue of fun itself. That's why any list of the enemies of play must begin with adults, who make the rules. If play is endangered, it's parents who have endangered it, particularly those who feel that less goofing off in the name of youthful achievement is a good thing. See Dick run. Well, that's fine for little Dick, but wouldn't most parents rather raise a Jane who sits still, studies and gets into Harvard?

If so, they're shortsighted, say the experts on play. Alvin Rosenfeld, co-author of *The Over-Scheduled Child: Avoiding the Hyper-Parenting Trap*, holds an old-fashioned view of play: it's joyful and emotionally nourishing. Stuart Brown, a retired psychiatrist and founder of the Institute for Play in Carmel Valley, Calif., believes that too little play may have a dark side. What Brown calls "play deprivation" can lead, he says, to depression, hostility and the loss of "the things that make us human beings."

Play doesn't just make kids happy, healthy and human. It may also make them smarter, says Rosenfeld. Today's mania for raising young Einsteins, he observes, might have destroyed the real Einstein—a notorious dreamer who earned poor grades in school but somewhere in his frolics divined the formula for the relationship between matter and energy. Play refreshes and stimulates the mind, it seems. And "frequent breaks may actually make kids more interested in learning," according to Rhonda Clements, a Hofstra University professor of physical education.

The case for play is simple and intuitive, which is what makes the decline of play a mystery. If Dick can run wild and get into Princeton too, then why isn't he out there running his little head off? That play has real value won't surprise most parents. That their kid horses around less than they did when they were young probably doesn't shock them either. The puzzle is, Where did all the playtime go?

Millie Wilcox, 60, thinks she knows. The retired nurse and mother of two grown boys (one of them being this writer) doesn't have a Ph.D. in child psychology, just a memory of her own Ohio childhood picking elderberries in the alley and once—imagine doing this today—playing house inside a cardboard box set smack dab in the middle of the street. "There wasn't so much traffic back then," says Wilcox, "and it seems like every neighborhood had a vacant lot. Vacant lots were important. Plus, our mothers were around during the day, and they knew everyone on the block, so they weren't scared for us."

There's common sense behind Wilcox's nostalgia for her old stamping grounds. After all, play needs to happen somewhere—preferably somewhere safe and open and not entirely dominated by grownups—but those idyllic somewheres are growing scarce. "In the huge rush to build shopping malls and banks," says Clements, "no one is thinking about where kids can play. That doesn't generate tax revenue."

What about those inviting vacant lots? "There's practically no such thing

anymore," laments urban planner Robin Moore, a former president of the International Association for the Child's Right to Play. Thanks to sidewalk-free subdivisions, congested roads and ubiquitous commercial developments, "all the free space has been spoken for," says Moore. Roger Hart, an environmental psychologist at the City University of New York, cites a general "disinvestment in public space" as one reason children are playing less outdoors. Even public sandboxes are vanishing. Says Hart: "People have become paranoid about animal waste." What's more, as the average family size gets smaller and suburban houses are built farther apart, "kids have a harder time finding each other than they used to," Moore says.

Parental fear is also a factor. Fear of molesters, bacteria, zooming SUVS. Neighbors who own guns. Neighbors who let their kids eat refined sugar. The list is as lengthy as last Sunday's newspaper, and it grows longer with every new edition. "It used to be," Hart says, "that in the presence of one another, kids formed a critical mass to keep each other safe. Gone are the days when children make any of their own plans." Their fearful, ambitious parents made plans for them, but these plans don't always mesh, unfortunately. A suburban Chicago mom who wishes to remain anonymous called up a school friend of her daughter's to arrange a play date. The kindergartner was booked solid. "It seems like kids today are always on the way to somewhere," complains the disillusioned mom

One place kids keep rushing to is Chuck E. Cheese, the chain of video game–crammed pizzerias where families can frolic in air-conditioned safety, separated by turnstiles from the Big Bad Wolf. Such enterprises fill the play vacuum with something far more modern and secure—"edutainment." It's a growing industry. Randy White is CEO of White Hutchinson Leisure & Learning Group in Kansas City, Mo. His company develops cavernous play facilities, up to 30,000 sq. ft. in area, that are Xanadus of prefabricated diversion, offering art projects, costumes, blocks and even simulated fishing. "We're reintroducing free play to families," says White. Free play at a price, that is. His facilities charge up

to $10 a head. "Parents feel that if they're not paying much for an experience, it's not worth it educationally," he says.

Screen Time
THESE DAYS, when kids do play, it's often indoors and with machines, limiting their opportunities for free exploration

When young fun has to prove itself in educational terms—when it's not sufficient that play be just playful—the world has reached a dreary spot. Yet here we are. Consider this: since the 1980s, with the rise of the academic-standards movement, hundreds of American elementary schools have eliminated recess. The Atlanta schools have dropped recess system-wide, and other districts are thinking of following suit. Does a no-recess day raise test scores or aid kids' mental performance? There's no evidence for it. There is plenty of evidence, however, that unbroken classwork drives children slightly batty, as Atlanta teachers are starting to note. Multiple studies show that when recess time is delayed, elementary-school kids grow increasingly inattentive. Goodbye recess, hello Ritalin.

Rebecca Lamphere, 25, of Virginia Beach, Va., is a play activist, to coin an awkward phrase. Her mission began three years ago after she noticed that the school playground adjacent to her house was always empty. School officials later instituted a "recess substitute" program called Walk 'n Talk that involved having children circle four orange cones set up on the grounds after lunchtime. "It was considered social time," Lamphere says, "but they all had to go in one direction and keep their voices down." Lamphere wasn't pleased—her daughter Charleen was about to start kindergarten—so she launched a protest. She circulated a petition, sought out experts in child development and ultimately attracted statewide attention. Last April, Virginia Beach mandated daily recess, and the state followed five months later.

Is that what we've come to—obligatory play? The defenders of unfettered recreation have a way of making it sound like broccoli, wholesome and vitamin packed but unenticing. "Kids need to learn how to navigate themselves and keep their bodies safe," says Richard Cohen, a child-development expert and play-programs manager at Brookfield Zoo outside Chicago. What fun! At their grimmest, the play scholars sound like Stuart Brown recounting a study of Texas prison inmates that found a common element in their childhoods. "They didn't engage in rough-and-tumble play," he says, offering anxious parents yet one more reason to live in mortal fear of almost everything.

Fear—the natural enemy of play. The fear that a French lesson missed is a Yale acceptance letter lost. The fear that sending junior outside to roam will end in reporting him missing to the police. Do we now have to add to these fears—some of them neurotic, others real—the fear that "play deprivation" will stunt kids' spirits, shrink their brains and even land them in jail? Such protective obsessing seems to be the problem, and doing more of it offers no solution. Parents should probably just tell kids that fooling around is bad for them, open the door and follow them outside. All work and no play can make adults dull too—sometimes even a little paranoid.

The Company They Keep: Friendships and Their Developmental Significance

HARTUP, WILLARD W. *The Company They Keep: Friendships and Their Developmental Significance.* CHILD DEVELOPMENT, 1996, **67**, 1–13.
Considerable evidence tells us that "being liked" and "being disliked" are related to social competence, but evidence concerning friendships and their developmental significance is relatively weak. The argument is advanced that the developmental implications of these relationships cannot be specified without distinguishing between *having friends, the identity of one's friends*, and *friendship quality.* Most commonly, children are differentiated from one another in diagnosis and research only according to whether or not they have friends. The evidence shows that friends provide one another with cognitive and social scaffolding that differs from what nonfriends provide, and having friends supports good outcomes across normative transitions. But predicting developmental outcome also requires knowing about the behavioral characteristics and attitudes of children's friends as well as qualitative features of these relationships.

Willard W. Hartup

University of Minnesota

On February 16, 1995, in the small Minnesota town of Delano, a 14-year-old boy and his best friend ambushed and killed his mother as she returned home. The circumstances surrounding this event were described in the next edition of the *Minneapolis Star Tribune* (February 18, 1995): The boy had "several learning disabilities—including attention deficit disorder." He had been "difficult" for a long time and, within the last year, had gotten in trouble with a step-brother by wrecking a car and carrying a gun to a movie theater. The mother was described as having a wonderful relationship with her daughter but having "difficulties" with her son. The family dwelling contained guns.

Against these child, family, and ecological conditions is a significant social history: The boy was "... a lonely and unliked kid who was the frequent victim of schoolmates' taunts, jeers, and assaults. He had trouble with school work and trouble with other kids.... He was often teased on the bus and at school because of his appearance and abilities.... He got teased bad. Every day, he got teased. He'd get pushed around. But he couldn't really help himself. He was kind of skinny.... He didn't really have that many friends."

The boy actually had two good friends: One appears to have had things relatively well put together. But with this friend, the subject "... passed [a] gun safety course for hunting; they took the class together." The second friend (with whom the murder was committed) was a troublesome child. These two boys described themselves as the "best of friends," and spent much time together. The boys have admitted to planning the ambush (one saying they had planned it for weeks, the other for a few hours). They were armed and waiting when the mother arrived home from work. One conclusion seems relatively certain: this murder was an unlikely event until these two antisocial friends reached consensus about doing it.

An important message emerges from this incident: Child characteristics, intersecting with family relationships and social setting, cycle through peer relations in two ways to affect developmental outcome: (*a*) through acceptance and rejection by other children in the aggregate, and (*b*) through dyadic relationships, especially with friends. Considerable evidence now tells us that "being liked" by other children (an aggregate condition) supports good developmental outcome; conversely, "being disliked" (another aggregate condition) is a risk factor (Parker & Asher, 1987). But the evidence concerning friendships and their developmental significance is weak—mainly because these relationships have not been studied extensively enough or with sufficient differentiation.

On the too-rare occasions in which friendships are taken into account developmentally— either in diagnosis or research— children are differentiated merely according to whether or not they have friends. This emphasis on having friends is based on two assumptions: First, making and keeping friends requires good reality-testing and social skills; "having friends" is thus a proxy for "being socially skilled." Second, friendships are believed to be developmental wellsprings in the sense that children must suspend egoism, embrace egalitarian attitudes, and deal with conflict effectively in order to maintain them (Sullivan, 1953). On two counts, then, having friends is thought to bode well for the future.

Striking differences exist, however, among these relationships—both from child to child and companion to companion. First, enormous variation occurs in who the child's friends are: Some companions are outgoing and rarely get into trouble; others are antisocial; still others are good children but socially clumsy. These choices would seem rather obviously to contribute to socialization—not only by affecting reputations (as the adage admonishes) but through what transpires between the children. Knowing that a teenager has friends tells us one thing, but the identity of his or her friends tells us something else.

Second, friendships differ from one another qualitatively, that is, in their *content* or normative foundations (e.g., whether or not the two children engage in antisocial behavior), their *constructiveness* (e.g., whether conflict resolution commonly involves negotiation or whether it involves power assertion), their *closeness* (e.g., whether or not the children spend much time together and engage in many different activities), their *symmetry* (e.g., whether social power is vested more or less equally or more or less unequally in the two children), and their *affective substrates* (e.g., whether the relationship is supportive and secure or whether it is nonsupportive and conflict ridden). Qualitative differences in these relationships may have developmental implications in the same way that qualitative variations in adult-child relationships do (Ainsworth, Blehar, Waters, & Wall, 1978).

This essay begins, then, with the argument that one cannot describe friendships and their developmental significance without distinguishing between *having friends, the identity of the child's friends* (e.g., personality characteristics of the child's friends), and *friendship quality*. In the sections that follow, these relationship dimensions are examined separately and in turn. Three conclusions emerge: First, having friends is a normatively significant condition during childhood and adolescence. Second, friendships carry both developmental advantages and disadvantages so that a romanticized view of these relationships distorts them and what they may contribute to developmental outcome. Third, the identity of the child's friends and friendship quality may be more closely tied to individual differences than merely whether or not the child has friends.

Having Friends

Measurement Issues

Children's friends can be identified in four main ways: (*a*) by asking the children, their mothers, or their teachers to name the child's friends and determining whether these choices are reciprocated; (*b*) by asking children to assess their liking for one another; (*c*) by observing the extent to which children seek and maintain proximity with one another; and (*d*) by measuring reciprocities and coordinations in their social interaction. Concor-

dances among various indicators turn out to be substantial, but method variance is also considerable; the "insiders" (the children themselves) do not always agree with the "outsiders" (teachers) or the observational record (Hartup, 1992; Howes, 1989).

Some variation among measures derives from the fact that social attraction is difficult for outsiders to know about. Method variance also derives from special difficulties connected with self-reports: First, children without friends almost always can name "friends" when asked to do so (Furman, in press). Second, friendship frequently seems to investigators to be a dichotomous condition (friend vs. nonfriend), whereas variation is more continuous (best friend/good friend/occasional friend/not friend). Third, whether these categories form a Guttman scale has not been determined, although researchers sometimes assume that they do (see Doyle, Markiewicz, & Hardy, 1994). Fourth, the status of so-called unilateral or unreciprocated friendship choice is unclear. Sometimes, when children's choices are not reciprocated, social interaction differs from when friendship choices are mutual; in other respects, the social exchange does not. Unilateral friends, for example, use tactics during disagreements with one another that are different from the ones used by mutual friends but similar to those used by nonfriends (e.g., standing firm). Simultaneously, conflict *outcomes* among unilateral friends (e.g., whether interaction continues) are more similar to those characterizing mutual friends than those characterizing nonfriends (Hartup, Laursen, Stewart, & Eastenson, 1988).

Developmental Significance

The developmental significance of having friends (apart from the identity of the child's friends or the quality of these relationships) has been examined in three main ways: (*a*) comparing the social interaction that occurs between friends and between nonfriends, (*b*) comparing children who have friends with those who don't and (*c*) examining the extent to which having friends moderates behavioral outcomes across certain normative transitions.

Behavior with friends and nonfriends.—Behaviors differentiating friends from nonfriends have been specified in more than 80 studies (Newcomb & Bagwell, 1995); four are cited here. In the first of these (Newcomb & Brady, 1982), school-aged children were asked to explore a "creativity box" with either a friend or a classmate who was not a friend. More extensive exploration was observed among the children with their friends; conversation was more vigorous and mutually oriented; the emotional exchange was more positive. Most important, when tested individually, the children who explored the box with a friend remembered more about it afterward.

Second, Azmitia and Montgomery (1993) examined problem solving among 11-year-olds (mainly their dialogues) working on "isolation of variables" problems either with friends or acquaintances (the children were required to deduce which pizza ingredients caused certain characters in a series of stories to get sick and die). Friends spontaneously justified their suggestions more frequently than acquaintances, elaborated on their partners' proposals, engaged in a greater percentage of conflicts during their conversations, and more often checked results. Most important, the children working with friends did better than children working with nonfriends—on the most difficult versions of the task only. Clearly, "a friend in need is a friend indeed." The children's conversations were related to their problem solving through engagement in transactive conflicts. That is, task performance was facilitated to a greater extent between friends than between nonfriends by free airing of the children's differences in a cooperative, task-oriented context.

Third, we recently examined conversations between friends and nonfriends (10-year-olds) in an inner-city magnet school while the children wrote stories collaboratively on a computer (Hartup, Daiute, Zajac, & Sholl, 1995). Stories dealt with the rain forest—subject matter that the children had studied during a 6-week science project. Baseline story writing was measured with the children writing alone; control subjects *always* wrote alone. Results indicate that friends did not talk more during collaboration than nonfriends but, nevertheless, (a) engaged in more mutually oriented and less individualistic utterances; (b) agreed with one another more often (but did not disagree more readily); (c) repeated their own and the other's assertions more often; (d) posed alternatives and provided elaborations more frequently; (e) spent twice as much time as nonfriends talking about writing content, the vocabulary being used, and writing mechanics; and (f) spent less time engaged in "off-task" talk. Principal component analyses confirm that the structure of friends' talk was strongly focused on the task (i.e., the text) and was assertively collaborative—reminiscent of the dialogs used by experts and novices as discovered in other social problem-solving studies (Rogoff, 1990). Our stories themselves show that, overall, the ones collaboratively written by friends were better than the ones written by nonfriends, a difference that seems to rest on better use of Standard English rather than the narrative elements included in the text. Results suggest, overall, that the affordances of "being friends" differ from the affordances of "being acquaintances" in social problem solving (Hartup, in press).

Fourth, we examined conflict and competition among school-aged children playing a board game when they had been taught different rules (Hartup, French, Laursen, Johnston, & Ogawa, 1993). Disagreements occurred more frequently between friends than between nonfriends and lasted longer. Conflict resolution, however, differed by friendship and sex: (a) boys used assertions *without rationales* more frequently than girls—but only when friends were observed; (b) girls, on the other hand, used assertions *with rationales* more frequently than boys but, again, only with friends. Sex differences in conflict talk, widely cited in the literature (see Maccoby, 1990), thus seem to be relationship manifestations rather than manifestations of individual children.

Based on these and the other available data sets, a recent meta-analysis identified significant friend versus nonfriend effects across four broad-band categories (Newcomb & Bagwell, 1995): *positive engagement* (i.e., talk, smiling, and laughter); *conflict management* (i.e., disengagement and negotiation vs. power assertion); *task activity* (i.e., being oriented to the task as opposed to being off task); and *relationship properties* (i.e., equality in the exchange as well as mutuality and affirmation). Behaviorally speaking, friendships clearly are "communal relationships" (Clark & Mills, 1979). Reciprocity constitutes their deep structure.

Existing data suggest that four cognitive and motivational conditions afford these distinctive interactions: (a) friends know one another better than nonfriends and are thus able to communicate with one another more efficiently and effectively (Ladd & Emerson, 1984); (b) friends and nonfriends have different expectations of one another, especially concerning assistance and support (Bigelow, 1977); (c) an affective climate more favorable to exploration and problem solving exists between friends than between nonfriends—namely, a "climate of agreement" (Gottman, 1983); and (d) friends more readily than nonfriends seek ways of resolving disagreements that support continued interaction between them (Hartup & Laursen, 1992).

Unfortunately, the developmental significance of these differences is not known, Only fragmentary information tells us about short-term consequences in problem solving and behavioral regulation. Recalled events (Newcomb & Brady, 1982), deductive reasoning (Azmitia & Montgomery, 1993), conflict rates (Hartup et al., 1988), creative writing (Hartup et al., 1995), and social/moral judgments (Nelson & Aboud, 1985) are better supported by transactions with friends than by transactions with nonfriends. But only a small number of investigations exists in each case—sometimes only one. The bottom line: Process-outcome studies are badly needed to tell us whether friends engage in better scaffolding than nonfriends, or whether it only seems like they do. Once process/outcome connections are established, we can then—and only then—conclude that friendships have normative significance (i.e., that children employ their friends adaptively on a daily basis as cognitive and social resources).

Having friends versus not having friends.—Does having friends contribute to developmental differentiation (i.e., contribute to individual differences)? For the answer to this question to be affirmative, children who have friends must differ from those who do not.

Cross-sectional comparisons show that, first, children who have friends are more socially competent and less troubled than children who do not; they are more sociable, cooperative, altruistic, self-confident, and less lonely (Hartup, 1993; Newcomb & Bagwell, in press). Second, troubled children (e.g., clinic-referred children) are more likely to be friendless than nonreferred control cases (Rutter & Garmezy, 1983). Friendlessness is not always assessed in the same manner in these studies, but the results are consistent: Not one data set suggests that children with friends are worse off than children who do not have them.

Although friended/friendless comparisons are consistent across data sets, the results are difficult to interpret. First, having friends in these studies usually means having good supportive friends; thus having friends is confounded with friendship quality. Second, causal direction is impossible to establish: Friendship experience may contribute to self-esteem, for example, but self-confident children may make friends more readily than less confident children.

Longitudinal studies can be more convincing concerning developmental significance. Unfortunately, few exist. Short-term studies suggest that certain benefits accrue across school transitions: First, attitudes toward school are better among kindergartners (5-year-olds) who have friends at the beginning and who maintain them than those who don't. Making new friends also predicts gains in school performance over the kindergarten year (Ladd, 1990). Second, with data collected from 10-year-olds across a 1-year interval, friendship experience enhanced self-esteem (Bukowski, Hoza, & Newcomb, 1991). Third, psychosocial disturbances have been reported less frequently when school changes occur in the company of good friends than when they don't (Berndt & Hawkins, 1991; Simmons, Burgeson, & Reef, 1988). Having friends thus seems to contribute specifically to affective outcomes across normative school transitions.

One long-term investigation (Bagwell, Newcomb, & Bukowski, 1994) raises questions, however, about "having friends" as a developmental predictor: Eleven-year-old children were identified as either friended or friendless on two separate occasions; subjects were re-evaluated at 23 years of age. Having friends and sociometric status (i.e., social acceptance) *together* predicted school success, aspirations, trouble with the law, and several other outcomes. Unique contributions to adult adjustment, however, were verified only for sociometric status. And even then, when stability in the childhood adjustment measures was taken into account, neither sociometric status nor friendship predicted adult outcomes.

Comment

Overall, the developmental significance of having friends is far from clear. Social interaction between friends differs from social interaction between nonfriends, but this does not tell us much more than that these relationships are unique social entities. Correlational studies are difficult to interpret because the effects of having friends are difficult to disentangle from the effects of friendship quality. Short-term longitudinal studies suggest that having friends supports adaptation during normative transitions, but more substantial evidence is needed concerning these effects. Child differences may interact with friendship experience in relation to developmental outcome rather than being main effects. Having friends, for example, may differentiate mainly among children who are vulnerable in some way prior to the transition. Stress associated with developmental transitions is known to accentuate differences among vulnerable children to a greater extent than among nonvulnerable ones (Caspi & Moffitt, 1991). Similarly, developmental interventions often have greater effects on vulnerable than on nonvulnerable individuals (see Crockenberg, 1981).

The Identity of the Child's Friends

We turn now to the identity of the child's friends. Several questions can be asked: With whom does the child become friends? Can the identity of a child's friends be forecast from what we know about the child? What is the developmental significance of the company a child keeps?

Who Are Children's Friends?

Consider, first, that children make friends on the basis of common interests and common activities. Common ground is a sine qua non in friendship relations throughout childhood and adolescence, suggesting that friends ought to be similar to one another in abilities and outlook. Folklore sometimes suggests that "opposites attract," but this notion has not found general support in the empirical literature. The weight of the evidence suggests that, instead, "Beast knows beast; birds of a feather flock together" (Aristotle, *Rhetoric*, Book 11).

Similarities between friends, however, vary from attribute to attribute, in most cases according to *reputational salience* (i.e., according to the importance of an attribute in determining the child's social reputation). Considerable evidence supports this "reputational salience hypothesis": Behavior ratings obtained more than 60 years ago by Robert Chailman (1932) showed that social cooperation (an attribute with considerable reputational salience) was more concordant among friends than nonfriends; intelligence (an attribute without reputational salience among young children) was not. Among boys, physical activity (reputationally salient among males) was more similar among friends than nonfriends. Among girls, attractiveness of personality and social network size (both more reputationally salient among females than among males) were more similar among friends than nonfriends.

More recent data also suggest that behavioral concordances among school-aged children and their friends are greater than among children and nonfriends (Haselager, Hartup, Van Lieshout, & Riksen-Walraven, 1995). Peer ratings were obtained in a large number of fifth-grade classrooms centering on three constructs: prosocial behavior, antisocial behavior, and social withdrawal (shyness). First, friends were more similar to one another than nonfriends within each construct cluster (i.e., mean difference scores were significantly smaller). Second, correlations between friends were greater for antisocial behavior (i.e., fighting, disruption, and bullying) than for prosocial behavior (i.e., cooperation, offering help to others) or social withdrawal (i.e., shyness, dependency, and being victimized). These differences may reflect differences among these three attributes in reputational salience: Fighting, for example, is more consistently related to reputation than either cooperation or shyness (Coie, Dodge, & Kupersmidt, 1990). Our results also show important sex differences: (a) Friends were more similar, to one another among girls than among boys in both prosocial and antisocial behavior (see also Cairns & Cairns, 1994), and (b) friends were more similar among boys than among girls in shyness. These gender variations are consistent with the reputational salience hypothesis, too: Being kind to others and being mean to them have greater implications for girls' social reputations than boys', whereas shyness/withdrawal has more to do with boys' reputations than girls' (Stevenson-Hinde & Hinde, 1986).

Concordance data from other studies are consistent with the reputational salience notion: Among adolescents, friends are most similar to one another in two general areas: (a) school-related attitudes, aspirations, and achievement (Epstein, 1983;

Kandel, 1978b) and (b) normative activities such as smoking, drinking, drug use, antisocial behavior, and dating (Dishion, Andrews, & Crosby, 1995; Epstein, 1983; Kandel, 1978b; Tolson & Urberg, 1993). Sexual activity among adolescents is also consistent with the reputational salience hypothesis. Among girls (both African-American and white) in the United States, friends have been found to be similar in sexual behavior and attitudes, even when age and antisocial attitudes are taken into account. Among boys, however, sexual activity (especially engaging in sexual intercourse) was not concordant (Billy, Rodgers, & Udry, 1984). The authors argue that sexual activity is more closely related to social reputation among adolescent girls than it is among boys, thus accounting for the gender differences in the results.

Still other investigators, employing the social network as a unit of analysis, have discovered that members of friendship networks are concordant on such salient dimensions as sports, academic activities, and drug use (Brown, 1989). Antisocial behavior also distinguishes social networks from one another beginning in middle childhood (Cairns, Cairns, Neckerman, Gest, & Garieppy, 1988).

Friendship Concordances: Sources and Developmental Implications

Similarities between friends are one thing, but where do they come from and where do they lead? Developmental implications cannot be specified without understanding that these similarities derive from three sources: (a) *sociodemographic conditions* that bring children into proximity with one another; (b) *social selection* through which children construct relationships with children who are similar to themselves rather than different; and (c) *mutual socialization* through which children become similar to their friends by interacting with them.

Sociodemographic conditions.—Demographic conditions determine the neighborhoods in which children live, the schools in which they enroll, and the classes they attend. Concordances among children and their friends in socioeconomic status, ethnicity, and chronological age thus derive in considerable measure from social forces that constrain the "peer pool" and the child's access to it. One should not underestimate, however, the extent to which some of these concordances derive from the children's own choices. Among children attending schools that are mixed-age, mixed-race, and mixed socioeconomically, friends are still more similar to one another in these attributes than nonfriends are (Goldman, 1981; McCandless & Hoyt, 1961).

Selection.—Some similarities among friends derive from the well-known tendency among human beings (not alone among the various species) for choosing close associates who resemble themselves. Recent studies confirm that the similarity-attraction hypothesis applies to children: Among elementary school children who began an experimental session as strangers, differential attraction was evident in some groups (40%). Within them, more social contact occurred between preferred than between nonpreferred partners, and correlations were higher between preferred than nonpreferred partners in sociability and the cog-

nitive maturity of their play (Rubin, Lynch, Coplan, Rose-Krasnor, & Booth, 1994).

But friendship selection is embedded in assortative processes occurring in larger social networks. Dishion and his colleagues (Dishion, Patterson, & Griesler, 1994) believe that these network concordances emerge through a process called "shopping" in which children and adolescents construct relationships that maximize interpersonal payoffs. Children are not believed to choose friends who are similar to themselves on a rational basis so much as on an experiential one. Accordingly, relationships become established when they "feel right." Similar individuals cleave to one another more readily than dissimilar individuals because they are more likely to find common ground in both their activities and their conversations. Antisocial children are thus most likely to make friends with other antisocial children and, in so doing, their common characteristics merge to create a "dyadic antisocial trait." Similarly, soccer players or musicians make friends, merge themselves dyadically, and set the stage for becoming even more similar to one another.

Selection thus acts simultaneously to determine the identity of the child's friends through two interlocking processes: (a) similarity and attraction occurring within dyads, and (b) assortative network formation occurring within groups. These processes undoubtedly combine differently from child to child in affecting developmental outcome: Cooperative, friendly, non-aggressive children can choose friends resembling themselves from a wide array of choices; antisocial children can also choose their friends on the basis of similarity and attraction—but frequently from a more restricted range of social alternatives.

Mutual socialization.—What behavioral outcomes stem from mutual socialization? The weight of the evidence suggests, first, that children and their friends who ascribe to conventional norms move further over time in the direction of normative behavior (Ball, 1981; Epstein, 1983; Kandel & Andrews, 1986). But does antisocial behavior increase over time among children in antisocial networks? Does troublesome behavior escalate among children—especially into criminal activity—through membership in these networks? Answers to these questions have been surprisingly difficult to provide, especially since children perceive their friends as exerting more pressure toward desirable than toward undesirable conduct (Brown, Clasen, & Eicher, 1986). Nevertheless, increases in undesirable behavior through antisocial friends among children who are themselves at risk for antisocial behavior is now relatively well documented (Ball, 1981; Berndt & Keefe, 1992; Dishion, 1990; Dishion et al., 1994). Conversely, "desisting" is forecast as strongly by a turning away from antisocial friends as by any other variable (Mulvey & Aber, 1988).

What occurs on a day-to-day basis between aggressive children and their friends? Jocks and their friends? "Brains" and their friends? One guesses that children model normative behaviors *for* their friends and simultaneously receive reinforcement *from* them. Antisocial children, for example, are known to engage in large amounts of talk with their friends—talk that is deviant even when the children are being videotaped in the laboratory (Dishion et al., 1994, 1995). Ordinary children talk a lot with their friends, too, but the content is not generally as deviant (Newcomb & Bagwell, 1995). Antisocial children use coercion with one another (Dishion et al., 1995); ordinary children, on the other hand, are freewheeling with their criticisms and persuasion but are less likely to be coercive (Berndt & Keefe, 1992; Hartup et al., 1993). Finally, one guesses that friends support one another in seeking environments that support their commonly held worldviews, although not much is known about this.

Other results show that selection *combines* with socialization to effect similarity between friends. Kandel (1978a) studied changes over the course of a year in drug use, educational aspirations, and delinquency in early adolescence, discovering that similarity stemmed from both sources in approximately equal amounts. Relative effects, however, vary according to the norms and the children involved (see Hartup, 1993).

Comment

Children and their friends are similar to one another, especially in attributes with reputational salience. One must acknowledge that effect sizes are modest and that friends are not carbon copies of one another. One must also acknowledge that the reputational salience hypothesis has never been subjected to direct test and it needs to be. Nevertheless, the identity of the child's friends is a significant consideration in predicting developmental outcome. Friends may be generally intimate, caring, and supportive, thus fostering good developmental prognosis. At the same time, the activities in which they support one another (the relationship *content*) may be extremely deviant, suggesting an altogether different prognosis.

Friendship Quality

Conceptual and Measurement Issues

Qualitative assessment of child and adolescent friendships currently involves two main strategies: (*a*) *dimensional analysis* through which one determines whether certain elements are present or absent in the social interaction between friends (e.g., companionship, intimacy, conflict, or power asymmetries), and (*b*) *typological* or *categorical* analysis through which one identifies patterns in social interaction believed to be critical to social development and adaptation (Furman, in press).

Dimensional assessment.—Most current dimensional assessments are based on "provisions" or "features" that children mention when talking about these relationships (Berndt & Perry, 1956; Bukowski, Hoza, & Boivin, 1994; Furman & Adler, 1982; Furman & Buhrmester, 1985; Parker & Asher, 1993); most instruments tap five or six domains. Domain scores, however, are correlated with one another (Berndt & Perry, 1986; Parker & Asher, 1993), and most factor analyses yield two-factor solutions. Both Berndt (in press) and Furman (in press) argue that "positive" and "negative" dimensions adequately describe most dimensional assessments, although some data sets suggest that more elaborate solutions are warranted (e.g., Ladd, Kochenderfer, & Coleman, in press).

Typological assessment.—Typological assessment is evolving slowly since the functional significance of friendships remains uncertain. Can one, for example, regard friendships as attachments? Probably not. No one has demonstrated that "the secure base phenomenon," so common among children and their caregivers, constitutes the functional core of children's friendships. Friends have been shown to be secure bases in one or two instances (Ipsa, 1981; Schwartz, 1972), but one is not overwhelmed with the evidence that children and their friends are bound to one another as attachment objects. Children describe their relationships with friends differently from their relationships with their caregivers—as *more* companionable, intimate, and egalitarian and, simultaneously, as *less* affectionate and reliable (Furman & Buhrmester, 1985). For these reasons, some writers describe friendships as affiliative relationships rather than attachments (Weiss, 1986). The challenge, then, is to describe what good-quality affiliative relationships are.

One new classification system has been devised on the basis of family systems theory (Shulman, 1993). Well-functioning friendships are considered to be balanced between closeness and intimacy, on the one hand, and individuality, on the other. The family systems model suggests three friendship types: *interdependent* ones, with cooperation and autonomy balanced; *disengaged* ones, in which friends are disconnected in spite of their efforts to maintain proximity with one another; and *consensus-sensitive* or *enmeshed* relationships, in which agreement and cohesion are maximized. Empirical data are based largely on children's interactions in a cooperative task adapted from family systems research (Reiss, 1981) and document the existence of interdependent and disengaged relationships—a promising beginning. Once again, however, caution should be exercised: Friendship networks may not revolve around the same equilibrative axes as families do.

Developmental Significance

Cross-sectional studies.—Among the various qualitative dimensions, *support* (positivity) and *contention* (negativity) have been examined most extensively in relation to child outcomes. Support is positively correlated with school involvement and achievement (Berndt & Hawkins, 1991; Cauce, 1986) and negatively correlated with school-based problems (Kurdek & Sinclair, 1988); positively correlated with popularity and good social reputations (Cauce, 1986); positively correlated with self-esteem (Mannarino, 1978; McGuire & Weisz, 1982; Perry, 1987) and psychosocial adjustment (Buhrmester, 1990) as well as negatively correlated with identity problems (Papini, Farmer, Clark, Micke, & Barnett, 1990) and depression—especially among girls (Compas, Slavin, Wagner, & Cannatta, 1986). Results are thus consistent but, once again, impossible to interpret. We cannot tell whether supportive relationships contribute to the competence of the individual child or vice versa.

Longitudinal studies.—Longitudinal studies dealing with friendship quality (positive vs. negative) emphasize school attitudes, involvement, and achievement. Studying children across the transition from elementary to junior high school, Berndt (1989) measured the size of the friendship network, friendship stability, and self-reported friendship quality (positivity) as well as popularity, attitudes toward school, and achievement. First, network size was negatively related to friendship support as reported by the children, suggesting that children recognize what researchers have been slow to learn, namely, that friendships are not all alike. Second, several nonsignificant results are illuminating: Neither number of friends nor friendship stability contributed to changes in school adjustment—either across the school transition or across the first year in the new school. School adjustment was relatively stable across the transition and was related to friendship stability cross-sectionally but not with earlier adjustment factored out. Third, the self-rated supportiveness of the child's friends, assessed shortly after entrance to the new school, predicted increasing popularity and increasingly positive attitudes toward classmates over the next year, suggesting that positive qualities in one's friendship relations support a widening social world in new school environments.

Other investigations focus on friendship qualities as predictors of school adaptation within the school year. Among 5-year-olds enrolled in kindergarten (Ladd et al., in press), for example, those having friendships characterized by "aid" and "validation" improved in school attitudes over the year with initial attitudes toward school factored out. Perceived conflict in friendships, on the other hand, predicted increasing forms of school maladjustment, especially among boys, including school loneliness and avoidance as well as school liking and engagement.

One other investigation (Berndt & Keefe, 1992) focused on both positive and negative friendship qualities and their correlations across time with school adjustment and self-esteem among adolescents (Berndt & Keefe, 1992). Students with supportive, intimate friendships became increasingly involved with school, while those who considered their friendships to be conflict-ridden and rivalrous became increasingly disruptive and troublesome. Friendship quality was not correlated with changes in self-esteem, possibly because self-esteem was relatively stable from the beginning to the end of the year. Additional analyses (Berndt, in press) suggest that developmental prediction is better for the negative dimensions in these relationships than the positive ones.

Other investigators have examined the interactions between stress and social support as related to behavioral outcome. With elementary school children, increases in peer support over several years predict both increasingly better adaptation and better grade point averages (Dubow, Tisak, Causey, Hryshko, & Reid, 1991). Other results, however, suggest that support from school personnel was associated with decreases in distress across a 2-year period but not support from friends (controlling for initial adjustment). Regression models showed that, actually, school grades predicted changes in friends' support rather than the reverse (DuBois, Felner, Brand, Adan, & Evans, 1992). Among adolescents, however, results are more complex: Windle (1992) reported that, among girls, friend support is positively correlated with alcohol use but negatively correlated with depression (with initial adjustment levels factored out). Among boys, friendship support is associated with outcome depending on

stress levels: When stress is high, friend support encourages both alcohol use and depression; when stress is low or moderate, both alcohol use and depression are associated with having *nonsupportive* friends.

The dissonances encountered in these results would be reduced considerably were the identity of the children's friends to be known. Children and adolescents with behavior difficulties frequently have friends who themselves are troublesome (Dishion et al., 1995). These friends may provide one another with emotional support, but the interactions that occur between them may not be the same as those occurring between nontroubled children and their friends. Knowing who the child's friends are might account for the empirical anomalies.

Other difficulties in accounting for these results derive from the fact that the referents used in measuring social support in these studies (except in Berndt's work) consisted of friendship networks (the child's "friends") rather than a "best friend." And still other complications arise from the use of one child's assessments of relationship qualities (the subject's) when the evidence suggests that discrepancies between partners may correlate more strongly with adjustment difficulties than the perceptions of either partner alone (East, 1991). Nevertheless, these studies provide tantalizing tidbits suggesting that friendship quality bears a causal relation to developmental outcome.

Comment

What kinds of research are needed to better understand the developmental implications of friendship quality? One can argue that we are not urgently in need of cross-time studies narrowly focused on friendships and their vicissitudes. Rather, we need comprehensive studies in which interaction effects rather than main effects are emphasized and that encompass a wide range of variables as they cycle through time: (a) measures of the child, including temperament and other relevant early characteristics; (b) measures of early relationships, especially their affective and cognitive qualities; (c) measures of early success in encounters with relevant institutions, especially the schools; (d) status and reputation among other children (sociometric status); *and*, (e) friendship measures that simultaneously include whether a child has friends, who the child's friends are, and what these relationships are like.

Coming close to this model are recent studies conducted by the Oregon Social Learning Center (e.g., Dishion et al., 1994; Patterson, Reid, & Dishion, 1992). Child characteristics and family relations in early childhood have not been examined extensively by these investigators, but their work establishes linkages between coerciveness and monitoring within parent-child and sibling relationships, on the one hand, and troublesomeness and antisocial behavior among school-aged boys on the other. These studies also establish that poor parental discipline and monitoring predict peer rejection and academic failures, and that these conditions, in turn, predict increasing involvement with antisocial friends. Among children with these early histories, the immediate connection to serious conduct difficulties in adolescence now seems to be friendship with another deviant child. Exactly these conditions existed in the social history of that Minnesota teenager who, together with his best friend, killed his mother early in 1995.

Conclusion

Friendships in childhood and adolescence would seem to be developmentally significant—both normatively and differentially. When children have friends, they use them as cognitive and social resources on an everyday basis. Normative transitions and the stress carried with them seem to be better negotiated when children have friends than when they don't, especially when children are at risk. Differential significance, however, seems to derive mainly from the identity of the child's friends and the quality of the relationships between them. Supportive relationships between socially skilled individuals appear to be developmental advantages, whereas coercive and conflict-ridden relationships are developmental disadvantages, especially among antisocial children.

Nevertheless, friendship and its developmental significance may vary from child to child. New studies show that child characteristics interact with early relationships and environmental conditions, cycling in turn through relations with other children to determine behavioral outcome (Hartup & Van Lieshout, 1995). The work cited in this essay strongly suggests that friendship assessments deserve greater attention in studying these developmental pathways than they are currently given. These assessments, however, need to be comprehensive. Along with knowing whether or not children have friends, we must know who their friends are and the quality of their relationships with them.

References

Ainsworth, M. D. S., Blehar, M. C., Waters, E., & Wall, S. (1978). *Patterns of attachment: A psychological study of the Strange Situation*. Hillsdale, NJ: Erlbaum.

Azmitia, M., & Montgomery, R. (1993). Friendship, transactive dialogues, and the development of scientific reasoning. *Social Development*, **2**, 202–221.

Bagwell, C., Newcomb, A. F., & Bukowski, W. M. (1994). *Early adolescent friendship as a predictor of adult adjustment: A twelve-year follow-up investigation*. Unpublished manuscript, University of Richmond.

Ball, S. J. (1981). *Beachside comprehensive*. Cambridge: Cambridge University Press.

Berndt, T. J. (1989). Obtaining support from friends during childhood and adolescence. In D. Belle (Ed.), *Children's social networks and social supports* (pp. 308–331). New York: Wiley.

Berndt, T. J. (in press). Exploring the effects of friendship quality on social development. In W. M. Bukowski, A. F. Newcomb, & W. W. Hartup (Eds.), *The company they keep: Friendships in childhood and adolescence*. Cambridge: Cambridge University Press.

Berndt, T. J., & Hawkins, J. A. (1991). *Effects of friendship on adolescents' adjustment to junior high school*. Unpublished manuscript, Purdue University.

Berndt, T. J., & Keefe, K. (1992). Friends' influence on adolescents' perceptions of themselves in school. In D. H. Schunk & J. L. Meece (Eds.), *Students' perceptions in the classroom* (pp. 51–73). Hillsdale, NJ: Erlbaum.

Berndt, T. J., & Perry, T. B. (1986). Children's perceptions of friendship as supportive relationships. *Developmental Psychology*, **22**, 640–648.

Bigelow, B. J. (1977). Children's friendship expectations: A cognitive developmental study. *Child Development*, **48**, 246–253.

Billy, J. O. G., Rodgers, J. L., & Udry, J. R. (1984). Adolescent sexual behavior and friendship choice. *Social Forces*, **62**, 653–678.

Brown, B. B. (1989). The role of peer groups in adolescents' adjustment to secondary school. In T. J. Berndt & C. W. Ladd (Eds.), *Peer relationships in child development* (pp. 188–215). New York: Wiley.

Brown, B. B., Clasen, D. R., & Eicher, S. A. (1986). Perceptions of peer pressure, peer conformity dispositions, and self-reported behavior among adolescents. *Developmental Psychology*, **22**, 521–530.

Buhrmester, D. (1990). Intimacy of friendship, interpersonal competence, and adjustment during preadolescence and adolescence. *Child Development*, **61**, 1101–1111.

Bukowski, W. M., Hoza, B., & Boivin, M. (1994). Measuring friendship quality during pre- and early adolescence: The development and psychometric properties of the Friendship Qualities Scale. *Journal of Personal and Social Relationships*, **11**, 471–484.

Bukowski, W. M., Hoza, B., & Newcomb, A. F. (1991). *Friendship, popularity, and the "self" during early adolescence*. Unpublished manuscript, Concordia University (Montreal).

Cairns, R. B., & Cairns, B. U. (1994). *Lifelines and risks*. Cambridge: Cambridge University Press.

Cairns, R. B., Cairns, B. D., Neckerman, H. J., Gest, S., & Garieppy, J.L. (1988). Peer networks and aggressive behavior: Peer support or peer rejection? *Developmental Psychology*, **24**, 815–823.

Caspi, A., & Moffitt, T. E. (1991). Individual differences are accentuated during periods of social change: The sample case of girls at puberty. *Journal of Personality and Social Psychology*, **61**, 157–168.

Cauce, A. M. (1986). Social networks and social competence: Exploring the effects of early adolescent friendships. *American Journal of Community Psychology*, **14**, 607–628.

Challman, R. C. (1932). Factors influencing friendships among preschool children. *Child Development*, **3**, 146–158.

Clark, M. S., & Mills, J. (1979). Interpersonal attraction in exchange and communal relationships. *Journal of Personality and Social Psychology*, **37**, 12–24.

Coie, J, U., Dodge, K. A., & Kupersmidt, J. B. (1990). Peer group behavior and social status. In S. R. Asher & J. D. Coie (Eds.), *Peer rejection in childhood* (pp. 17–59). Cambridge: Cambridge University Press.

Compas, B. E., Slavin, L. A., Wagner, B. A., & Cannatta, K. (1986). Relationship of life events and social support with psychological dysfunction among adolescents. *Journal of Youth and Adolescence*, **15**, 205–221.

Crockenberg, S. B. (1981). Infant irritability, mother responsiveness, and social support influences on the security of mother-infant attachment. *Child Development*, **52**, 857–865.

Dishion, T. J. (1990). The peer context of troublesome child and adolescent behavior. In P. Leone (Ed.), *Understanding troubled and troublesome youth*. Newbury Park, CA: Sage.

Dishion, T. J., Andrews, D. W., & Crosby, L. (1995). Anti-social boys and their friends in early adolescence: Relationship characteristics, quality, and interactional process. *Child Development*, **66**, 139–151.

Dishion, T. J., Patterson, G. R., & Griesler, P. C. (1994). Peer adaptations in the development of antisocial behavior: A confluence model. In L. R. Huesmann (Ed.), *Current perspectives on aggressive behavior* (pp. 61–95). New York: Plenum.

Doyle, A. B., Markiewicz, U., & Hardy, C. (1994). Mothers' and children's friendships: Intergenerational associations. *Journal of Social and Personal Relationships*, **11**, 363–377.

DuBois, D. L., Felner, R. D., Brand, S. Adan, A. M., & Evans, E. C. (1992). A prospective study of life stress, social support, and adaptation in early adolescence. *Child Development*, **63**, 542–557.

Dubow, E. F., Tisak, J., Causey, D., Hryshko, A., & Reid, G. (1991). A two-year longitudinal study of stressful life events, social support, and social problem-solving skills: Contributions to children's behavioral and academic adjustment. *Child Development*, **62**, 583–599.

East, P. L. (1991). The parent-child relationships of withdrawn, aggressive, and sociable children: Child and parent perspectives. *Merrill-Palmer Quarterly*, **37**, 425–444.

Epstein, J. L. (1983). Examining theories of adolescent friendship. In J. L. Epstein & N. L. Karweit (Eds.), *Friends in school* (pp. 39–61). San Diego: Academic Press.

Furman, W. (in press). The measurement of friendship perceptions: Conceptual and methodological issues. In W. M. Bukowski, A. F. Newcomb, & W. W. Hartup (Eds.), *The company they keep: Friendships in childhood and adolescence*. Cambridge: Cambridge University Press.

Furman, W., & Adler, T. (1982). *The Friendship Questionnaire*. Unpublished manuscript, University of Denver.

Furman, W., & Buhrmester, D. (1985). Children's perceptions of the personal relationships in their social networks. *Developmental Psychology*, **21**, 1016–1022.

Goldman, J. A. (1981). The social interaction of preschool children in same-age versus mixed-age groupings. *Child Development*, **52**, 644–650.

Gottman, J. M. (1983). How children become friends. *Monographs of the Society for Research in Child Development*, **48** (3, Serial No. 201).

Hartup, W. W. (1992). Friendships and their developmental significance. In H. McGurk (Ed.), *Childhood social development* (pp. 175–205). Gove, UK: Erlbaum.

Hartup, W. W. (1993). Adolescents and their friends. In B. Laursen (Ed.), *Close friendships in adolescence* (pp. 3–22). San Francisco: Jossey-Bass.

Hartup, W. W. (in press). Cooperation, close relationships, and cognitive development. In W. M. Bukowski, A. F. Newcomb, & W. W. Hartup (Eds.), *The company they keep: Friendships in childhood and adolescence*. Cambridge: Cambridge University Press.

Hartup, W. W., Daiute, C., Zajac, R., & Sholl, W. (1995). *Collaboration in creative writing by friends and nonfriends*. Unpublished manuscript, University of Minnesota.

Hartup, W. W., French, D. C., Laursen, B., Johnston, K. M., & Ogawa, J. (1993). Conflict and friendship relations in middle childhood: Behavior in a closed-field situation. *Child Development*, **64**, 445–454.

Hartup, W. W., & Laursen, B. (1992). Conflict and context in peer relations. In C. H. Hart (Ed.), *Children on playgrounds: Research perspectives and applications* (pp. 44–84). Albany: State University of New York Press.

Hartup, W. W., Laursen, B., Stewart, M. I., & Eastenson, A. (1988). Conflict and the friendship relations of young children. *Child Development*, **59**, 1590–1600.

Hartup, W. W., & Van Lieshout, C. F. M. (1995). Personality development in social context. In J. T. Spence (Ed.), *Annual Review of Psychology*, **46**, 655–687.

Haselager, C. J. T., Hartup, W. W., Van Lieshout, C. F. M., & Riksen-Walraven, M. (1995). *Friendship similarity in middle childhood as a function of sex and sociometric status*. Unpublished manuscript, University of Nijmegen.

Howes, C. (1989). Peer interaction of young children. *Monographs of the Society for Research in Child Development*, **53** (Serial No. 217).

Ipsa, J. (1981). Peer support among Soviet day care toddlers. *International Journal of Behavioral Development*, **4**, 255–269.

Kandel, D. B. (1978a). Homophily, selection, and socialization in adolescent friendships. *American Journal of Sociology*, **84**, 427–436.

Kandel, D. B. (1978b). Similarity in real-life adolescent pairs. *Journal of Personality and Social Psychology*, **36**, 306–312.

Kandel, D. B., & Andrews, K. (1986). Processes of adolescent socialization by parents and peers. *International Journal of the Addictions*, **22**, 319–342.

Kurdek, L. A., & Sinclair, R. J. (1988). Adjustment of young adolescents in two-parent nuclear, stepfather, and mother-custody families. *Journal of Consulting and Clinical Psychology*, **56**, 91–96.

Ladd, G. W. (1990). Having friends, keeping friends, making friends, and being liked by peers in the classroom: Predictors of children's early school adjustment? *Child Development*, **61**, 1081–1100.

Ladd, G. W., & Emerson, E. S. (1984). Shared knowledge in children's friendships. *Developmental Psychology*, **20**, 932–940.

Ladd, G. W., Kochenderfer, B. J., & Coleman, C. C. (in press). Friendship quality as a predictor of young children's early school adjustment. *Child Development*.

Maccoby, E. E. (1990). Gender and relationships: A developmental account. *American Psychologist*, **45, 513–520**.

Mannarino, A. P. (1978). Friendship patterns and self-concept development in preadolescent males. *Journal of Genetic Psychology*, **133**, 105–110.

McCandless, B. R., & Hoyt, J. M. (1961). Sex, ethnicity and play preferences of preschool children. *Journal of Abnormal and Social Psychology*, **62**, 683–685.

McGuire, K. D., & Weisz, J. R. (1982). Social cognition and behavior correlates of preadolescent chumship. *Child Development*, **53**, 1478–1484.

Mulvey, E. P., & Aber, M. S. (1988). Growing out of delinquency: Development and desistance. In R. Jenkins & W. Brown (Eds.), *The abandonment of delinquent behavior: Promoting the turn-around*. New York: Praeger.

Nelson, J., & Aboud, F. E. (1985). The resolution of social conflict between friends. *Child Development*, **56**, 1009–1017.

Newcomb, A. F., & Bagwell, C. (1995). Children's friendship relations: A meta-analytic review. *Psychological Bulletin*, **117**, 306–347.

Newcomb, A. F., & Bagwell, C. (in press). The developmental significance of children's friendship relations. In W. M. Bukowski, A. F. Newcomb, & W. W. Hartup (Eds.), *The company they keep: Friendship in childhood and adolescence*. Cambridge: Cambridge University Press.

Newcomb, A. F., & Brady, J. E. (1982). Mutuality in boys' friendship relations. *Child Development*, **53**, 392–395.

Papini, D. R., Farmer, F. F., Clark, S. M., Micke, J. C., & Barnett, J. K. (1990). Early adolescent age and gender differences in patterns of emotional self-disclosure to parents and friends. *Adolescence*, **25**, 959–976.

Parker, J. G., & Asher, S. R. (1987). Peer relations and later personal adjustment: Are low-accepted children at risk? *Psychological Bulletin*, **102**, 357–389.

Parker, J. G., & Asher, S. R. (1993). Friendship and friendship quality in middle childhood: Links with peer group acceptance and feelings of loneliness and social dissatisfaction. *Developmental Psychology*, **29**, 611–621.

Patterson, G. R., Reid, J. B., & Dishion, T. J. (1992). *Antisocial boys*. Eugene, OR: Castalia.

Perry, T. B. (1987). *The relation of adolescent self-perceptions to their social relationships*. Unpublished doctoral dissertation, University of Oklahoma.

Reiss, D. (1981). *The family's construction of reality*. Cambridge, MA: Harvard University Press.

Rogoff, B. (1990). *Apprenticeship in thinking*. New York: Oxford University Press.

Rubin, K. H., Lynch, D., Coplan, R., Rose-Krasnor, L., & Booth, C. L. (1994). "Birds of a feather...": Behavioral concordances and preferential personal attraction in children. *Child Development*, **65**, 1778–1785.

Rutter, M., & Garmezy, N. (1983). Developmental psychopathology. In E. M. Hetherington (Ed.), P. H. Mussen (Series Ed.), *Handbook of child psychology: Vol.* **4**. *Socialization, personality, and social development* (pp. 775–911). New York: Wiley.

Schwartz, J. C. (1972). Effects of peer familiarity on the behavior of preschoolers in a novel situation. *Journal of Personality and Social Psychology*, **24**, 276–284.

Shulman, S. (1993). Close friendships in early and middle adolescence: Typology and friendship reasoning. In B. Laursen (Ed.), *Close friendships in adolescence* (pp. 55–72). San Francisco: Jossey-Bass.

Simmons, R. C., Burgeson, R., & Reef, M. J. (1988). Cumulative change at entry to adolescence. In M. Gunnar & W. A. Collins (Eds.), *Minnesota symposia on child psychology* (Vol. **21**, pp. 123–150). Hillsdale, NJ: Erlbaum.

Stevenson-Hinde, J., & Hinde, R. A. (1986). Changes in associations between characteristics and interaction. In R. Plomin & J. Dunn (Eds.), *The study of temperament: Changes, continuities and challenges* (pp. 115–129). Hillsdale, NJ: Erlbaum.

Sullivan, H. S. (1953). *The interpersonal theory of psychiatry*. New York: Norton.

Tolson, J. M., & Urberg, K. A. (1993). Similarity between adolescent best friends. Journal of *Adolescent Research*, **8**, 274–288.

Weiss, R. S. (1986). Continuities and transformations in social relationships from childhood to adulthood. In W. W. Hartup & Z. Rubin(Eds.), *Relationships and development* (pp. 95–110). Hillsdale, NJ: Erlbaum.

Windle, M. (1992). A longitudinal study of stress buffering for adolescent problem behaviors. *Developmental Psychology*, **28**, 522–530.

Presidential address to the biennial meetings of the Society for Research in Child Development, April 1, 1995, Indianapolis, IN. The author is grateful to W. Andrew Collins, Rosemary K. Hartup, Gary W. Ladd, Brett Laursen, and Andrew F. Newcomb for their comments on this manuscript. Requests for reprints may be sent to Willard W. Hartup, Institute of Child Development, University of Minnesota, 51 E. River Road, Minneapolis, MN 55455-0345.

The Adjustment of Children from Immigrant Families

Andrew J. Fuligni[1]

Department of Psychology, New York University, New York, New York

The dramatic rise in immigration to the United States in the past 30 years has resulted in a burgeoning population of children with foreign-born parents. In 1997, there were approximately 3 million children who were foreign-born themselves and an additional 10.8 million who were born in the United States after their parents had entered the country (Rumbaut, 1998). Together, these children from immigrant families represent almost one fifth of the total population of American children. Today's immigrant families exhibit greater ethnic, linguistic, and socioeconomic diversity than ever before in American history (Portes & Rumbaut, 1996). Unlike the predominantly European immigrants in the early 1900s, the majority of recent immigrant families hail from Asian and Latin American countries such as Mexico, the Philippines, El Salvador, Vietnam, Cuba, and Korea.

Social scientists, policymakers, and practitioners alike have expressed concern as to how such a large and diverse group of children will adapt to American society. How will they perform in school, given the dramatic variations in their cultural and linguistic backgrounds? Will the transition to a new and different society have a negative impact on their psychological and behavioral adjustment? Research has only recently caught up with the rapid increase in immigration, but a number of studies have begun to paint a surprising portrait of the children from immigrant families. Rather than asking whether these unique children will adjust to American society, the question now

seems to be, how can they be doing so well?

PATTERNS OF ADJUSTMENT

In systematic studies of nonclinical populations, the children from immigrant families demonstrate a remarkable level of general adjustment. In fact, they often appear to be better off than their peers from American-born families. Students with immigrant parents, including children who themselves are foreign-born, tend to receive grades in school that are equal to or even higher than those of students whose parents were born in the United States (Kao & Tienda, 1995). The students' success is evident across many different subjects, including English. Similarly surprising results have been found regarding the age at which foreign-born children enter the United States. The secondary school performance of relatively recent arrivals tends to equal or even surpass the achievement of foreign-born students who entered this country at younger ages (Fuligni, 1997; Rumbaut, 1997).

Fewer studies have been conducted on the broader behavioral and psychological adjustment of immigrant children. Yet findings that are beginning to emerge are consistent with those from the research on academic achievement. Recent analyses of data from the National Longitudinal Study of Adolescent Health (Add Health), a nationally representative study of more than 20,000 adolescents,

indicate that across a variety of outcome measures, youths from immigrant families exhibit healthier adjustment than their peers from American-born families (Harris, in press). First-generation (foreign-born) and second-generation (American-born with immigrant parents) adolescents are less likely to engage in delinquent and violent acts, to use drugs and alcohol, and to have had sex. In addition, teens from immigrant families are less likely to be in poor health, to be obese, to have asthma, and to have missed school because of a health or emotional problem. Among immigrant families themselves, first-generation youths tend to be healthier and less likely to engage in risky behavior than their second-generation counterparts. Analyses looking at children's age when they immigrated show a pattern similar to the one for academic achievement: Foreign-born adolescents who came to the United States at later ages evidence fewer problem behaviors and better physical health than those who immigrated at younger ages.

The findings regarding the psychological health of children from immigrant families tend to be more complex, but there is little evidence that this group suffers the great distress commonly expected of them. Despite feeling that they have less control over their lives and that they are less popular, youths from immigrant families report a level of self-esteem equal to that of their peers from native-born families (Kao, in press). The Add Health study has found no overall differences in depressive feelings and positive well-being according to the adolescents' generation (Harris, in press). Other studies have observed that adolescents from immigrant families tend to have fewer psychosomatic problems and less psychological distress than those from native-born families (Steinberg, 1996).

Children from immigrant families tend to exhibit positive adjustment even when they are compared with American-born children of the same ethnic backgrounds. For example, immigrant Mexican youths are less likely to have engaged in delinquent or violent acts, to have used drugs or alcohol, and to have asthma than their Mexican peers from the second and third generations (Harris, in press). The same is true for adolescents from other Latin American and Asian backgrounds. In addition, the psychological well-being of youths from immigrant families is similar to or even higher than that of youths from native-born families of the same ethnic group (Harris, in press; Steinberg, 1996). The findings regarding academic achievement, however, tend to be somewhat mixed. Some studies have observed consistent generational differences among all ethnic groups (Steinberg, 1996), but others have reported that the success of immigrant students relative to their peers from the same ethnic group tends to be most evident among Asian youths and less apparent among Latin American adolescents (Fuligni, 1997; Kao & Tienda, 1995). In addition, the rate at which immigrant Latin American students drop out from U.S. schools is slightly higher (24%) than the rate for American-born Latin American youths (18%; McMillen, 1997).[2]

Despite the overall success of the children from immigrant families, important variations in adjustment exist within the population itself. Children in families from Asia receive higher grades than those in families from Europe, who in turn have more academic success than students from Latin American families (Fuligni, 1997; Kao & Tienda, 1995). Similarly, children in immigrant Chinese families tend to exhibit lower rates of risky behavior and better physical health outcomes than children in families from Latin America (Harris, in press). Differences also exist among children in immigrant Asian and Latin American families themselves. Immigrant Filipino youths engage in more risky behavior than Chinese adolescents, with rates comparable to those among Latin American adolescents (Harris, in press). In addition, Mexican students do worse on standardized

tests than other Latin American students, such as those from Cuban and Colombian families (Rumbaut, 1997).

These variations, although significant, do not change the picture of generally positive adjustment among children from immigrant families. When compared with children from native-born families of similar ethnic backgrounds, those from immigrant families exhibit better physical health, less involvement in risky behavior, and similar or even greater academic achievement and psychological well-being. The only exception to this trend seems to be that immigrant Latin American students have more difficulty completing high school in the United States than their second- and third-generation peers.

SOCIOECONOMIC FACTORS

Given the many challenges of adjusting to a new and different society, how do the children from immigrant families present such a consistent picture of successful development? One possible explanation could be that these children come from relatively advantaged family backgrounds. Indeed, some immigrant parents received advanced education in their home countries and have come to the United States seeking greater professional opportunities. More than 40% of foreign-born Filipinos have received bachelor's degrees, compared with only 20% of the general American-born population (U. S. Bureau of the Census, 1993). But many other immigrant parents, such as those from Latin America and Southeast Asia, tend to be of much lower educational backgrounds. For example, only 4% of immigrant Mexican adults have graduated from college. Variations in educational attainment produce major differences in annual family income, with the immigrant Filipinos and Mexicans earning approximately $48,000 and $22,000, respectively (U. S. Bureau of the Census, 1993).

Socioeconomic factors alone do not explain the differences in adjustment between children from immigrant and American-born families. Generational differences in academic achievement, behavioral adjustment, and psychological well-being remain after the effects of parental education and income have been removed statistically (Fuligni, 1997; Harris, in press; Kao & Tienda, 1995; Steinberg, 1996). In fact, generational differences often become greater

after such controls, reflecting the fact that many children from immigrant families do better than would be expected given their backgrounds. When youths with parents of similar levels of education and income were compared, children from immigrant Latin American families evidenced slightly higher educational outcomes than students from native-born families of the same ethnic background (Kao, in press). In the Add Health study, youths from immigrant families reported significantly less emotional distress and more positive well-being than their peers from American-born families after families' socioeconomic status was taken into account (Harris, in press).

Rather than explaining generational differences in adjustment, socioeconomic factors seem to be more important for the ethnic variations within the population of children from immigrant families. Immigrant families differ dramatically in their economic backgrounds, with parents from Asia tending to be more educated and to work in higher paying occupations than those from Latin America (U. S. Bureau of the Census, 1993). Families from Laos, Cambodia, Mexico, and El Salvador find themselves in worse economic conditions than other Asian and Latin American groups. These variations, along with differences in the manner in which the families are treated and afforded opportunities in this country, are likely to be important sources of the generally poorer outcomes for children in families from Latin America and certain countries in Southeast Asia (Portes & Rumbaut, 1996).

PSYCHOSOCIAL FACTORS

To explain the success of children from immigrant families, one must turn to a collection of psychosocial factors that seem to motivate the children to seek success in school while protecting them from psychological and behavioral difficulties.

Value of Education

Immigrant families see education as the best way that their children can succeed in American society. Regardless of their ethnic or socioeconomic backgrounds, foreign-born parents tend to place a great importance on school achievement (Caplan, Choy, & Whitmore, 1991; Gibson & Bhachu, 1991; Suarez-Orozco & Suarez-

Orozco, 1995). Families from countries as different as India, Mexico, China, and Cuba all emphasize academic success and aspire for their children to attend college. Acutely aware of the challenges that their children face, immigrant parents try to minimize these difficulties by contrasting them to the relative lack of educational opportunities in their native countries (Matute-Bianchi, 1991; Ogbu, 1991). Some parents also encourage their children to view education as a way to avoid the often menial jobs in which the parents find themselves.

The children from immigrant families quickly internalize their parents' emphasis on educational achievement. In a study of adolescents from Latin American and Asian backgrounds, students from immigrant families endorsed every attitude and value regarding education more strongly then their peers with American-born parents (Fuligni, 1997). First- and second-generation students placed more importance on learning mathematics and English, aspired to higher levels of educational attainment, valued academic success more, and spent more time studying and doing homework than those from American-born families. These attitudes and behaviors, in turn, statistically accounted for the higher grades of immigrant students. Similarly high levels of academic motivation have been observed in numerous ethnographies of specific immigrant populations (e.g., Gibson & Bhachu, 1991; Suarez-Orozco & Suarez-Orozco, 1995).

The educational emphasis of immigrant families likely enhances more than just their children's academic achievement. In general, students who value educational success and put effort into their studies tend to have better psychological well-being and less frequent involvement in risky behaviors such as substance use and delinquency (Steinberg, 1996). Focusing on education, therefore, probably prevents the children from immigrant families from getting involved in activities that may threaten their psychological and behavioral adjustment. Instead of creating undue pressure, the motivation to achieve may provide immigrant students with a clear direction that helps them to navigate a new and different society.

Family Obligation

Many immigrant families, such as those from Asia and Latin America, come from collectivistic traditions that empha-size family members' responsibilities and obligations to one another (Chilman, 1993; Shon & Ja, 1982). With immigration, these traditions take on immediate and practical importance because foreign-born parents often know very little about American society. Children, who assimilate more quickly, help their families with negotiating the official tasks and more informal demands of the new country (Zhou, 1997). The children from immigrant families feel a profound sense of duty and obligation to their families, both in the present and in the future. They are more likely than those from American-born families to believe that they should help their parents financially and have their parents live with them when the children become adults (Fuligni, Tseng, & Lam, in press).

Children from immigrant families view school success as one of the most important ways that they can assist their families. Parents often emigrate to the United States in order to provide their children with better opportunities, including the chance to pursue education through and even beyond secondary school. Some students say that they would feel guilty about not trying hard in school, given the many personal and professional sacrifices their parents made to come to this country (Caplan et al., 1991; Suarez-Orozco & Suarez-Orozco, 1995). Other children believe that their educational attainment will help them to secure employment and support the family in the future. Students from immigrant families often cite such indebtedness and responsibility as their primary motivations to do well in school (Zhou & Bankston, 1998).

The sense of responsibility to the family likely keeps children from immigrant families from engaging in the relatively more risky activities of those from American-born families. At a basic level, children and youths who assist and spend time with their families have fewer opportunities to become involved in delinquency or substance use. In addition, the obligations associated with immigrant families provide children with integral roles within the family. These roles delineate a set of expectations, such as supporting the family's reputation and well-being, that may keep children from immigrant families from engaging in activities that would disappoint or embarrass the family in the larger immigrant community (Zhou & Bankston, 1998).

Nevertheless, there is some recent evidence that very high levels of family obligations may not be so advantageous for children. My colleagues and I (Fuligni et al., in press) found that although a moderate sense of responsibility was associated with higher academic achievement, those adolescents who felt the strongest obligations tended to receive school grades just as low as or even lower than those of adolescents with the weakest sense of obligation. This curvilinear association is exemplified by the poor Latin American immigrants, studied by Suarez-Orozco and Suarez-Ocozco (1995), who feel the need to cut back on their studies when their families face economic distress. The students value education, but the more immediate need to help their families at home or on the job can interfere with the students' progress at school. It is currently unknown how such a high level of responsibility to the family may affect the students' broader psychological and behavioral adjustment.

Cultural Identity

Despite the pressure to conform to Americanized ethnic and racial categories, immigrant families and their children tend to avoid such labels and instead retain their original cultural identities. Adolescents from immigrant families relate more to nationalistic identities, such as Mexican or Chinese, than to pan-ethnic or combination labels such as Latino or Asian American (Rumbaut, 1994). It is not surprising that immigrant families would claim identities tied to their cultures of origin. But immigrant parents sometimes employ such identifications as a way to keep their children from adopting undesirable "American" attitudes and behaviors, such as laziness, materialism, and selfishness (Gibson & Bhachu, 1991; Sung, 1987). Certain immigrant groups also feel the need to distance themselves from the negative stereotypes associated with American ethnic categories. For example, some West Indian adolescents with African backgrounds prefer not to be identified with American blacks because of the low expectations that American society has for such youths (Waters, 1994). Similarly, immigrant Mexican youths sometimes resist labels such as Mexican American, Latino, or Chicano (Matute-Bianchi, 1991).

Studies have recently suggested that such cultural identifications have important implications for children's adjustment. West Indian and Mexican youths who identify with their parents' cultural origins tend to be more attached to school and attain greater academic success than their peers who assume the more Americanized ethnic identities (Matute-Bianchi, 1991; Waters, 1994). It is unclear, however, what produces an association between identity and adjustment. Distancing themselves from American ethnic labels may enable immigrant children to avoid the negative stereotypes that act to depress the achievement of minority students (Steele, 1997). Cultural labels chosen by immigrant children and adolescents can also be confounded with social class, and such identifications can be just as much reactions to as producers of experiences in American society. For example, Waters (1994) observed that the West Indian youths who did not identify with their parents' cultural origin tended to be from lower socioeconomic backgrounds and were more likely to report that they had experienced discrimination in the United States. The dynamics of cultural identification among children from immigrant families presents a particular challenge to researchers. The process appears to be of great significance for the children's adjustment, but it is currently not well understood.

CONCLUSION

Despite the concerns of many observers, the children from immigrant families display a truly remarkable degree of adjustment across a variety of domains. These children do well with the help of a collection of values and traditions that provide the children with a clear direction, a responsible role, and a strong cultural identity. Children from Latin American families tend to have more difficulties than their counterparts from Asian families, but even those from Latin American families appear to be adjusting more successfully than their peers from American-born families of similar socioeconomic and ethnic backgrounds.

The question remains as to whether the children from immigrant families will maintain their successful adjustment through adolescence and into adulthood. Up to this point, research on this population has relied almost exclusively on cross-sectional designs that compare different children according to their and their parents' birthplaces or the children's

age of immigration. Despite the implication from these studies that more time spent in the United States diminishes children's overall adjustment, we currently do not know whether exposure to American society brings about changes in the attitudes and behaviors of individual children. On the one hand, the children's value of education and identifications with their families and cultures may remain constant through their lives, enabling them to overcome challenges to their attainments as adults. On the other hand, the children's cumulative experiences in this country may lead them to acculturate to the seemingly less advantageous values and activities of their peers from American-born families. Many of the studies cited in this review are following their subjects longitudinally, so we should soon discover whether the children from immigrant families continue their impressive adaptation to the United States. Alternatively, we may find that exposure to American society can actually compromise the development of a particularly motivated and industrious group of children.

Acknowledgments—I am grateful to Joshua Aronson, Allison Sidle Fuligni, and Diane Ruble for reading an earlier version of this manuscript.

Notes

1. Address correspondence to Andrew J. Fuligni, New York University, 6 Washington Pl., 2nd Floor, New York, NY 10003; e-mail: fuligni@ psych.nyu.edu.

2. The percentage of all foreign-born Latin American youths aged 16 through 24 years who are not enrolled in school and have not received a high school diploma (the traditional criteria used to determine dropout rates) is actually 46%. Yet this high figure is misleading because almost half (43%) of the Latin American immigrants in this age range have never enrolled in U.S. schools because they entered this country after the age of 18 or because they came in search of employment rather than education. Therefore, the dropout rate among those immigrant youths who actually enrolled in a U. S. school (24%) is a better indicator of their adjustment to U. S. schools and a fairer comparison to the dropout rate among

American-born youths (McMillen, 1997).

References

Caplan, N., Choy, M. H., & Whitmore, J. K. (1991). *Children of the boat people: A study of educational success*. Ann Arbor: University of Michigan Press.

Chilman, C. S. (1993). Hispanic families in the United States: Research perspectives. In H. P. McAdoo (Ed.), *Family ethnicity: Strength in diversity* (pp. 141–163). Newbury Park, CA: SAGE.

Fuligni, A. J. (1997). The academic achievement of adolescents from immigrant families: The roles of family background, attitudes, and behavior. *Child Development, 68*, 261–273.

Fuligni, A. J., Tseng, V., & Lam, M. (in press). Attitudes toward family obligations among American adolescents from Asian, Latin American, and European backgrounds. *Child Development*.

Gibson, M. A., & Bhachu, P. K. (1991). The dynamics of educational decision making: A comparative study of Sikhs in Britain and the United States. In M. A. Gibson & J. U. Ogbu (Eds.), *Minority status and schooling: A comparative study of immigrant and involuntary minorities* (pp. 63–96). New York: Garland.

Harris, K. M. (in press). The health status and risk behavior of adolescents in immigrant families. In D. J. Hernandez (Ed.), *Children of immigrants: Health, adjustment, and public assistance*. Washington, DC: National Academy Press.

Kao, G. (in press). Psychological well-being and educational achievement among immigrant youth. In D. J. Hernandez (Ed.), *Children of immigrants: Health, adjustment, and public assistance*. Washington, DC: National Academy Press.

Kao, G., & Tienda, M. (1995). Optimism and achievement: The educational performance of immigrant youth. *Social Science Quarterly, 76*, 1–19.

Matute-Bianchi, M. E. (1991). Situational ethnicity and patterns of school performance among immigrant and non-immigrant Mexican-descent students. In M. A. Gibson & J. U. Ogbu (Eds.), *Minority status and schooling: A comparative study of immigrant and invol-*

untary minorities (pp. 205–248). New York: Garland.

McMillen, M. (1997). *Dropout rates in the United States: 1995.* Washington, DC: U. S. Government Printing Office.

Ogbu, J. U. (1991). Immigrant and involuntary minorities in comparative perspective. In M. A. Gibson & J. U. Ogbu (Eds.), *Minority status and schooling: A comparative study of immigrant and involuntary minorities* (pp. 3–36). New York: Garland.

Portes, A., & Rumbaut, R. G. (1996). *Immigrant America: A portrait* (2nd ed.). Berkeley: University of California Press.

Rumbaut, R. G. (1994). The crucible within: Ethnic identity, self-esteem and segmented assimilation among children of immigrants. *International Migration Review, 28,* 748–794.

Rumbaut, R. G. (1997). Ties that bind: Immigration and immigrant families in the United States. In A. Booth, A. C. Crouter, & N. Landale (Eds.), *Immigration and the family: Research and policy on U.S. immigrants* (pp. 3–46). Mahwah, NJ: Erlbaum.

Rumbaut, R. G. (1998, March). *Transformations: The post-immigrant generation in an age of diversity.* Paper presented at the annual meeting of the Eastern Sociological Society, Philadelphia.

Shon, S. P., & Ja, D. Y. (1982). Asian families. In M. McGoldrick, J. K. Pearce, & J. Giordano (Eds.), *Ethnicity and family therapy* (pp. 208–228). New York: Guilford Press.

Steele, C. M. (1997). A threat in the air: How stereotypes shape intellectual identity and performance. *American Psychologist, 52,* 613–629.

Steinberg, L. (1996). *Beyond the classroom: Why school reform has failed and what parents need to do.* New York: Simon & Schuster.

Suarez-Orozco, C., & Suarez-Orozco, M. M. (1995). *Transformations: Immigration, family life, and achievement motivation among Latino adolescents.* Stanford, CA: Stanford University Press.

Sung, B. L. (1987). *The adjustment experience of Chinese immigrant children in New York City.* New York: Center for Migration Studies.

U.S. Bureau of the Census. (1993). *We the American: Foreign born.* Washington, DC: U.S. Government Printing Office.

Waters, M. C. (1994). Ethnic and racial identities of second-generation black immigrants in New York City. *International Migration Review, 28,* 795–820.

Zhou, M. (1997). Growing up American: The challenge confronting immigrant children and children of immigrants. *Annual Review of Sociology, 23,* 63–95.

Zhou, M., & Bankston, C. L. (1998). *Growing up American: How Vietnamese children adapt to life in the United States.* New York: Russell Sage Foundation.

Recommended Reading

Booth, A., Crouter, A. C., & Landale, N. (Eds.). (1997). *Immigration and the family: Research and policy on U.S. immigrants.* Mahwah, NJ: Erlbaum.

Gibson, M. A., & Ogbu, J. U. (Eds.). (1991). *Minority status and schooling: A comparative study of immigrant and involuntary minorities.* New York: Garland.

Hernandez, D. J. (Ed.). (in press). *Children of immigrants: Health, adjustment, and public assistance.* Washington, DC: National Academy Press.

From *Current Directions in Psychological Science,* August 1998, pp. 99–103. © 1998 by the American Psychological Society. Reprinted by permission of Blackwell Publishers, Ltd.

UNIT 4

Parenting and Family Issues

Unit Selections

Key Points to Consider

- Where did you get your ideas, values, and beliefs about how a parent behaves? If you were unsure about how to respond to a particular parenting situation, whom would you consult? How do you think your own experience of parenting has affected your attitudes or possible parenting practices? Do you think your parents had a significant effect on your growing up?

- Virtually no one has a family network that has not been touched by divorce and remarriage. Since divorce and remarriage affect boys and girls differently and at different ages, how might you handle these transitions in the best interest of a child?

- If you were to put your own children in child care, how would you know what features to look for that signal a high quality experience? Do you think raising a child at home with the mother is always the best situation? Why or why not?

- Do you think religion is a critical ingredient in family life? Why or why not?

 **Links: www.dushkin.com/online/**
These sites are annotated in the World Wide Web pages.

Facts for Families
http://www.aacap.org/publications/factsfam/index.htm
Families and Work Institute
http://www.familiesandworkinst.org
The National Academy for Child Development
http://www.nacd.org
National Council on Family Relations
http://www.ncfr.com
The National Parent Information Network (NPIN)
http://ericps.ed.uiuc.edu/npin/
Parenting and Families
http://www.cyfc.umn.edu/Parenting/parentlink.html
Parentsplace.com: Single Parenting
http://www.parentsplace.com/family/singleparent/
Stepfamily Association of America
http://www.stepfam.org

Few people today realize that the potential freedom to choose parenthood—deciding whether to become a parent, deciding when to have children, or deciding how many children to have—is a development due to the advent of reliable methods of contraception and other recent sociocultural changes. Moreover, unlike any other significant job to which we may aspire, few, if any, of us will receive any formal training or information about the lifelong responsibility of parenting. For most of us, our behavior is generally based on our own conscious and subconscious recollections of how we were parented as well as on our observations of the parenting practices of others around us. In fact, our society often behaves as if the mere act of producing a baby automatically confers upon the parents an innate parenting ability and as if a family's parenting practices should remain private and not be subjected to scrutiny or criticism by outsiders.

Given this climate, it is not surprising that misconceptions about many parenting practices continue to persist today. Only within the last 35 years or so have researchers turned their lenses on the scientific study of the family. Social, historical, cultural, and economic forces also have dramatically changed the face of the American family today. For example, significant numbers of children in our country will experience the divorce and/or remarriage of their parents at some point during their lifetimes. In "What Matters? What Does Not? Five Perspectives on the Association Between Marital Transitions and Children's Adjustment," E. Mavis Hetherington and colleagues describe the effects of divorce and remarriage on children. Interestingly, the role of fathering today does not resemble the Hollywood version of "Father Knows Best." Researcher Ronald Rohner reviews some of these historical and research changes in "Father Love and Child Development: History and Current Evidence."

Most parents never take courses or learn of the research on parenting. In the seminal article "Contemporary Research on Parenting: The Case for Nature *and* Nurture" a distinguished panel of researchers summarize recent parenting research and describe the importance of considering the interaction of genetics and environment, a child's temperament, and peer and neighborhood interactions when determining parental influence.

Similarly, the author of "Discipline: The New Rules," discusses data on the differences in current and past disciplinary approaches that mothers and fathers use when disciplining their children.

The majority of mothers in the United States rely on some form of child care. Sandra Scarr, a leading scholar on the issue, reviews the research on the effects of child care on children's social, academic, and emotional development in "American Child Care Today." Ellen Galinsky interviewed children from their perspective about their views and wishes of their working parents in "Do Working Parents Make The Grade?"

With alarming frequency, news reports bring us accounts of tragedies and other unspeakable acts that are committed increasingly by young adults and now even by children. How do children and adults learn to behave in a moral and responsible way? In "The Moral Development of Children" William Damon discusses research on the origins of morality in children and the key role that parents play in promoting their children's moral development.

Religious exposure and training is present in many families. One family's personal account of discussing religion, science, and God with their child is chronicled in "Playing With God." This account highlights the active nature of a child's own spiritual socialization and the give and take between parents and children in this process.

Contemporary Research on Parenting

The Case for Nature and Nurture

W. Andrew Collins *University of Minnesota,* **Eleanor E. Maccoby** *Stanford University,*
Laurence Steinberg *Temple University,* **E. Mavis Hetherington** *University of Virginia,*
Marc H. Bornstein *National Institute of Child Health and Human Development*

Current findings on parental influences provide more sophisticated and less deterministic explanations than did earlier theory and research on parenting. Contemporary research approaches include (a) behavior-genetic designs, augmented with direct measures of potential environmental influence; (b) studies distinguishing among children with different genetically influenced predispositions in terms of their responses to different environmental conditions; (c) experimental and quasi-experimental studies of change in children's behavior as a result of their exposure to parents' behavior, after controlling for children's initial characteristics; and (d) research on interactions between parenting and nonfamilial environmental influences and contexts, illustrating contemporary concern with influences beyond the parent-child dyad. These approaches indicate that parental influences on child development are neither as unambiguous as earlier researchers suggested nor as insubstantial as current critics claim.

> The heredity and environment of an organism
> can be completely separated only in analytic
> thinking, for in actual nature such separation
> would lead to instant death of the organism,
> even though the philosopher making the analysis might himself survive. (Gesell & Thompson,
> 1934, p. 293)

Research on parenting has been the centerpiece of longstanding efforts in psychology to understand socialization processes. As the field moves into its second century, however, this focus on parental influence faces several high-profile challenges. One challenge comes from the charge that there is little compelling evidence of parents' influence on behavior and personality in adolescence and adulthood (Harris, 1995, 1998; Rowe, 1994). Another is the allegation that socialization researchers have neglected significant forces other than parenting—forces that may contribute more extensively than parenting to

individual differences in adult behavior. The most commonly cited sources of alternative influences are heredity (Harris, 1995, 1998; Rowe, 1994) and peers (Harris, 1995, 1998), although some writers emphasize the relatively greater importance of concurrent environmental forces more generally (e.g., Lewis, 1997).

These criticisms of socialization research generally invoke studies of parenting published before the early 1980s. Neither the assumptions nor the research paradigms that dominated the field as recently as a decade ago, however, represent research on parenting today. Contemporary students of socialization largely agree that early researchers often overstated conclusions from correlational findings; relied excessively on singular, deterministic views of parental influence; and failed to attend to the potentially confounding effects of heredity. Contemporary researchers have taken steps to remedy many of those shortcomings. Unfortunately, the weaknesses of old studies still permeate presentations of socialization research in introductory textbooks and the mass media, partly because they appeal to preferences for simple generalizations instead of the conditional effects that capture the reality of socialization.

Leading-edge approaches to social development and personality no longer rely exclusively on correlational designs, overly simple laboratory analogs, or additive models for assigning variance to one source or another. Contemporary studies, including research on parenting, turn on complex statistical methods and research designs that capture real-world complexity without sacrificing the rigor necessary to infer causal relations. Moreover, conceptual models increasingly encompass multiple sources of influence. Researchers draw on emerging knowledge in behavior genetics, neuroendocrine studies, studies of animal behavior, and intervention and prevention science to recognize the complex interplay between inherited and experiential components of individual development. The result is both a more complete and a more differentiated picture of parenting and its likely effects (for comprehensive reviews of contemporary socialization research, see Bornstein, 1995b; Eisenberg & Damon, 1998).

One goal of this article is to outline key features of contemporary approaches to studies of parental socialization. We also show how current researchers have, for some time, been identifying and responding to the very challenges pointed to by recent critics. We pay particular attention to research designs that estimate inherited and other dispositional factors, as well as experiential ones, in estimating influence. We describe several lines of evidence that address issues of causality regarding the scope and nature of parental influences. Finally, we propose that responsible conclusions about the significance of parenting can be based on only the emerging body of research findings that incorporate both individual and social factors and their interrelations.

Contemporary Approaches to Parenting Research

Research during the past two decades has undermined the once tacit assumption that environment should be the sole starting point in explaining individual differences in development. The relevant evidence comes from comparisons of the degree of similarity between individuals who vary in degree of genetic relatedness (e.g., identical vs. fraternal twins). Typical results imply that heredity accounts for a substantial proportion of this similarity, even though a recent meta-analysis (McCartney, Harris, & Bernieri, 1990) concluded that heredity rarely accounts for as much as 50% of the variation among individuals in a particular population, perhaps even less when personality characteristics are the focus. Although these findings also imply that environment contributes substantially to individual differences, behavior-genetics researchers typically infer environmental effects from the residual after estimates of genetic contributions are computed. The sources of the apparent environmental influences are not specified.

Efforts to understand the role of parents in socialization are constrained severely by the traditional analytic model on which the most cited behavior-genetic findings are based. This "additive" model regards hereditary and environmental components as independent and separable and holds that these two components together account for 100% of the variance in a characteristic (Plomin, 1990). Consequently, most behavior-genetic research has allowed for only main effects of genes and environment, ignoring the possibility that genes may function differently in different environments. A primary problem in disentangling heredity and measures of environmental influences, however, is that genetic and environmental factors are correlated (Plomin, 1990). Researchers consis-

tently find that parenting of identical twins is more similar than parenting of fraternal twins and that two biological siblings typically experience more similar parenting than do two adopted children (Dunn & Plomin, 1986; Plomin, DeFries, & Fulker, 1988; Reiss, Niederhiser, Hetherington, & Plomin, in press; Rowe, 1983). Parents' genotypes, as well as children's genotypes, contribute to these contrasting patterns. That individuals who are more closely related genetically also have more similar shared parental environments means that observed associations between parenting and measures of child characteristics cannot be assumed to be either entirely genetic or entirely environmental in origin. As Rose (1995) stated it, the central question in development is "how genetic effects are modulated across lifespans of environmental interactions" (p. 627).

A related problem further limits the usefulness of traditional behavior-genetic approaches to research on parenting. Estimating the effects of heredity versus environment ignores the potential for malleability, even in characteristics heavily influenced by heredity. When environmental conditions change substantially over time, mean levels of a characteristic also may change, although heritability coefficients (which are based on correlations) may or may not change (Plomin & Rutter, 1998). The problem comes from the failure to recognize that means and correlations can vary independently. Thus, although intelligence has been shown to have a high heritability coefficient, individuals' cognitive abilities can improve or decline as a function of experience (for an explanation of this point, see Weinberg, 1989).

Migration studies often reveal similar paradoxes. For example, height is highly heritable, with heritability coefficients in the 90s, showing that within a given population, the variation in children's heights is closely linked with the variations in their parents' heights. By inference, very little variance remains to be attributed to environmental factors. At the same time, grandparents born in Japan are, on the average, considerably shorter than their grandchildren born and reared in the United States (Angoff, 1988). In the same way, genetic factors that are highly important in a behavior do not show up in a study of the heritability of that behavior because this genetic factor is uniform for all members of a population. Thus, analyzing the variation of a factor within a population does not provide exhaustive information concerning either the genetic or the environmental contributions to the factor. Large-scale societal factors, such as ethnicity or poverty, can influence group means in parenting behavior—and in the effects of parenting behaviors—in ways that are not revealed by studies of within-group variability. In addition, highly heritable traits also can be highly malleable. Like traditional correlational research on parenting, therefore, commonly used behavior-genetic methods have provided an incomplete analysis of differences among individuals.

To acknowledge the importance of the interplay of heredity and environment, four lines of contemporary research on parenting have emerged. One line of research adopts the additive model of behavior-genetics research but augments it with direct measures of potential environmental influences in an effort to document environmental effects more precisely (Plomin et al., 1988; Reiss et al., in press). A second line of research addresses the insensitivity of additive models to Gene 5 Environment effects (Plomin & Rutter, 1998; Rutter et al., 1997) by distinguishing among children with different genetic predispositions on a characteristic to see whether they respond differently to different environmental conditions. The distinctions among genetically different groups often rely on measures of temperament or the parent's carrying a known genetic risk factor. A third line of research examines the effect of parental practices after controlling for any initial dispositional characteristics of children. This kind of research is intended to permit inferences about the direction of effects when parent and child characteristics are initially correlated. Evidence on this point comes from three types of research designs: (a) longitudinal studies in which child characteristics at Time 1 are controlled statistically, (b) experiments in which nonhuman animals are exposed to selected rearing environments, and (c) intervention studies either in which "experiments of nature" have resulted in marked changes in parenting experiences or in which families are randomly assigned to different treatment programs designed to improve parenting with resulting changes in child behavior. A fourth line of contemporary studies addresses the possibility that extrafamilial environmental conditions with which parenting is correlated contribute to individual differences in development and behavior.

Augmented Behavior-Genetic Designs

Traditional behavior-genetic designs give primacy to the effects of heredity, relying on a series of computations to reveal which portions of the variance should be labeled as contributions of the shared environment or assigned to nonshared, "other," or "unknown" sources. Although evidence of shared family influences and experiences has appeared for some characteristics such as health habits, alcohol patterns, smoking patterns (McGue, 1994), depression in later life (Gatz, Pedersen, Plomin, Nesselroade, & McLearn, 1992), delinquency as reported by siblings (Rowe, Chassin, Presson, Edwards, & Sherman, 1992), and autonomy and sociability (Reiss et al., in press), the most frequent conclusion has been that shared environments play a small, inconsequential role in children's development.

Many scholars, however, have challenged this inference. One criticism is that the assumptions, methods, and truncated samples used in behavior-genetic studies maximize the effects of heredity and features of the environment that are different for different children and minimize the effects of shared family environments (Goodman, 1991; Hoffman, 1991; Patterson, 1999; Rose, 1995; Stoolmiller, 1999). For example, Stoolmiller (1999) noted that recent adoption studies have been impaired by pronounced range restrictions (about 67%) in the family environments sampled. Stoolmiller argued that the estimated contribution of shared environment likely would be as much as 50% higher if appropriate corrections for range restriction were applied to data from such studies.

A second criticism is that estimates of the relative contributions of environment and heredity vary greatly depending on the source of data (Turkheimer & Waldron, in press). Twin studies typically yield higher heritability estimates for a trait than adoption studies do (Wachs & Plomin, 1991). Moreover, in both types of studies, heritability estimates vary considerably depending on the measures used to assess similarity between children or between parents and children. The largest effect sizes for environmental influences on social development are found with the relatively rarely used method of direct behavioral observations, whereas the smallest effect sizes for environmental influences are found with parental reports, which are the most commonly used measure in behavior-genetic studies of behavioral outcomes (Emde et al., 1992; Ghodsion-Garpey & Baker, 1997; Miles & Carey, 1997; Rutter et al., 1997; Wachs, 1992). The sizable variability in estimates of genetic and environmental contributions depending on the paradigms and measures used means that no firm conclusions can be drawn about the relative strength of these influences on development.

Traditional twin and adoption studies have been criticized on the grounds that they estimate environmental effects only as a residual: the effects remaining after genetic effects have been estimated and subtracted from 100%. Efforts to rectify this problem by measuring environment directly, however, have failed to clarify the contributions of environment relative to heredity. Most such efforts were stimulated by Plomin and Daniels's (1987) proposal that the environmental variance in behavior-genetic studies emanates largely from experiences that differ for children in the same family. By measuring such differences, researchers hoped to better understand the portion of the variance in behavior-genetic studies not attributed specifically to genetic relatedness. Behavior-genetic analyses, however, can establish that nonshared environment contributes to individual differences in a domain but cannot document the connections between objectively measured nonshared environmental events and development (Turkheimer & Waldron, in press). Most studies with direct measures of the environment and of the development of multiple siblings within a family, moreover, have not used designs that permit heritability estimates (e.g., Brody & Stoneman, 1994; Tejerina-Allen, Wagnere, & Cohen, 1994).

Thus, researchers' attempts to work within the traditional additive model, while augmenting it with direct measures of environment, have yielded findings that are conditional on a series of methodological problems in assessing the relevant environmental factors and in the inherent limitations of the additive model for identifying Gene X Environment interactions. The remainder of this article is devoted to recent investigations of how processes of influence operate and interact.

The Search for Gene X Environment Effects

Traditional behavior-genetic models do not afford comparisons of the effects of differing environments on individuals who vary on genetically influenced characteristics. For example, in twin and adoption studies, degree of biological relatedness between individuals, not specific markers of genetically linked characteristics in the two individuals, is the primary focus, and variations in environments are rarely assessed. The most likely possibility is that the forced estimates of main effects for genetic relatedness and environment in the additive model mask virtually ubiquitous correlations and statistical interactions between the two in existing research. Such interactions are notably difficult to detect because of low statistical power in most relevant studies (McCall, 1991; McClelland & Judd, 1993; Wahlsten, 1990). Although some writers (e.g., Harris, 1998) have elected to subsume evidence of Gene X Environment correlations and interactions under genetic contributions to behavioral development, responsible scholarship requires closer attention to emerging evidence that these effects involve direct parental influences as well (O'Connor, Deater-Deckard, Fulker, Rutter, & Plomin, 1998; Plomin & Rutter, 1998).

The search for Gene X Environment effects often takes the form of using measures of temperament for the purpose of distinguishing among children with different genetic predispositions to see whether they respond differently to given environmental conditions (Bornstein, 1995b; Plomin & Rutter, 1998; Rutter et al., 1997). Studies that pool parenting effects across children with very different temperaments inevitably obscure actual parental effects. Even when parenting effects are apparent, it is not reasonable to expect that a given style or quality of parenting would have the same effect on every child. Moreover, different parental strategies or degrees of parental effort may be required to bring about the same outcome in different children. Two types of recent studies attempt to disentangle individual children's heredity and the nature of their rearing experiences: (a) studies of the effect of rearing experiences on the behavior of children who differ on measures of temperament and (b) studies comparing the effect of high- versus low-risk environments on children of differing vulnerability.

Temperament and parenting. Temperamental characteristics, defined as "constitutionally based individual differences in reactivity and self-regulation" (Rothbart & Ahadi, 1994, p. 55), are thought to emerge early, to show some stability over time, but to be modifiable by experience. In general, statistical associations between early temperamental characteristics and later adjustment are modest (see Rothbart & Bates, 1998, for a review), suggesting that these associations also may be moderated by environmental factors. A difficult temperament, characterized by intense negative affect and repeated demands for attention, is associated with both later externalizing and internalizing disorders (Bates & Bayles, 1988; Bates, Bayles, Bennett, Ridge, & Brown, 1991). Early resistance to control, impulsivity, irritability, and distractibility predicts later externalizing and social alienation (Caspi, Henry, McGee, Moffitt, & Silva, 1995; Hagekull, 1989, 1994), whereas early shy, inhibited, or distress-prone behaviors predict later anxiety disorders, harm avoidance, and low aggression and social potency (Caspi & Silva, 1995).

Correlations between temperamental characteristics and parental behavior reflect bidirectional interactive processes, as well as genetic linkages between parent and child characteristics. Temperamental characteristics may set in motion a chain of reactions from others that put children at risk or protect them from developing behavior and psychological problems (Caspi & Elder, 1988; Hetherington, 1989, 1991; Quinton, Pickles, Maughan, & Rutter, 1993; Rutter, 1990; Rutter & Quinton, 1984; Werner, 1990). Difficultness, irritability, and distress proneness in infants evoke hostility, criticism, a tendency to ignore the child, avoidance, coercive discipline, and a lack of playfulness in mothers (Lee & Bates, 1985; Rutter & Quinton, 1984; Van den Boom, 1989). These reactions, in turn, are associated with avoidant (Grossman, Grossman, Spangler, Suess, & Unzner, 1985; Van den Boom, 1989) or insecure-ambivalent attachment (Goldsmith & Alansky, 1987; Miyake, Chen & Campos, 1985). Bates, Pettit, and Dodge (1995), in a longitudinal study, found that infants' characteristics (e.g., hyperreactivity, impulsivity, and difficult temperament) significantly predicted externalizing problems 10 years later. Although this finding at first seems to support the lasting effects of physiologically based characteristics, Bates et al. (1995) also showed that predictive power increased when they added information about parenting to the equation. Infants' early characteristics elicited harsh parenting at age 4, which in turn predicted externalizing problems when the children were young adolescents, over and above the prediction from infant temperament. Similarly, this and other findings imply that even though parental behavior is influenced by child behavior, parents' actions contribute distinctively to the child's later behavior. For example, in a longitudinal adoption design, O'Connor et al. (1998) confirmed that children at genetic risk for antisocial behavior elicited more negative parenting from adoptive parents than did children not at risk. They also found, however, that "most of the association between negative parenting and children's externalizing behavior was not explicable on the basis of an evocative gene-environment correlation and that an additional environmentally mediated parental effect on children's behavior was plausible" (p. 970).

Bidirectional and interactive effects of this kind now appear to carry significant implications for distinctive effects of parenting variations on children who differ in temperamental characteristics. In longitudinal work on the socialization of "conscience," Kochanska (1995, 1997) found that maternal use of gentle childrearing techniques that deemphasized power assertion was more effective with temperamentally fearful children than with bolder, more exploratory children in promoting the development of conscience. With bolder children, maternal responsiveness and a close emotional bond with the child were more important in fostering conscience. Similarly, the quality of parenting to some extent moderates associations between early temperamental characteristics of difficultness, impulsivity, and unmanageability and later externalizing disorders (Bates, Pettit, Dodge, & Ridge, 1998; Rothbart & Bates, 1998). Firm, restrictive parental control has been linked to lower levels of later externalizing in early difficult, unmanageable children (Bates et al., 1998). Although only a few studies have examined the moderating effects of parenting on the links between temperamental predispositions and later adjustment, and although not all of these studies have had positive results (Rothbart & Bates, 1998), the evidence nevertheless suggests that parenting moderates these associations.

Studies of risk and resiliency. Parallels to these differential relations between parenting and child behavior can be found in studies of risk and resiliency. Children who showed early developmental problems because of risk factors such as perinatal damage (Werner & Smith, 1992) improved in adjustment under authoritative parenting. Parenting, moreover, appears to play a mediating role between parental psychopathology and child symptoms of disorder (R. Conger, Ge, Elder, Lorenz, & Simons, 1994; Ge, Conger, Lorenz, Shanahan, & Elder, 1995; Ge, Lorenz, Conger, Elder, & Simons, 1994). For example, Downey and Walker (1992) demonstrated that children with a psychiatrically ill parent who were not exposed to parental maltreatment, in contrast to those who were, showed very low levels of both externalizing and internalizing. That different outcomes for children are associated with differential parental responses to the same risk factor implies parental influence, although Downey and Walker cannot rule out evocative behavior on the part of the child.

A Finnish adoption study (Tienari et al., 1994) further illustrates how a genetic predisposition can either manifest itself or not, depending on whether certain triggering environmental conditions are present. Adoptees who had a schizophrenic biological parent were more likely to develop a range of psychiatric disorders (including schizophrenia) than were adoptees not at genetic risk, but only if they were adopted into dysfunctional families (see also Cadoret, 1985). Similar findings have been reported from studies of adopted children whose biological parents had

a history of criminality (Bohman, 1996). If adopted into well-functioning homes, 12% of these children displayed petty criminality in adulthood. However, if adopted into families carrying environmental risk, their rate of petty criminality in adulthood rose to 40%. These findings suggest that well-functioning parents can buffer children at genetic risk and circumvent the processes that might ordinarily lead from genotype to phenotype. The more general point is that genetic vulnerabilities (or strengths) may not be manifested except in the presence of a pertinent environmental trigger such as parenting.

Studies of Parental Influence, Controlling for Initial Child Characteristics

A third line of research attempts to provide a basis for examining instances in which parental behavior may exert a causal influence in changing children's behavior. Studies of this type subsume several research strategies. One strategy is longitudinal research in which children's initial characteristics can be observed to change over time in relation to specific parenting experiences. Even more compelling evidence for determining the causal status of parenting, however, involves experimental manipulations. In some recent experiments, young nonhuman animals were exposed to measurably different rearing conditions. Some experiments of nature with humans also have provided evidence of this kind. The most compelling evidence, however, comes from interventions in which parents are assigned randomly to behavior-change treatment groups, with resulting changes in the behavior of both the parents and their otherwise untreated children. Random assignment is the means for ensuring that treatment groups are not initially different.

Longitudinal studies of parenting and child development. The most widely used strategy in contemporary studies of socialization uses short-term longitudinal designs to better distinguish parenting effects from the characteristics of the child (e.g., Ge et al., 1996; Steinberg, Lamborn, Darling, Mounts, & Dornbusch, 1994). In these studies, aspects of child functioning and development are measured at more than one point in time. Statistical procedures, such as the analysis of covariance or multiple regression, are then used to estimate the relation between parenting at one point in time and child outcomes at some subsequent point, after taking into account characteristics of the child at the time that parenting was assessed. Studies showing that the over-time effect of parenting on child development holds even after controlling for earlier child characteristics are important for several reasons. First, in the absence of a randomized experimental design, this strategy provides indirect evidence that parenting conceivably affects—rather than simply accompanying or following from—child adjustment. Such indirect evidence is important because one cannot randomly assign children to different home environments. These analyses do not rule out the possibility that different children elicit different parental responses, but they do provide evidence that the correlation between child adjustment and parenting is not due *solely* to the effect of children on parenting behavior.

Significant longitudinal relations between parenting and child adjustment after taking into account their concurrent relation also help rule out a number of third-variable explanations, including the possibility that the observed association is due to factors that parents and their children share, such as genes or socioeconomic status. To be a viable explanation for the observed association, a third variable would have to be correlated with the measures of child adjustment at the time of the longitudinal follow-up but not correlated with the same measures taken earlier. Any genetically mediated link between parenting and child adjustment, for example, would be taken into account by controlling for the concurrent relation between parenting and child adjustment before examining their relation over time.

Rearing experiments with animals. Recent work with nonhuman animals points clearly to the fact that experience—that is, encountering or engaging with the environment—influences brain development in young organisms and that these changes in the brain are associated with changes in behavior (Greenough & Black, 1992). Although some of the relevant environmental events must occur during a sensitive period to affect development (Bornstein, 1989), the mammalian brain generally remains malleable by environmental inputs well into adulthood (Huttenlocher, 1994; Nelson, in press). Environmental events that have to do with the amount or kind of "parenting" that a young organism receives are essential for survival in all mammalian species. The presence and activities of the infant stimulate a set of maternal behaviors needed by the infant (including but not confined to feeding), and these reciprocal maternal behaviors serve to facilitate the infant's adaptation and development (e.g., Stern, 1985). Studies of higher mammals confirm that, as these interactions continue to occur, an intense emotional bond is formed such that separation of the pair produces distress and behavioral disruption in each member of the pair. Studies in which young animals have been deprived of "mothering" have shown clearly that such deprivation not only disrupts the ongoing behavior of the young animal at the time of deprivation but also leads to dysfunctional outcomes for the offspring in the long term.

Current animal work is addressing implications of naturally occurring variation, within the "normal" range, in maternal behavior. Meaney and Plotsky and their colleagues (Caldji et al., 1998; Liu et al., 1997) have studied styles of mothering in rats, relating variations in these styles to behavioral outcomes in their offspring. Maternal animals differ considerably in the frequency with which they lick and groom their newborn pups and in whether they arch their backs to facilitate nursing or lie passively on top of or next to the pups. Individual differences in these mothering styles have been shown to be quite stable. In adulthood, moreover, the offspring of mothers who had done more licking and grooming and had nursed with arched backs (high LG-ABN mothers, whom we can call *nurturant*) were less timid in leaving their home cages to obtain food or explore a novel environment than were the offspring of low LG-ABN mothers. These outcomes are correlated with neuroendocrine processes. As adults, rats who had experienced high levels of maternal licking and grooming as newborns showed reduced levels of adrenocorticotropic hormone and corticosterone in response to a stressful condition (close restraint). Furthermore, differences emerged in the densities of receptors for stress hormones in several loci in the brains of animals that had experienced the two different kinds of maternal styles in their first 10 days of life. Thus, early mothering styles apparently affected the neural circuitry that governs behavioral stress responses in the offspring as they grow into adulthood.

To determine whether there is an independent effect of maternal styles per se on these outcomes, apart from any genetic mediation, researchers have cross-fostered infants born to a low-nurturant mother to rearing by a high-nurturant mother. Early findings (Anisman, Zaharia, Meaney, & Merali, 1998) show that these infants manifest the benefits of their early rearing in their modified adult stress reactions, by comparison with infants born to low-nurturant mothers and reared by them.

Corroborating evidence comes from studies with nonhuman primates (Suomi, 1997). Suomi and colleagues initially observed naturally occurring individual differences in "emotional reactivity" among Rhesus monkeys. In early life, some animals are hesitant about exploring new environments and show extreme reactions to separation from their mothers, whereas others characteristically react more calmly. Individual animals' reactivity patterns remain quite stable over many years. These patterns of behavior are accompanied by distinctive neuroendocrine patterns. The behavioral and physiological indicators that distinguish highly reactive animals from less reactive ones are especially apparent under environmentally stressful conditions (Suomi, 1997).

When young Rhesus monkeys with clearly different reactivity patterns are cross-fostered to mothers who are either reactive (easily distressed) or nonreactive (calm), their adult behavior is quite different from that shown by the biological offspring of each type of mother. Genetically reactive young animals that are reared by calm mothers for the first six months of their lives and then placed in large social groups made up of peers and non-related older adults develop normally and indeed rise to the top of their dominance hierarchy. Further, these cross-fostered animals are adept at avoiding stressful situations and at recruiting social support that enables them to cope with stress. By contrast, genetically reactive infants who are raised by reactive mothers typically are socially incompetent when placed in the larger living group at the age of six months and are particularly vulnerable to stress. In general, the introduction of stressful conditions seems to make the effects of early rearing experience especially perceptible (Suomi, 1997). Thus, variations in mothering style have a lasting effect on the reactivity of the young animals when they move into new social contexts. Moreover, the quality of early mothering now has been found to affect the way genetically at-risk females parent their own offspring. If cross-fostered to low-reactive mothers, they are competent parents with their own offspring; if raised by high-reactive mothers, they manifest mothering deficits.

Recent work (Suomi, in press) has shown that the genetic make-up of young monkeys influences how large an effect early rearing conditions will have. A gene has been identified for which one allele is associated with a highly reactive temperament and the other allele with a calmer temperament. Certain aspects of the neuroendocrine system (i.e., serotonergic functioning) are controlled by this gene. Maternal deprivation has a powerful effect on the genetically reactive monkeys, producing deficits in their neuroendocrine functioning and in their behavioral and emotional reactions. For the animals not carrying the genetically risky allele, however, maternal deprivation has little effect.

These recent studies trace some of the complex steps in the long pathway between genes and phenotypic behavior. The findings show that both genes and parenting affect brain processes and neuroendocrine systems. These studies point to a future in which researchers will be able to provide more detailed information about the interplay of heredity and parenting influences than traditional twin and adoption studies can yield.

Experiments of nature. No extensively controlled rearing experiments have been conducted with human children, but several natural experiments have yielded information that is strikingly parallel to the findings of the cross-fostering work. A recent example is found with the children who lived in Romanian orphanages for some months or years in early childhood, during which time they were deprived of the opportunity to form a close bond with a single trusted adult caregiver. Some of these children have been adopted into middle-class homes in other cultures. The effects of the early deprivation appear to depend on its duration. Recent follow-up measures at age six in a group of Romanian orphans adopted by Canadian families show that children adopted during approximately the first half-year of life manifest no lasting effects of their early experience. But children adopted later have been found to have abnormally high levels of cortisol during the ordinary daily routine of their adoptive homes, indicating that the neuroendocrine system involved in stress regulation has not developed normally (Chisholm, 1998; Chisholm, Carter, Ames, & Morison, 1995; Gunnar, in press; see also Rutter & the ERA study team, 1998).

An example of variations in parenting that are more within the normal range comes from France, where 20 children were located who had been abandoned in infancy by their low-socioeconomic-status parents and adopted by upper-middle-class parents (Schiff, Duyme, Dumaret, & Tomkiewitz, 1982). These children all had biological siblings or half-siblings who remained with the biological mother and were reared by her in impoverished circumstances. The researchers were unable to find any selective factors that might have made the abandoned children more genetically promising than the ones retained at home. When tested in middle childhood, however, the adopted children's IQs averaged 14 points higher than those of their natural siblings. By contrast, children who remained with their biological mothers were four times more likely to exhibit failures in their school performance. These results are consistent with those of several other early adoption studies (e.g., Skodak & Skeels, 1949; Scarr & Weinberg, 1976, 1978) showing that adoption into well-functioning middle-class homes can provide a "bonus" in cognitive functioning for the children involved.

What aspects of living in more advantaged homes were responsible for these children's cognitive and educational gains is not known. Was it the more stimulating, more cultured, more educated environments provided by the adoptive parents, or were there greater amounts of parent-child interaction or more secure attachments? We can only suspect that something about the way these adoptive parents dealt with the children contributed to the effect. Evidence from the Colorado Adoption Project provides some suggestive evidence for a bidirectional process. The Colorado project included data on rates of communicative development in groups of 12-month-olds either born or adopted into intact families (Hardy-Brown, 1983; Hardy-Brown & Plomin, 1985; Hardy-Brown, Plomin, & DeFries, 1981). Biological mothers' verbal intelligence correlated with the language competencies of children they had not seen since birth. Reciprocally, however, adoptive mothers' activities, like imitating their infants' vocalizations and vocalizing responsively and contingently to infants' vocalizations, also predicted child language competencies. Similarly, another comparison of children with their biological and their adoptive parents (Scarr & Weinberg, 1978) showed that correlations between the vocabulary scores of adoptive mothers and children were as high as those between the vocabulary scores of biological mothers and their children. Like other examples cited earlier, these findings clearly show the distinct contribution of parental behavior over and above the contribution of heredity.

Interventions with human parents. Finally, interventions that seek to change the mean level of a behavioral or personality characteristic in children provide additional evidence of the efficacy of parenting. Efforts to manipulate parental behavior for the purpose of influencing child behavior are surprisingly rare. Laboratory analog studies (e.g., Kuczynski, 1984), although documenting short-term effects of specific behaviors of parents, cannot establish that such behaviors significantly influence broadband outcomes for offspring. The primary source of relevant information for human children comes from evaluations of programs designed to remediate or prevent socialization problems. Such programs typically target the behavior of either children alone or both children and parents. Of particular relevance to socialization, however, are studies in which the behavior of parents, but not the children, is the target of the manipulation. If the manipulation produces desired changes in the parent's behavior and if the degree of change, in turn, is associated with changes in the child's behavior, the evidence for the causal influence of parents is compelling. Unfortunately, only a few such programs focus on improving parental behavior, and even fewer estimate the causal influences of changes in parental behavior on child outcomes (for reviews, see Cowan, Powell, & Cowan, 1998; McMahon & Wells, 1998).

An exception is a recent prevention program intended to foster more effective parenting following divorce (Forgatch & DeGarmo, 1999). School-age sons of recently divorced single mothers often manifest increased academic, behavioral, social, and emotional problems relative to sons of nondivorced mothers, and the divorced mothers themselves commonly behave toward their sons in a more coercive and less positive manner than nondivorced mothers do (Chase-Lansdale, Cherlin, & Kiernan, 1995; Hetherington, 1993; Zill, Morrison, & Coiro, 1993). In most reports, however, the direction of causality is unclear. Forgatch and DeGarmo sought both to address the causality issue and to test a method for preventing these apparently negative sequelae of divorce. They designed group-intervention and individual follow-up procedures for 153 recently divorced mothers who met three criteria: they had been separated from their partners within the prior 3 to 24 months, they resided with a biological son in Grades 1 through 3, and they did not cohabit with a new partner. Initial observational, self-report, and teacher report measures of both mothers' parenting and children's behaviors were used to control for possible genetically influenced differences among parent-child pairs. Random assignment ensured that the treatment group was not systematically different from the control group of 85 mothers and sons who also met the screening criteria. No intervention was provided to the children. At the end of 12 months, treatment-group mothers generally showed less coercive behavior toward children and less decline in positive behavior than control-group mothers did (although both treatment- and control-group mothers manifested at least temporary declines in positive behavior during the year following divorce). Moreover, the degree of change in the mothers' behavior over the course of 12 months significantly predicted the degree of change in the children's behaviors. Changes in parenting practices were associated significantly with changes in teacher-reported school adjustment and with changes in both child-reported and parent-reported maladjustment. Estimated effect sizes for these correlated changes ranged from .032 to .144 (M. Forgatch, personal communication, November 1, 1999). These effect sizes are small to medium, according to Cohen's (1988) criteria.

Other intervention attempts with parents have yielded similarly impressive evidence. Cowan and Cowan (in press), in a randomized design, showed that parents' participation in a 16-week series of discussion groups on effective parenting just prior to their children's kindergarten entry resulted in better school adjustment and higher academic achievement for children in kindergarten and first grade, compared with children whose parents attended a series of discussion groups without the effective-parenting emphasis. The relative advantage for the children of intervention-group parents has persisted through age 10, a period of six years. With parents of infants, Van den Boom (1989, 1994) demonstrated that an intervention to train lower-class mothers to respond sensitively to their infants irritability and reduced the extent of avoidant attachment in distress-prone infants. Similarly, Belsky, Goode, and Most (1980) found that interventions to increase mothers' didactic interactions with infants during play resulted in significantly higher exploratory play among infants, compared with a no-treatment control group. In interventions to improve the behavioral-training skills of parents of noncompliant children, Forehand and colleagues demonstrated both improvements in parental behavior and behavioral changes in the children, as well as increased parental perceptions of improved child behavior and decreased parental depression (Forehand & King, 1977; Forehand, Wells, & Griest, 1980). Depending on the content of the maternal training, children have been shown to manifest differing patterns of competence. Riksen-Walraven (1978) showed that infants of mothers trained in responding demonstrated higher levels of exploratory competence, whereas infants of mothers trained on improving sensory stimulation habituated more efficiently. When interventions are effective, behavior change tends to be long-lasting (Patterson, 1975).

Findings from studies of parenting-focused interventions provide the strongest evidence available on the efficacy of parenting behavior in humans. Whether naturally occurring behaviors of the kind encouraged by these experimental programs account for behavioral development is more difficult to establish. Nevertheless, the increasing use of multimethod, multi-informant assessments and structural equation modeling is helping to overcome some of the shortcomings of traditional correlational studies of socialization and behavior-genetic studies using single informants (Rutter et al., 1997). These more methodologically rigorous studies (e.g., R. Conger & Elder, 1994; Forgatch, 1991; Kim, Hetherington, & Reiss, 1999) generally yield associations between parenting and child outcomes, with appropriate controls for Time 1 status on outcome measures, that meet Cohen's (1988) criteria for small or medium effect sizes. Some studies (e.g., Kochanska, 1997) yield impressively large effect sizes. Even small effects of parenting, however, are likely to become large effects over time (Abelson, 1985). Parental behavior has been shown to be highly stable across time (Holden & Miller, 1999). Thus, specific parental influences, consistently experienced, likely accumulate to produce larger meaningful outcomes over the childhood and adolescent years.

Studies of Links Between Parenting and Other Influences

Current investigations address a further challenge from recent critics of parenting research as well: the need to consider environmental influences other than parents in accounting for differences among children. Socialization research today is guided by an ecological perspective on human development (Bronfenbrenner, 1979; for recent reviews, see Bornstein 1995a, 1995b; Bronfenbrenner & Morris, 1998). Families are seen as important influences on children, the effect of which can be understood only in light of the simultaneous influence of social spheres such as peer groups and schools. These influences occur within broad contexts (e.g., neighborhood, cultural context, historical epoch) that add to, shape, and moderate the effect of the family. The ecological perspective not only emphasizes the potential significance of extrafamilial influences on the child's development but also, more importantly, stresses the interactive and synergistic, rather than additive and competitive, nature of the links between the family and other influences. In this section we consider the implications of this view for parenting in relation to two extrafamilial influences on socialization: peers and macrocontexts of parent-child relations.

Relations of parental and peer influence. In an earlier era, socialization researchers cast families and peers as opposing forces vying for influence over the child's behavior. In much the same way that recent developments in behavior genetics have challenged the wisdom of attempting to estimate how much variance in a trait is attributable to genes versus the environment, contemporary models of socialization no longer ask whether children are influenced more by parents or by peers. Today, socialization researchers develop and test models that examine how parents and peers exert conjoint influence on the developing child (e.g., Brown, Mounts, Lamborn, & Steinberg, 1993; Cairns & Cairns, 1994; Kishion, Patterson, Stoolmiller, & Skinner, 1991; Fuligni & Eccles, 1993; Mounts & Steinberg, 1995).

This new direction rests on four findings that have emerged consistently from research on parent and peer influences. The first finding is that the observed similarity between adolescents and their friends across a wide array of variables, including school achievement (Epstein, 1983), aggression (Cairns, Cairns, Neckerman, Gest, & Gariepy, 1988), internalized distress (Hogue & Steinberg, 1995), and drug use (Kandel, 1978), is due mostly to the tendency for individuals to select like-minded friends, as well as to the influence that friends have over each other (Berndt, 1999; Berndt, Hawkins, & Jiao, 1999). Children are not randomly assigned to peer groups. Although unambiguous estimates of the relative effect of selection and influence effects are not available, a child with antisocial inclinations may be far more likely to fall into a similarly inclined peer group than an antisocial peer group is to corrupt a well-behaved youngster. Similarly, an academically oriented child may be more likely to select academically oriented friends than a child who is not interested in school is to develop a passion for achievement because his or her friends are so inclined. Equating peer influence with peer similarity overstates considerably the extent of peer influence, because the equation fails to take account of the selection effect (Bauman & Fisher, 1986).

The second finding is that peer influence often operates with respect to everyday behaviors and transient attitudes, not enduring personality traits or values (Brown, 1990). Most studies examining individuals' religiosity, educational plans, and occupational choices, for example, reveal that parental influence on adolescent personality development is deeper and more enduring than that of peers (Brown, 1990). To be sure, even transient peer influences over day-to-day behaviors can have enduring sequelae that are opposed to what parents might desire (e.g., peer influence to become sexually active can result in an unplanned pregnancy and foreshortened educational attainment; peer influence to engage in criminal activity can result in a jail sentence). However, because peer influence tends to be immediate, its content changes with shifts in friendships. Studies that track individuals through adolescence often reveal that young adults are more similar to their parents than they had appeared to be as teenagers (J. Conger, 1971).

The third finding is evidence of the significance of parents and parent-child relationships in influencing which peers children select. Any psychological snapshot taken during adolescence, when peers are undeniably an important force in children's lives, rightly should be viewed as the end of a long process of socialization that began early in childhood and most likely has its origins in the family. Parke and Bhavnagri (1989) indicated that parents influence children's peer experiences in two general ways. During elementary school parents propel their children toward certain peers by managing their youngsters' social activities (which has the effect of increasing contact with some peers and diminishing it with others); during both childhood and adolescence, parents actively steer children toward certain friends and away from others. In addition, throughout the child's development parents indirectly influence the child's attitudes, values, personality, and motives, which in turn affect the child's interactions and affiliations with particular peers (Brown et al., 1993). For all of these reasons, parental and peer influence tend to be complementary, not antithetical (Brown, 1990).

Finally, and perhaps most importantly, adolescents differ considerably in their susceptibility to peer influence, and one of the most important contributors to this differential susceptibility is the quality of the parent-child relationship. Adolescents whose parents are authoritative (i.e., responsive and demanding) are less swayed by peer pressure to misbehave than are adolescents whose parents are permissive (Devereux, 1970) or authoritarian (Fuligni & Eccles, 1993). Indeed, adolescents from authoritative homes are more susceptible to prosocial peer pressure (e.g., pressure to do well in school) but less susceptible to antisocial peer pressure (e.g., pressure to use illicit drugs and alcohol; Mounts & Steinberg, 1995). In other words, the particular peers a youngster selects as friends and the extent to which he or she is susceptible to their influence are both affected by parenting.

A compelling illustration of indirect effects of parents comes from research on the development of antisocial behavior and aggression (DeBaryshe, Patterson, & Capaldi, 1993; Dishion et al., 1991; Patterson, DeBaryshe, & Ramsey, 1989). Researchers consistently have confirmed that adolescents' involvement in antisocial activity is influenced significantly by their relationships with antisocial peers but that the chain of events that leads some adolescents into antisocial peer groups begins at home during childhood. The links in this chain include exposure to harsh and coercive parenting, which contributes to the development of aggression and to academic difficulties in school; these problems, in late childhood, lead to the selection of antisocial peers. Even when selection effects are controlled, much of what appears to be peer influence is actually the end result of familial influence at an earlier point in the child's development.

Macrocontexts of parenting. Parents also mediate the association between broader social, cultural, economic, and historical contexts and children's behavior and personality. These broad contextual forces affect how parents behave and may accentuate or attenuate the effect of parental behavior on children's development. R. Conger (e.g., R. Conger et al., 1994) and McLoyd (1990), for example, have demonstrated that many of the deleterious effects of poverty on children's development are mediated through the effect of poverty on parenting; economic stress and disadvantage increase parental punitiveness, which in turn adversely affects the child. One implication of this for understanding the results of research on parenting is that estimates of the strength of parental influence are likely specific to particular communities in particular cultures at particular points in time. Many apparent "effects" of social class or economic disadvantage are mediated through the effect of these factors on parenting practices.

An example comes from recent research on the effects of neighborhood contexts on children's behavior and personality (Brooks-Gunn, Duncan, & Aber, 1997; Brooks-Gun, Duncan, Klebanov, & Sealand, 1993; Chase-Lansdale & Gordon, 1996). Neighborhood characteristics have been shown both to influence parents' behavior and to moderate the effect of parenting practices on the child's development (Klebanov, Brooks-Gunn, & Duncan, 1994). The effect of neighborhoods on parental practices is evident in the finding that parents adjust their management strategies to suit the demands of the neighborhood context within which they live (Furstenberg, Eccles, Elder, Cook, & Sameroff, 1997). Parents who live in dangerous neighborhoods tend to be more controlling and restrictive, which protects the child's physical well-being but which also may have the unintended consequence of squelching the child's sense of autonomy. With respect to moderating effects, Darling and Steinberg (1997) have shown that the links between parental involvement in school and children's achievement vary as a function of the behavior of other parents in the neighborhood, with parental involvement having more potent effects within neighborhoods with high concentrations of involved parents. Similarly, the beneficial effects of authoritative parenting are accentuated when adolescents affiliate with peers who themselves have authoritative parents (Fletcheer, Darling, Steinberg, & Dornbusch, 1995).

The documented relations between parental and other influences are consistent with recent criticisms (e.g., Harris, 1995, 1998) that socialization researchers have overemphasized the role of parents and underemphasized the role of nonfamilial influences, most notably, the peer group. Studies of the broader context of parental socialization, however, neither support nor refute claims about the potency of parental influence. These studies do amply illustrate that, far from a myopic focus on the influence of parents, contemporary researchers have for some time amassed evidence that socialization can be fully understood only by examining the role of parents in light of the influence of other settings in which children and families function.

Conclusions

The lines of research just described imply a concept of parenting and parental influence that is more differentiated and complex than the dominant models of earlier eras. Whereas socialization researchers often depicted parents as "molding" children to function adequately in the society (Hartup, 1989; Maccoby, 1992), contemporary evidence clearly points toward multiple roles for parents that often do not imply the deterministic effect once attributed to them. Whereas researches using behavior-genetic paradigms imply determinism by heredity and correspondingly little parental influence (e.g., Rowe, 1994), contemporary evidence confirms that the expression of heritable traits depends, often strongly, on experience, including specific parental behaviors, as well as predispositions and age-related factors in the child. Whereas both older traditions typically limited ideas about environmental effects to parents, contemporary researchers have shown the interrelated effects of parenting, nonfamilial influences, and the role of the broader context in which families live (e.g., Bronfenbrenner, 1979; Bronfenbrenner & Ceci, 1994; Brooks-Gunn et al., 1997; Darling & Steinberg, 1997; Wachs, 1999).

This new generation of evidence on the role of parenting should add to the conviction, long held by many scholars, that broad, general main effects for either heredity or environment are unlikely in research on behavior and personality. Statistical interactions and moderator effects are the rule, not the exception. Information of this kind, unfortunately, fits poorly with the desire of the popular media for facile sound bites about parenting or the yearning of some writers of introductory textbooks for general, causal statements about behavioral development. Contrary to criticisms of socialization research, the difficulty today is not that the evidence is inadequate to show parenting effects but that the evidence has revealed a reality that is far more complex than critics expected or that writers can convey in most popular media outlets. For psychologists, the challenge is to make that reality a compelling foundation for the science and practice of the future and to find ways of disseminating this knowledge to a public eager to understand the forces that shape children's development.

REFERENCES

Abelson, R. (1985). A variance explanation paradox: When a little is a lot. *Psychological Bulletin, 97*, 129–133.

Angoff, W. H. (1988). The nature-nurture debate, aptitudes, and group differences. *American Psychologist, 43*, 713–720.

Anisman, H., Zaharia, M. D., Meaney, M. J., & Merali, Z. (1998). Do early-life events permanently alter behavioral and hormonal responses to stressors? *International Journal of Developmental Neuroscience, 16*, 149–164.

Bates, J., & Bayles, K. (1988). The role of attachment in the development of behavior problems. In J. Belsky & T. Nezworski (Eds.), *Clinical implications of attachment* (pp. 253–299). Hillsdale, NJ: Erlbaum.

Bates, J., Bayles, K., Bennett, D. S., Ridge, B., & Brown, M. M. (1991). Origins of externalizing behavior problems at eight years of age. In E. J. Pepler & K. H. Rubin (Eds.), *The development and treatment of childhood aggression* (pp. 197–216). New York: Academic Press.

Bates, J., Pettit, G., & Dodge, K. (1995). Family and child factors in stability and change in children's aggressiveness in elementary school. In J. McCord (Ed.), *Coercion and punishment in long-term perspectives* (pp. 124–138). New York: Cambridge University Press.

Bates, J., Pettit, G., Dodge, K., & Ridge, B. (1998). Interaction of temperamental resistance to control and restrictive parenting in the development of externalizing behavior. *Developmental Psychology, 34*, 982–995.

Bauman, K., & Fisher, L. (1986). On the measurement of friend behavior in research on friend influence and selection: Findings from longitudinal studies of adolescent smoking and drinking. *Journal of Youth and Adolescence, 15*, 345–353.

Belsky, J., Goode, M. K., & Most, R. K. (1980). Maternal stimulation and infant exploratory competence: Cross-sectional, correlational, and experimental analyses. *Child Development, 51*, 1168–1178.

Berndt, T. J. (1999). Friends' influence on children's adjustment to school. In W. A. Collins & B. Laursen (Eds.), *Relationships as developmental contexts: The Minnesota Symposia on Child Psychology* (Vol. 30, pp. 85–108). Mahwah, NJ: Erlbaum.

Berndt, T. J., Hawkins, J. A., & Jiao, Z. (1999). Influence of friends and friendship on adjustment to junior high school. *Merrill-Palmer Quarterly, 45*, 13–41.

Bohman, M. (1996). Predispositions to criminality: Swedish adoption studies in retrospect. In G. R. Bock & J. A. Goode (Eds.), *Genetics of criminal and antisocial behavior, Ciba Foundation Symposium 194* (pp. 99–114). Chichester, England: Wiley.

Bornstein, M. H. (1989). Sensitive periods in development: Structural characteristics and causal interpretations. *Psychological Bulletin, 105*, 179–197.

Bornstein, M. H. (1995a). Form and function: Implications for studies of culture and human development. *Culture and Psychology, 1*, 123–137.

Bornstein, M. H. (Ed.). (1995b). *Handbook of parenting.* Mahwah, NJ: Erlbaum.

Brody, G., & Stoneman, Z. (1994). Sibling relations and their association with parental differential treatment. In E. M. Hetherington, D. Reiss, & R. Plomin (Eds.), *Separate social worlds of siblings: The impact of nonshared environment on development* (pp. 129–142). Hillsdale, NJ: Erlbaum.

Bronfenbrenner, U. (1979). *The ecology of human development.* Cambridge, MA: Harvard University Press.

Bronfenbrenner, U., & Ceci, S. J. (1994). Nature-nurture reconceptualized in developmental perspective: A bioecological model. *Psychological Review, 101*, 568–586.

Bronfenbrenner, U., & Morris, P. A. (1998). The ecology of developmental processes. In W. Damon & R. M. Lerner (Eds.), *Handbook of child psychology: Theoretical models of human development* (5th ed., Vol. 1, pp. 993–1028). New York: Wiley.

Brooks-Gunn, J., Duncan, G., & Aber, L. (Eds.). (1997). *Neighborhood poverty: Context and consequences for children.* New York: Russell Sage Foundation.

Brooks-Gunn, J., Duncan, G., Klebanov, P., & Sealand, N. (1993). Do neighborhoods influence child and adolescent development? *American Journal of Sociology, 99*, 353–395.

Brown, B. (1990). Peer groups. In S. Feldman & G. Elliott (Eds.), *At the threshold: The developing adolescent* (pp. 171–196). Cambridge, MA: Harvard University Press.

Brown, B., Mounts, N., Lamborn, S., & Steinberg, L. (1993). Parenting practices and peer group affiliation in adolescence. *Child Development, 64*, 467–482.

Cadoret, R. (1985). Genes, environment and their interaction in the development of psychopathology. In T. Sakai & T. Tsuboi (Eds.), *Genetic aspects of human development* (pp. 165–175). Tokyo: Igaku-Shoin.

Cairns, R., & Cairns, B. (1994). *Lifelines and risks: Pathways of youth in our time.* New York: Cambridge University Press.

Cairns, R., Cairns, B., Neckerman, H., Gest, S., & Gariepy, J. L. (1988). Social networks and aggressive behavior: Peer support or peer rejection? *Developmental Psychology, 24*, 815–823.

Caldjii, C., Tannenbaum, B., Sharma, S., Francis, D., Plotsky, P. M., & Meaney, M. J. (1998). Maternal care during infancy regulates the development of neural systems mediating the expression of fearfulness in the rat. *Proceedings of the National Academy of Science, 95*, 5335–5340.

Caspi, A., & Elder, G. (1988). Emergent family patterns: The intergenerational construction of problem behavior and relationships. *International Journal of Behavioral Development, 5,* 81–94.

Caspi, A., Henry, B., McGee, R. O., Moffitt, T. E., & Silva, P. A. (1995). Temperamental origins of child and adolescent behavior problems: From age 3 to age 15. *Child Development, 66,* 55–68.

Caspi, A., & Silva, P. (1995). Temperamental qualities at age 3 predict personality traits in young adulthood: Longitudinal evidence from a birth cohort. *Child Development, 66,* 486–498.

Chase-Lansdale, P. L., Cherlin, A., & Kiernan, K. (1995). The long-term effects of parental divorce on the mental health of young adults: A developmental perspective. *Child Development, 66,* 1614–1634.

Chase-Lansdale, P. L., & Gordon, R. A. (1996). Economic hardship and the development of five- and six-year-olds: Neighborhood and regional perspectives. *Child Development, 67,* 3338–3367.

Chisholm, K. (1998). A three-year follow-up of attachment and indiscriminate friendliness in children adopted from Romanian orphanages. *Child Development, 69,* 1092–1106.

Chisholm, K., Carter, M., Ames, E. W., & Morison, S. J. (1995). Attachment security and indiscriminately friendly behavior in children adopted from Romanian orphanages. *Development and Psychopathology, 7,* 283–294.

Cohen, J. (1988). *Statistical power analysis for the behavioral sciences* (2nd ed.). Hillsdale, NJ: Erlbaum.

Conger, J. (1971). A world they never knew: The family and social change. *Daedalus, 100,* 1105–1138.

Conger, R., & Elder, G. E. (1994). *Families in troubled times: Adapting to change in rural America.* New York: Aldine.

Conger, R., Ge, X., Elder, G. H., Lorenz, F., & Simons, R. (1994). Economic stress, coercive family process and developmental problems of adolescents. *Child Development, 65,* 541–561.

Cowan, P. A., & Cowan, C. P. (in press). What an intervention design reveals about how parents affect their children's academic achievement and social competence. In J. Borkowski, S. Landesman-Ramey, & M. Bristol (Eds.), *Parenting and the child's world: Multiple influences on intellectual and social-emotional development.* Hillsdale, NJ: Erlbaum.

Cowan, P. A., Powell, D., & Cowan, C. P. (1998). Parenting interventions: A family systems perspective. In W. Damon, I. Sigel, & K. A. Renninger (Eds.), *Handbook of child psychology: Child psychology in practice* (Vol. 4, pp. 3–72). New York: Wiley.

Darling, N., & Steinberg, L. (1997). Community influences on adolescent achievement and deviance. In J. Brooks-Gunn, G. Duncan, & L. Aber (Eds.), *Neighborhood poverty: context and consequences for children: Conceptual, methodological, and policy approaches to studying neighborhoods* (Vol. 2, pp. 120–131). New York: Russell Sage Foundation.

DeBaryshe, B., Patterson, G., & Capaldi, D. (1993). A performance model for academic achievement in early adolescent boys.] *Developmental Psychology, 29,* 795–804.

Devereux, E. C. (1970). The role of peer group experience in moral development. In J. P. Hill (Ed.), *Minnesota Symposia on Child Psychology* (Vol. 4, pp. 94–140). Minneapolis: University of Minnesota Press.

Dishion, T., Patterson, G., Stoolmiller, M., & Skinner, M. (1991). Family, school, and behavioral antecedents to early adolescent involvement with antisocial peers. *Developmental Psychology, 27,* 172–180.

Downey, G., & Walker, E. (1992). Distinguishing family-level and child-level influences on the development of depression and aggression. *Development and Psychopathology 4,* 81–96.

Dunn, J., & Plomin, R. (1986). Determinants of maternal behavior toward three-year-old siblings. *British Journal of Developmental Psychology, 57,* 348–356.

Eisenberg, N., & Damon, W. (Eds.), (1998). *Handbook of child psychology: Social, emotional, and personality development* (Vol. 3). New York: Wiley.

Emde, R., Plomin, R., Robinson, J., Corley, R., DeFries, J., Fulker, D., Reznick, J. S., Campos, J., Kagan, J., & Zahn-Waxler, C. (1992). Temperament, emotion, and cognition at fourteen months: The MacArthur longitudinal twin study. *Child Development, 63,* 1437–1455.

Epstein, J. L. (1983). The influence of friends on achievement and affective outcomes. In J. L. Epstein & N. Karweit (Eds.), *Friends in school* (pp. 177–200). New York: Academic Press.

Fletcher, A., Darling, N., Steinberg, L., & Dornbusch, S. (1995). The company they keep: Relation of adolescents' adjustment and behavior to their friends' perceptions of authoritative parenting in the social network. *Developmental Psychology, 31,* 300–310.

Forehand, R., & King, H. E. (1977). Noncompliant children: Effects of parent training on behavior and attitude change. *Behavior Modification, 1,* 93–108.

Forehand, R., Wells, K. C., & Griest, D. L. (1980). An examination of the social validity of a parent training program. *Behavior Therapy, 11,* 488–502.

Forgatch, M. S. (1991). The clinical science vortex: A developing theory of antisocial behavior. In D. Pepler & K. Rubin (Eds.), *The development and treatment of childhood aggression* (pp. 291–315). Hillsdale, NJ: Erlbaum.

Forgatch, M. S., & DeGarmo, D. S. (1999). Parenting through change: An effective prevention program for single mothers. *Journal of Consulting and Clinical Psychology, 67,* 711–724.

Fuligni, A., & Eccles, J. (1993). Perceived parent-child relationships and early adolescents' orientation toward peers. *Developmental Psychology, 29,* 622–632.

Furstenberg, F., Jr., Eccles, J., Elder, G., Jr., Cook, T., & Smaeroff, A. (1997). *Managing to make it.* Chicago: University of Chicago Press.

Gatz, M., Pedersen, N. L., Plomin, R., Nesselrade, J. R., & McLearn, G. E. (1992). Importance of shared genes and shared environments for symptoms of depression in older adults. *Journal of Abnormal Psychology, 101,* 701–708.

Ge, X., Conger, R., Cadoret, R., Neiderhiser, J., Yates, W., Troughton, E., & Stewart, M. (1996). The developmental interface between nature and nurture: A mutual influence model of child antisocial behavior and parent behavior. *Developmental Psychology, 32,* 547–598.

Ge, X., Conger, R., Lorenz, F., Shanahan, M., & Elder, G. (1995). Mutual influences in parent and adolescent psychological distress. *Developmental Psychology, 31,* 406–419.

Ge, X., Lorenz, F., Conger, R., Elder, G., & Simons, R. (1994). Trajectories of stressful life events and depressive symptoms during adolescence. *Developmental Psychology, 30,* 467–483.

Gesell, A., & Thompson, H. (1934). *Infant behavior: Its genesis and growth.* New York: McGraw-Hill.

Ghodsion-Carpey, J., & Baker, L. A. (1997). Genetic and environmental influences on aggression in 4- to 7-year-old twins. *Aggressive Behavior, 13,* 173–186.

Goldsmith, H., & Alansky, J. (1987). Maternal and infant temperamental predictors of attachment: A meta-analytic review. *Journal of Consulting and Clinical Psychology, 55,* 805–816.

Goodman, R. (1991). Growing together and growing apart: The non-genetic forces on children in the same family. In R. McGuffin & R. Murry (Eds.), *The new genetics of mental illness* (pp. 212–224). Oxford, England: Oxford University Press.

Greenough, W., & Black, J. (1992). Induction of brain structure by experience: Substrates for cognitive development. In M. R. Gunnar & C. A. Nelson (Eds.), *Developmental neuroscience: Minnesota Symposia on Child Psychology* (Vol. 24, pp. 155–200). Hillsdale, NJ: Erlbaum.

Grossmann, K., Grossman, K., Spangler, G., Suess, G., & Unzner, L. (1985). Maternal sensitivity and newborns' orientation responses as related to quality of attachment in Northern Germany. *Monographs of the Society for Research in Child Development, 50*(1–2, Serial No. 209), 233–256.

Gunnar, M. (in press). Early adversity and the development of stress reactivity and regulation. In C. A. Nelson (Ed.), *The effects of adversity on neurobehavioral development: Minnesota Symposia on Child Psychology* (Vol. 31). Mahwah, NJ: Erlbaum.

Hagekull, B. (1989). Longitudinal stability of temperament within a behavioral style framework. In G. A. Kohnstamm, J. E. Bates, & M. K. Rothbart (Eds.), *Temperament in childhood* (pp. 283–297). Chichester, England: Wiley.

Hagekull, B. (1994). Infant temperament and early childhood functioning: Possible relations to the five-factor models. In C. J. Halverson, Jr., G. A. Kohnstamm, & R. P. Martin (Eds.), *The developing structure of temperament and personality* (pp. 227–240). Hillsdale, NJ: Erlbaum.

Hardy-Brown, K. (1983). Universals in individual differences: Disentangling two approaches to the study of language acquisition. *Developmental Psychology, 19*, 610–624.

Hardy-Brown, K., & Plomin, R. (1985). Infant communicative development: Evidence from adoptive and biological families for genetic and environmental influences on rate differences. *Developmental Psychology, 21*, 378–385.

Hardy-Brown, K., Plomin, R., & DeFries, J. C. (1981). Genetic and environmental influences on rate of communicative development in the first year of life. *Developmental Psychology, 17*, 704–717.

Harris, J. R. (1995). Where is the child's environment? A group socialization theory of development. *Psychological Review, 102*, 458–489.

Harris, J. R. (1998). *The nurture assumption: Why children turn out the way they do.* New York: Free Press.

Hartup, W. W. (1989). Social relationships and their developmental significance. *American Psychologist, 44*, 120–126.

Hetherington, E. M. (1989). Coping with family transitions: Winners, losers, and survivors. *Child Development, 60*, 1–14.

Hetherington, E. M. (1991). The role of individual differences in family relations in coping with divorce and remarriage. In P. Cowan & E. M. Hetherington (Eds.), *Advances in family research: Family transitions* (Vol. 2, pp. 165–194). Hillsdale, NJ: Erlbaum.

Hetherington, E. M. (1993). A review of the Virginia Longitudinal Study of Divorce and Remarriage: A focus on early adolescence. *Journal of Family Psychology, 7*, 39–56.

Hoffman, L. W. (1991). The influence of the family environment on personality: Accounting for sibling differences. *Psychological Bulletin, 110*, 187–203.

Hogue, A., & Steinberg, L. (1995). Homophily of internalized distress in adolescent peer groups. *Developmental Psychology, 31*, 897–906.

Holden, G. W., & Miller, P. C. (1999). Enduring and different: A meta-analysis of the similarity in parents' child rearing. *Psychological Bulletin, 125*, 223–254.

Huttenlocher, P. R. (1994). Synaptogenesis, synapse elimination, and neural plasticity in human cerebral cortex. In C. A. Nelson (Eds.), *Minnesota Symposia on Child Psychology: Threats to optimal development: Integrating biological, psychological, and social risk factors* (Vol. 27, pp. 35–54). Hillsdale, NJ: Erlbaum.

Kandel, D. (1978). Homophily, selection, and socialization in adolescent friendships. *American Journal of Sociology, 84*, 427–436.

Kim, J. E., Hetherington, E. M., & Reiss, D. (1999). Associations between family relationships, antisocial peers and adolescent's externalizing behaviors: Gender and family type differences. *Child Development, 70*, 1209–1230.

Klebanov, P. K., Brooks-Gunn, J., & Duncan, G. T. (1994). Does neighborhood and family poverty affect mothers' parenting, mental health and social support? *Journal of Marriage and the Family, 56*, 441–455.

Kochanska, G. (1995). Children's temperament, mothers' discipline, and the security of attachment: Multiple pathways to emerging internalization. *Child Development, 66*, 597–615.

Kochanska, G. (1997). Multiple pathways to conscience for children with different temperaments: From toddlerhood to age 5. *Developmental Psychology, 33*, 228–240.

Kuczynski, L. (1984). Socialization goals and mother-child interaction: Strategies for long-term and short-term compliance. *Developmental Psychology, 20*, 1061–1073.

Lee, C. L., & Bates, J. (1985). Mother-child interaction at age two years and perceived difficult temperament. *Child Development, 56*, 1314–1325.

Lewis, M. (1997). *Altering fate: Why the past does not predict the future,* New York: Guilford Press.

Liu, D., Diorio, J., Tannenbaum, B., Caldji, C., Francis, D., Freedman, M. A., Sharma, S., Pearson, P., Plotsky, P. M., & Meaney, M. J. (1997, September 12). Maternal care, hippocampal glucocorticoid receptors and hypothalamic-pituitary-adrenal responses to stress. *Science, 277*, 1659–1662.

Maccoby, E. E. (1992). The role of parents in the socialization of children: An historical overview. *Developmental Psychology, 28*, 1006–1017.

McCall, R. (1991). So many interactions, so little evidence: Why? In T. Wachs & R. Plomin (Eds.), *Conceptualization and measurement of organism-environment interactions* (pp. 142–161). Washington, DC: American Psychological Association.

McCartney, K., Harris, M., & Bernieri, F. (1990). Growing up and growing apart: A developmental meta-analysis of twin studies. *Psychological Bulletin, 107*, 226–237.

McClelland, G., & Judd, C. (1993). Statistical difficulties of detecting interactions and moderator effects. *Psychological Bulletin, 114*, 376–390.

McGue, M. (1994). Genes, environment, and the etiology of alcoholism. In R. Zucker, G. Boyd, & J. Howard (Eds.), *The development of alcohol problems: Exploring the biopsychosocial matrix of risk* (National Institute of Alcohol Abuse and Alcoholism Research Monograph No. 26, pp. 1–40). Rockville, MD: U. S. Department of Health and human Services.

McLoyd, V. (1990). The impact of economic hardship on Black families and children: Psychological distress, parenting, and socioemotional development. *Child Development, 61*, 311–346.

McMahon, R. J., & Wells, K. C. (1998). Conduct problems. In E. J. Mash & R. A. Barkley (Eds.), *Treatment of childhood disorders* (2nd ed., pp. 111–151). New York: Guilford Press.

Miles, D., & Carey, G. (1997). Genetic and environmental architecture of human aggression. *Journal of Personality and Social Psychology, 72*, 207–217.

Miyake, K., Chen, S. J., & Campos, J. (1985). Infant temperament, mother's mode of interaction and attachment in Japan: An interim report. *Monographs of the Society for Research in Child Development, 50* (1–2, Serial No. 209), 276–297.

Mounts, N., & Steinberg, L. (1995). An ecological analysis of peer influence on adolescent grade point average and drug use. *Developmental Psychology, 31*, 915–922.

Nelson, C. A. (in press). The neurobiological bases of early intervention. In S. J. Meisels & J. P. Shonkoff (Eds.), *Handbook of early childhood intervention* (2nd ed.). New York: Cambridge University Press.

O'Connor, T. G., Deater-Deckard, K., Fulker, D., Rutter, M. L., & Plomin, R. (1998). Genotype-environment correlations in late childhood and early adolescence: Antisocial behavioral problems and coercive parenting. *Developmental Psychology, 34*, 970–981.

Parke, R., & Bhavnagri, N. P. (1989). Parents as managers of children's peer relationships. In D. Belle (Ed.), *Children's social networks and social support* (pp. 241–259). New York: Wiley.

Patterson, G. R. (1975). Multiple evaluations of a parent-training program. In T. Thompson & W. S. Dockens (Eds.), *Applications of behavior modification* (pp. 299–322). New York: Academic Press.

Patterson, G. R. (1999). *Recent news concerning the demise of parenting may be a bit premature.* Unpublished manuscript, Oregon Social Learning Center, Eugene, OR.

Patterson, G. R., DeBaryshe, B. D., & Ramsey, E. (1989). A developmental perspective on antisocial behavior. *American Psychologist, 44*, 329–335.

Plomin, R. (1990). *Nature and nurture: An introduction to human behavioral genetics.* Pacific Grove, CA: Brooks/Cole.

Plomin, R., & Daniels, D. (1987). Why are children in the same family so different from each other? *Behavioral and Brain Science, 10*, 1–16.

Plomin, R., DeFries, J., & Fulker, D. (1988). *Nature and nurture during infancy and early childhood.* New York: Cambridge University Press.

Plomin, R., & Rutter, M. (1998). Child development, molecular genetics, and what to do with genes once they are found. *Child Development, 69*, 1223–1242.

Quinton, D., Pickles, A., Maughan, B., & Rutter, M. (1993). Partners, peers, and pathways: Assortative pairing and continuities in conduct disorder. *Development and Psychopathology, 5*, 763–783.

Reiss, D., Niederhiser, J., Hetherington, E. M., & Plomin, R. (in press). *The relationship code: Deciphering genetic and social patterns in adolescent development.* Cambridge, MA: Harvard University Press.

Riksen-Walraven, J. (1978). Effects of caregiver behavior on habituation rate and self-efficacy in infants. *International Journal of Behavioral Development, 1*, 105–130.

Rose, R. (1995). Genes and human behavior. *Annual Review of Psychology, 46*, 625–654.

Rothbart, M., & Ahadi, S. (1994). Temperament and the development of personality. *Journal of Abnormal Psychology, 103*, 55–66.

Rothbart, M., & Bates, J. (1998). Temperament. In W. Damon & N. Eisenberg (Eds.), *Handbook of child psychology: Social, emotional, and personality development* (Vol. 3, pp. 105–176). New York: Wiley.

Rowe, D. (1983). A biometrical analysis of perceptions of family environment: A study of twin and singleton sibling kinship. *Child Development, 54*, 416–423.

Rowe, D. (1994). *The limits of family influence: Genes, experience, and behavior.* New York: Guilford Press.

Rowe, D., Chassin, L., Presson, C., Edwards, D., & Sherman, S. J. (1992). An "epidemic" model of adolescent cigarette smoking. *Journal of Applied Social Psychology, 22*, 261–285.

Rutter, M. (1990). Psychosocial resilience and protective mechanisms. In J. Rolf, A. S. Masten, D. Cicchetti, K. H. Nuechterlein, & S. Weintraub (Eds.), *Risk and protective factors in the development of psychopathology* (pp. 181–214). New York: Cambridge University Press.

Rutter, M., Dunn, J., Plomin, R., Simonoff, E., Pickles, A., Maughan, B., Ormel, H., Meyer, J., & Eaves, L. (1997). Integrating nature and nurture: Implications of person-environment correlations and interactions for developmental psychopathology. *Development and Psychopathology, 9*, 335–364.

Rutter, M., & the English and Romanian Adoptees (ERA) study team. (1998). Developmental catch-up, and deficit, following adoption after severe global early privation. *Journal of Child Psychology and Psychiatry and Allied Disciplines, 39*, 465–476.

Rutter, M., & Quinton, D. (1984). Parental psychiatric disorder: Effects on children. *Psychological Medicine, 14*, 853–880.

Scarr, S., & Weinberg, R. A. (1976). IQ test performance of Black children adopted by White families. *American Psychologist, 31*, 726–739.

Scarr, S., & Weinberg, R. A. (1978). The influence of "family background" on intellectual attainment. *American Sociological Review, 43*, 674–692.

Schiff, M., Duyme, M., Dumaret, A., & Tomkiewitz, S. (1982). How much could we boost scholastic achievement and IQ scores? A direct answer from a French adoption study. *Cognition, 12*, 165–196.

Skodak, M., & Skeels, H. (1949). A final follow-up of one hundred adopted children. *Journal of Genetic Psychology, 75*, 85–125.

Steinberg, L., Lamborn, S., Darling, N., Mounts, N., & Dornbusch, S. (1994). Over-time changes in adjustment and competence among adolescents from authoritative, authoritarian, indulgent, and neglectful families. *Child Development, 65*, 754–770.

Stern, D. N. (1985). *The interpersonal world of the infant.* New York: Basic Books.

Stoolmiller, M. (1999). Implications of the restricted range of family environments for estimates of heritability and nonshared environment in behavior-genetic adoption studies. *Psychological Bulletin, 125*, 392–409.

Suomi, S. J. (1997). Long-term effects of different early rearing experiences on social, emotional and physiological development in nonhuman primates. In M. S. Kesheven & R. M. Murra (Eds.), *Neurodevelopmental models of adult psychopathology* (pp. 104–116). Cambridge, England: Cambridge University Press.

Suomi, S. J. (in press). A biobehavioral perspective on developmental psychopathology: Excessive aggression and serotonergic dysfunction in monkeys. In A. J. Sameroff, M. Lewis, & S. Miller (Eds.), *Handbook of developmental psychopathology.* New York: Plenum.

Tejerina-Allen, M., Wagner, B. M., & Cohen, P. (1994). A comparison of across-family and within-family parenting predictors of adolescent psychopathology and suicidal ideation. In E. M. Hetherington, D. Reiss, & R. Plomin (Eds.), *Separate social worlds of siblings: The impact of nonshared environment on development* (pp. 143–158). Hillsdale, NJ: Erlbaum.

Tienari, P., Wynne, L. C., Moring, J., Lahti, I., Naarala, M., Sorri, A., Wahlberg, K. E., Saarento, O., Seitma, M., Kaleva, M., & Lasky, K. (1994). The Finnish adoptive family study of schizophrenia: Implications for family research. *British Journal of Psychiatry, 23*(Suppl. 164), 20–26.

Turkheimer, E., & Waldron, M. C. (in press). Nonshared environment: A theoretical, methodological, and quantitative review. *Psychological Bulletin.*

Van den Boom, D. C. (1989). Neonatal irritability and the development of attachment. In G. A. Kohnstamm, J. E. Bates, & M. K. Rothbart (Eds.), *Temperament in childhood* (pp. 299–318). Chichester, England: Wiley.

Van den Boom, D. C. (1994). The influence of temperament and mothering on attachment and exploration: An experimental manipulation of sensitive responsiveness among lower-class mothers with irritable infants. *Child Development, 65*, 1457–1477.

Wachs, T. D. (1992). *The nature of nurture.* Newbury Park, CA: Sage.

Wachs, T. D. (1999). Celebrating complexity: Conceptualization and assessment of the environment. In S. Friedman & T. D. Wachs (Eds.), *Measuring environment across the life span: Emerging methods and concepts* (pp. 357–392). Washington, DC: American Psychological Association.

Wachs, T. D., & Plomin, R. (1991). *Conceptualization and measurement of organism–environment interaction.* Washington, DC: American Psychological Association.

Wahlsten, D. (1990). Insensitivity of the analysis of variance to heredity-environment interaction. *Behavior and Brain Science, 13,* 109–161.

Weinberg, R. A. (1989). Intelligence and IQ: Landmark issues and great debates. *American Psychologist, 44,* 98–104.

Werner, E. (1990). Protective factors and individual resilience. In S. Meisels & J. Shonkoff (Eds.), *Handbook of early childhood intervention* (pp. 97–116). Cambridge, MA: Harvard University Press.

Werner, E., & Smith, R. (1992). *Overcoming the odds: High risk children from birth to adulthood.* Ithaca, NY: Cornell University Press.

Zill, N., Morrison, D., & Coiro, M. (1993). Long-term effects of parental divorce on parent-child relationships, adjustment, and achievement in young adulthood. *Journal of Family Psychology, 7,* 91–103.

Editor's note. Jerome Kagan served as action editor for this article.

Authors' note. W. Andrew Collins, Institute of Child Development, University of Minnesota; Eleanor E. Maccoby, Department of Psychology, Stanford University; Laurence Steinberg, Department of Psychology, Temple University; E. Mavis Hetherington, Department of Psychology, University of Virginia; Marc H. Bornstein, Child and Family Research, National Institute of Child Health and Human Development.

Preparation of this article was supported in part by the Rodney S. Wallace Professorship for the Advancement of Teaching and Learning, College of Education and Human Development, University of Minnesota. We thank the following for helpful comments on the manuscript: Marion S. Forgatch, Ben Greenberg, Megan R. Gunnar, Willard W. Hartup, Jerome Kagan, Gerald Patterson, Stephen Suomi, Deborah Vandell, Theodore Wachs, and Richard A. Weinberg.

Correspondence concerning this article should be addressed to W. Andrew Collins, Institute of Child Development, University of Minnesota, 51 East River Road, Minneapolis, MN 55455–0345. Electronic mail may be sent to wcollins@tc.umn.edu.

What Matters? What Does Not?

Five Perspectives on the Association Between Marital Transitions and Children's Adjustment

E. Mavis Hetherington, Margaret Bridges, and Glendessa M. Insabella
University of Virginia

This article presents an analysis of 5 views of factors that contribute to the adjustment of children in divorced families or stepfamilies. These perspectives are those that emphasize (a) individual vulnerability and risk; (b) family composition; (c) stress, including socioeconomic disadvantage; (d) parental distress; and (e) disrupted family process. It is concluded that all of these factors contribute to children's adjustment in divorced and remarried families and that a transactional model examining multiple trajectories of interacting risk and protective factors is the most fruitful in predicting the well-being of children.

In the past 30 years, there has been a significant decline in the proportion of two-parent families in first marriages and a complementary increase in the number of single-parent households and stepfamilies. These changes are the result of a rapid rise in the divorce rate that began during the 1960s (Simons, 1996) and also, to a lesser extent, of an increase in births to single mothers. Although there has been a modest decrease in the divorce rate since the late 1970s, almost one half of marriages end in divorce in the United States, and one million children experience their parents' divorce each year (U.S. Bureau of the Census, 1992). It is projected that between 50% and 60% of children born in the 1990s will live, at some point, in single-parent families, typically headed by mothers (Bumpass & Sweet, 1989; Furstenberg & Cherlin, 1991). Currently, stepfamilies make up approximately 17% of all two-parent families with children under 18 years of age (Glick, 1989).

Although the high divorce rate has been interpreted as a rejection of the institution of marriage, 75% of men and 66% of women eventually will remarry, suggesting that although people are rejecting specific marital partners, most are not rejecting marriage itself (Booth & Edwards, 1992; Bumpass, Sweet, & Castro-Martin, 1990; Cherlin & Furstenberg, 1994; Ganong & Coleman, 1994). Since the 1960s, however, the annual rate of remarriage has actually declined as the divorce rate has increased. Moreover, divorces are more frequent in remarriages and occur at a rate 10% higher than that in first marriages (Bumpass et al., 1990; Cherlin & Furstenberg, 1994). Couples with remarried wives are almost twice as likely to divorce as are couples with remarried husbands. This association may be attributable to the 50% higher rate of dissolution in remarriages in which children from previous marriages are present (Tzeng & Mare, 1995), although the presence of children appears to be less relevant to the marital quality of African American couples (Orbuch, Veroff, & Hunter, in press). As a result of their parents' successive marital transitions, about half of all children whose parents divorce will have a stepfather within four years of parental separation, and 1 out of every 10 children will experience at least two divorces of their residential parent before turning 16 years of age (Furstenberg, 1988). These numbers underestimate the actual number of household reorganizations to which children are exposed because many couples cohabit before remarriage or cohabit as an alternative to remarriage (Bumpass & Raley, 1995; Bumpass, Sweet, & Cherlin, 1991; Cherlin & Furstenberg, 1994; Ganong & Coleman, 1994).

The national figures for marital transitions and family structure mask very different patterns among racial and ethnic groups because the social context of marriage varies across communities (Orbuch et al., in press). African American children are twice as likely as White children to experience at least one parental divorce (National Center for Health Statistics, 1988) and also are more likely to bear children out of wedlock in adolescence and adulthood (Demo & Acock, 1996; Tzeng & Mare, 1995; U.S. Bureau of the Census, 1992). In addition, African Americans and Hispanic Whites are less likely to divorce after separation and to remarry than are non-Hispanic Whites (Castro-Martin & Bumpass, 1989; Cherlin, 1992). Thus, in comparison with White children, more African American children spend longer periods of time in single-parent households, which often include kin and cohabiting partners.

As marriage has become a more optional, less permanent institution in contemporary American society, children in all ethnic groups are encountering stresses and adaptive challenges associated with their parents' marital transitions. Children from divorced and remarried families, in contrast to those from never-divorced families, exhibit more problem behaviors and lower psychological well-being. Little agreement exists, however, about the extent, severity, and duration of these problems because there is great diversity in children's responses to parental marital transitions (Amato & Keith, 1991a; Emery & Forehand, 1994; Hetherington, 1991b; McLanahan & Sandefur, 1994). Furthermore, although it is clear that marital dissension and dissolution, life in single-parent households, and remarriage present families and children with new experiences, risks, and resources, there is some disagreement on how these factors undermine or enhance the well-being of children.

Theoretical Perspectives on Marital Transitions and the Adjustment of Children

Five main theoretical perspectives have been proposed to explain the links between divorce and remarriage and children's adjustment. These perspectives are those emphasizing (a) individual risk and vulnerability; (b) family composition; (c) stress, including socioeconomic disadvantage; (d) parental distress; and (e) family process.

Individual Risk and Vulnerability

It has been proposed that some characteristics of parents and children may influence their exposure and vulnerability to adversity. Some adults possess characteristics (e.g., antisocial behavior) that place them at increased risk for marital discord, multiple marital transitions, and other adverse life experiences (Capaldi & Patterson, 1991; Kitson & Morgan, 1990; Patterson & Dishion, 1988; Simons, Johnson, & Lorenz, 1996). Adults with psychological problems such as depression or antisocial behavior often select partners who also experience psychological difficulties (Merikangas, Prusoff, & Weissman, 1988), thereby increasing their risk for marital problems and dissolution. This is called the marital selectivity hypothesis.

In addition, some children have attributes that increase their vulnerability or protect them from deleterious consequences of stresses associated with their parents' marital transitions (Amato & Keith, 1991a; Emery & Forehand, 1994; Hetherington, 1989, 1991b).

Family Composition

It is commonly assumed that two biological parents provide the optimal family environment for healthy child development and that any deviation from this family structure, such as single-parent families or stepfamilies, is problematic for children (Amato & Keith, 1991a; Kitson & Holmes, 1992; Simons, 1996). Much of the early theorizing about divorce and family structure focused on father absence.

Stress and Socioeconomic Disadvantage

This perspective emphasizes that marital transitions trigger a series of negative social and economic changes, stresses, and practical problems that can interfere with the well-being of parents and children. For custodial mothers and their children, divorce is related to a notable economic decline that is associated with living conditions that make raising children more difficult (McLanahan & Sandefur, 1994), whereas remarriage is associated with an increase in household income for single mothers. Although much of the research on stress has focused on economic stresses, both divorced and remarried families encounter other stresses related to changing family roles and relationships (Cherlin & Furstenberg, 1994; Hetherington & Stanley Hagen, 1995; Simons, 1996).

Parental Distress

This perspective suggests that stressful life experiences, including economic decline and adaptive challenges associated with divorce and remarriage, lead to parental strain, distress, and diminished well-being, which are reflected in psychological problems such as depression, anxiety, irritability, and antisocial behaviors, as well as stress-related health problems (Capaldi & Patterson, 1991; Forgatch, Patterson, & Ray, 1995; Hetherington, 1989, 1991b; Kiecolt-Glaser et al., 1987; Lorenz, Simons, & Chao, 1996; Simons & Johnson, 1996). There is great individual variability in response to negative life changes; some parents cope with such changes with apparent equanimity, whereas others exhibit marked affective disruption and distress.

Family Process

Finally, many researchers have emphasized that differences between nondivorced families and divorced and remarried families on process variables such as conflict, control, expression of positive and negative affect, and problem solving largely explain the effects of divorce and remarriage. It is argued that more proximal variables, such as discipline and child-rearing practices, are most important in affecting children's adjustment.

Although these perspectives often are presented as competing with each other, empirical support can be found for each, suggesting that they may best be considered as complementary hypotheses (Amato & Keith, 1991a; Simons, 1996). In this article, research on the five perspectives is reviewed, and the direct and indirect effects of the five factors on the adjustment of children and parents in divorced and remarried families are examined. Finally, a transactional model of marital transitions involving relationships among the factors is presented.

Adjustment of Children in Divorced and Remarried Families

There is general agreement among researchers that children, adolescents, and adults from divorced and remarried families, in comparison with those from two-parent, nondivorced families, are at increased risk for developing problems in adjustment (for meta-analyses, see Amato & Keith, 1991a, 1991b) and that those who have undergone multiple divorces are at a greater risk (Capaldi & Patterson, 1991; Kurdek, Fine, & Sinclair, 1995). For the most part, the adjustment of children from divorced and remarried families is similar (Amato & Keith, 1991a; Cherlin & Furstenberg, 1994). Children from divorced and remarried families are more likely than children from nondivorced families to have academic problems, to exhibit externalizing behaviors and internalizing disorders, to be less socially responsible and competent, and to have lower self-esteem (Amato & Keith, 1991a; Cherlin & Furstenberg, 1994; Hetherington, 1989). They have problems in their relationships with parents, siblings, and peers (Amato & Keith, 1991b; Hetherington, 1997).

Normative developmental tasks of adolescence and young adulthood, such as attaining intimate relationships and increasing social and economic autonomy, seem to be especially difficult for youths from divorced and remarried families. Adolescents from divorced and remarried families exhibit some of the same behavior problems found in childhood and, in addition, are more likely to drop out of school, to be unemployed, to become sexually active at an earlier age, to have children out of wedlock, to be involved in delinquent activities and substance abuse, and to associate with antisocial peers (Amato & Keith, 1991a; Conger & Chao, 1996; Demo & Acock, 1996; Elder & Russell, 1996; Hetherington & Clingempeel, 1992; McLanahan & Sandefur, 1994; Simons & Chao, 1996; Whitbeck, Simons, & Goldberg, 1996). Increased rates of dropping out of high school and of low socioeconomic attainment in the offspring of divorced and remarried families extend across diverse ethnic groups (Amato

& Keith, 1991b); however, the effect is stronger for females than for males (Hetherington, in press).

Adult offspring from divorced and remarried families continue to have more adjustment problems (Chase-Lansdale, Cherlin, & Kiernan, 1995; Hetherington, in press), are less satisfied with their lives, experience lower socioeconomic attainment, and are more likely to be on welfare (Amato & Keith, 1991b). Marital instability also is higher for adults from divorced and remarried families (Amato & Keith, 1991b; Glenn & Kramer, 1985; Hetherington, in press; McLanahan & Bumpass, 1988; Tzeng & Mare, 1995), in part because of the presence of a set of risk factors for divorce, including early sexual activity, adolescent childbearing and marriage, and cohabitation (Booth & Edwards, 1990; Hetherington, 1997). In addition, in comparison with young adults from nondivorced families, young adults from divorced and remarried families exhibit more reciprocated, escalating, negative exchanges, including denial, belligerence, criticism, and contempt, and less effective problem solving during their marital interactions (Hetherington, in press). This pattern is probably related to the intergenerational transmission of divorce, which is reported to be 70% higher in the first five years of marriage from adult women from divorced families than for those whose parents have remained married (Bumpass, Martin, & Sweet, 1991).

Although there is considerable consensus that, on average, offspring from divorced and remarried families exhibit more problems in adjustment than do those in nondivorced, two-parent families, there is less agreement on the size of these effects. Some researchers report that these effects are relatively modest, have become smaller as marital transitions have become more common (Amato & Keith, 1991a), and are considerably reduced when the adjustment of children preceding the marital transition is controlled (Block, Block, & Gjerde, 1986, 1988; Cherlin et al., 1991). However, others note that approximately 20%–25% of children in divorced and remarried families, in contrast to 10% of children in nondivorced families, have these problems, which is a notable twofold increase (Hetherington, 1989, 1991b; Hetherington & Clingempeel, 1992; Hetherington & Jodl, 1994; McLanahan & Sandefur, 1994; Simons & Associates, 1996; Zill, Morrison, & Coiro, 1993). Because these difficulties in adjustment tend to co-occur and appear as a single behavior-problem cluster (Jessor & Jessor, 1977; Mekos, Hetherington, & Reiss, 1996), the vast majority of children from divorced families and stepfamilies do not have these problems and eventually develop into reasonably competent individuals functioning within the normal range of adjustment (Emery & Forehand, 1994). This argument is not intended to minimize the importance of the increase in adjustment problems associated with divorce and remarriage nor to belittle the fact that children often report their parents' marital transitions to be their most painful life experience. It is intended to underscore the research evidence supporting the ability of most children to cope with their parents' divorce and remarriage and to counter the position that children are permanently blighted by their parents' marital transitions.

We turn now to an examination of some of the individual, social, economic, and family factors that contribute to the diversity in children's adjustment in divorced and remarried families. Each factor is discussed as it relates to the five perspectives on marital transitions.

Individual Risk and Vulnerability of Parents Associated With Divorce and Remarriage

Some adults have attributes that increase their probability not only of having dysfunctional marital relationships but also for having other problematic social relationships within and outside of the family, displaying inept parenting behaviors, encountering stressful life events, and having decreased psychological well-being (Amato & Booth, 1996; Block et al., 1986). Longitudinal studies have found that, in adults as well as in children, many of the problems attributed to divorce and remarriage and their concomitant life changes were present before these transitions occurred.

Although psychological distress and disorders may increase after divorce, parents who later divorce are more likely preceding divorce to be neurotic, depressed, antisocial, or alcoholic; to have economic problems (Amato, 1993; Capaldi & Patterson, 1991; Forgatch et al., 1995; Gotlib & McCabe, 1990); and to have dysfunctional beliefs about relationships (Baucom & Epstein, 1990; Kelly & Conley, 1987; Kurdek, 1993). In their marital interactions, they exhibit poor problem-solving and conflict resolution skills, thus escalating reciprocation of negative affect, contempt, denial, withdrawal, and stable, negative attributions about their spouses' behavior, which in turn significantly increase their risk for marital dissolution and multiple divorces (Bradbury & Fincham, 1990; Fincham, Bradbury, & Scott, 1990; Gottman, 1993, 1994; Gottman & Levenson, 1992; Matthews, Wickrama, & Conger, 1996). Sometimes these patterns are later found in the marital relationships of their adult offspring (Hetherington, in press). In relationships with their children, parents whose marriages will later be disrupted are more irritable, erratic, and nonauthoritative as much as 8–12 years prior to divorce (Amato & Booth, 1996; Block et al., 1988). These factors contribute to problems in children's adjustment and family relations in nondivorced families, single-parent families, and stepfamilies.

Children's Individual Risk, Vulnerability, and Resiliency Associated With Adjustment to Divorce and Remarriage

In accord with the individual risk perspective, characteristics of children may make them vulnerable or protect them from the adverse consequences or risks associated with their parents' divorce or remarriage. Some of these attributes influence the experiences and adjustment of children long before marital transitions occur.

Children's Adjustment Preceding Divorce and Remarriage

Children whose parents later divorce exhibit poorer adjustment before the breakup (Amato & Booth, 1996; Amato & Keith, 1991a; Block et al., 1986; Cherlin et al., 1991). When antecedent levels of problem behaviors are controlled, differences in problem behaviors between children from divorced and nondivorced families are greatly reduced (Cherlin et al., 1991; Guidubaldi, Perry, & Nastasi, 1987). Several alternative interpretations of these findings can be made. First, it is likely that maladapted parents, dysfunctional family relationships, and inept parenting already have taken their toll on children's adjustment before a divorce occurs. Second, divorce may be, in part, a result of having to deal with a difficult child. Third, personality problems in a parent, such as emotionality and lack of self-regulation, that lead to both divorce and inept socialization practices also may be genetically linked to behavior problems in children (Jockin, McGue, & Lykken, 1996; McGue & Lykken, 1992).

Children in stepfamilies also exhibit more behavior problems before remarriage occurs, and some researchers have speculated that the adaptive difficulties of stepchildren may be largely the result of experiences in divorced families (Furstenberg, 1988). This seems unlikely, because there is an increase in adjustment problems immediately after a marital transition, and because children in newly married families show more problems than those in stabilized, divorced, one-parent households (Hetherington & Clingempeel, 1992) or than those in longer remarried, stabilized stepfamilies (Hetherington & Jodl, 1994).

Personality and Temperament

Children who have easy temperaments; who are intelligent, socially mature, and responsible; and who exhibit few behavior problems are better able to cope with their parents' marital transitions. Stresses associated with divorce and remarriage are likely to exacerbate existing problems in children (Block et al., 1986; Elder, Caspi, & Van Nguyen, 1992; Hetherington, 1989, 1991b). In particular, children with difficult temperaments or behavior problems may elicit negative responses from their parents who are stressed in coping with their marital transitions. These children also may be less able to adapt to parental negativity when it occurs and may be less adept at gaining the support of people around them (Hetherington, 1989, 1991b; Rutter, 1987). Competent, adaptable children with social skills and attractive personal characteristics, such as an easy temperament and a sense of humor, are more likely to evoke positive responses and support and to maximize the use of available resources that help them negotiate stressful experiences (Hetherington, 1989; Werner, 1988).

Developmental Status

Developmental status and gender are the child characteristics most extensively researched in relation to adaptation to divorce and remarriage; however, the results of these studies have been inconsistent. Investigations of children's age at divorce must consider both age at the time of the marital transition and age at the time of assessment. In most studies, these variables are confounded with the length of time since the divorce or remarriage occurred. Some researchers have found that preschool-age children whose parents divorce are at greater risk for long-term problems in social and emotional development than are older children (Allison & Furstenberg, 1989; Zill et al., 1993). It has been suggested that younger children may be less able to appraise realistically the causes and consequences of divorce, may be more anxious about the possibility of total abandonment, may be more likely to blame themselves for the divorce, and may be less able to utilize extrafamilial protective resources (Hetherington, 1989). This greater vulnerability of young children to divorce has not been reported by other investigators (Amato & Keith, 1991a).

In contrast, early adolescence seems to be an especially difficult time in which to have a remarriage occur. Early adolescents are less able to adapt to parental remarriage than are younger children or late adolescents (Hetherington, 1993; Hetherington & Clingempeel, 1992), perhaps because the presence of a stepparent exacerbates normal early adolescent concerns about autonomy and sexuality. In addition, adolescence and young adulthood are periods in which problems in adjustment may emerge or increase, even when divorce or remarriage has occurred much earlier (Amato & Keith, 1991a, 1991b; Bray & Berger, 1993; Hetherington, 1993, in press; Hetherington & Clingempeel, 1992; Hetherington & Jodl, 1994).

Gender

Although earlier studies frequently reported gender differences in response to divorce and remarriage, with divorce being more deleterious for boys and remarriage for girls (Hetherington, 1989), more recent studies have found that gender differences in response to divorce are less pronounced and consistent than was previously believed (Amato & Keith, 1991a). Some of the inconsistencies may be attributable to the fact that fathers' custody, joint custody, and the involvement of noncustodial fathers are increasing and that involvement of fathers may

be more important for boys than for girls (Amato & Keith, 1991a; Clarke-Stewart & Hayward, 1996; Lindner-Gunnoe, 1993; Zill, 1988).

Some research has shown that boys respond to divorce with increases in conduct disorders and girls with increases in depression (Emery, 1982); however, both male and female adolescents from divorced and remarried families show higher rates of conduct disorders and depression than do those from nondivorced families (Amato & Keith, 1991a; Hetherington, 1993; Hetherington & Clingempeel, 1992; Hetherington & Jodl, 1994). Female adolescents and young adults from divorced and remarried families are more likely than their male counterparts to drop out of high school and college. Male and female adolescents are similarly affected in the likelihood of becoming teenage parents; however, single parenthood has more adverse effects on the lives of female adolescents (McLanahan & Sandefur, 1994). Female young adults from divorced and remarried families are vulnerable to declining socioeconomic status because of the sequelae of adolescent childbearing and school dropout. These sequelae are compounded in stepdaughters by early home leaving, which they attribute to family conflict (Cherlin & Furstenberg, 1994; Hetherington, 1997, in press).

Some girls in divorced, mother-headed families emerge as exceptionally resilient individuals, enhanced by confronting the increases in challenges and responsibilities that follow divorce (Hetherington, 1989, 1991b; Werner, 1993). Such enhancement is not found for boys following marital transitions or for girls in stepfamilies (Hetherington, 1989, 1991b). Boys, especially preadolescent boys, are more likely than girls to benefit from being in stepfather families (Amato & Keith, 1991a; Hetherington, 1993). Close relationships with supportive stepfathers are more likely to reduce antisocial behavior and to enhance the achievement of stepsons than of stepdaughters (Amato & Keith, 1991a; Hetherington, 1993; Lindner-Gunnoe, 1993; Zimiles & Lee, 1991). Girls are at greater increased risk than are boys for poor adjustment and low achievement when they are in either stepfather or stepmother families rather than in nondivorced families (Lee, Burkam, Zimiles, & Ladewski, 1994; Zimiles & Lee, 1991).

Some research suggests that living in stepfamilies is more beneficial to Black adolescents than to White adolescents, although these effects vary by gender. In contrast to the findings for White youths, young Black women in stepfamilies have the same rate of teenage parenthood as do those in two-parent, nondivorced families, and young Black men in stepfamilies are at no greater risk to drop out of high school than are those in two-parent families (McLanahan & Sandefur, 1994). McLanahan and Sandefur proposed that the income, supervision, and role models provided by stepfathers may be more advantageous for Black children because they are more likely than White children to live in more disorganized neighborhoods with fewer resources and social controls.

Family Composition-Parental Absence and the Adjustment of Children

The family composition or parental absence perspective proposed that a deviation in structure from a family with two first-married parents, biologically related to their children, is associated with increases in problem behavior in children. Two parents can provide support to each other, especially in their child rearing, as well as multiple role models and increased resources, supervision, and involvement for their children (Amato, 1995; Demo & Acock, 1996; Dornbusch et al., 1985; Furstenberg, Morgan, & Allison, 1987; Lamb, 1997). If father unavailability or absence is a critical factor in divorce, father custody or contact with a noncustodial parent, stepfather, or father surrogate should enhance children's adjustment. Furthermore, children who experience loss of their fathers through divorce or death should exhibit similar adjustment problems. Less theorizing has focused on mother absence, although similar hypotheses might be proposed for mothers.

Children and adults from homes with an absent parent due to either divorce or death have more problems in adjustment than do those in nondivorced families; however, significantly more problems are found in academic achievement, socioeconomic attainment, and conduct disorders for offspring from divorced families (Amato & Keith, 1991a; Felner, Ginter, Boike, & Cowen, 1981; Felner, Stolberg, & Cowen, 1975; Hetherington, 1972). Although children of both divorced and widowed women suffer the loss of their fathers and economic declines, the finding suggests that other factors moderate the differences in their outcomes. One of these factors may be greater support and involvement with the extended family, especially that of the lost parent's family, following death but not divorce (Hetherington, 1972). Another may be the greater conflict in families preceding divorce but not the death of a parent (Amato & Keith, 1991a).

The parental absence hypothesis also suggests that contact with noncustodial parents or joint custody should promote children's well-being; however, contact with both noncustodial mothers and fathers diminishes rapidly following divorce. More than 20% of children have no contact with their noncustodial fathers or see them only a few times a year, and only about one quarter of children have weekly visits with their divorced fathers (Seltzer, 1991). Black noncustodial fathers have higher rates of both regular contact and no contact with their children than do non-Hispanic White fathers (McLanahan & Sandefur, 1994). Decreased paternal involvement is related to residential distance, low socioeconomic status, and parental remarriage (Seltzer, 1991). Seltzer and Brandreth (1994) noted that custodial mothers serve as "gatekeepers" (Ahrons, 1983), controlling noncustodial fathers' access to and the conditions of visits with their children. When conflict, resentment, and anger are high,

the "gate" may be closed, and fathers may be discouraged or shut out. In contrast, when there is low conflict between divorced spouses, when mediation is used (Dillon & Emery, 1996), or when noncustodial fathers feel they have some control over decisions in their children's lives (Braver et al., 1993; Seltzer, 1991), paternal contact and child support payments are more likely to be maintained.

In contrast, noncustodial mothers are more likely than noncustodial fathers to sustain contact with their children and to rearrange their living situations to facilitate children's visits. They maintain approximately twice as much contact with their children as noncustodial fathers do and are less likely to completely drop out of their children's lives or to diminish contact when either parent remarries (Furstenberg & Nord, 1987; Furstenberg, Nord, Peterson, & Zill, 1983; Lindner-Gunnoe, 1993; Santrock, Sitterle, & Warshak, 1988; White, 1994; Zill, 1988). In addition, there is some evidence that noncustodial mothers, like noncustodial fathers, are more likely to maintain contact with sons than with daughters (Lindner-Gunnoe, 1993), although the preferential contact of fathers with sons is larger and more consistently obtained than that of mothers (Amato & Booth, 1991).

There is little support for the position that sheer frequency of contact facilitates positive adjustment in children (Amato & Keith, 1991a; King, 1994a, 1994b). However, as we discuss at greater length in the Family Process and the Adjustment to Divorce and Remarriage section, under conditions of low interparental conflict, contact with competent, supportive, authoritative noncustodial parents can have beneficial effects for children, and these effects are most marked for noncustodial parents and children of the same sex (Hetherington, 1989; Lindner-Gunnoe, 1993; Zill, 1988) Thus, it is the quality of contact, rather than the frequency, that is important (Amato, 1993; Emery, 1988; Furstenberg & Cherlin, 1991).

Research on custodial arrangements also has found few advantages of joint custody over sole residential custody. In a large study of custody in California, Maccoby and Mnookin (1992) found adolescents in the custody of their fathers had higher rates of delinquency, perhaps because of poorer monitoring by fathers. A meta-analysis of divorce by Amato and Keith (1991a), however, did not support the findings of poorer adjustment in children in families in which fathers have custody.

A corollary to the parental absence hypothesis would suggest that the addition of a stepparent might compensate for the loss of a parent. However, the family composition perspective implies that it is not only the presence of two parents but also biological relatedness to the parents that matter. Although divorce involves the exit of a family member, remarriage involves the restructuring of the family constellation with the entrance of a stepparent and sometimes stepsiblings. Predictions made about stepfamilies on the basis of the family composition hypothesis are unclear. On the one hand, the presence of a stepparent might compensate for the loss of the noncustodial parent by restoring a two-parent household. On the other hand, the child must confront an additional transition to another family with a nontraditional composition involving the addition of nonbiologically related family members to the household. In a family in which both divorced parents remarry, much more complex kin networks are created within and outside the household in a linked family system (Jacobson, 1982) or a binuclear family (Ahrons, 1979). A child's expanded kin networks may include stepsiblings, half siblings, and stepgrandparents, as well as stepparents and biologically related kin, and represent a marked deviation from the composition of the nondivorced nuclear family (Booth & Edwards, 1992; Bray, 1987, 1988; Bray, Berger, & Boethel, 1994; Burrell, 1995; Cherlin & Furstenberg, 1994; Giles-Sims, 1987).

Stress, Socioeconomic Disadvantage, and the Adjustment to Divorce and Remarriage

The stress perspective attributes problems in the adjustment of children from divorced and remarried families to the increased stresses experienced in these families. Parents and children living in divorced families encounter a diverse array of stressful life events (Hetherington, Cox, & Cox, 1985; Simons et al., 1996). Both custodial mothers and fathers complain of task overload and social isolation as they juggle household, child-care, and financial responsibilities that are usually dealt with by two parents (Hetherington & Stanley Hagan, 1997). Noncustodial parents express concerns associated with the establishment of new residences, social networks, and intimate relationships; loss of children; problems with visitation arrangements; and continued difficulties in relations with their ex-spouses (Hetherington, 1989, 1991b; Hetherington & Stanley Hagan, 1997; Hoffman, 1995; Minton & Pasley, 1996).

In spite of the diversity in stresses associated with divorce, most attention by sociologists and economists has focused on the marked decrement in the income of custodial mothers following marital dissolution and its accompanying risk factors. Those investigators who support a socioeconomic disadvantage perspective suggest that controlling for income will eliminate or greatly diminish the association between family structure and children's well-being (McLanahan & Sandefur, 1994). In addition, because custodial fathers do not encounter the financial decrements experienced by custodial mothers and because remarriage is the fastest way out of poverty for single mothers, it might be expected that children in father-custody families and stepfamilies will exhibit fewer behavior problems than those in divorced mother-custody households.

Because of increased enforcement of noncustodial fathers' child support payments and changes in the labor force for women, it has been speculated that custodial mothers and their children may no longer experience such drastic economic declines following divorce. A recent review (Bianchi, Subaiya, & Kahn, 1997) suggests, however, that custodial mothers still experience the loss of approximately one quarter to one half of their predivorce income in comparison to only 10% by custodial fathers following divorce (Arendell, 1986; Cherlin, 1992; Emery, 1994; McLanahan & Booth, 1989). For custodial mothers, this loss in income is accompanied by increased workloads; high rates of job instability; and residential moves to less desirable neighborhoods with poor schools, inadequate services, often high crime rates, and deviant peer populations (McLanahan & Booth, 1989; McLanahan & Sandefur, 1994).

Although father-only families have substantially higher incomes than do families with divorced custodial mothers, a significant number of father-only families (18%) live in poverty, and fathers rarely receive child support (Meyer & Garasky, 1993). However, most father-custody families have financial, housing, child-care, and educational resources not available to divorced custodial mothers. Custodial fathers report less child-rearing stress than do custodial mothers, and their children show fewer problems (Amato & Keith, 1991a; Clarke-Stewart & Hayward, 1996). This could be attributed to economic advantages in father-custody families; however, even with income controlled, children in father-custody families—especially boys—show greater well-being than those in mother-custody families (Clarke-Stewart & Hayward, 1996).

Newly repartnered parents and their children report higher levels of both positive and negative life changes than do those in never-divorced families (Forgatch et al., 1995; Hetherington et al., 1985). Although there is a marked increase in income for divorced mothers following remarriage, conflicts over finances, child rearing, and family relations remain potent problems in stepfamilies (Bray & Berger, 1993; Hetherington, 1993; Hetherington & Jodl, 1994). The economic improvement conferred by remarriage is not reflected in the improved adjustment of children in stepfamilies, and the new stresses associated with remarriage often counter the benefits associated with increased income (Amato & Booth, 1991; Bray & Berger, 1993; Cherlin & Furstenberg, 1994; Demo & Acock, 1996; Forgatch et al., 1995; Hetherington & Clingempeel, 1992; Hetherington & Jodl, 1994).

Parental Distress and the Adjustment to Divorce and Remarriage

Investigators taking the parental distress perspective propose that stressors affect children's adjustment through parental distress and diminished well-being (Bank, Duncan, Patterson, & Reid, 1993; Forgatch et al., 1995; Lorenz et al., 1996; Simons & Beaman, 1996; Simons, Beaman, Conger, & Chao, 1992; Simons & Johnson, 1996). In this view, it is the parents' response to stress, rather than the stress itself, that is most salient for children's adjustment.

Signs of diminished parental well-being and distress, including anger, anxiety, depression, loneliness, impulsivity, feelings of being externally controlled, and emotional liability, may emerge or increase in the immediate aftermath of divorce (Hetherington, 1989, 1993; Pearlin & Johnson, 1977). In addition, newly remarried parents are often depressed or preoccupied as they cope with the challenges of their new family life (Hetherington & Clingempeel, 1992; Hetherington & Jodl, 1994). The mental health of parents in divorced and remarried families is related to children's adjustment through diminished competence in their parenting (Clarke-Stewart & Hayward, 1996; Forgatch et al., 1995; Hetherington, 1993; Lorenz et al., 1996; Simons, 1996).

The stresses associated with marital transitions place both residential and nonresidential parents at risk not only for psychological disorders (Hetherington, 1989, 1991b; Kitson & Morgan, 1990; Stack, 1989; Travato & Lauris, 1989) but also for disruption in immune system functioning (Kiecolt-Glaser et al., 1988) and concomitant increased rates of illness and morbidity, which are notable in divorced adults, especially in men (Burman & Margolin, 1992; Hu & Goldman, 1990; Riessman & Gerstel, 1985). Nonresidential fathers engage in more health-compromising and impulsive behaviors, such as alcohol consumption, than do fathers in any other family type (Umberson, 1987; Umberson & Williams, 1993) and are overrepresented among suicides and homicides (Bloom, Asher, & White, 1978).

Although depression remains higher in divorced women than in nondivorced women, by two years after divorce, women show less depression and more psychological well-being than do those who remain in conflict-ridden marriages with husbands who undermine their discipline and feelings of competence. The well-being of both men and women increases after the formation of a mutually caring, intimate relationship, such as a remarriage (Hetherington, 1993). Most parents do adapt to their new marital situation, with concomitant decreases in psychological and physical problems. In support of the parental distress perspective, even temporary disruptions in parents' health, social, and psychological functioning may make it difficult to be competent in parenting children who may be confused, angry, and apprehensive about a divorce or remarriage, and this inept parenting adversely affects children's adjustment (Chase-Lansdale & Hetherington, 1990; Emery, 1988; Emery & Dillon, 1994; Hetherington, 1989; Hetherington & Stanley Hagan, 1995; Maccoby & Mnookin, 1992).

Family Process and the Adjustment to Divorce and Remarriage

Divorce and remarriage confront families with changes and challenges associated with pervasive alterations in family roles and functioning. The changes in family relationships can support or undermine the efforts of children to adapt to their new family situations. Proponents of the family process perspective argue that the impact of parental attributes, changes in family structure, socioeconomic disadvantage, and parental distress on children's adjustment is largely mediated by disruptions in family relationships and interactions, such as those involved in discipline and child-rearing practices (Demo & Acock, 1996; Forgatch et al., 1995; Hetherington, 1993; Simons & Beaman, 1996; Simons & Johnson, 1996). Without disruptions in family functioning, the former risk factors are less likely to compromise children's adjustment.

Relationships Between Divorced Couples

Marital conflict is associated with a wide range of deleterious outcomes for children, including depression, poor social competence and academic performance, and conduct disorders (Amato & Keith, 1991a; Cowan & Cowan, 1990; Davies & Cummings, 1994; Forehand, Brody, Long, Slotkin, & Fauber, 1986; Gottman & Katz, 1989; Peterson & Zill, 1986). Conflict, contempt, anger, and acrimony often antecede divorce, and in the immediate aftermath of marital disruption, conflict may escalate. Consequently, one of the most frequently asked questions about divorce is whether parents should stay together in an unhappy, conflict-ridden marriage for the sake of the children.

The hypothesis that conflict is a major contributor to problems in divorced families is substantiated by evidence that children in high-conflict, nondivorced families have more problems in psychological adjustment and self-esteem than do those in divorced families or in low-conflict, nondivorced families (Amato & Keith, 1991a; Amato, Loomis, & Booth, 1995). In addition, longitudinal prospective studies of divorce indicate that divorce improves the adjustment of children removed from contentious marriages but is deleterious for children whose parents had less overtly conflictual relationships preceding divorce (Amato et al., 1995). When measures of marital dissatisfaction rather than conflict are used, the advantages of divorce over unhappy marital situations are less marked (Simons, 1996) because many couples in unsatisfying marriages may not exhibit overt conflict (Gottman, 1994).

Although contact and conflict between divorced couples diminish over time, they remain higher for couples with children as they attempt to negotiate coparenting relationships and economic responsibilities (Masheter, 1991). Despite the fact that cooperative, mutually supportive, and nonconfrontational coparenting relationships are advantageous to parents and children, only about one quarter of divorced parents attain such relationships and an approximately equal number maintain acrimonious relationships (Maccoby & Mnookin, 1992). Most coparenting relationships after divorce evolve into parallel coparenting relationships not only with little communication or coordination of parenting but also with lessened conflict because of the disengaged relationships. Cooperative coparenting is most likely to occur when family size is small and when there was little conflict at the time of divorce (Maccoby, Buchanan, Mnookin, & Dornbusch, 1993). With little conflict and cooperative coparenting, children adapt better not only to their parents' divorce but also to their parents' remarriages, and they tend to have more positive relations with their stepparents (Bray & Berger, 1993; Crosbie-Burnett, 1991).

The sheer frequency of conflict may not be as detrimental as the type of conflict. Conflicts in which children are caught in the middle while parents denigrate each other, precipitate loyalty conflicts, communicate through the children, or fight about the children are most destructive to children's well-being (Buchanan, Maccoby, & Dornbusch, 1991; Maccoby et al., 1993; Maccoby & Mnookin, 1992). Children in highly conflicted families not only are more distressed but also may learn to exploit and mislead their parents and to escape monitoring of their activities when they are older (Hetherington, Law, & O'Connor, 1992). Even when children are not directly involved in their parents' conflicts, the adverse effects of conflicts may be experienced through increased parental irritability and diminished monitoring, support, and involvement (Patterson, 1991).

Relationships of Custodial Mothers and Children

Children in both mother- and father-custody families show more problems than do children in nondivorced families; however, most offspring in both types of divorced families eventually are reasonably well-adjusted. Because approximately 84% of children reside with their mothers following divorce (Seltzer, 1994), most studies of parent-child relations following marital dissolution have involved custodial mothers. Close relationships with supportive, authoritative mothers who are warm but exert firm, consistent control and supervision are generally associated with positive adjustment in children and adolescents (Bray & Berger, 1993; Forehand, Thomas, Wierson, Brody, & Fauber, 1990; Hetherington, 1989, 1993; Hetherington & Clingempeel, 1992; Maccoby et al., 1993; Simons & Johnson, 1996). In the immediate aftermath of divorce, there is a period of disrupted parenting characterized by irritability and coercion and diminished communication, affection, consistency, control, and monitoring (Hetherington, 1991a, 1991b, 1993; Simons & Johnson, 1996).

The parenting of divorced mothers improves over the course of the two years following divorce but remains less authoritative than that of nondivorced mothers, and problems in control and coercive exchanges between divorced mothers and sons may remain high (Hetherington, 1991a). Even in adulthood, relationships between sons and divorced mothers are less close than those in nondivorced families, whereas differences in closeness are not found for daughters (Booth & Amato, 1994). Preadolescent girls and their divorced mothers often have close, companionate, confiding relationships; however, in adolescence, there is a notable increase in conflict in these relationships (Hetherington, 1991a; Hetherington & Clingempeel, 1992). In comparison with adolescents in nondivorced, two-parent families, adolescents in divorced families and in stepfamilies experience the highest levels of mother-adolescent disagreements and the lowest levels of parental supervision (Demo & Acock, 1996). Both conflictive, negative parent-adolescent relationships and lack of monitoring are associated with involvement with antisocial peers—one of the most potent pathways to the development of delinquency, alcoholism, substance abuse, and teenage sexual activity and childbearing (Conger & Reuter, 1996; Hetherington, 1993; Simons & Chao, 1996; Whitbeck et al., 1996).

About one quarter to one third of adolescents in divorced and remarried families, in comparison with 10% of adolescents in nondivorced families, become disengaged from their families, spending as little time at home as possible and avoiding interactions, activities, and communication with family members (Hetherington, 1993; Hetherington & Jodl, 1994). This incidence is greater for boys in divorced families and for girls in stepfamilies. If disengagement is associated with lack of adult support and supervision and with involvement in a delinquent peer group, it leads to both antisocial behavior and academic problems in adolescents (Hetherington, 1993; Patterson, DeBaryshe, & Ramsey, 1989). However, if there is a caring adult involved with the adolescent outside of the home, such as the parent of a friend, a teacher, a neighbor, or a coach, disengagement may be a positive solution to a disrupted, conflictual family situation (Hetherington, 1993).

It has been noted that children in divorced families grow up faster, in part, because of early assignment of responsibilities (Weiss, 1979), more autonomous decision making (Dornbusch et al., 1985), and lack of adult supervision (Hetherington, 1991a; Thomson, McLanahan, & Curtin, 1992). Assignment of responsibility may be associated with resilience and unusual social competence in girls from divorced families; yet, if the task demands are beyond the children's capabilities, they also may be associated with low self-esteem, anxiety, and depression (Hetherington, 1989, in press). Furthermore, if adolescents perceive themselves as being unfairly burdened with responsibilities that interfere with their other activities, they may respond with resentment, rebellion, and noncompliance.

The restabilizing of family relations following a remarriage takes considerably longer than that following a divorce (Cherlin & Furstenberg, 1994). Whereas a new homeostasis is established in about two to three years following divorce, it has been estimated that the adjustment to remarriage may take as long as five to seven years (Cherlin & Furstenberg, 1994; Papernow, 1988; Visher & Visher, 1990). Because more than one quarter of remarriages are terminated within five years, with higher rates for families with children, restablization never occurs in many stepfamilies.

In the first year following a remarriage, custodial mothers engage in less affective involvement, less behavior control and monitoring, and more negativity than nondivorced mothers (Bray & Berger, 1993; Hetherington, 1993; Hetherington & Clingempeel, 1992). Negative mother-child interactions are related to more disengagement, dysfunctional family roles, poorer communication, and less cohesion in stepfamilies (Bray, 1990). However, in long-established remarriages, the parenting of custodial mothers with their biological offspring becomes increasingly similar to that in nondivorced families (Bray & Berger, 1993; Hetherington, 1993; Hetherington & Clingempeel, 1992; Hetherington & Jodl, 1994).

Relationships of Custodial Fathers and Children

Although children usually live with their mothers following the dissolution of their parents' marriage, father-headed families have tripled since 1974, making them the fastest growing family type in the United States (Meyer & Garasky, 1993). Arrangements about physical custody are often made on the basis of personal decisions by parents and not on judicial decree, and the preponderance of maternal physical custody, even when joint legal custody has been granted, may reflect concerns fathers have about assuming full-time parenting (Maccoby et al., 1993; Maccoby & Mnookin, 1992). Boys and older children are more likely to be placed in father-only custody, but some girls and young children do live with their fathers. In contrast to custodial mothers, custodial fathers are a very select group of fathers who may be more child-oriented than most fathers. Fathers who seek custody of their children are more involved and capable than those fathers who have custody thrust on them because the mothers were unwilling or incompetent to parent (Hanson, 1988; Mendes, 1976a, 1976b). Once their families have restabilized, custodial fathers report less child-rearing stress, better parent-child relations, and fewer behavior problems in their children than do custodial mothers (Amato & Keith, 1991a; Clarke-Stewart & Hayward, 1996; Furstenberg, 1988).

There are different strengths and weaknesses in the parenting of custodial mothers and fathers. Although custodial mothers and custodial fathers are perceived to be similarly warm and nurturing with younger children (Warshak, 1986), mothers have more problems with control and with assignment of household tasks, whereas fathers have more problems with communication, self-disclosure, and monitoring of their children's activities (Chase-Lansdale & Hetherington, 1990; Furstenberg, 1988; Warshak, 1986). Moreover, fathers have special difficulties with monitoring adolescents' behavior, especially that of daughters (Buchanan, Maccoby, & Dornbusch, 1992; Maccoby et al., 1993).

Recent evidence indicates that adolescent adjustment is more predictable from the parenting of a custodial parent of the same sex than one of the opposite sex (Lindner-Gunnoe, 1993). This evidence parallels findings of the greater salience of same-sex parents in the adjustment of adolescents in nondivorced families (Furman & Buhrmester, 1992; Kurdek & Fine, 1993). In spite of this greater influence of same-sex custodial parents, both sons and daughters report feeling closer to their custodial parent than their noncustodial parent, regardless of whether the parent is a mother or a father (Hetherington & Clingempeel, 1992; Maccoby et al., 1993; White, Brinkerhoff, & Booth, 1985).

As has been found with mothers, when custodial fathers remarry, there are disruptions in father-child relationships, especially with daughters (Clingempeel, Brand, & Ievoli, 1984). Fathers may alter their caretaking relationships more radically than mothers do because fathers are more likely to expect a stepmother to play a major role in household tasks and parenting (Hetherington & Stanley Hagen, 1995). However, in long-established stepfamilies, there are few differences in parent-child relations between remarried fathers and their residential biological children and those fathers and children in nondivorced families (Hetherington & Jodl, 1994).

Relationships of Noncustodial Mothers and Children

Although less is known about noncustodial mothers than noncustodial fathers, nonresidential mothers maintain more contact with their children than do nonresidential fathers. It is not only in the quantity but also in the quality of parent-child relationships that these mothers and fathers differ. Noncustodial mothers are less adept than custodial mothers in controlling and monitoring their children's behavior, but they are more effective in these parenting behaviors than are noncustodial fathers (Furstenberg & Nord, 1987; Lindner-Gunnoe, 1993). Children report that noncustodial mothers are more interested in and informed about their activities; are more supportive, sensitive, and responsive to their needs; and are more communicative than noncustodial fathers (Furstenberg & Nord, 1987; Lindner-Gunnoe, 1993; Santrock & Sitterle, 1987). Therefore, it is not surprising that children report talking more about their problems and activities and feeling closer to noncustodial mothers than to noncustodial fathers (Lindner-Gunnoe, 1993), nor that noncustodial mothers have more influence over their children's development, especially their daughters' adjustment, than do noncustodial fathers (Brand, Clingempeel, & Bowen-Woodward, 1988; Lindner-Gunnoe, 1993; Zill, 1988). Noncustodial mothers' warmth, support, and monitoring enhance their children's scholastic achievement and diminish antisocial, externalizing problems (Lindner-Gunnoe, 1993). In appraising some research findings that children have fewer problems in the custody of fathers than in the custody of mothers (Amato & Keith, 1991a; Clarke-Stewart & Hayward, 1996), it must be considered that part of this effect may be attributable to the more active involvement of noncustodial mothers.

When a custodial father remarries, closeness to the noncustodial mother can have some disadvantages because it is related to children's lack of acceptance of a stepmother. In contrast, there is no association between the relationship with a noncustodial father and building a close relationship with a stepfather (Hetherington, 1993; Hetherington & Jodl, 1994; White, 1994).

Relationships of Noncustodial Fathers and Children

In contrast to mothers' behavior, the postdivorce parenting behavior of fathers is less predictable from their predivorce behavior (Hetherington et al., 1985). Some previously attached and involved fathers find the enforced marginality and intermittent contact in being noncustodial fathers to be painful, and they drift away from their children. Other fathers, especially custodial fathers, rise to the occasion and increase their involvement and parenting competence. However, most nonresidential fathers have a friendly, egalitarian, companionate relationship rather than a traditional parental relationship with their children (Arendell, 1986; Furstenberg & Nord, 1987; Hetherington, Cox, & Cox, 1979; Munsch, Woodward, & Darling, 1995). They want their visits to be pleasant and entertaining and are hesitant to assume the role of disciplinarian or teacher. They are less likely than nondivorced fathers to criticize, control, and monitor their children's behavior or to help them with tasks such as homework (Bray & Berger, 1993; Furstenberg & Nord, 1987; Hetherington, 1991b).

Frequency of contact with noncustodial fathers and the adjustment of children are usually found to be unrelated (Amato & Keith, 1991a). Although obviously some degree of contact is essential, it seems to be the quality of the relationship and the circumstances of contact rather than frequency of visits that are most important (Amato, 1993; Emery, 1988; Furstenberg & Cherlin, 1991; Simons & Beaman, 1996). When noncustodial fathers are not just "tour guide" fathers but maintain more parent-like contact,

participate in a variety of activities with their children, and spend holidays together, the well-being of children is promoted (Clarke-Stewart & Hayward, 1996). Under conditions of low conflict, the involvement of authoritative noncustodial fathers can enhance children's adjustment (Hetherington, 1989), especially that of boys (Lindner-Gunnoe, 1993). It can even, to some extent, protect the children from the adverse consequences of rejecting or incompetent noncustodial mothers (Hetherington, 1989). In contrast, under conditions of high conflict, frequent contact with noncustodial parents may exacerbate children's problems (Kline, Johnston, & Tschann, 1991).

Relationships Between Stepparents and Stepchildren

Papernow (1998) commented that the typical starting point for a stepfamily involving "a weak couple subsystem, a tightly bonded parent-child alliance, and potential interference in family functioning from an outsider" (p. 56) would be considered problematic in a traditional nondivorced family. Clinicians have remarked that any stepfamily that uses a traditional nuclear family as its ideal is bound for disappointment (Visher & Visher, 1990). Similar patterns of relationships in traditional families and stepfamilies may lead to different outcomes. Patterns of functioning and family processes that undermine or promote positive adjustment may differ in the two types of families (Bray & Berger, 1993). The complex relationships between families following remarriage may require less rigid family boundaries and more open, less integrated relations among the family subsystems.

Although both stepfathers and stepmothers feel less close to stepchildren than do nondivorced parents to their children, they, if not the stepchildren, want the new marriage to be successful (Brand et al., 1988; Bray & Berger, 1993; Hetherington, 1993; Kurdek & Fine, 1993). In the early stages of a remarriage, stepfathers have been reported to be like polite strangers, trying to ingratiate themselves with their stepchildren by showing less negativity but also less control, monitoring, and affection than do fathers in nondivorced families (Bray & Berger, 1992; Hetherington & Clingempeel, 1992). In longer established stepfamilies, a distant, disengaged parenting style remains the predominant one for stepfathers, but conflict and negativity, especially between stepparents and stepdaughters, can remain high or increase, especially with adolescents (Brand et al., 1988; Bray & Berger, 1993; Hetherington, 1993; Hetherington & Jodl, 1994). Some of the conflict in stepfamilies is due to the negative rejecting behavior of stepchildren toward stepparents (Bray & Berger, 1993; Hetherington & Clingempeel, 1992; Hetherington & Jodl, 1994). Even stepparents with the best intentions may give up in the face of persistent hostile behavior by stepchildren.

Conflict between stepfathers and stepchildren is not necessarily precipitated by the children. In fact, rates of physical abuse perpetrated by stepfathers on their stepchildren are 7 times higher than those by fathers on their biological children, and homicide rates for stepfathers are 100 times higher than those for biological fathers (Daly & Wilson, 1996; Wilson, Daly, & Weghorst, 1980). These differential rates are most marked with infants and preschool-age children (Daly & Wilson, 1996).

Stepmothers have a more difficult time integrating themselves into stepfamilies than do stepfathers. Remarried fathers often expect that the stepmothers will participate in child rearing, forcing the stepmothers into more active, less distant, and more confrontational roles than those required of stepfathers (Brand et al., 1988). Support by the fathers for the stepmothers' parenting and parental agreement on child rearing are especially important in promoting effective parenting in stepmothers (Brand et al., 1988). The assumption of the dominant disciplinarian role is fraught with problems for stepparents (Brand et al., 1988; Bray & Berger, 1993; Hetherington, 1991a), and although authoritative parenting can have salutary effects on stepchildren's adjustment, especially with stepfathers and stepsons, authoritative parenting is not always a feasible option in stepfamilies (Bray & Berger, 1993). When custodial parents are authoritative and when stepparents are warm and involved and support the custodial parents' discipline rather than making independent control attempts, children can be responsive and adjust well (Bray & Berger, 1993; Hetherington, 1989).

It is not only parent-child relationships but also relationships between siblings that are more conflictual and less supportive in divorced families and stepfamilies than in nondivorced families (Hetherington, 1991a). These effects are more marked for biologically related siblings than for stepsiblings (Hetherington & Jodl, 1994). Less involved, harsher parenting is associated with rivalrous, aggressive, and unsupportive sibling relationships in divorced and remarried families (Conger & Conger, 1996; Hetherington, 1991a, 1993; Hetherington & Clingempeel, 1992), and, in turn, these negative sibling relations lead to low social competence and responsibility and to more behavior problems in children (Hetherington & Clingempeel, 1992).

Conclusion: What Matters? What Doesn't

In reviewing the five perspectives, it is clear that each may influence children's adjustment. The first perspective, the individual risk and vulnerability hypothesis, is supported by evidence suggesting that children and their parents have attributes that directly contribute to their experiencing marital transitions and to having more difficulties in adjusting to them. These problems may be transmitted genetically from parents to children, or the effect on children's adjustment may be indirect, due to

parents' ineffective child-rearing strategies. However, individual vulnerability to the adverse outcomes of divorce and remarriage seems to involve a complex interaction among an array of individual attributes, including personality, age, gender, and ethnicity, and the effects of these interactions have been difficult to differentiate.

The family composition—parental absence hypothesis is not as well supported by the evidence. Generally, children in never-divorced families with two parents are more competent than children whose parents have divorced. However, this theory would suggest that children's adjustment should benefit from the addition of a stepparent, yet there are few indications of lower levels of problems in children in stepfamilies as compared with children in divorced families. Furthermore, some studies indicate that especially in the early stages of a remarriage, stepchildren exhibit more difficulties than do children in stabilized, divorced, single-parent families (Amato & Keith, 1991a; Hetherington, 1993; Hetherington & Clingempeel, 1992; Hetherington & Jodl, 1994).

These comments must be qualified by findings indicating that the presence of a stepfather, especially with preadolescent boys, can attenuate problems in adjustment for stepsons, whereas the presence of either a stepmother or a stepfather may be associated with higher levels of problem behaviors for girls (Amato & Keith, 1991a; Hetherington, 1989; Hetherington & Jodl, 1994; Lee et al., 1994). These results, in conjunction with the somewhat inconsistent evidence that boys may also fare better in a father-custody family than in a mother-custody family (Amato & Keith, 1991a; Clarke-Stewart & Hayward, 1996; Zill, 1988), indicate that the presence of a father may have positive effects on the well-being of boys. Rather than rejecting the family composition-parental absence perspective, it should be concluded that there is not a simple main effect of family composition or parental absence but that it is modified by the reason for parental unavailability, the quality of family relationships, and the child's gender.

The findings thus far yield only modest support for marked direct effects of life stress and economic deprivation on children's adjustment. Even when income is controlled, children in divorced families show more problems than do those in nondivorced families (Amato & Keith, 1991a; Clarke-Stewart & Hayward, 1996; Demo & Acock, 1996; Guidubaldi et al., 1987; Hetherington, 1997, in press; Simons & Associates, 1996). In addition, although the income in stepfamilies is only slightly lower than that in nondivorced families, children in these families show a similar level of problem behavior to that in divorced mother-custody families (Amato & Keith, 1991a; Demo & Acock, 1996; Forgatch et al., 1995; Henderson, Hetherington, Mekos, & Reiss, 1996; Simons & Johnson, 1996). Thus, the effects of income do not seem to be primary and are largely indirect.

Some investigators using large-scale survey data report that as much as half of the effects of divorce on children's adjustment is attributable to economic factors (McLanahan & Sandefur, 1994); others find no direct effects of income but a major effect of the quality of family relationships that may alter children's adjustment (Demo & Acock, 1996). Furthermore, in studies in which income has been controlled, differences between offspring in divorced and nondivorced families remain (Amato & Keith, 1991a; Clarke-Stewart & Hayward, 1996; Demo & Acock, 1996; Guidubaldi et al., 1987; Hetherington, in press; Simons & Associates, 1996). Some of the inconsistencies in findings are due to methodological differences in studies. Surveys often have large representative samples but inadequate measures, sometimes involving only two or three items and single informants, to assess parental and family characteristics and family process variables. Studies using smaller, less representative samples but more reliable multimethod, multi-informant assessment, including observations, have found that much of the effects of family structure and economic stress are mediated by inept parenting (Forgatch et al., 1995; Simons & Johnson, 1996). Furthermore, there is some support in the research on stress, economic deprivation, and marital transitions for the individual risk position. As stated earlier, antisocial individuals are at greater risk not only for job instability, economic problems (Simons et al., 1992), and stressful life events but also for divorce (Capaldi & Patterson, 1991; Kitson & Holmes, 1992; Lahey et al., 1988), problems in successive marital relationships (Capaldi & Patterson, 1991), and incompetent parenting (Forgatch et al., 1995; Simons & Johnson, 1996).

Although it is true that parental distress increases in the aftermath of a divorce, research indicates that the effect of parents' well-being is largely mediated through their parenting. Even temporary disruptions in parents' physical and psychological functioning due to a marital transition interfere with their ability to offer support and supervision at a time when children need them most.

Although attributes of parents and children, family composition, stress and socioeconomic disadvantage, and parental distress impact children's adjustment, their effects may be mediated through the more proximal mechanism of family process. Dysfunctional family relationships, such as conflict, negativity, lack of support, and nonauthoritative parenting, exacerbate the effects of divorce and remarriage on children's adjustment. Certainly if divorced or remarried parents are authoritative and their families are harmonious, warm, and cohesive, the differences between the adjustment of children in these families and those in nondivorced families are reduced. However, marital transitions increase the probability that children will not find themselves in families with such functioning. Research on the relationships between family members in nondivorced families and stepfamilies supports the family process hypothesis, suggesting that, in large part, it is negative, conflictual, dysfunctional family relationships between parents, parents and children, and siblings that account for differences in children's adjustment.

It has become fashionable to attempt to estimate the relative contributions of individual attributes, family structure, stresses, parental distress, and family process

Figure 1

A Transactional Model of the Predictors of Children's Adjustment Following Divorce and Remarriage

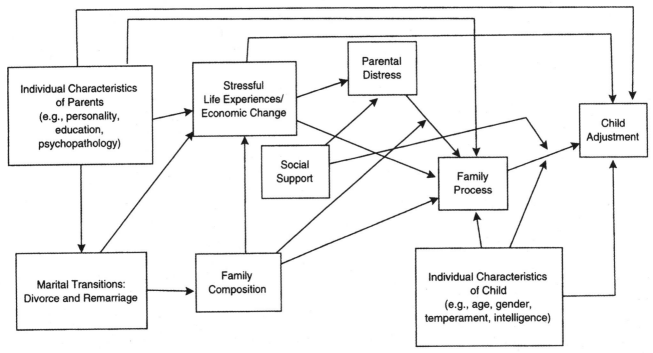

to the adjustment of children in divorced and remarried families. These attempts have led to conflicting results, futile controversies, and misleading conclusions because the amount of variance explained by the factors differs from sample to sample and varies with the methods and the data analytic strategies used. Moreover, different risk and vulnerability factors are likely to come into play and to vary in salience at different points in the transitions from an unhappy marriage to divorce, to life in a single-parent household, through remarriage, and into subsequent marital transitions. These risk factors will be modified by shifting protective factors and resources.

A transactional model of risks associated with marital transitions is perhaps most appropriate (see Figure 1). Divorce and remarriage increase the probability of parents and children encountering a set of interrelated risks. These risks are linked, interact, and are mediated and moderated in complex ways. These effects are illustrated in the model in different ways. For example, parental distress (e.g., maternal depression) does not have a direct effect on children's adjustment, which is not to say it does not have an impact. Instead, its influence is mediated through its link to family process, specifically the depressed mothers' diminished ability to effectively parent. In contrast, some variables moderate the relationship between other variables, such that the relationship depends on the level of the moderator. For example, children with difficult temperaments are expected to be more adversely affected by disruptions in family functioning than are children with easy temperaments. Thus, individual variables such as temperament can moderate the effect of family process on children's adjustment.

All family members encounter stresses associated with marital transitions, and it may be the balance between risks and resources that determines the impact of stresses on divorced and remarried parents and their children. All five of the factors described at the beginning of this article are associated with divorce and remarriage and with adverse outcomes for children. Studies using path analyses (e.g., Conger & Conger, 1996; Forgatch et al., 1995; Simons & Associates, 1996) have helped illuminate the patterns of linkages among these risks and have suggested that many of the risk factors are mediated by proximal experiences such as disruptions in parent-child or sibling relationships. However, the fact that a path is indirect does not reduce its importance. Figure 1 presents the theoretical model describing the linkages among these factors. A set of individual attributes, such as antisocial behavior, is associated with an increased risk of divorce and an unsuccessful remarriage; problems in social relationships, including parent-child relationships; and stressful life events. All family members encounter stresses as they deal with the changes, challenges, and restructuring of the family associated with marital transitions, but these vary for different family members and for divorce and remarriage. Divorce usually leads to the loss or the diminished availability of a father and the economic, social, and

emotional resources he can provide, which increases the probability of poverty and its concomitant environmental and experiential adversities for divorced custodial mothers and their children. Although some of the effects of stresses, such as living in neighborhoods with high crime rates, poor schools, antisocial peers, and few job opportunities or resources, may impact directly on children's adjustment and attainment, other effects of stress in divorced families may be indirect and mediated through parental psychological distress, inept or altered parenting, and disrupted family processes. Stresses associated with the changes and complexities in stepfamilies may also lead to distress and dysfunctional family functioning. Children, because of individual characteristics such as gender, temperament, personality, age, and intelligence, vary in their influence on family process and their vulnerability or resilience in dealing with their parents' divorce and remarriage and concomitant changes in family roles, relationships, and process. Thus, effects of the earlier risk factors on children's adjustment are mediated or moderated by associated transactional risk factors and often eventually by disruptions in family functioning. These indirect or mediated effects do not negate the importance of the earlier risk factors as a link in the transactional path of adversity leading to problems in child adjustment.

Static, cross-sectional slices out of the lives of parents and children in divorced or remarried families give a misleading picture of how risk and protective factors combine to influence the adjustment of children. An examination of the dynamic trajectories of interacting risk and protective factors associated with divorce and remarriage will yield a more valid and fruitful view of the multiple pathways associated with resiliency or adverse outcomes for children who have experienced their parents' marital transactions.

REFERENCES

Ahrons, C. R. (1979). The binuclear family: Two households, one family. *Alternative Lifestyles, 2,* 499–515.

Ahrons, C. R. (1983). Predictors of paternal involvement postdivorce: Mothers' and fathers' perceptions. *Journal of Divorce, 6,* 55–69.

Allison, P. D., & Furstenberg, F. F., Jr. (1989). How marital dissolution affects children: Variations by age and sex. *Developmental Psychology, 25,* 540–549.

Amato, P. R. (1993). Children's adjustment to divorce: Theories, hypotheses, and empirical support. *Journal of Marriage and the Family, 55,* 23–38.

Amato, P. R. (1995). Single-parent households as settings for children's development, well-being, and attainment: A social network/resources perspective. *Sociological Studies of Children, 7,* 19–47.

Amato, P. R., & Booth, A. (1991). Consequences of parental divorce and marital happiness for adult well-being. *Social Forces, 69,* 895–914.

Amato, P. R., & Booth, A. (1996). A prospective study of divorce and parent-child relationships. *Journal of Marriage and the Family, 58,* 356–365.

Amato, P. R. & Keith, B. (1991a). Parental divorce and adult well-being: A meta-analysis. *Journal of Marriage and the Family, 53,* 43–58.

Amato, P. R., & Keith, B. (1991b). Parental divorce and the well-being of children: A meta-analysis. *Psychological Bulletin, 110,* 26–46.

Amato, P. R., Loomis, L. S., & Booth, A. (1995). Parental divorce, marital conflict, and offspring well-being during early adulthood. *Social Forces, 73,* 895–915.

Arendell, T. (1986). *Mothers and divorce: Legal, economic, and social dilemmas.* Berkeley: University of California Press.

Bank, L., Duncan, T., Patterson, G. R., & Reid, J. (1993). Parent and teacher ratings in the assessment and prediction of antisocial and delinquent behaviors. *Journal of Personality, 61,* 693–709.

Baucom, D. H., & Epstein, N. (1990). *Cognitive-behavioral marital therapy.* New York: Brunner/Mazel.

Bianchi, S. M., Subaiya, L., & Kahn, J. (1997, March). *Economic well-being of husbands and wives after marital disruption.* Paper presented at the annual meeting of the Population Association of America, Washington, DC.

Block, J. H., Block, J., & Gjerde, P. F. (1986). The personality of children prior to divorce: A prospective study. *Child Development, 57,* 827–840.

Block, J. H., Block, J., & Gjerde, P. F. (1988). Parental functioning and the home environment in families of divorce: Prospective and concurrent analyses. *Journal of the American Academy of Child and Adolescent Psychiatry, 27,* 207–213.

Bloom, B. L., Asher, S. J., & White, S. W. (1978). Marital disruption as a stressor: A review and analysis. *Psychological Bulletin, 85,* 867–894.

Booth, A., & Amato, P. R. (1994). Parental marital quality, parental divorce, and relations with parents. *Journal of Marriage and the Family, 56,* 21–34.

Booth, A., & Edwards, J. N. (1990). Transmission of marital and family quality over the generations: The effects of parental divorce and unhappiness. *Journal of Divorce, 13,* 41–58.

Booth, A., & Edwards, J. N. (1992). Starting over: Why remarriages are more unstable. *Journal of Family Issues, 13,* 179–194.

Bradbury, T. N., & Fincham, F. D. (1990). Attributions in marriage: Review and critique. *Psychological Bulletin, 107,* 3–33.

Brand, E., Clingempeel, W. G., & Bowen-Woodward, K. (1988). Family relationships and children's psychosocial adjustment in stepmother and stepfather families. In E. M. Hetherington & J. D. Arasteh (Eds.), *Impact of divorce, single parenting, and stepparenting on children* (pp. 299–324). Hillsdale, NJ: Erlbaum.

Braver, S. L., Wolchik, S. A., Sandler, I. N., Sheets, V. L., Fogas, B., & Bay, R. C. (1993). A longitudinal study of noncustodial parents: Parents without children. *Journal of Family Psychology, 7,* 9–23.

Bray, J. H. (1987, August–September). *Becoming a stepfamily: Overview of The Developmental Issues in Stepfamilies Research Project.* Paper presented at the 95th Annual Convention of the American Psychological Association, New York.

Bray, J. H. (1988). Children's development during early remarriage. In E. M. Hetherington & J. D. Arasteh (Eds.), *Impact of divorce, single parenting, and stepparenting on children* (pp. 279–288). Hillsdale, NJ: Erlbaum.

Bray, J. H. (1990, August). *The developing stepfamily II: Overview and previous findings.* Paper presented at the 98th Annual Convention of the American Psychological Association, Boston.

Bray, J. H., & Berger, S. H. (1992). Nonresidential family-child relationships following divorce and remarriage. In C. E. Depner & J. H. Bray (Eds.), *Nonresidential parenting: New vistas in family living* (pp. 156–181). Newbury Park, CA: Sage.

Bray, J. H., & Berger, S. H. (1993). Developmental Issues in Stepfamilies Research Project: Family relationships and parent-child interactions. *Journal of Family Psychology, 7,* 76–90.

Bray, J. H., Berger, S. H., & Boethel, C. L. (1994). Role integration and marital adjustment in stepfather families. In K. Pasley & M. Ihinger-Tallman (Eds.), *Stepparenting: Issues in theory, research, and practice* (pp. 69–86). Westport, CT: Greenwood Press.

Buchanan, C. M., Maccoby, E. E., & Dornbusch, S. M. (1991). Caught between parents: Adolescents' experience in divorced homes. *Child Development, 62,* 1008–1029.

Buchanan, C. M., Maccoby, E. E., & Dornbusch, S. M. (1992). Adolescents and their families after divorce: Three residential arrangements compared. *Journal of Research on Adolescence, 2,* 261–291.

Bumpass, L. L., Martin, T. C., & Sweet, J. A. (1991). The impact of family background and early marital factors on marital disruption. *Journal of Family Issues, 12,* 22–42.

Bumpass, L. L., & Raley, R. K. (1995). Redefining single-parent families: Cohabitation and changing family reality. *Demography, 32,* 97–109.

Bumpass, L. L., & Sweet, J. A. (1989). *Children's experience in single-parent families: Implications of cohabitation and marital transitions* (National Study of Families and Households Working Paper No. 3). Madison: University of Wisconsin, Center for Demography and Ecology.

Bumpass, L. L., Sweet, J. A., & Castro-Martin, T. (1990). Changing patterns of remarriage. *Journal of Marriage and the Family, 52,* 747–756.

Bumpass, L. L., Sweet, J. A., & Cherlin, A. (1991). The role of cohabitation in declining rates of marriage. *Journal of Marriage and the Family, 53,* 913–927.

Burman, P., & Margolin, G. (1992). Analysis of the association between marital relationships and health problems: An interactional perspective. *Psychological Bulletin, 112,* 39–63.

Burrell, N. A. (1995). Communication patterns in stepfamilies: Redefining family roles, themes, and conflict styles. In M. A. Fitzpatrick & A. L. Vangelisti (Eds.), *Explaining family interactions* (pp. 290–309). Thousand Oaks, CA: Sage.

Capaldi, D. M., & Patterson, G. R. (1991). Relation of parental transitions to boys' adjustment problems: I. A linear hypothesis. II. Mothers at risk for transitions and unskilled parenting. *Developmental Psychology, 27,* 489–504.

Castro-Martin, T., & Bumpass, L. (1989). Recent trends and differentials in marital disruption. *Demography, 26,* 37–51.

Chase-Lansdale, P. L., Cherlin, A. J., & Kiernan, K. E. (1995). The long-term effects of parental divorce on the mental health of young adults: A developmental perspective. *Child Development, 66,* 1614–1634.

Chase-Lansdale, P. L., & Hetherington, E. M. (1990). The impact of divorce on life-span development: Short and long term effects. In P. B. Baltes, D. L. Featherman, & R. M. Lerner (Eds.), *Life-span development and behavior* (Vol. 10, pp. 105–150). Hillsdale, NJ: Erlbaum.

Cherlin, A. (1992). *Marriage, divorce, remarriage: Social trends in the U.S.* Cambridge, MA: Harvard University Press.

Cherlin, A. J., & Furstenberg, F. F. (1994). Stepfamilies in the United States: A reconsideration. In J. Blake & J. Hagen (Eds.), *Annual review of sociology* (pp. 359–381). Palo Alto, CA: Annual Reviews.

Cherlin, A. J., Furstenberg, F. F., Chase-Lansdale, P. L., Kiernan, K. E., Robins, P. K., Morrison, D. R., & Teitler, J. O. (1991). Longitudinal studies of effects of divorce in children in Great Britain and the United States. *Science, 252,* 1386–1389.

Clarke-Stewart, K. A., & Hayward, C. (1996). Advantages of father custody and contact for the psychological well-being of school-age children. *Journal of Applied Developmental Psychology, 17,* 239–270.

Clingempeel, W. G., Brand, E., & Ievoli, R. (1984). Stepparent-stepchild relationships in stepmother and stepfather families: A multimethod study. *Family Relations, 33,* 465–473.

Conger, R. D., & Chao, W. (1996). Adolescent depressed mood. In R. L. Simons & Associates (Eds.), *Understanding differences between divorced and intact families: Stress, interaction, and child outcome* (pp. 157–175). Thousand Oaks, CA: Sage.

Conger, R. D., & Conger, K. J. (1996). Sibling relationships. In R. L. Simons & Associates (Eds.), *Understanding differences between divorced and intact families: Stress, interaction, and child outcome* (pp. 104–124). Thousand Oaks, CA: Sage.

Conger, R. D., & Reuter, M. A. (1996). Siblings, parents, and peers: A longitudinal study of social influences in adolescent risk for alcohol use and abuse. In G. H. Brody (Ed.), *Sibling relationships: Their causes and consequences* (pp. 1–30). Norwood, NJ: Ablex.

Cowan, P. A., & Cowan, C. P. (1990). Becoming a family: Research and intervention. In I. Sigel & G. A. Brody (Eds.), *Family research* (pp. 246–279). Hillsdale, NJ: Erlbaum.

Crosbie-Burnett, M. (1991). Impact of joint versus sole custody and quality of the co-parental relationship on adjustment of adolescents in remarried families. *Behavioral Sciences and the Law, 9,* 439–449.

Daly, M., & Wilson, M. I. (1996). Violence against stepchildren. *Current Directions in Psychological Science, 5,* 77–81.

Davies, P. T., & Cummings, E. M. (1994). Marital conflict and child adjustment: An emotional security hypothesis. *Psychological Bulletin, 116,* 387–411.

Demo, D. H., & Acock, A. C. (1996). Family structure, family process, and adolescent well-being. *Journal of Research on Adolescence, 6,* 457–488.

Dillon, P. A., & Emery, R. E. (1996). Divorce mediation and resolution of child custody disputes: Long-term effects. *American Journal of Orthopsychiatry, 66,* 131–140.

Dornbusch, S. M., Carlsmith, J. M., Bushwall, S. J., Ritter, P. L., Liederman, H., Hastrof, A. H., & Gross, R. T. (1985). Single parents, extended households, and the control of adolescents. *Child Development, 56,* 326–341.

Elder, G., Caspi, A., & Van Nguyen, R. (1992). Resourceful and vulnerable children: Family influences in stressful times. In R. K. Silbereisen & K. Eyferth (Eds.), *Development in context: Integrative perspectives on youth development* (pp. 165–194). New York: Springer.

Elder, G. H., Jr., & Russell, S. T. (1996). Academic performance and future aspirations. In R. L. Simons & Associates (Eds.), *Understanding differences between divorced and intact families: Stress, interaction, and child outcome* (pp. 176–192). Thousand Oaks, CA: Sage.

Emery, R. E. (1982). Interpersonal conflict and the children of discord and divorce. *Psychological Bulletin, 92,* 310–330.

Emery, R. E. (1988). *Marriage, divorce, and children's adjustment.* Newbury Park, CA: Sage.

Emery, R. E. (1994). *Renegotiating family relationships.* New York: Guilford Press.

Emery, R. E., & Dillon, P. A. (1994). Conceptualizing the divorce process: Renegotiating boundaries of intimacy and power in the divorced family system. *Family Relations, 43,* 374–379.

Emery, R. E., & Forehand, R. (1994). Parental divorce and children's well-being: A focus on resilience. In R. J. Haggerty, L. R. Sherrod, N. Garmezy, & M. Rutter (Eds.), Stress, risk, and resilience in children and adolescents (pp. 64–99). Cambridge, England: Cambridge University Press.

Felner, R. D., Ginter, M. A., Boike, M. F., & Cowen, E. L. (1981). Parental death or divorce and the school adjustment of young children. *American Journal of Community Psychology, 9,* 181–191.

Felner, R. D., Stolberg, A., & Cowen, E. L. (1975). Crisis events and school mental health referral patterns of young children. *Journal of Consulting and Clinical Psychology, 43,* 305–310.

Fincham, F. D., Bradbury, T. N., & Scott, C. K. (1990). Cognition in marriage. In F. D. Fincham & T. N. Bradbury (Eds.), *The psychology of marriage* (pp. 118–149). New York: Guilford Press.

Forehand, R., Brody, G., Long, N., Slotkin, J., & Fauber, R. (1986). Divorce/divorce potential and interparental conflict: The relationship to early adolescent social and cognitive functioning. *Journal of Adolescent Research, 1,* 389–397.

Forehand, R., Thomas, A. M., Wierson, M., Brody, G., & Fauber, R. (1990). Role of maternal functioning and parenting skills in adolescent functioning following divorce. *Journal of Abnormal Psychology, 99,* 278–283.

Forgatch, M. S., Patterson, G. R., & Ray, J. A. (1995). Divorce and boys' adjustment problems: Two paths with a single model. In E. M. Hetherington & E. A. Blechman (Eds.), *Stress, coping, and resiliency in children and families* (pp. 67–105). Mahwah, NJ: Erlbaum.

Furman, W., & Buhrmester, D. (1992). Age and sex differences in perceptions of networks of personal relationships. *Child Development, 63,* 103–115.

Furstenberg, F. F., Jr. (1988). Child care after divorce and remarriage. In E. M. Hetherington & J. D. Arasteh (Eds.), *Impact of divorce, single parenting, and stepparenting on children* (pp. 245–261). Hillsdale, NJ: Erlbaum.

Furstenberg, F. F., Jr., & Cherlin, A. J. (1991). Divided families: *What happens to children when parents part.* Cambridge, MA: Harvard University Press.

Furstenberg, F. F., Jr., Morgan, S. P., & Allison, P. D. (1987). Paternal participation and children's well-being after marital dissolution. *American Sociological Review, 52,* 695–701.

Furstenberg, F. F., Jr., & Nord, C. W. (1987). Parenting apart: Patterns of childrearing after marital disruption. *Journal of Marriage and the Family, 47,* 893–904.

Furstenberg, F. F., Jr., Nord, C. W., Peterson, J. L., & Zill, N. (1983). The life course of children of divorce: Marital disruption and parental contact. *American Sociological Review, 48,* 656–668.

Ganong, L. H., & Coleman, M. (1994). *Remarried family relationships.* Thousand Oaks, CA: Sage.

Giles-Sims, J. (1987). Social exchange in remarried families. In K. Pasley & M. Ihinger-Tallman (Eds.), *Remarriage and stepparenting: Current research and theory* (pp. 141–163). New York: Guilford Press.

Glenn, N. D., & Kramer, K. B. (1985). The psychological well-being of adult children of divorce. *Journal of Marriage and the Family, 47,* 905–912.

Glick, P. C. (1989). Remarried families, stepfamilies, and stepchildren: A brief demographic profile. *Family Relations, 38,* 24–27.

Gotlib, I., & McCabe, S. B. (1990). Marriage and psychopathology. In F. D. Fincham & T. N. Bradbury (Eds.), *The psychology of marriage* (pp. 226–257). New York: Guilford Press.

Gottman, J. M. (1993). A theory of marital dissolution and stability. *Journal of Family Psychology, 7,* 57–75.

Gottman, J. M. (1994). *What predicts divorce?* Hillsdale, NJ: Erlbaum.

Gottman, J. M., & Katz, L. F. (1989). Effects of marital discord on young children's peer interaction and health. *Developmental Psychology, 25,* 373–381.

Gottman, J. M., & Levenson, R. W. (1992). Marital processes predictive of later dissolution: Behavior, physiology, and health. *Journal of Personality and Social Psychology, 63,* 221–233.

Guidubaldi, J., Perry, J. D., & Nastasi, B. K. (1987). Growing up in a divorced family: Initial and long-term perspectives on children's adjustment. In S. Oskamp (Ed.) *Applied social psy-*

chology annual: Vol. 7. Family processes and problems (pp. 202–237). Newbury Park, CA: Sage.

Hanson, S. M. H. (1988). Single custodial fathers and the parent-child relationship. Nursing Research, 30, 202–204.

Henderson, S. H., Hetherington, E. M., Mekos, D., & Reiss, D. (1996). Stress, parenting, and adolescent psychopathology in nondivorced and stepfamilies: A within-family perspective. In E. M. Hetherington & E. H. Blechman (Eds.), Stress, coping, and resiliency in children and families (pp. 39–66). Mahwah, NJ: Erlbaum.

Hetherington, E. M. (1972). Effects of father absence on personality development in adolescent daughters. Developmental Psychology, 7, 313–326.

Hetherington, E. M. (1989). Coping with family transitions: Winners, losers, and survivors. Child Development, 60, 1–14.

Hetherington, E. M. (1991a). Families, lies, videotapes. Journal of Research on Adolescence, 1, 323–348.

Hetherington, E. M. (1991b). The role of individual differences in family relations in coping with divorce and remarriage. In P. Cowan & E. M. Hetherington (Eds.), Advances in family research: Vol. 2, Family transitions (pp. 165–194). Hillsdale, NJ: Erlbaum.

Hetherington, E. M. (1993). An overview of the Virginia Longitudinal Study of Divorce and Remarriage with a focus on early adolescence. Journal of Family Psychology, 7, 39–56.

Hetherington, E. M. (1997). Teenaged childbearing and divorce. In S. Luthar, J. A. Burack, D. Cicchetti, & J. Wiesz (Eds.), Developmental psychopathology: Perspectives on adjustment, risk, and disorders (pp. 350–373). Cambridge, England: Cambridge University Press.

Hetherington, E. M. (in press). Social capital and the development of youth from nondivorced, divorced, and remarried families. In A. Collins (Ed.), Relationships as developmental contexts: The 29th Minnesota Symposium on Child Psychology. Hillsdale, NJ: Erlbaum.

Hetherington, E. M., & Clingempeel, W. G. (1992). Coping with marital transitions: A family systems perspective. Monographs of the Society for Research in Child Development, 57, (2–3, Serial No. 227).

Hetherington, E. M., Cox, M., & Cox, R. (1979). Family interaction and the social, emotional, and cognitive development of children following divorce. In V. Vaughn & T. Brazelton (Eds.), The family: Setting priorities (pp. 89–128). New York: Science and Medicine.

Hetherington, E. M. Cox, M., & Cox, R. (1985). Long-term effects of divorce and remarriage on the adjustment of children. Journal of the American Academy of Child Psychiatry, 24, 518–539.

Hetherington, E. M., & Jodl, K. M. (1994). Stepfamilies as settings for child development. In A. Booth & J. Dunn (Eds.), Stepfamilies: Who benefits? Who does not? (pp. 55–79). Hillsdale, NJ: Erlbaum.

Hetherington, E. M., Law, T. C., & O'Connor, T. G. (1992). Divorce: Challenges, changes, and new chances. In F. Walsh (Ed.), Normal family processes (2nd ed., pp. 219–246). New York: Guilford Press.

Hetherington, E. M., & Stanley Hagan, M. S. (1995). Parenting in divorced and remarried families. In M. Bornstein (Ed.), Handbook of parenting (pp. 233–255). Hillsdale, NJ: Erlbaum.

Hetherington, E. M., & Stanley Hagan, M. S. (1997). The effects of divorce on fathers and their children. In M. Bornstein (Ed.), The role of the father in child development (pp. 191–211). New York: Wiley.

Hoffman, C. D. (1995). Pre- and post-divorce father-child relationships and child adjustment: Noncustodial fathers' perspectives. Journal of Divorce and Remarriage, 23, 3–20.

Hu, Y., & Goldman, N. (1990). Mortality differentials by marital status: An international comparison. Demography, 27, 233–250.

Jacobson, D. S. (1982, August). Family structure in the age of divorce. Paper presented at the 90th Annual Convention of the American Psychological Association, Washington, DC.

Jessor, R., & Jessor, S. L. (1977). Problem behavior and psycho-social development. New York: Academic Press.

Jockin, V., McGue, M., & Lykken, D. T. (1996). Personality and divorce: A genetic analysis. Journal of Personality and Social Psychology, 71, 288–299.

Kelly, E. L., & Conley, J. J. (1987). Personality and compatibility: A prospective analysis of marital stability and marital satisfaction. Journal of Personality and Social Psychology, 52, 27–40.

Kiecolt-Glaser, J. K., Fisher, L. D., Ogrocki, P., Stout, J. C., Speicher, C. E., & Glaser, R. (1987). Marital quality, marital disruption, and immune function. Psychosomatic Medicine, 49, 13–34.

Kiecolt-Glaser, J. K., Kennedy, S., Malkoff, S., Fisher, L. D., Speicher, C. E., & Glaser, R. (1988). Marital discord and immunity in males. Psychosomatic Medicine, 50, 213–229.

King, V. (1994a). Nonresidential father involvement and child well-being: Can dads make a difference? Journal of Family Issues, 15, 78–96.

King, V. (1994b). Variation in the consequences of nonresidential father involvement for children's well-being. Journal of Marriage and the Family, 56, 964–972.

Kitson, G. C., & Holmes, W. M. (1992). Portrait of divorce: Adjustment to marital breakdown. New York: Guilford Press.

Kitson, G. C., & Morgan, L. A. (1990). The multiple consequences of divorce. Journal of Marriage and the Family, 52, 913–924.

Kline, M., Johnston, J. R., & Tschann, J. M. (1991). The long shadow of marital conflict: A model of children's post-divorce adjustment. Journal of Marriage and the Family, 53, 297–309.

Kurdek, L. A. (1993). Predicting marital dissolution: A 5-year prospective longitudinal study of newlywed couples. Journal of Personality and Social Psychology, 64, 221–242.

Kurdek, L. A., & Fine, M. A. (1993). Parent and nonparent residential family members as providers of warmth, support, and supervision to young adolescents. Journal of Family Psychology, 7, 245–249.

Kurdek, L. A., Fine, M. A., & Sinclair, R. J. (1995). School adjustment in sixth graders: Parenting transitions, family climate, and peer norm effects. Child Development, 66, 430–445.

Lahey, B. B., Hartdagen, S. E., Frick, P. J., McBurnett, K., Connor, R., & Hynd, G. W. (1988). Conduct disorder: Parsing the confounded relation to parental divorce and antisocial personality. Journal of Abnormal Psychology, 97, 334–337.

Lamb, M. E. (1997). Fathers and child development: An introductory overview and guide. In M. E. Lamb (Ed.), The role of the father in child development (pp. 1–18). New York: Wiley.

Lee, V. E., Burkam, D. T., Zimiles, H., & Ladewski, B. (1994). Family structure and its effect on behavioral and emotional problems in young adolescents. Journal of Research on Adolescence, 4, 405–437.

Lindner-Gunnoe, M. (1993). Noncustodial mothers' and fathers' contributions to the adjustment of adolescent stepchildren. Unpublished doctoral dissertation. University of Virginia.

Lorenz, F. O., Simons, R. L., & Chao, W. (1996). Family structure and mother's depression. In R. L. Simons & Associates (Eds.), Understanding differences between divorced and intact families: Stress, interaction, and child outcome (pp. 65–77). Thousand Oaks, CA: Sage.

Maccoby, E. E., Buchanan, C. M., Mnookin, R. H., & Dornbusch, S. M. (1993). Post-divorce roles of mothers and fathers in the lives of their children. Journal of Family Psychology, 7, 24–38.

Maccoby, E. E., & Mnookin, R. H. (1992). *Dividing the child: Social and legal dilemmas of custody.* Cambridge, MA: Harvard University Press.

Masheter, C. (1991). Post-divorce relationships between ex-spouses: The roles of attachment and interpersonal conflict. *Journal of Marriage and the Family, 53,* 101–110.

Matthews, L. S., Wickrama, K. A. S., & Conger, R. D. (1996). Predicting marital instability from spouse and observer reports of marital interaction. *Journal of Marriage and the Family, 58,* 641–655.

McGue, M., & Lykken, D. T. (1992). Genetic influence on risk of divorce. *Psychological Science, 6,* 368–373.

McLanahan, S. S., & Booth, K. (1989). Mother-only families: Problems, prospects, and politics. *Journal of Marriage and the Family, 51,* 557–580.

McLanahan, S. S., & Bumpass, L. (1988). Intergenerational consequences of family disruption. *American Journal of Sociology, 94,* 130–152.

McLanahan, S., & Sandefur, G. (1994). *Growing up with a single parent: What hurts, what helps?* Cambridge, MA: Harvard University Press.

Mekos, D., Hetherington, E. M., & Reiss, D. (1996). Sibling differences in problem behavior and parental treatment in nondivorced and remarried families. *Child Development, 67,* 2148–2165.

Mendes, H. A. (1976a). Single fatherhood. *Social Work, 21,* 308–312.

Mendes, H. A. (1976b). Single fathers. *Family Coordinator, 25,* 439–444.

Merikangas, K. R., Prusoff, B. A., & Weissman, M. M. (1988). Parental concordance for affective disorders: Psychopathology in offspring. *Journal of Affective Disorders, 15,* 279–290.

Meyer, D. R., & Garasky, S. (1993). Custodial fathers: Myths, realities, and child support policy. *Journal of Marriage and the Family, 55,* 73–89.

Minton, C., & Pasley, K. (1996). Fathers' parenting role identity and father involvement: A comparison of nondivorced and divorced, nonresident fathers. *Journal of Family Issues, 17,* 26–45.

Munsch, J., Woodward, J., & Darling, N. (1995). Children's perceptions of their relationships with coresiding and non-custodial fathers. *Journal of Divorce and Remarriage, 23,* 39–54.

National Center for Health Statistics. (1988). *Current estimates from the National Health Interview Survey: United States, 1987* (DHHS Publication No. 88–1594). Washington, DC: U.S. Government Printing Office.

Orbuch, T. L., Veroff, J., & Hunter, A. G. (in press). Black couples, White couples: The early years of marriage. In E. M. Hetherington (Ed.), *Coping with divorce, single-parenting, and remarriage: A risk and resiliency perspective.* Mahwah, NJ: Erlbaum.

Papernow, P. L. (1988). Stepparent role development: From outsider to intimate. In W. R. Beer (Ed.), *Relative strangers: Studies of stepfamily processes* (pp. 54–82). Totowa, NJ: Rowman & Littlefield.

Patterson, G. (1991, March). *Interaction of stress and family structure and their relation to child adjustment.* Paper presented at the biennial meetings of the Society for Research on Child Development, Seattle, WA.

Patterson, G., DeBaryshe, B., & Ramsey, E. (1989). A developmental perspective on antisocial behavior. *American Psychologist, 44,* 329–335.

Patterson, G., & Dishion, T. J. (1988). Multilevel family process models: Traits, interactions, and relationships. In R. Hinde & J. Stevenson-Hinde (Eds.), *Relationships within families: Mutual influences* (pp. 283–310). Oxford, England: Clarendon Press.

Pearlin, L. I., & Johnson, J. S. (1977). Marital status, life-stresses and depression. *American Sociological Review, 42,* 704–715.

Peterson, J. L., & Zill, N. (1986). Marital disruption, parent-child relationships, and behavior problems in children. *Journal of Marriage and the Family, 48,* 295–307.

Riessman, C. K., & Gerstel, N. (1985). Marital dissolution and health: Do males or females have greater risk? *Social Science and Medicine, 20,* 627–635.

Rutter, M. (1987). Psychosocial resilience and protective mechanisms. *American Journal of Orthopsychiatry, 57,* 316–331.

Santrock, J. W., & Sitterle, K. A. (1987). Parent-child relationships in stepmother families. In K. Pasley & M. Ihinger-Tallman (Eds.), *Remarriage and stepparenting: Current research and theory* (pp. 273–299). New York: Guilford Press.

Santrock, J. W., Sitterle, K. A., & Warshak, R. A. (1988). Parent-child relationships in stepfather families. In P. Bronstein & C. P. Cowan (Eds.), *Fatherhood today: Men's changing roles in the family* pp. 144–165). New York: Wiley.

Seltzer, J. A. (1991). Relationships between fathers and children who live apart: The father's role after separation. *Journal of Marriage and the Family, 53,* 79–101.

Seltzer, J. A. (1994). Consequences of marital dissolution for children. *Annual Review of Sociology, 20,* 235–266.

Seltzer, J. A., & Brandreth, Y. (1994). What fathers say about involvement with children after separation. *Journal of Family Issues, 15,* 49–77.

Simons, R. L. (1996). The effect of divorce on adult and child adjustment. In R. L. Simons & Associates (Eds.), *Understanding differences between divorced and intact families: Stress, interaction, and child outcome* (pp. 3–20). Thousand Oaks, CA: Sage.

Simons, R. L., & Associates. (Eds. (1996). *Understanding differences between divorced and intact families: Stress, interaction, and child outcome.* Thousand Oaks, CA: Sage.

Simons, R. L., & Beaman, J. (1996). Father's parenting. In R. L. Simons & Associates (Eds.), *Understanding differences between divorced and intact families: Stress, interaction, and child outcome* (pp. 94–103). Thousand Oaks, CA: Sage.

Simons, R. L., Beaman, J., Conger, R. D., & Chao, W. (1992). Childhood experience, conceptions of parenting, and attitudes of spouse as determinants of parental behavior. *Journal of Marriage and the Family, 55,* 91–106.

Simons, R. L., & Chao, W. (1996). Conduct problems. In R. L. Simons & Associates (Eds.), *Understanding differences between divorced and intact families: Stress, interaction, and child outcome* (pp. 125–143). Thousand Oaks, CA: Sage.

Simons, R. L., & Johnson, C. (1996). Mother's parenting. In R. L. Simons & Associates (Eds.), *Understanding differences between divorced and intact families: Stress, interaction, and child outcome* (pp. 81–93). Thousand Oaks, CA: Sage.

Simons, R. L., Johnson, C., & Lorenz, F. O. (1996). Family structure differences in stress and behavioral predispositions. In R. L. Simons & Associates (Eds.), *Understanding differences between divorced and intact families: Stress, interaction, and child outcome* (pp. 45–63). Thousand Oaks, CA: Sage.

Stack, S. (1989). The impact of divorce on suicide in Norway, 1951–1980. *Journal of Marriage and the Family, 51,* 229–238.

Thomson, E., McLanahan, S. S., & Curtin, R. B. (1992). Family structure, gender, and parental separation. *Journal of Marriage and the Family, 54,* 368–378.

Travato, F., & Lauris, G. (1989). Marital status and mortality in Canada: 1951–81. *Journal of Marriage and the Family, 51,* 907–922.

Tzeng, J. M., & Mare, R. D. (1995). Labor market and socioeconomic effects on marital stability. *Social Science Research, 24,* 329–351.

Umberson, D. (1987). Family status and health behaviors: Social control as a dimension of social integration. *Journal of Health and Social Behavior, 28,* 306–319.

Umberson, D., & Williams, C. L. (1993). Divorced fathers: Parental role strain and psychological distress. *Journal of Family Issues, 14*, 378–400.

U.S. Bureau of the Census. (1992). *Marital status and living arrangements: March, 1992* (No. 468, Tables G & 5, Current Population Reports, Series P–20). Washington, DC: U.S. Government Printing Office.

Visher, E. B., & Visher, J. S. (1990). Dynamics of successful stepfamilies. *Journal of Divorce and Remarriage, 14*, 3–11.

Warshak, R. A. (1986). Father custody and child development: A review and analysis of psychological research. *Behavioral Sciences and the Law, 4*, 185–202.

Weiss, R. S. (1979). Growing up a little faster: The experience of growing up in a single-parent household. *Journal of Social Issues, 35*, 97–111.

Werner, E. E. (1988). Individual differences, universal needs: A 30-year study of resilient high-risk infants. *Zero to Three: Bulletin of National Center for Clinical Infant Programs, 8*, 1–15.

Werner, E. E. (1993). Risk, resilience, and recovery: Perspectives from the Kauaii Longitudinal Study. *Development and Psychopathology, 54*, 503–515.

Whitbeck, L. B., Simons, R. L., & Goldberg, E. (1996). Adolescent sexual intercourse. In R. L. Simons & Associates (Eds.), *Understanding differences between divorced and intact families: Stress, interaction, and child outcome* (pp. 144–156). Thousand Oaks, CA: Sage.

White, L. (1994). Stepfamilies over the life course: Social support. In A. Booth & J. Dunn (Eds.), *Stepfamilies: Who benefits? Who does not?* (pp. 109–137). Hillsdale, NJ: Erlbaum.

White, L. K., Brinkerhoff, D. B., & Booth, A. (1985). The effect of marital disruption on children's attachment to parents. *Journal of Family Issues, 6*, 5–22.

Wilson, M. I., Daly, M., & Weghorst, S. J. (1980). Household composition and the risk of child abuse and neglect. *Journal of Biosocial Science, 12*, 333–340.

Zill, N. (1988). Behavior, achievement, and health problems among children in stepfamilies. In E. M. Hetherington & J. D. Arasteh (Eds.), *Impact of divorce, single parenting, and stepparenting on children* (pp. 324–368). Hillsdale, NJ: Erlbaum.

Zill, N. Morrison, D. R., & Coiro, M. J. (1993). Long-term effects of parental divorce on parent-child relationships, adjustment, and achievement in young adulthood. *Journal of Family Psychology, 7*, 91–103.

Zimiles, H., & Lee, V. E. (1991). Adolescent family structure and educational progress. *Developmental Psychology, 27*, 314–320.

E. Mavis Hetherington, Margaret Bridges, and Glendessa M. Insabella, Department of Psychology, University of Virginia.

Correspondence concerning this article should be addressed to E. Mavis Hetherington, Department of Psychology, University of Virginia, 102 Gilmer Hall, Charlottesville, VA 22903–2477. Electronic mail may be sent to emh2f@virginia.edu.

From *American Psychologist*, February 1998, pp. 167–184. © 1998 by the American Psychological Association. Reprinted by permission.

American Child Care Today

Sandra Scarr

University of Virginia and KinderCare Learning Centers, Inc.

Child care has 2 purposes: mothers' employment and children's development. These are conflicting goals, because the first focuses on the quantity and affordability of child care whereas the second favors expensive quality services. Affordable child care fosters maternal employment and gender equality. With welfare reform demanding more child-care places to move mothers from welfare to work, the pressure for larger quantities of child care is great. Demanding regulations raise the quality of care and give more assurance of children's well-being, but they also increase the cost. More expensive regulations price more working parents out of licensed care and force them to use unregulated home care. Widely varying qualities of child care have been shown to have only small effects on children's current development and no demonstrated long-term impact, except on disadvantaged children, whose homes put them at developmental risk. Parents have far greater impact on their children's development through both the genes and environments they provide. Thus, greater quantities of affordable, regulated child care may be possible.

Care of American children by anyone other than their own mothers needs to have a name. Even care of children by their own fathers is counted by the U.S. Labor Department as "other relative care." Cultural anxiety about nonmaternal child care is revealed in every aspect of research, practices, and policies that are reviewed in this article.

Terms for the care of children by people other than mothers include *child care, family day care, home care, center care, nanny care, babysitting, preschool education, after-school care,* and others. *Day care* is probably the most frequently used term, although early childhood professionals prefer the term *child care,* because "we take care of *children,* not *days*" (M. Guddemi, personal communication, July 6, 1996). Different terms relate to the age of the child (infant, toddler, preschool or school age), the setting (e.g., home versus center), and the primary purpose (babysitting, when the focus is on working mothers' needs, versus preschool education, when the focus is on benefits to the

child). The term *child care* is used throughout this article to include all varieties of nonmaternal care of children who reside with their parent(s) or close family members; it excludes foster care and institutional care.

The assumption of all the nomenclature is that child care provided by anyone other than the child's mother deserves special notice, because it is a nonnormative event that needs definition. In fact, shared child care is the normative experience for contemporary American children, the vast majority of whose mothers are employed. More than half the mothers of infants under 12 months of age are in the labor force; three quarters of school-age children's mothers are working (Behrman, 1996).

History of Child Care

Nonmaternal shared child care is, in fact, normative for the human young, both historically and worldwide: "Nonparental care is a universal practice with a long history, not a dangerous innovation representing a major deviation from species-typical and species-appropriate patterns of child care" (Lamb, in press). Exclusive maternal care of infants and young children is a cultural myth of an idealized 1950s, not a reality anywhere in the world either now or in earlier times. Child care has always been shared, usually among female relatives. Until recently, most American children of working parents were cared for by other female relatives, but high rates of female employment have reduced that source of babysitters. What has changed over time and varies cross-nationally is the degree to which child care is bought in the marketplace rather than shared among female relatives.

Today, more American children are cared for by paid providers than by relatives. Relatives have, presumably, some emotional commitment to the health and safety of relatives' offspring; therefore, quality of care was seldom raised as an issue of concern. The predominance of nonrelative care in the last decade has alerted consumers, governments, and the research community to the possibly damaging effects of poor quality care on children's development; the zeitgeist called for critical appraisal of non-maternal care (Scarr, 1985).

In agricultural societies, infants are typically left in the care of siblings, grandmothers, or female neighbors, who are also caring for their own children. In industrialized societies, mothers' employment outside the home has necessitated nonmaternal care of various types. Demand for child care is driven entirely by the economic need for women in the labor force (Lamb, Sternberg, Hwang, & Broberg, 1992), although occasional subgroups, such as upper-class mothers with heavy social schedules, may use extensive nonmaternal child care (Lamb, in press). Tracing historical changes in maternal employment provides a guide to the demand for and use of nonmaternal child care.

Employment Moved Out of the Home and Into the Workplace

Prior to the Industrial Revolution, and in nonindustrial parts of the world today, women are both economically productive workers and primary child caregivers. When employment moved outside the home and into the factory and office, men followed work into new settings, and women generally remained at home, without a direct economic role.

In a correlated development, mothers' roles as knowledgeable caregivers began to be stressed. In the late 19th and early 20th centuries, child rearing was no longer a natural species response but a role that required extensive education and knowledge. Children began to have tender psyches that required maternal attention to develop well. Mothers were given an important emotional role in the home that complemented fathers' economic productivity (Kagan, 1980; Scarr, 1984).

Prior to World War II, few women remained in the labor force after childbearing. The need for industrial workers during the war brought many mothers into factories and offices to replace men away at war. Mothers' employment was culturally sanctioned and supported by the government provision of child-care centers attached to war factories. Mothers, as Rosie the Riveter, took on the many paid work roles that had previously been denied them.

After the war, government and cultural supports for mothers' employment were withdrawn, child-care centers were closed, and mothers were told to go home to make way in the workplace for returning veterans. The birthrate soared and new suburbs were built as federally sponsored highway programs fueled a boom in housing outside of cities. All of this was a direct result of government policy that held as ideal a two-parent family with a working father and a nonworking mother, ensconced in single-family dwelling.

Erroneous predictions about an economic recession after the war, which became instead an economic boom fueled by unfulfilled consumer demand for cars, refrigerators, and housing, left many jobs open to women. Many mothers did not follow official advice to go home, and female employment has grown steadily since. Goods and services that used to be homemade (e.g., clothing, canned goods, and cleaning) came to be increasingly purchased, requiring additional family income. As the divorce rate and single motherhood soared, more mothers needed jobs to support their families. Today most mothers are employed.

In 1995, 62% of mothers with children under six years were employed. This rate was up more than 2% from 1994 and nearly 5% from 1993. Among mothers with children under two years, 58% were working in March 1995, up 4% from 1993 (1996 Green Book, as cited in Hofferth, 1996). The ideal of a nonemployed mother remained strong, however. One legacy for working mothers of the baby-boom generation and beyond is guilt about their employment.

Purposes of Child Care

Three major, often conflicting, purposes for child care create the child-care dilemma we as a society suffer today (Scarr & Weinberg, 1986; Stoney & Greenberg, 1996). First, child care supports maternal employment, which for individual families and for the economy has become a necessity. It is assumed that U.S. working families will pay for their own child-care services. Second, child care serves children's development, which can be enhanced by high-quality early childhood programs, whether or not children's mothers are employed. Again, families are expected to pay for early childhood programs, unless they are poor. Third, child care has been used throughout this century to intervene with economically disadvantaged and ethnic minority children to socialize them to the cultural mainstream. Poor and immigrant children could be fed, immunized, given English language experience, behaviorally trained, given an orderly schedule, and so forth (Scarr & Weinberg, 1986; Stoney & Greenberg, 1996). Taxpayers have paid for these services to the poor.

The roots of child care are in the welfare and reform movements of the 19th century. Day nurseries, which evolved into the child-care centers of today, began in Boston in the 1840s to care for the children of widows and working wives of seamen, two groups of women who had to work outside the home. Reformers, such as Jane Addams, founded day nurseries to care for poor and immigrant children, whose mothers had to work (Scarr & Weinberg, 1986). Preteen school-age children required adult supervision to be safely occupied and kept out of trouble. The primary purpose of day nurseries was to keep children safe and fed while their poor mothers worked. Other benefits, such as early education, were secondary.

By contrast, kindergartens and nursery schools began in the early 20th century to enhance the social development of middle- and upper-class children. For a few hours a week, the children could play with others and experience an enriched learning environment under the tutelage of trained early childhood teachers. Nursery school existed to serve the developmental needs of middle- and upper-class children, whose mothers were not employed (Scarr & Weinberg, 1986).

By the late 1960s, educators and child development researchers recognized the value of nursery schools for poor children, who needed the stimulation and learning opportunities that such early childhood settings afforded children from affluent families. Head Start was designed, in large part, to enhance the learning of poor and minority children—to provide the same kinds of early childhood opportunities that middle-class children had enjoyed for decades. Because many of their mothers were supported by welfare, Head Start could involve mothers in early childhood programs and serve children's developmental needs. As part-day, part-year programs, Head Start did not serve the child-care needs of working mothers.

These three purposes for child care set quite different priorities for the services to be offered and have different assumptions about who will pay for them. Thus, disputes continue about whose goals are to be served by child-care services, who shall pay for them, and what form child care should take. Conflicting advocacy for (a) high-quality, low-cost caregiving, versus (b) high-quality, high-cost, child-centered preschool education, versus (c) intervention and compensation for poor children continues to compete for attention in debates about American child care.

Varieties of Child-Care Arrangements

When the focus is on early childhood education, whether for higher or lower income children, the setting is usually a center or preschool. When the focus is on care while parents work, the setting is often a home. In fact, these distinctions have blurred in recent years, as more and more children move from homes to center-based programs, where they receive both extended care and early education.

Family day care versus center care. Family day-care providers care for children in their own homes. The providers' own children are often included in the mix of children, which can include infants through school-age children who come before and after school. Most family day-care homes accommodate 6 or fewer children and have one caregiver. Some larger homes care for 6 to 20 children and employ aides to assist the family day-care

providers. States generally regulate larger homes. Family day-care homes are for-profit independent providers.

Child-care centers provide group care for children from infancy to school age in age-segregated groups, with smaller ratios of children at younger ages to adults. Facilities vary from church basements to purpose-built centers with specialized spaces and equipment. The most notable differences between homes and centers are educational curricula and staff training, which centers are required to provide and homes are not. Parents prefer center-based care for preschool children and home care for infants and toddlers.

Licensed versus unlicensed care. In all states, child-care centers must be licensed by a state department of social services or its equivalent.[1] Licensure includes regulations on health and safety, ratios of children to adults, group sizes, staff training, and often required play materials. Regular inspections are done semiannually or annually or more frequently if problems have been noted.

Family homes that care for more than six children are usually required to be licensed, although regulations vary considerably from state to state. Most family day-care providers care for fewer than six children and are therefore exempt from any state regulation or inspection. Availability of federal food subsidies to licensed homes, however, has encouraged more family day-care homes to seek licensure or registration. Family day-care homes are rarely visited by state regulators.

Nonprofit versus for-profit centers. In the United States, child-care centers are sponsored by churches, nonprofit community groups, public schools, Head Start, employers, for-profit independent providers, and corporations. Public schools and Head Start serve older preschool children only, whereas other centers usually include younger children as well. Only about half of all centers, however, provide infant care, because the required low ratios of infants to providers make infant care prohibitively expensive.

The mix of public provision and private enterprise in U.S. child care reflects the ambivalence Americans feel about whether child care should be primarily a publicly supported service for children or a business expense for working families (partially offset by tax credits). Should tax dollars be used to supply child care only to poor children, or should all children be eligible for publicly supported child care? Should family day care and privately owned centers profit from the child-care business, or should child care be a nonprofit service (as in Hawaii) like primary education?

Where Are Children Today?

In 1995, there were nearly 21 million children under the age of five years who were not yet enrolled in school. Of these, about 40% were cared for regularly by parents, 21% by other relatives, 31% in child-care centers, 14% in family day-care homes, and 4% by sitters in the child's home. These figures total more than 100% because 9% of children have more than one regular care arrangement, such as enrollment in a part-time preschool program and parental care at home during other hours (Hofferth, 1996). The distribution of center sponsorship is shown in Figure 1.

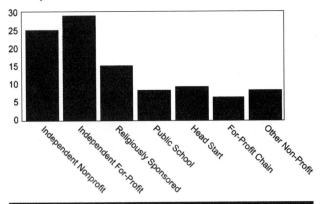

Figure 1
Administrative Auspices of Child-Care Centers (by Percentage) in the United States, 1990 (Willer et al., 1991)

Over the last 30 years, children have been shifted gradually from home to center-based care. In 1965, only 6% of children were cared for in centers; by 1995, 31% were. Use of family day care and care by parents, other relatives, and sitters all declined. Figure 2 shows historical trends in use of different forms of child care. By 1990, in families with employed mothers (three fifths of families with young children), only 37% of infants and 32% of children from one to two years of age were cared for primarily by parents. Of three- to four-year-olds, only 25% were primarily in parental care, and 37% were in child-care centers (Hofferth, 1996).

In surveys by *Working Mother* magazine in 1995 and 1996, readers expressed strong preferences for center-based care over home care, whether by relatives or not. Child safety and parental control over the arrangement were prominent reasons for the preference. Home care is unsupervised and usually unlicensed. Television exposés of abuse and neglect in day-care homes have appeared regularly over the last decade. Relatives do not always abide by parents' child-rearing preferences, such as toilet-training techniques and feeding routines. Paid help is more dependable and controllable. Child-care centers are open even if one caregiver is ill or on vacation (Mason & Kuhlthau, as cited in Mason & Duberstein, 1992).

Relative care is, in general, less costly than other care (Hofferth, 1996). About half of relative care involves payment, but the rates tend to be lower than market rates. Although 23% of parents express a preference for relative care, 77% of mothers prefer another kind of child care (Mason & Kuhlthau, as cited in Mason & Duberstein,

1992). Economic factors play the major role in use of relative care. The more preschool children in the family, the more likely relatives will supply the care, because market discounts for multichild families do not substantially reduce the total cost of child care. The higher the family income, the less likely parents are to choose relative care (Blau & Robbins, 1990).

Older preschool children are more likely than infants and toddlers to be enrolled in center care, but from 1965 to 1995, the use of center care for infants and toddlers grew exponentially, from about 3% in 1965 to 23% in 1993. Parental care of infants and toddlers declined dramatically across that period. School-age care has lagged behind the need for this service and enjoys little public support.

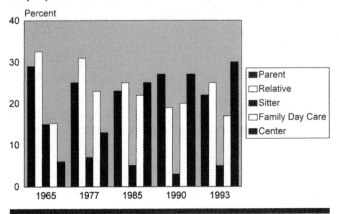

Figure 2
Primary Care for Youngest Preschool Child of Employed Mothers, 1965–1993 (Hofferth, 1996)

Children from more affluent families and those from families on welfare are most likely to be enrolled in centers rather than cared for in homes. Families with an annual income of more than $50,000 can afford center-based programs; those below the poverty line receive subsidies for child care and enroll their children without charge in Head Start. Working families with annual incomes below $25,000 but above the poverty line are the least likely to be able to afford and to use center-based child care.

Nearly 10% of mothers work nonstandard hours; they have fewer choices of child-care arrangements. Only 3% of centers and about 17% of family day-care homes provide evening and weekend care (Hofferth, 1996). In two-parent families, children of evening-shift and weekend workers may be cared for by the other parent or by another relative in the case of single-parent families. Father care is a seldom recognized choice that minimizes costs of child care in a dual-income family.

Presser's data from Detroit suggest that child-care preferences often determine whether mothers work shifts other than 9-to-5. Fully one third of dual-income families have one parent working nonstandard hours to offset child-care costs (Presser, 1992b). When mothers work nights and weekends, and when they have more than one preschool child, fathers are more likely to supply some of the child care. As child-care costs rise, parents are more likely to arrange schedules to provide the care themselves (Mason & Duberstein, 1992).

Much has been said about the shortage of child-care spaces in this country (Hofferth, 1992). With annual increases in the percentage and numbers of working mothers (soon to increase dramatically with welfare reform), the child-care supply is not growing sufficiently to meet the demand for the care of infants and toddlers, of mildly sick children, or of children whose parents work nonstandard hours. Infant and toddler care are scarce nationally; because of low ratio requirements of children to staff, infant and toddler care are very expensive and therefore in particularly short supply. Preschool and after-school care are less costly and more readily available. It is also difficult to find suitable care for disabled children. Even with the Americans With Disabilities Act to encourage nondiscrimination, few facilities can provide competent care for disabled children, particularly those with severe behavior disorders and multiple physical handicaps.

The primary problem is that the market for child care is poorly funded, both by limited parental incomes and by low state subsidies. The price of child care cannot be set high enough in many communities to encourage investment in new facilities or quality programs. Low-income communities have a smaller child-care supply than more affluent ones because of parents' inability to pay for care.

Child-Care Regulations

The 50 states and the District of Columbia display amazing differences in the regulations they have developed to affect cost and quality of child care. Ratios of children to adults in some states (e.g., Maryland, Massachusetts) are less than half of those approved in other states (e.g., Ohio, Texas). Permissible ratios for children under 12 months of age range from 3 to 8 per caregiver. For children ages 12 to 35 months the range among states is from 4 to 13 children per caregiver! Teacher training requirements vary from none (e.g., Georgia, Alabama) to college degrees or advanced credentials (e.g., Illinois, New Jersey). Group sizes permitted for younger children vary from 4 or 6 children, to 20 children, to legally unlimited numbers.

There is a significant cultural and economic gradient from North to South, whereby parents and state regulators in the Northern tier of states demand better quality preschool and child-care programs and are willing to pay more for lower ratios and more highly trained staff. However, in some Northern states with very low ratios and high training requirements, few parents can afford center-based care. Massachusetts, for example, has less than one third the number of child-care center spaces per capita than Texas, a high-ratio, low-training state, has. Low

ratios and teacher training requirements raise the cost of center care to such levels that the vast majority of parents in Massachusetts are forced to use unregulated family day care. By contrast, parents in Texas have the highest provision of center-based programs in the country. The trade-off of quantity and quality in center-based care is a recurring dilemma.

A Labor Force Perspective on Child-Care Research

Despite national ambivalence about maternal employment, the U.S. economy could not function without women employees and entrepreneurs. Today, 48% of workers are women. It is inconceivable that the 80% of these women who are mothers could stay home. Seldom do developmental psychologists consider the economic legitimacy of child care to serve the goal of maternal employment.

There are two major reasons for maternal employment: (a) economic well-being of the family and (b) gender equality (Scarr, 1996). "Child care policies in many countries have been designed at least in part to promote female employment and to equalize potential employment opportunities of men and women" (Lamb, in press).

First and foremost, mothers (and fathers) are employed because their families need or want the income to enhance their standard of living. In today's economy, it is most often a necessity to have two employed parents to support a family with children. Two thirds of mothers are working to keep their families out of poverty (Scarr, Phillips, & McCartney, 1990). With welfare reform, this proportion will increase.

The second reason for maternal employment—to promote economic, social, and political gender equality—is a more complicated issue. The major reason for discrepancies in men's and women's work compensation and career achievements is that family responsibilities fall more heavily on women, especially when there are small children in the home (Scarr, 1996). Most mothers do not maintain full-time employment or have the same commitment to careers that childless women have or that men have, whether they are fathers or not. Unequal child-care responsibilities lead mothers to be less invested in career development and less motivated to maintain continuous, full-time employment. As several commentators have noted, there cannot be gender equality in the workforce until men take more responsibility for child care. According to Supreme Court Justice Ruth Bader Ginsburg, "Women will not be truly liberated until men take equal care of children. If I had an affirmative action plan to design, it would be to give men every incentive to be concerned about the rearing of children" ("Justice Ginsburg Takes on," 1995, p. A4).

Although mothers in the Western industrialized world have increased their economic activity, the gendered division of responsibility and work involved in child-care provision is still the norm in families with young children. When tested for anxiety about leaving their children in child care, fathers expressed more anxiety than mothers, but when asked to rate how their wives felt about leaving children in care, fathers greatly exaggerated their wives' worries about employment and child care (Deater-Deckard, Scarr, McCartney, & Eisenberg, 1994). By inference, fathers think it is the mother's job to worry more about child care, even today. Men's collective choice of nonparticipation in child care helps to maintain men's privileged position in society and in relation to the market and the state (Leira, 1992; Presser, 1992a).

Child Care and Other Family Supports

One often hears liberal policy analysts yearn for the federal government to provide more family-friendly policies that make balancing work and family life less stressful. Corporations vie each year to be on the *Working Mother* magazine list of the top 100 most family-friendly companies. The world's role models of countries with the most family-friendly policies are the Nordic countries.

Family-friendly government policies in the Nordic countries (Sweden, Norway, Finland, Denmark, and Iceland) help mothers to balance work and family life by granting paid, job-guaranteed maternity and parental leaves, child allowances to supplement family income, and part-time work for mothers when their children are young. Although parental leave and part-time employment opportunities can be used by either fathers or mothers, mothers take more than 95% of the leave time and make up virtually all of the part-time workers.

The collective effect of these family-friendly policies is to increase gender inequality to such an extent that Swedish women earn only half of men's wages (in the United States, women earn 77% of men's wages; "Women's Figures," 1997) and hold virtually none of the top jobs in corporations or universities (Cherlin, 1992; Leira, 1992; Scarr, 1996).

Government policies that support maternal absences from the labor force, such as paid parental leaves and child allowances, make balancing work and family life easier for mothers of young children, but they have long-term deleterious consequences for mothers' careers (Scarr, 1996). Although many admire the Swedish system of extensive supports for working parents, including part-time work opportunities when children are young, Cherlin (1992) cited some of the disadvantages:

> Note that you cannot make Partner in a Stockholm law firm working six hours a day. The cost of the system is that its solutions may impede the ability of well-educated mothers to rise up the managerial and professional hierarchies.... That still leaves the problem that women... may lose

experience and continuity in the labor force and the associated promotions and wage increases. (p. 213)

In the United States, where there are few family supports, mothers are more often employed full-time even when their children are infants, thus maintaining more continuous labor force participation, which leads to career advancement, higher incomes, retirement benefits, and other markers of gender equality. Most mothers want to be employed for a variety of reasons. Women's labor force participation is associated with higher family income, greater personal satisfaction, and more social support. However, the double burdens of home and family also lead to role overload and excessive work hours for young mothers in the United States (Scarr, Phillips, & McCartney, 1989). Although working mothers experience greater time stress and role strain (Staines & Pleck, 1983), they express greater satisfaction with their multiple roles than stay-at-home mothers (Scarr, Phillips, & McCartney, 1989).

Significant problems with child-care arrangements and high child-care costs discourage mothers' labor force participation and can lead to depression and marital problems (Ross & Mirowsky, 1988; White & Keith, 1990). If child-care costs were more reasonable, national surveys show that 10–20% more mothers would return to the labor force after giving birth (Mason & Duberstein, 1992). Child-care problems impair women's long-term earning prospects by limiting their participation in the labor force (Cherlin, 1992; Collins & Hofferth, 1996; Mason & Duberstein, 1992; Scarr, 1996).

Income inequalities between men and women are largely explained by the lower labor force participation of mothers in their childbearing years. In 1995, childless women in their 20s and 30s earned 98% of men's wages ("Women's Figures," 1997). In addition, women are less likely than men to be given advanced training opportunities, promotions, and managerial responsibility because they are perceived to have less commitment to careers (Scarr, 1996). Subsidized child care is the one family-friendly government policy that supports gender equality and women's career achievements.

Welfare Reform, or Why Shouldn't Poor Mothers Work Too?

The idea that mothers should be paid to stay at home with children arose during the 1930s, when widows and a few divorcees needed support to rear their children at least to school age. Aid to Families With Dependent Children (AFDC) was the last in a series of programs that was initiated to accomplish this goal. Support levels were generally low, so that a mother and her children could live at the poverty level, but they were provided with medical insurance, food stamps, often housing and clothing allowances, and social services. Gradually, over the past 50 years, welfare (AFDC) recipients came to be identified with never-married minority women and poor White women who had children in their teens and early 20s and were never employed.

As the majority of middle-class mothers entered the labor force in the 1980s, there was a sea-change in thinking about AFDC. By the early 1990s, the majority of middle-class mothers of infants and young children were employed: two thirds when their children were under six years of age and three quarters by the time their children were school age, with most of these mothers working full-time. Married mothers were working at the same rate as single mothers (Scarr, Phillips, & McCartney, 1989). Public empathy for mothers supported by AFDC to stay home with their children evaporated. Why should the taxes of working mothers go to support poor mothers to enjoy the privilege of staying home with their children? Reform of the welfare system rose to the top of the political agenda and was passed in 1996. Welfare will no longer be an open-ended, lifetime entitlement. It will provide time-limited support in emergencies, but mothers of children over three years of age can expect to be employed. Child-care assistance for low-income mothers is the key to welfare reform, because single low-income mothers cannot pay market rates for child care.

"Workfare Means Day Care"

Child care is the essential ingredient in welfare reform and mothers' employment, as indicated by the above heading taken from a recent *Time* magazine article (1996). State by state, policies are being developed to provide child care to permit poor mothers to work. The major intent is to care for children while their mothers are employed, but what quality of care will be afforded by the states? There are no necessary quality assurances, beyond basic health and safety, in the provision of child care that allows mothers to work. Only when one is concerned about the children's development do other qualities of the child-care experience matter.

The Quality/Cost/Affordability Dilemma

Child care is critical to working parents' well-being (Mason & Duberstein, 1992). The availability and affordability of child care of acceptable quality directly affect parents' ability to manage both work and family life. Location, hours of operation, and flexibility (with respect to rules, mildly ill children, and the like) are major factors in the perceived availability of child care. Many parents find their choices quite limited (Galinsky, 1992).

Cost in relation to family income is the major affordability issue (Scarr, 1992b). As in any market-driven service, quality depends on what consumers are willing and able to pay for child care, which economists refer to as the *cost per quality unit of care* (Mason & Duberstein, 1992;

Morris & Helburn, 1996). Consumers who are able to pay a high price will find someone willing to provide the service. Low-income families struggle to find acceptable quality care at a price they can afford, although they pay a higher percentage of their income for child care (23% versus 6% in high-income families). The trade-off of cost and quality of services is a major dilemma in American child care (Morris & Helburn, 1996).

Accessibility and cost of child care per quality unit are overriding issues in evaluating the impact of child care on parents (Prosser & McGroder, 1992). Ease of access, measured in travel time to a child-care center, directly affects how likely a mother is to stay in the labor force (Collins & Hofferth, 1996). Middle- and upper income mothers are much more likely to keep their jobs if they use formal child-care arrangements (day-care centers) than if they have informal or no stable arrangements. Labor force participation among low-income mothers is more sensitive to the availability of relatives to care for children, because they cannot afford to pay market rates for child care (Collins & Hofferth, 1996).

Absenteeism and Productivity Effects

Mothers with secure child care are absent from work and tardy less often and are more productive in the workplace.

> When child care arrangements break down, employed parents are more likely to be absent, to be late, to report being unable to concentrate on the job, to have higher levels of stress and more stress-related health problems, and to report lower parental and marital satisfaction. (Galinsky, 1992, p. 167)

Breakdowns in child-care arrangements are frequent and stressful; in a Portland, Oregon study, 36% of fathers and 46% of mothers who used out-of-home care reported child-care-related stress. Leading causes of child-care breakdown are child illness and a provider who quits (Galinsky, 1992). The greater the number of child-care arrangements, the more likely they are to break and the greater the parental stress. Stable, reliable child care of acceptable quality is clearly related to mothers returning to work and staying in the labor force; this is especially true of middle- and high-income mothers (Collins & Hofferth, 1996; Phillips, 1992).

A Child Development Perspective on Child-Care Research

Three Waves of Research

The ecology of child-care research has undergone some important changes in the past two decades. Three waves of child-care research have been identified (Belsky, 1984; Clarke-Stewart, 1988; McCartney & Marshall, 1989). In the 1970s, the first wave compared maternal care with any kind of nonmaternal care, without assessment of the quality of either setting in which the care took place. The implicit research question was "How much damage is done to infants and young children by working mothers?" There was no consideration of whether variation in child development depended on variation in kind and quality of care, at home or in other child-care settings.

The second wave examined the quality and variety of child-care settings and introduced the idea that children's responses to child care may be individually different. In the 1980s, many child-care studies actually observed child care in process, evaluated quality of care, and assessed children individually.

The third wave of research included not only proximal influences on the child but distal influences as well. McCartney and Marshall (1989) suggested the inclusion of three systems to describe a true ecological study of the child-care experience: first, variation of child-care quality and type; second, family characteristics; and, third, individual differences among children. Although considerable attention has been devoted to evaluating child-care settings, characteristics of parents and family settings have seldom been integrated into child-care research.

A special note should be made on child-care-as-intervention with children from low-income and disadvantaged families. The best studied interventions, such as the Carolina Abecedarian Project (Ramey, Bryant, Sparling, & Wasik, 1985), used child care to enrich poor children's lives with positive results both concurrently and into primary school. Children with poor learning opportunities at home and without sufficient emotional support are particularly benefited by early childhood programs (McCartney, Scarr, Phillips, & Grajek, 1985), and the more intensive the intervention, the better the results (Ramey & Ramey, 1992).

Dimensions of Quality

There is an extraordinary international consensus among child-care researchers and practitioners about what quality child care is: It is warm, supportive interactions with adults in a safe, healthy, and stimulating environment, where early education and trusting relationships combine to support individual children's physical, emotional, social, and intellectual development (Bredekamp, 1989).

Although quality of care is a multifaceted concept, the most commonly used measures of center quality are remarkably similar in the dimensions of quality they stress and in their measurement characteristics (Scarr, Eisenberg, & Deater-Deckard, 1994). Determinations of child-care quality are based on a number of criteria, but the most commonly agreed on are health and safety requirements, responsive and warm interaction between staff and children, developmentally appropriate curricula, limited group size, age-appropriate caregiver: child ratios, adequate indoor and outdoor space, and adequate staff training in either early childhood education or child development (Bredekamp, 1989; Kontos & Fiene, 1987). Caregivers with specific training in child care and child development provide more sensitive and responsive care than do those without such training. In sum, the quality of child care is affected by lower ratios, smaller group sizes, and better qualified teachers (Cost, Quality, and Child Outcomes Study Team, 1995; Scarr, Eisenberg, & Deater-Deckard, 1994; Whitebook, Howes, & Phillips, 1991).

Staff turnover is another common measure of the quality of care. High turnover means that children have fewer opportunities to develop stable, affectionate relationships with caregivers. Stability of care appears to be especially important for infants and toddlers who display more appropriate social behaviors in stable than in unstable care arrangements (Howes & Stewart, 1987; Suwalsky, Zaslow, Klein, & Rabinovich, 1986). Recently, a tri-state study has shown that quality of care is more closely related to teacher wages than to other structural center-care variables (Phillips, Mekos, Scarr, McCartney, & Abbott-Shim, in press; Scarr, Eisenberg, & Deater-Deckard, 1994).

Variations in Quality of Care

Few experienced observers would doubt that center quality in the United States varies from excellent to dreadful and is, on average, mediocre (Cost, Quality, and Child Outcomes Study Team, 1995; Hofferth, Brayfield, Deich, & Holcomb, 1991; National Institute of Child Health and Human Development [NICHD] Early Child Care Research Network, 1996; Scarr, Phillips, McCartney, & Abbott-Shim, 1993). Quality in child-care centers is measured, by observation and interview, in units that are regulated (such as ratios of teachers to children, group sizes, and teacher training) and in dimensions that are process-oriented (such as adult–child interactions and developmentally appropriate activities; Phillips, 1987). In European studies, child-care quality also varies but not as dramatically as in the United States (Lamb, Sternberg, Hwang, & Broberg, 1992).

Family day-care homes have seldom been studied, and those that have been sampled may not be representative of the enormous number of unlicensed, unregulated homes. Studies of family day care have found quality to be highly variable (Galinsky, Howes, Kontos, & Shinn, 1994). In the recent NICHD study (NICHD Early Child Care Research Network, 1996), day-care home quality was, on average, fair to good but again highly variable.

Poor quality child care has been reported to put children's development at risk for poorer language and cognitive scores and lower ratings of social and emotional adjustment (for reviews, see Lamb, in press; Scarr &

Eisenberg, 1993). Studies of center quality and child outcomes, which controlled statistically for family background differences, have found that overall quality has small but reliable effects on language and cognitive development (Goelman & Pence, 1987; McCartney, 1984; Wasik, Ramey, Bryant, & Sparling, 1990), social competence, and social adjustment (McCartney et al., 1997). Parents and caregivers rated children as more considerate, sociable, intelligent, and task-oriented when caregivers engaged in more positive verbal interactions with the children.[2] Other studies have found that children with involved and responsive caregivers display more exploratory behaviors, are more positive (Clarke-Stewart, Gruber, & Fitzgerald, 1994; Holloway & Reichhart-Erickson, 1989), and display better peer relations (Howes, Phillips, & Whitebook, 1992) than children with uninvolved, unresponsive caregivers. The inferences from these findings are not straightforward, however.

Predictably, quality of care selected by parents has been found to be correlated with parents' personal characteristics (Bolger & Scarr, 1995), thereby complicating interpretations of any effects of child care per se. The confound of family and child-care characteristics leads to overestimation of child-care effects that result instead from family differences. For example, children from families with single employed mothers and low incomes were more likely to be found in lower quality care (Howes & Olenick, 1986). Children in high-quality care had parents who were more involved and interested in compliance than parents of children in lower quality care, and behavioral differences were evident in the center. Parents who use more punitive forms of discipline and hold more authoritarian attitudes toward children were found to choose lower quality care for their children (Bolger & Scarr, 1995; Scarr et al., 1993).

In a recent large study, less sensitive mothers who value work more chose poorer quality child care in the infants' first six months, enrolled their infants in centers at earlier ages for more hours per week, and were more likely to have insecurely attached infants (NICHD Early Child Care Research Network, in press). Of course, variations in parents' interactions with their children and in parents' personality, intelligence, and attitudes determine the characteristics that will be transmitted to children genetically as well as environmentally (Scarr, 1992a; 1993). How can these confounds be sorted out?

Many studies statistically covary out measured family characteristics from associations between child care and child outcomes and look at residual associations. When family and child-care qualities are truly confounded, however, it is impossible to covary out all family effects, because one has only a limited set of measures of the families—typically parents' education, income, and occupation, and some personality, cognitive, or attitudinal test scores. Parents who differ on any one of these measures are very likely to differ on many other unmeasured traits that affect associations between child care and child outcomes. Thus, the small, statically reliable associations that have been found between child-care quality and child outcomes are exceedingly difficult to interpret.

Nonmaternal Care

Nonmaternal infant care has been the most controversial issue in the entire child-care research field, but it may soon be laid to rest. Throughout the 1980s and early 1990s, dramatic claims were made about the damaging effects of early entry into "day care" (not defined or measured) on infants' attachments to their mothers (Belsky, 1986, 1988, 1992; Belsky & Rovine, 1988). Reanalyses of data on day care versus "home-reared" infants revealed a slight difference in rates of insecure attachments as measured by the Strange Situation: 37% versus 29% (Clarke-Stewart, 1988, 1989; Lamb, Sternberg, & Prodromidis, 1992). Other measures of attachment showed no relationship to age at entry or amount of infant child care.

Arguments swirled in the public press and developmental literature about whether the results applied only to boys; to infants with insensitive mothers; to infants who experience more than 20, 30, or 35 hours of nonmaternal care a week; or to infants who experience poor quality care (Phillips, McCartney, Scarr, & Howes, 1987). Working mothers were tormented with doubt and guilt (Bowman, 1992). Finally, the NICHD Early Child Care Research Study (NICHD Early Child Care Research Network, in press) of more than 1,000 infants has shown no relationship between age at entry or amount of infant care and attachments as measured by the Strange Situation (for a full review, see Lamb, in press). Naturally, less sensitive, less well-adjusted mothers were much more likely to have insecurely attached infants (NICHD Early Child Care Research Network, in press). Several interaction effects suggested that higher quality care may help to offset poor mothering. Let us hope that is the end of the early child-care controversy.

Lack of Long-Term Effects

Researchers have explored the possible long-term effects of day-care experiences in different qualities of care for children from different kinds of backgrounds. Children from low-income families are definitely benefited by quality child care, which has been used as an intervention strategy (Field, 1991; Ramey et al., 1985; Ramey & Ramey, 1992). Poor children who experience high-quality infant and preschool care show better school achievement and socialized behaviors in later years than similar children without child-care experience or with experience in lower quality care. For poor children, quality child care offers learning opportunities and social and emotional supports that many would not experience at home.

For children from middle- and upper income families, the long-term picture is far less clear. With a few exceptions that can be explained by the confounding of family with child-care characteristics in the United States, research results show that the impact on development from poorer versus better care within a broad range of safe environments is small and temporary. Given the learning opportunities and social and emotional supports that their homes generally offer, child care is not a unique or lasting experience for these children.

Long-term effects of day-care quality were reported in longitudinal studies by Vandell Henderson, and Wilson (1988) and by Howes (1988). The former researchers reported that children who attended better quality day-care centers in the preschool period were better liked by their peers and exhibited more empathy and social competence at age eight than children form poorer quality preschool centers. Howes found that after controlling for the effects of some family characteristics, good school skills and few behavior problems were predicted by high-quality care for both boys and girls. However, age at entry and amount of day care were not related to later academic achievement or to social behaviors, so that one suspects the family effects, confounded with child-care quality (Bolger & Scarr, 1995), accounted for the long-term results.

In contrast to the U.S. findings, the results of two longitudinal studies conducted in Sweden indicated that early age of entry into day care was associated with better school performance and positive teacher ratings from childhood to early adulthood (Andersson, 1989; Hartmann, 1995). Of the many differences in family background that could be only partially controlled, early entrants into child care had better educated mothers who returned to work earlier than less achieving mothers. Again, one suspects that unmeasured family effects account for the long-term positive effects of child care in the Swedish study, as they did for negative effects in the U.S. studies.

A more thorough Swedish study (Broberg, Hwang, & Chace, 1993) reported no long-term effects of differences in child-care environments on children's adjustments or achievement at eight to nine years of age. It should be noted, however, that Sweden's uniformly high-quality child-care centers (Hennessy & Melhuish, 1991) do not really test for the effects of poor child care on later development.

No effects of quality of preschool care on school-age development were also reported in a Dutch retrospective study (Goosens, Ottenhoff, & Koops, 1991). However, there was very little variance in the measure of quality in this study, which may account for that finding.

Four Studies of Long-Term Impact of Varied Child-Care Quality

Study 1. In a large U.S. study of highly varied child-care centers (McCartney et al., 1997; Scarr et al., 1993), 720 young children (ages 12 to 60 months) who were enrolled in 120 child-care centers in three states were evaluated for social adjustment. Quality of care in the centers and family characteristics were used to predict differences in parents' and teachers' ratings of children's adjustment and observations of social behaviors.

Both structural (e.g., staff to child ratios, teachers' wages, education, training) and process (interactions, programs) measures were used to evaluate quality of care in the centers. Family structural characteristics (e.g., income, educational levels, race, number of children) and processes (e.g., parenting stress, work—family interference, parental attitudes, separation anxieties) represented family effects. Children's own characteristics of age, gender, and child-care history were also used to predict adjustment and social behavior. Thus, center-care quality, family, and child characteristics were jointly used to predict children's social adjustment and social behaviors.

Results showed substantial effects of child and family characteristics on both teachers' and parents' ratings of children's adjustment and social behaviors and very small, but statistically reliable, effects of quality of child care on social adjustment ratings. In a four-year follow-study of 141 children, Deater-Deckard, Pinkerton, and Scarr (1996) reported no longer-term effects of differences in quality of preschool child care on these school-age children's social, emotional, or behavioral adjustment.

Study 2. A study of day-care centers in Bermuda (McCartney, 1984; McCartney et al., 1985; Phillips, McCartney, & Scarr, 1987) emphasized the importance of quality care for infants, toddlers, and preschool children. The major question addressed longitudinally was whether or not the effects of differences in quality of child care in the preschool years continue to be seen at ages five through nine years.

In a follow-up study (Chin-Quee & Scarr, 1994), teacher ratings of social competence and academic achievement were obtained from 127 of the children at ages five, six, seven, and eight years. In hierarchical and simultaneous regressions, family background characteristics, not child-care amounts or qualities, were found to be predictive of social competence and academic achievement in the primary grades. By the school-age years, the effects of infant and preschool child-care experiences were no longer influential in children's development, but family background continued to be important.

Study 3. In another longitudinal study in Bermuda (Scarr, Lande, & McCartney, 1989), the child-care experiences of 117 children, who had been assessed for cognitive and social development at two and four years of age, were examined for long-term effects. At 24 months of age, children in center-based care, where the ratio of infants to caregivers was 8:1, had poorer cognitive and language development than children in family day care or at home with their mothers (who did not differ from each other). These results persisted after controlling for maternal education, IQ, income, and occupational status. However, at 42 to 48 months, no differences were found between children in center care and other children.

Study 4. In Bermuda, an islandwide screening, assessment, and treatment program was implemented to help children with developmental problems (Scarr, McCartney, Miller, Hauenstein, & Ricciuti, 1994). Child-care histories were also ascertained. Two samples were studied: a population sample of 1,100 Bermudian children and a small subsample of children, most of whom were determined to be at risk for developmental problems.

To assess the effects of maternal employment (Scarr & Thompson, 1994), infants with mothers who worked 20 or more hours a week were compared with infants with mothers who worked less than 20 hours a week. To address the effects of entry into nonmaternal care before the age of one, infants who were placed in regular nonmaternal care before the age of one were compared with infants who did not experience regular nonmaternal care before the age of one. Teacher ratings of social competence and academic achievement were obtained for the children at ages five, six, seven, and eight years.

Results revealed that family background variables frequently predicted child social competence and academic achievement measures in both samples. After controlling for family characteristics, no differences in school-age outcomes were found between children whose mothers worked 20 or more hours a week when they were infants and children with mothers who worked less than 20 hours a week in either sample. In addition, age of entry into nonmaternal care before the age of one did not significantly predict any child outcome measures.

Conclusions

In studies in Sweden and Holland, in a large study of child-care centers in the United States, and in three separate studies in Bermuda, differences in child-care experience, both qualitative and quantitative, did not have persistent effects on children's development. In these studies, child-care centers in Bermuda and the United States included both good- and poor-quality care, whereas centers in Sweden and Holland included only good-quality care. Research to date on quality differences does not show a major impact on the development of children from ordinary homes. These results may differ for the children from socioeconomically disadvantaged homes, for whom quality child-care programs may supply missing elements in their lives.

Public Policy and the Quality/Cost Trade-Off

Quality/Cost/Affordability Trade-Off

In general, higher quality child care costs more than lower quality care. Fifty to seventy percent of the cost is in staff salaries, and higher quality centers spend proportionately more on labor (Morris & Helburn, 1996). For ex-

ample, center-based child care costs twice as much in Massachusetts, which has among the most demanding regulations in the United States, as in Georgia, which has more lenient regulations. In a study of 120 centers in three states, centers in Massachusetts had higher quality care, on average, than those in Georgia, but comparisons of costs of living and incomes showed that families in Massachusetts are economically disadvantaged by the high cost of child care (Hancock, Eisenberg, & Scarr, 1993). Whereas the 1990 media family income for Georgia parents who used center-based care was $50,000, in Massachusetts the median income of families who could afford center care was nearly $80,000. Massachusetts families with an annual income of less than about $60,000 were unable to afford state-regulated quality care.

The more stringent the child-care regulations, the less licensed child care will be available and the more families will be forced to use unregulated care for their children. When regulations become so stringent that most families are priced out of the regulated child-care market, one has to wonder about the wisdom of having such expensive regulations.

Unfortunately, regulations have only tangential effects on the actual quality of care. States cannot legislate warm, sensitive interactions or rich learning opportunities provided by talented teachers. Aside from safety and health considerations, which can be effectively regulated, observed quality of child care is correlated only .30 to .40 with regulated variables, such as ratios and teacher qualifications (Scarr, Eisenberg, & Deater-Deckard, 1994). Therefore, regulations directly produce higher costs but only indirectly improve quality of care.

In addition, parents may not agree that quality defined by professionals is what they want or are willing to pay for in the child care they choose (Cost, Quality, and Child Outcomes Study Team, 1995; Haskins, 1992). Whereas early childhood professionals value discovery learning and hands-on experience, many working class and more traditional parents prefer structured learning and direct instruction for their preschool children. Individual attention to each child requires more staff than a classroom organized for group instruction. Lower ratios equal higher staff costs, which some parents are not willing to support, especially if the program is not what they want anyway.

States should examine the cost:benefit ratio of their regulations and their impact on making child care affordable, available, and of sufficient quality to support good child development without driving most families into the underground market of unregulated care. Surely, we all expect state regulations to protect children and to assure them a supportive environment in child care. That is the minimum government responsibility. Given the wide variation in regulations among the states, however, it should be possible to examine the benefits of greater and lesser costs of child care.

Equity in Child Care

In the United States, a two-tier system is evolving—a higher quality one for both affluent families and the poor, who get public support for child care, and a lower quality one for middle- and lower income working families, who cannot pay for high-quality care (Maynard & McGinnis, 1992; Whitebook et al., 1991). In my opinion and in that of many other child advocates, public support for child care should make quality services available to all children of working families.

To make this dream a reality, we must spend tax moneys efficiently. Government-provided services are the least-cost-effective means to provide quality child care. Compare Head Start expenditures per child with those of a typical child-care center with excellent early educational programs. Head Start spends approximately $5,000 per child annually for part-day (typically three to four hours), part-year (public school calendar) programs.[3] For exactly the same amount of money, the government could give poor parents vouchers to purchase quality child care and education in full-day, full-year child-care programs (Cost, Quality, and Child Outcomes Study Team, 1995). Another benefit of vouchers is the reduction in socioeconomic segregation, which results from programs that only poor children may attend. In most nonprofit and for-profit centers, between 5% and 40% of the children are on child-care assistance, whereas in Head Start centers, nearly 100% of the children are on child-care assistance.

Edward Zigler (Zigler & Finn-Stevenson, 1996) has proposed that public schools, well-entrenched institutions in all communities, be used to implement child-care services for preschool children (not infants or toddlers). With varying mixes of federal, state, local, and private funding, including parental fees, Zigler has prompted more than 400 schools to incorporate child care in their educational programs. Public schools can be one mechanism to increase the child-care supply for older children, but critics complain that most schools need to focus exclusively on improving their existing educational programs, which international surveys show to be of poor quality.

States are currently setting child-care reimbursement rates under the new welfare reform legislation. If they are pressured to serve more children, their rates will be too low to give poor parents access to quality care. If they set rates high enough to give poor parents access to quality care, they may not be able to serve all eligible families. Inadequate funding drives states to make Solomonic choices.

Whither Child Care in America?

Repeatedly, international research results have shown only small concurrent effects of child care on children's development and no evidence for long-term effects, un-less the children are seriously disadvantaged. Observation about the small effects on children of differences in quality of care can be enhanced beyond their practical importance by liberal politicians and child advocates, who may demand high-quality child care regardless of cost. Conservatives, however, will ask the logically obvious question: What is the minimal expense for child care that will allow mothers to work and not do permanent damage to children? Conservative politicians will find the research results conveniently permissive of mediocre quality. Mediocre is not the same as deleterious, unsafe, and abusive care, however, and there is some of that in the United States that must be eliminated. Government standards that prevent terrible care are essential for our nation's well-being.

Debates about welfare reform, working mothers, and child care reflect broad societal conflicts about women, families, and children.

- Is child care in America primarily meant to serve the needs of working parents, with little regard for the education of preschoolers, especially disadvantaged children?
- Will nonwelfare working families have to pay for the child care they need, discouraging many women from entering the labor force, or will the public decide that, like primary education, child care is a public service that deserves broad taxpayer support?
- Will regulations on licensed care be made so expensive that most parents will be priced out of the center-care market and forced to use unregulated care in homes? Or, will state regulations be so lax that American child care will be little better than custodial warehousing?

In summary, I hope the United States will decide that child care is both an essential service for working families and an important service to America's children, especially to the poorest among them. Governments have the responsibility to make child care affordable for all working parents and to regulate child care to assure that children are afforded opportunities to develop emotionally, socially, and intellectually. Regardless of who their parents are, children are the next generation for all of us.

NOTES

1. In 11 states, church-sponsored child care is exempt from all but health and safety licensure.
2. Paradoxically, in one study, children's social adjustment was positively related to poorer quality care, but this finding has not been replicated and is probably sample-specific (Phillips, McCartney, & Scarr, 1987).
3. Costs of medical, dental, and social service programs are additional.

REFERENCES

Andersson, B. E. (1989). Effects of public day care—A longitudinal study. *Child Development, 60*, 857–866.

Behrman, R. E. (Ed.). (1996). Financing child care. *The Future of Children, 6*(2).

Belsky, J. (1984). Two waves of day care research: Developmental effects and conditions of quality. In R. C. Ainslie (Ed.), *The child and the day care setting* (pp. 24–42). New York: Praeger.

Belsky, J. (1986). Infant day care: A cause for concern? *Zero to Three. 6*, 1–9.

Belsky, J. (1988). The "effects" of infant day care reconsidered. *Early Childhood Research Quarterly, 3*, 235–272.

Belsky, J. (1992). Consequences of child care for children's development: A deconstructionist view. In A. Booth (Ed.), *Child care in the 1990s: Trends and consequences* (pp. 83–94). Hillsdale, NJ: Erlbaum.

Belsky, J., & Rovine, M. J. (1988). Nonmaternal care in the first year of life and the infant–parent attachment. *Child Development, 59*, 157–167.

Blau, D. M., & Robbins, P. K. (1990, April). *Child care demand and labor supply of young mothers over time.* Paper presented at the annual meeting of the Population Association of America, Toronto. Ontario, Canada.

Bolger, K. E., & Scarr, S. (1995). Not so far from home: How family characteristics predict child care quality. *Early Development and Parenting, 4*(3), 103–112.

Bowman, B. (1992). Child development and its implications for day care. In A. Booth (Ed.), Child care in the 1990s: Trends and consequences (pp. 95–100). Hillsdale, NJ: Erlbaum.

Bredekamp, S. (1989, November). *Measuring quality through a national accreditation system for early childhood programs.* Paper presented at the annual meeting of the American Educational Research Association, San Francisco, CA.

Broberg, A. G., Hwang, C. P., & Chace, S. V. (1993, March). *Effects of day care on elementary school performance and adjustment.* Paper presented at the biennial meetings of the Society for Research in Child Development, New Orleans, LA.

Cherlin, A. (1992). Infant care and full-time employment. In A. Booth (Ed.), *Child care in the 1990s: Trends and consequences* (pp. 209–214). Hillsdale, NJ: Erlbaum.

Chin-Quee, D., & Scarr, S. (1994). Lack of longitudinal effects of infant and preschool child care on school-age children's social and intellectual development. *Early Development and Parenting, 3* (2), 103–112.

Clarke-Stewart, A. (1988). The "effects" of infant day care reconsidered: Risks for parents, children, and researchers. *Early Childhood Research Quarterly, 3*, 293–318.

Clarke-Stewart, K. A. (1989). Infant day care: Maligned or malignant? *American Psychologist, 44*, 266–273.

Clarke-Stewart, K. A., Gruber, C. P., & Fitzgerald, L. M. (1994). *Children at home and in day care.* Hillsdale, NJ: Erlbaum.

Collins, N., & Hofferth, S. (1996, May). *Child care and employment turnover.* Paper presented at the annual meeting of the Population Association of America, New Orleans, LA.

Cost, Quality, and Child Outcomes Study Team. (1995). *Cost, quality and child outcomes in child care centers* (Public Report, 2nd ed.) Denver: University of Colorado at Denver, Economics Department.

Deater-Deckard, K., Pinkerton, R., & Scarr, S. (1996). Child care quality and children's behavioral adjustment: A four-year longitudinal study. *Journal of Child Psychology & Psychiatry, 37*(8), 937–948.

Deater-Deckard, K., Scarr, S., McCartney, K., & Eisenberg, M. (1994). Paternal separation anxiety: Relationships with parenting stress, child-rearing attitudes, and maternal anxieties. Psychological Science, 5(6), 341–346.

Field, T. (1991). Quality infant day-care and grade school behavior and performance. *Child Development, 62*, 863–870.

Galinsky, E. (1992). The impact of child care on parents. In A. Booth (Ed.), *Child care in the 1990s: Trends and consequences* (pp. 159–171). Hillsdale, NJ: Erlbaum.

Galinsky, E., Howes, C., Kontos, S., & Shinn, M. (1994). *The study of children in family child care and relative care.* New York: Families and Work Institute.

Goelman, H., & Pence, A. R. (1987). Effects of child care, family and individual characteristics on children's language development: The Victoria Day Care Research Project. In D. Phillips (Ed.), *Quality in child care: What does research tell us? Research monographs of the National Association for the Education of Young Children* (pp. 43–56). Washington, DC: National Association for the Education of Young Children.

Goosens, F. A., Ottenhoff, G., & Koops, W. (1991). Day care and social outcomes in middle childhood: A retrospective study. *Journal of Reproductive and Infant Psychology, 9*, 137–150.

Hancock. T., Eisenberg, M., & Scarr, S. (1993, March). *Cost of child care and families' standard of living.* Paper presented at the biennial meetings of the Society for Research in Child Development, New Orleans, LA.

Hartmann, E. (1995). *Long-term effects of day care and maternal teaching on educational competence, independence and autonomy in young adulthood.* Unpublished manuscript, University of Oslo, Oslo, Norway.

Haskins, R. (1992). Is anything more important than day-care quality? In A. Booth (Ed.), *Child care in the 1990s: Trends and consequences* (pp. 101–115). Hillsdale, NJ: Erlbaum.

Hennessy, E., & Melhuish, E. C. (1991). Early day care and the development of school-age children: A review. *Journal of Reproductive and Infant Psychology, 9*, 117–136.

Hofferth, S. (1992). The demand for and supply of child care in the 1990s. In A. Booth (Ed.), *Child care in the 1990s: Trends and consequences* (pp. 3–25). Hillsdale, NJ: Erlbaum.

Hofferth, S. (1996). Child care in the United States today. *The Future of Children: 6*(2), 41–61.

Hofferth, S., Brayfield, A., Deich, S., & Holcomb, P. (1991). *National child care survey 1990.* Washington, DC: The Urban Institute.

Holloway, S. D., & Reichhart-Erickson, M. (1989). Child care quality, family structure, and maternal expectations: Relationship to preschool children's peer relations. *Journal of Applied Developmental Psychology, 4*, 99–107.

Howes, C. (1988). Relations between early child care and schooling. *Developmental Psychology, 24*, 53–57.

Howes, C., & Olenick, M. (1986). Family and child care influences on toddlers' compliance. *Child Development, 57*, 202–216.

Howes, C., Phillips, D. A., & Whitebook, M. (1992). Thresholds of quality: Implications for the social development of children in center-based child care. *Child Development, 63*, 449–460.

Howes, C., & Stewart, P. (1987). Child's play with adults, toys, and peers: An examination of family and child-care influences. *Developmental Psychology, 23*, 423–430.

Justice Ginsburg takes on affirmative action. (1995, April 17). *The Washington Post*, p. A4.

Kagan, J. (1980). Perspectives on continuity. In O. G. Brim & J. Kagan (Eds.), *Constancy and change in human development* (pp. 1–15). Cambridge, MA: Harvard University Press.

Kontos, S., & Fiene, R. (1987). Child care quality, family background, and children's development. *Early Childhood Research Quarterly, 6*, 249–262.

Lamb, M. (in press). Nonparental child care: Context, quality, correlates, and consequences. In W. Damon (Series Ed.) & I. E. Sigel & K. A. Renniger (Vols. Eds.), *Handbook of child psychology: Child psychology in practice* (4th ed.). New York: Wiley.

Lamb, M., Sternberg, K. J., Hwang, P., & Broberg, A. (Eds.). (1992). *Child care in context*. Hillsdale, NJ: Erlbaum.

Lamb, M., Sternberg, K. J., & Prodromidis, M. (1992). The effects of day care on infant–mother attachment: A re-analysis of the data. *Infant Behavior and Development, 15*, 71–83.

Leira, A. (1992). *Welfare states and working mothers*. Cambridge, England: Cambridge University Press.

Mason, K., & Duberstein, L. (1992). Consequences of child care for parents' well-being. In A. Booth (Ed.), *Child care in the 1990s: Trends and consequences* (pp. 127–158). Hillsdale, NJ: Erlbaum.

Maynard, R., & McGinnis, E. (1992). Policies to enhance access to high-quality child care. In A. Booth (Ed.), *Child care in the 1990s: Trends and consequences* (pp. 189–208). Hillsdale, NJ: Erlbaum.

McCartney, K. (1984). The effect of quality of day care environment upon children's language development. *Developmental Psychology, 20*, 244–260.

McCartney, K., & Marshall, N. (1989). The development of child care research. *Newsletter of the Division of Children, Youth, and Family Services, 12*(4), 14–15.

McCartney, K., Scarr, S., Phillips, D., & Grajek, S. (1985). Day care as intervention: Comparisons of varying quality programs. *Journal of Applied Developmental Psychology, 6*, 247–260.

McCartney, K., Scarr, S., Rocheleau, A., Phillips, D., Eisenberg, M., Keefe, N., Rosenthal, S., & Abbott-Shim, M. (1997). Social development in the context of typical center-based child care. *Merrill-Palmer Quarterly, 43*(3), 426–450.

Morris, J., & Helburn, S. (1996, July). How centers spend money on quality. *Child Care Information Exchange*, 75–79.

National Institute of Child Health and Human Development Early Child Care Research Network. (1996). Characteristics of infant child care: Factors contributing to positive caregiving. *Early Childhood Research Quarterly, 11*, 269–306.

National Institute of Child Health and Human Development Early Child Care Research Network. (in press). The effects of infant child care on infant–mother attachment security: Results of the NICHD Study of Early Child Care. *Child Development*.

Phillips, D. (Ed.). (1987). *Quality in child care: What does research tell us? Research monographs of the National Association for the Education of Young Children*. Washington, DC: National Association for the Education of Young Children.

Phillips, D. (1992). Child care and parental well-being: Bringing quality of care into the picture. In A. Booth (Ed.), *Child care in the 1990s: Trends and consequences* (pp. 172–179). Hillsdale, NJ: Erlbaum.

Phillips, D., McCartney, K., & Scarr, S. (1987). Child care quality and children's social development. *Developmental Psychology, 23*, 537–543.

Phillips, D., McCartney, K., Scarr, S., & Howes, C. (1987). Selective review of infant day care research: A cause for concern. *Zero to Three, 7*, 18–21.

Phillips, D., Mekos, D., Scarr, S., McCartney, K., & Abbott-Shim, M. (in press). Paths to quality in child care: Structural and contextual influences on classroom environments. *Early Childhood Research Quarterly*.

Presser, H. (1992a). Child care and parental well-being: A needed focus on gender trade-offs. In A. Booth (Ed.), *Child care in the 1990s: Trends and consequences* (pp. 180–185). Hillsdale, NJ: Erlbaum.

Presser, H. (1992b). Child-care supply and demand: What do we really know? In A. Booth (Ed.), *Child care in the 1990s: Trends and consequences* (pp. 26–32). Hillsdale, NJ: Erlbaum.

Prosser, W., & McGroder, S. (1992). The supply and demand for child care: Measurement and analytic issues. In A. Booth (Ed.), *Child care in the 1990s: Trends and consequences* (pp. 42–55). Hillsdale, NJ: Erlbaum.

Ramey, C., Bryant, D., Sparling, J., & Wasik, B. (1985). Project CARE: A comparison of two early intervention strategies to prevent retarded development. *Topics in Early Childhood Special Education, 5* (2), 12–25.

Ramey, C., & Ramey, S. (1992). Early educational intervention with disadvantaged children—to what effect? *Applied and Preventive Psychology, 1*, 131–140.

Ross, C. E., & Mirowsky, J. (1988). Child care and emotional adjustment to wives' employment. *Journal of Health and Social Behavior, 29*, 127–138.

Scarr, S. (1984). Mother care/other care. New York: Basic Books.

Scarr, S. (1985). Constructing psychology: Making facts and fables for our times. *American Psychologist, 40*, 499–512.

Scarr, S. (1992a). Developmental theories for the 1990s: Development and individual differences. *Child Development, 63*, 1–19.

Scarr, S. (1992b). Keep our eyes on the prize: Family and child care policy in the United States, as it should be. In A. Booth (Ed.), *Child care in the 1990s: Trends and consequences* (pp. 215–222). Hillsdale, NJ: Erlbaum.

Scarr, S. (1993). Biological and cultural diversity: The legacy of Darwin for development. *Child Development, 64*, 1333–1353.

Scarr, S. (1996). Family policy dilemmas in contemporary nation-states: Are women benefited by family-friendly governments? In S. Gustavsson & L. Lewin (Eds.), *The future of the nation state: Essays on cultural pluralism and political integration* (pp. 107–129). London: Routledge.

Scarr, S., & Eisenberg, M. (1993). Child care research: Issues, perspectives, and results. *Annual Review of Psychology, 44*, 613–644.

Scarr, S., Eisenberg, M., & Deater-Deckard, K. (1994). Measurement of quality of child care centers. *Early Childhood Research Quarterly, 9*, 131–151.

Scarr, S., Lande, J., & McCartney, K. (1989). Child care and the family: Cooperation and interaction. In J. Lande, S. Scarr, & N. Guzenhauser (Eds.), *Caring for children: Challenge to America* (pp. 21–40). Hillsdale, NJ: Erlbaum.

Scarr, S., McCartney, K., Miller, S., Hauenstein, E., & Ricciuti, A. (1994). Evaluation of an islandwide screening, assessment and treatment program. *Early Development and Parenting, 3*(4), 199–210.

Scarr, S., Phillips, D., & McCartney, K. (19890). Working mothers and their families. *American Psychologist, 44*, 1402–1409.

Scarr, S., Phillips, D., & McCartney, K. (1990). Facts, fantasies, and the future of child care in the United States. *Psychological Science, 1*, 26–35.

Scarr, S., Phillips, D., McCartney, K., & Abbott-Shim, M. (1993). Quality of child care as an aspect of family and child care policy in the United States. *Pediatrics, 91*(1), 182–188.

Scarr, S., & Thompson, W. (1994). Effects of maternal employment and nonmaternal infant care on development at two and four years. Early Development and Parenting, 3(2), 113–123.

Scarr, S., & Weinberg, R. A. (1986). The early childhood enterprise: Care and education of the young. *American Psychologist, 41*, 1140–1146.

Staines, G. L., & Pleck, J. H. (1983). *The impact of work schedules on the family*. Ann Arbor, MI: Institute for Social Research, Survey Research Center.

Stoney, L., & Greenberg, M. H. (1996). The financing of child care: Current and emerging trends. *The Future of Children, 6*, 83–102.

Suwalsky, J., Zaslow, M., Klein, R., & Rabinovich, B. (1986, August). *Continuity of substitute care in relation to infant–mother attachment.* Paper presented at the 94th Annual Convention of the American Psychological Association, Washington, DC.

Vandell, D. L., Henderson, V. K., & Wilson, K. S. (1988). A longitudinal study of children with day-care experiences of varying quality. *Child Development, 59,* 1286–1292.

Wasik, B. H., Ramey, C. T., Bryant, D. M., & Sparling, J. J. (1990). A longitudinal study of two early intervention strategies: Project CARE. *Child Development, 61,* 1682–1696.

White, L., & Keith, B. (1990). The effect of shift work on the quality and stability of marital relations. *Journal of Marriage and the Family, 52,* 453–462.

Whitebook, M., Howes, C., & Phillips, D. (1991). *Who cares? Child care teachers and the quality of care in America.* Final Report of the National Child Care Staffing Study. Oakland, CA: Center on Child Care Staffing.

Willer, B., Hofferth, S., Kisker, E. E., et al. (1991). *The demand and supply of child care in 1990.* Washington, DC: National Association for the Education of Young People.

Women's figures. (1997, January 15). *Wall Street Journal,* p. A15.

Workfare means day care. (1996, December 23). *Time,* 38–40.

Zigler, E. F., & Finn-Stevenson, M. (1996). Funding child care and public education. *The Future of Children, 6,* 104–121.

Sandra Scarr, Department of Psychology, University of Virginia, and KinderCare Learning Centers, Inc., Montgomery, AL.

Correspondence concerning this article should be addressed to Sandra Scarr, 77–6384 Halawai Street, Kailua-Kona, HI 96740. Electronic mail may be sent to sandrascar@aol.com.

From *American Psychologist,* February 1998, pp. 95–108. © 1998 by the American Psychological Association. Reprinted with permission.

Do Working Parents Make The Grade?

Book Excerpt: In the debates over quality time and how to balance work and family, kids are rarely heard. A new 'Ask the Children' study reveals how kids rate their moms and dads—and what children really want.

By Ellen Galinsky

WHENEVER I MENTION THAT I AM STUDYING HOW kids see their working parents, the response is electric. People are fascinated. Parents want to know what I have found, but inevitably they are nervous, too. Sometimes they say, "I wonder what other people's children would say. I'm not sure that I'm ready to hear what mine have to say!"

Why has a comprehensive, in-depth study of this question never been conducted? Because we have been afraid to ask, afraid to know. But now I feel the time is right. The answers of children are illuminating, not frightening. They help us see that our assumptions about children's ideas are often at odds with reality. Ultimately, this information will help us be better parents—and better employees, too. In fact, adding children's voices to our national conversation about work and family life will change the way we think about them forever.

Many of the debates we've been having about work and family miss the mark. For example, we have been locked in a longstanding argument about whether it is "good or bad" for children if their mothers work. Numerous observational studies have found that having a working mother doesn't harm children, yet the debate still rages. Another way to assess this issue is to see whether children of mothers who are not employed and children of working mothers differ in the way they feel they are being parented. In our "Ask the Children" study, we had a representative group of more than 1,000 children in grades three through 12 to evaluate their parents in 12 areas strongly linked to children's healthy development, school readiness and school success. In their responses—rendered in actual letter grades—having a mother who worked was never once predictive of how children assess their mothers' parenting skills. We also found

that while the amount of time children and parents spend together is very important, most children don't want more time with their parents. Instead, they give their mothers and fathers higher grades if the time they do spend together is not rushed but focused and rich in shared activities.

Family Values

56% of parents think their kids want more time together; only 10% of kids want more time with Mom, 15.5% with Dad. Most kids, however, feel they have enough time.

62.5% of parents say they like their work a lot. Only 41% of children say Dad enjoys his job, and 42% say the same about Mom.

44.5% of kids say time with Mom is rushed, 37% say so with Dad. Only 33% of parents think time with their kids is rushed.

23% of kids want their parents to earn more; 14% of parents think kids want this.

It may seem surprising that children whose mothers are at home caring for them full time fail to see them as more supportive. But a mother who is employed can be there for her child or not, just as mothers who are not employed can be. Indeed, children of nonworking fathers see their dads less positively when it comes to making them feel important and loved and to participating in important events in the children's lives. Fathers who work part time are less likely to be seen as encouraging their children's learning. Perhaps fathers who work less than full time or who are unemployed are feeling financial and role strain, which could affect how they interact with their children.

Grading
Dad

He instills good values, but doesn't always know what 'really' goes on

SUBJECT	A	B	C	D	F
Raising me with good values	69%	18%	8%	4%	2%
Appreciating me for who I am	58	21	11	8	2
Encouraging me to enjoy learning	57.5	24	12	4	2
Making me feel important and loved	57	22	13	6	2
Being able to go to important events	55	22	13	5	5.5
Being there for me when I am sick	51.5	20	16	8	4
Spending time talking with me	43	24	19	10	4
Establishing traditions with me	41	26	15	11	7
Being involved in school life	38	24	19	12	7
Being someone to go to when upset	38	22	15	12	13
Controlling his temper	31	27	20	10	12
Knowing what goes on with me	31	30	17	12.5	10

NOTE: GRADES GIVEN BY CHILDREN IN SEVENTH THROUGH 12TH GRADES

That children can appreciate the efforts of working parents is clear. Said one 12-year-old son of working parents: "If parents wish to provide some of the better things in life, both parents need to work and share the home and children responsibilities." A 15-year-old girl whose father works full time and whose mother does not said: "Your children may not like you working now, but it will pay off later on."

The problem isn't that mothers (and fathers) work: it is how we work and how work affects our parenting. For example, we asked the children in this study, "If you were granted one wish to change the way that your mother's or your father's work affects your life, what would that wish be?" We also asked more than 600 parents to guess what their child's response would be. Taken together, 56 percent of parents assume that their children would wish for more time together and less parental time at work. And 50 percent of parents with children up to 18 years old say they feel that they have too little time with their child—fathers (56 percent) even more so than mothers (44 percent).

But only 10 percent of children wish that their mothers would spend more time with them, and 15.5 percent say the same thing about their fathers. And surprisingly, children with employed mothers and those with mothers at home do not differ on whether they feel they have too little time with Mom.

What the largest proportion of children (23 percent) say that they want is for their mothers and their fathers to make more money. I suspect that money is seen as a stress-reducer, given children's other answers. The total number of children who wish that their parents would be less stressed or less tired by work is even larger: 34 percent make this wish for their mothers and 27.5 percent for their fathers. Sympathy for working parents comes through loud and clear: "I would like to thank the parents of America for working so hard to earn money," says

one 15-year-old girl. "I know that a working parent goes through so much for their children."

The study also reveals what children learn from their parents about the world of work. Only about two in five children think their parents like their work a lot, compared with 62.5 percent of parents who say they do. That's probably because many of us have said to our kids, "I have to go to work." Or "I wish I didn't have to leave." We seem to talk around children rather than with them about our jobs. And our reluctance to talk to our children about our work has meant that young people are getting haphazard rather than intentional information, sometimes blaming themselves for distress we pick up on the job, and not fully appreciating the potential of their own future careers.

As a result, many children play detective to figure out what is going on in our jobs that upsets or elates us. They study our moods at the end of the workday. One of our young subjects says you can tell if your parents are in a bad mood "because you get a short and simple answer. If they had a bad day, they won't talk. Or they will just go off by themselves."

What makes a good parent? Through our interviews with parents and children, eight critical parenting skills emerged. We then asked the children in our national survey to grade their own mothers and dads on those criteria. They are:

1. Making the child feel important and loved
2. Responding to the child's cues and clues
3. Accepting the child for who he or she is, but expecting success
4. Promoting strong values
5. Using constructive discipline
6. Providing routines and rituals to make life predictable and create positive neural patterns in developing brains
7. Being involved in the child's education
8. Being there for the child

Grading

Mom

She's there during illness, but sometimes loses her temper

SUBJECT	A	B	C	D	F
Being there for me when I am sick	81%	11%	5%	2%	1%
Raising me with good values	75	15	6	3	2
Making me feel important and loved	64	20	10	5	1
Being able to go to important events	64	20	10	3	3.5
Appreciating me for who I am	64	18	8	6	5
Encouraging me to enjoy learning	59	23	11.5	3	3
Being involved in school life	46	25	14	10	6
Being someone to go to when upset	46	22	14	8	9
Spending time talking with me	43	33	14	6	4
Establishing traditions with me	38	29	17	10	6
Knowing what goes on with me	35	31	15	10	9
Controlling her temper	29	27.5	20.5	12	11

Which of these skills earned parents the highest—and lowest—grades? Among children in the seventh through the 12th grades, mothers are given the highest grades for being there when the child is sick (81 percent gave their mothers an A) and for raising their children with good values (75 percent). They receive the lowest grades for controlling their tempers when their children make them angry (only 29 percent gave their mothers an A) and for knowing what is really going on in their children's lives (35 percent). The age of the child makes a difference. Younger children consistently rate their parents more favorably than older ones, which no doubt reflects the way teenagers separate emotionally from their parents.

Money also matters. In analysis after analysis, the children's perception of their families' economic health is strongly linked to how they rate their moms' and dads' parenting skills. Although the public often views the problems of children as primarily moral in nature, our analyses show that families that do not have to worry about putting bread on the table may have more to give to their children emotionally. They also may be able to raise their children in more positive, cohesive communities.

These findings illustrate why it is so important to ask the children rather than to rely on our own assumptions. The issue of time with children has typically been framed in the public debate as a mothers' issue. But when we ask the children, we see that fathers need to be front and center in this discussion, as well.

Children in the seventh through the 12th grades judge their fathers less favorably than their mothers in some important respects, such as making their child feel important and loved and being someone whom the child can go to if upset. Teenagers are more likely than their younger counterparts to want more time with their fathers. Thirty-nine percent of children 13 through 18 years old feel they have too little time with their fathers, compared with 29 percent of children 8 through 12 years old.

Time spent in shared activities wins parents high marks—but not if it feels hurried or rushed

We found that the quantity of time with mothers and fathers does matter a great deal. Children who spend more time with their mothers and fathers on workdays and nonworkdays see their parents more positively, feel that their parents are more successful at managing work and family responsibilities, and see their parents as putting their families first. "I think that if the parents spend more time with their children, they will become better people in life," says a 12-year-old boy whose father works part time while his mom stays home.

But to move beyond simply cataloging the number of hours children and parents spend together, we looked at what parents and children do while they are together, such as eating a meal, playing a game or sport or exercising, doing homework (together) and watching TV. For all these activities, the same pattern holds: the more frequently parents and children engaged in them together, the more positive the assessment parents got from their children.

But spending time together isn't enough. Many children said their interactions with parents feel rushed and hurried, and they gave their mothers and fathers lower marks as a result. More than two in five (44.5 percent) children feel that their time with their mother is rushed, while 37 percent feel their time with their father is rushed. Some mentioned mornings as particularly hectic times for their families. One 12-year-old girl said of her mother: "She's rushing and telling me to rush.... And my backpack weighs a ton, so if she walks me to school, it's like running down the street. I'm like, 'wait up…'"

Kids who think their families are financially secure feel more positive about Mom and Dad

Predictably, children are more likely to see their parents positively if their time together is calmer. For example: of children 8 through 18 years of age who rate their time with their mothers as very calm, 86 percent give their mothers an A for making them feel important and loved, compared with 63 percent of those who rate their time with their mothers as very rushed. And 80 percent of children who feel their time with their fathers is very calm give them an A for "appreciating me for who I am," compared with only 50.5 percent of those who rate their time with their fathers as very rushed.

The flip side of feeling rushed and distracted with children is concentration and focus. In one-on-one interviews, we asked parents to describe moments when they felt particularly successful at home. Over and over, we heard the word "focus." The mother of a 12-year-old says: "It's the time you spend with your children [when] you are really focused on them that's good; not a distracted time."

Of children in the seventh through 12th grades, 62 percent say that mothers find it "very easy" and 52 percent say that fathers find it very easy to focus on them when they are together.

And children are very attuned to the times when their parents are truly focused on them: "They're not just saying normal things like 'uh huh… uh hmmm.' They seem to be very intent on what I'm saying, they're not just looking away," said a 10-year-old boy. Some children even have "tests" of whether their parent is focusing on them. For example, one 13-year-old boy throws nonsense statements — like "a goldfish on the grass"— into the middle of a sentence to check out whether his parents are really listening to him.

Every analysis we conducted revealed that when children feel that their mothers and fathers can focus on them, they are much more likely to feel that their parents manage their work and family responsibilities more successfully and put their families before their work. And they give their parents much higher marks for all of the parenting skills we examined.

So, is it quantity time or quality time? Clearly, the words we're using to describe time within the family are wrong. To change the debate, we need new words. Since "focus" is the word that parents use to describe the quality of time they treasure most, I suggest we use it. And since parents and children highly value the quantity of time they spend being together, whether sharing a meal or just being around each other in a non-rushed way, we need a phrase for that, too. Children need focused times and hang-around times.

I hope that, as a result of this book, the conversations around work and family will change. When parents and children talk together about these issues, reasonable changes can be made. Children will tell us how some things could be better. Yes, they will still try to push our guilt buttons. Yes, they will still read our moods and plead their case for what they want because kids will be kids. But we are the adults, and we set the tone for our relationships with our children.

I repeat the wisdom of a 12-year-old child: "Listen. Listen to what your kids say, because you know, sometimes it's very important. And sometimes a kid can have a great idea and it could even affect you." So let's ask the children.

Father Love and Child Development: History and Current Evidence

Abstract
Six types of studies show that father love sometimes explains as much or more of the variation in specific child and adult outcomes as does mother love. Sometimes, however, only father love is statistically associated with specific aspects of offsprings' development and adjustment, after controlling for the influence of mother love. Recognition of these facts was clouded historically by the cultural construction of fatherhood and fathering in America.

Keywords
father love; paternal acceptance; parental acceptance-rejection theory

Ronald P. Rohner[1]

Research in every major ethnic group of America (Rohner, 1998b), in dozens of nations internationally, and with several hundred societies in two major cross-cultural surveys (Rohner 1975, 1986, 1998c; Rohner & Chaki-Sircar, 1988) suggests that children and adults everywhere—regardless of differences in race, ethnicity, gender, or culture—tend to respond in essentially the same way when they experience themselves to be loved or unloved by their parents. The overwhelming bulk of research dealing with parental acceptance and rejection concentrates on mothers' behavior, however. Until recently, the possible influence of father love has been largely ignored. Here, I concentrate on evidence showing the influence of fathers' love-related behaviors—or simply, *father love*—in relation to the social, emotional, and cognitive development and functioning of children, adolescents, and adult offspring. Moreover, I focus primarily, but not exclusively, on families for which information is available about both fathers and mothers—or about youths' perceptions of both their fathers' and mothers' parenting. My principal objective is to

identify evidence about the relative contribution to offspring development of father love vis-à-vis mother love.

I define father love in terms of paternal acceptance and rejection as construed in parental acceptance-rejection theory (Rohner, 1986, in press). Paternal acceptance includes such feelings and behaviors (or children's perceptions of such feelings and behaviors) as paternal nurturance, warmth, affection, support, comfort, and concern. Paternal rejection, on the other hand, is defined as the real or perceived absence or withdrawal of these feelings and behaviors. Rejection includes such feelings as coldness, indifference, and hostility toward the child. Paternal rejection may be expressed behaviorally as a lack of affection toward the child, as physical or verbal aggression, or as neglect. Paternal rejection may also be experienced in the form of undifferentiated rejection; that is, there may be situations in which individuals feel that their fathers (or significant male caregivers) do not really care about, want, or love them, even though there may not be observable behavioral indicators showing that the fathers are neglect-

ing, unaffectionate, or aggressive toward them. Mother love (maternal acceptance-rejection) is defined in the same way.

FATHERHOOD AND MOTHERHOOD ARE CULTURAL CONSTRUCTIONS

The widely held cultural construction of fatherhood in America—especially prior to the 1970s—has two strands. Historically, the first strand asserted that fathers are ineffective, often incompetent, and maybe even biologically unsuited to the job of child-rearing. (The maternal counterpoint to this is that women are genetically endowed for child care.) The second strand asserted that fathers' influence on child development is unimportant, or at the very most peripheral or indirect. (The maternal counterpoint here is that mother love and competent maternal care provide everything that children need for normal, healthy development.) Because researchers internalized these cultural beliefs as their own personal beliefs, fathers were essentially ignored by mainstream behavioral science until late in the 20th century. The 1970s through the 1990s, however, have seen a revolution in recognizing fathers and the influence of their love on child development. Three interrelated lines of influence I have discussed elsewhere (Rohner, 1998a) seem to account for this revolution. The net effect of these influences has been to draw attention to the fact that father love sometimes explains a unique, independent portion of the variation in specific child outcomes, over and above the portion explained by mother love. In fact, a few recent studies suggest that father love is the sole significant predictor of specific outcomes, after removing the influence of mother love.

STUDIES SHOWING THE INFLUENCE OF FATHER LOVE

Six types of studies (discussed at greater length in Rohner, 1998a) demonstrate a strong association between father love and aspects of offspring development.

Studies Looking Exclusively at Variations in the Influence of Father Love

Many of the studies looking exclusively at the influence of variations in father love deal with one of two topics: gender role development, especially of sons, and father involvement. Studies of gender role development emerged prominently in the 1940s and continued through the 1970s. Commonly, researchers assessed the masculinity of fathers and of sons, and then correlated the two sets of scores. Many psychologists were surprised at first to discover that no consistent results emerged from this research. But when they examined the quality of the father-son relationship, they found that if the relationship between masculine fathers and their sons was warm and loving, the boys were indeed more masculine. Later, however, researchers found that the masculinity of fathers per se did not seem to make much difference because "boys seemed to conform to the sex-role standards of their culture when their relationships with their fathers were warm, regardless of how 'masculine' the fathers were" (Lamb, 1997, p. 9).

Paternal involvement is the second domain in which there has been a substantial amount of research on the influence of variations in father love. Many studies have concluded that children with highly involved fathers, in relation to children with less involved fathers, tend to be more cognitively and socially competent, less inclined toward gender stereotyping, more empathic, psychologically better adjusted, and the like. But "caring for" children is not necessarily the same thing as "caring about" them. And a closer examination of these studies suggests that it was not the simple fact of paternal engagement (i.e., direct interaction with the child), availability, or responsibility for child care that was associated with these positive outcomes. Rather, it appears that the quality of the father-child relationship—especially of father love—makes the greatest difference (Lamb, 1997; Veneziano & Rohner, 1998).

Father Love Is as Important as Mother Love

The great majority of studies in this category deal with one or a combination of the following four issues among children, adolescents, and young adults: (a) personality and psychological adjustment problems, including issues of self-concept and self-esteem, emotional stability, and aggression; (b) conduct problems, especially in school; (c) cognitive and academic performance issues; and (d) psychopathology. Recent studies employing multivariate analyses have allowed researchers to conclude that fathers' and mothers' behaviors are sometimes each associated significantly and uniquely with these outcomes. The work of Young, Miller, Norton, and Hill (1995) is one of these studies. These authors employed a national sample of 640 12- to 16-year-olds living in two-parent families. They found that perceived paternal love and caring was as predictive of sons' and daughters' life satisfaction—including their sense of well-being—as was maternal love and caring.

Father Love Predicts Specific Outcomes Better Than Mother Love

As complex statistical procedures have become more commonplace in the 1980s and 1990s, it has also become more common to discover that the influence of father love explains a unique, independent portion of the variation in specific child and adult outcomes, over and above the portion of variation explained by mother love. Studies drawing this conclusion tend to deal with one or more of the following four issues among children, adolescents, and young adults: (a) personality and psychological adjustment problems, (b) conduct problems, (c) delinquency, and (d) psychopathology. For example, evidence is mounting that fathers may be especially salient in the development of such forms of psychopathology as substance abuse (drug and alcohol use and abuse), depression and depressed emotion, and behavior problems, including conduct disorder and externalizing behaviors (including aggression toward people and animals, property destruction, deceitfulness, and theft) (Rohner, 1998c). Fathers are also being increasingly implicated in the etiology of borderline personality disorder (a pervasive pattern of emotional and behavioral instability, especially in interpersonal relationships and in self-image) and borderline personality organization (a less severe form of borderline personality disorder) (Fowler, 1990; Rohner & Brothers, in press).

Father love appears to be uniquely associated not just with behavioral and psychological problems, however, but also with health and well-being. Amato (1994), for example, found in a national sample that perceived closeness to fathers made a significant contribution—over and above the contribution made by perceived closeness to mothers—to adult sons' and daughters' happiness, life satisfaction, and low psychological distress (i.e., to overall psychological well-being).

Father Love Is the Sole Significant Predictor of Specific Outcomes

In the 1990s, a handful of studies using a variety of multivariate statistics have concluded that father love is the sole significant predictor of specific child outcomes, after removing the influences of mother love. Most of these studies have dealt with psychological and behavioral problems of adolescents. For example, Cole and McPherson (1993) concluded that father-child conflict but not mother-child conflict (in each case, after the influence of the other was statistically controlled) was positively associated with depressive symptoms in adolescents. Moreover, father-adolescent cohesion was positively associated with the absence of depressive symptoms in adolescents. These results are consistent with Barrera and Garrison-

Jones's (1992) conclusion that adolescents' satisfaction with fathers' support was related to a lowered incidence of depressive symptoms, whereas satisfaction with mothers' support was not. Barnett, Marshall, and Pleck (1992), too, found that when measures of the quality of both mother-son and father-son relationships were entered simultaneously into a regression equation, only the father-son relationship was related significantly to adult sons' psychological distress (a summed measure of anxiety and depression).

Father Love Moderates the Influence of Mother Love

A small but growing number of studies have concluded that fathers' behavior moderates and is moderated by (i.e., interacts with) other influences within the family. Apparently, however, only one study so far has addressed the issue of whether mother love has different effects on specific child outcomes depending on the level of father love. This study, by Forehand and Nousiainen (1993), found that when mothers were low in acceptance, fathers' acceptance scores had no significant impact on youths' cognitive competence. But when mothers were high in acceptance, fathers' acceptance scores made a dramatic difference: Fathers with low acceptance scores tended to have children with poorer cognitive competence, whereas highly accepting fathers tended to have children with substantially better cognitive competence.

Paternal Versus Maternal Parenting Is Sometimes Associated With Different Outcomes for Sons, Daughters, or Both

Many of the studies in this category were published in the 1950s and 1960s, and even earlier. Many of them may be criticized on methodological and conceptual grounds. Nonetheless, evidence suggests that serious research questions should be raised in the future about the possibility that associations between love-related parenting and child outcomes may depend on the gender of the parent and of the child. Three different kinds of studies tend to be found in this category.

First, some research shows that one pattern of paternal love-related behavior and a different pattern of maternal love-related behavior may be associated with a single outcome in sons, daughters, or both. For example, Barber and Thomas (1986) found that daughters' self-esteem was best predicted by their mothers' general support (e.g., praise and approval) but by their fathers' physical affection. Sons' self-esteem, however, was best predicted by their mothers' companionship (e.g., shared activities) and by their fathers' sustained contact (e.g., picking up the boys for safety or for fun).

Second, other research in this category shows that a single pattern of paternal love-related behavior may be associated with one outcome for sons and a different outcome for daughters. For example, Jordan, Radin, and Epstein (1975) found that paternal nurturance was positively associated with boys' but not girls' performance on an IQ test. Finally, the third type of research in this category shows that the influence of a single pattern of paternal love-related behaviors may be more strongly associated with a given outcome for one gender of offspring than for the other. For example, Eisman (1981) reported that fathers' love and acceptance correlated more highly with daughters' than with sons' self-concept.

DISCUSSION

The data reported here are but a minuscule part of a larger body of work showing that father love is heavily implicated not only in children's and adults' psychological well-being and health, but also in an array of psychological and behavioral problems. This evidence punctuates the need to include fathers (and other significant males, when appropriate) as well as mothers in future research, and then to analyze separately the data for possible father and mother effects. It is only by separating data in this way that behavioral scientists can discern when and under what conditions paternal and maternal factors have similar or different effects on specific outcomes for children. This recommendation explicitly contradicts a call sometimes seen in published research to merge data about fathers' and mothers' parenting behaviors.

Finally, it is important to note several problems and limitations in the existing research on father love. For example, even though it seems unmistakably clear that father love makes an important contribution to offsprings' development and psychological functioning, it is not at all clear what generative mechanisms pro-

duce these contributions. In particular, it is unclear why father love is sometimes more strongly associated with specific offspring outcomes than is mother love. And it is unclear why patterns of paternal versus maternal parenting may be associated with different outcomes for sons, daughters, or children of both genders. It remains for future research to inquire directly about these issues. Until then, we can know only that father love is often as influential as mother love—and sometimes more so.

Note

1. Address correspondence to Ronald P. Rohner, Center for the Study of Parental Acceptance and Rejection, School of Family Studies, University of Connecticut, Storrs, CT 06269-2058; e-mail: rohner@uconnvm.uconn.edu or http://vm.uconn.edu/~rohner.

References

Amato, P. R. (1994). Father-child relations, mother-child relations and offspring psychological well-being in adulthood. *Journal of Marriage and the Family, 56*, 1031–1042.

Barber, B. & Thomas, D. (1986). Dimensions of fathers' and mothers' supportive behavior: A case for physical affection. *Journal of Marriage and the Family, 48*, 783–794.

Barnett, R. C., Marshall, N. L., & Pleck, J. H. (1992). Adult son-parent relationships and the associations with sons' psychological distress. *Journal of Family Issues, 13*, 505–525.

Barrera, M., Jr., & Garrison-Jones, C. (1992). Family and peer social support as specific correlates of adolescent depressive symptoms. *Journal of Abnormal Child Psychology, 20*, 1–16.

Cole, D., & McPherson, A. E. (1993). Relation of family subsystems to adolescent depression: Implementing a new family assessment strategy. *Journal of Family Psychology, 7*, 119–133.

Eisman, E. M. (1981). Sex-role characteristics of the parent, parental acceptance of the child and child self-concept. (Doctoral dissertation, California School of Professional Psychology at Los Angeles, 1981). *Dissertation Abstracts International, 24*, 2062.

Forehand, R., & Nousiainen, S. (1993). Maternal and paternal parenting: Critical dimensions in adolescent functioning. *Journal of Family Psychology, 7*, 213–221.

Fowler, S. D. (1990). *Paternal effects on severity of borderline psychopathology.* Unpublished doctoral dissertation, University of Texas, Austin.

Jordan, B., Radin, N., & Epstein, A. (1975). Paternal behavior and intellectual functioning in preschool boys and girls. *Developmental Psychology, 11*, 407–408.

Lamb, M. E. (1997). Fathers and child development: An introductory overview and guide. In M. E. Lamb (Ed.), *The role of the father in child development* (pp. 1–18). New York: John Wiley & Sons.

Rohner, R. P. (1975). *They love me, they love me not: A worldwide study of the effects of parental acceptance and rejection.* New Haven, CT: HRAF Press.

Rohner, R. P. (1986). *The warmth dimension: Foundations of parental acceptance-rejection theory.* Newbury Park, CA: SAGE.

Rohner, R. P. (1998a). *The importance of father love: History and contemporary evidence.* Manuscript submitted for publication.

Rohner, R. P. (1998b). *Parental acceptance-rejection bibliography* [On-line]. Available: http://vm.unconn.edu/~rohner

Rohner, R. P. (1998c). *Worldwide mental health correlates of parental acceptance-rejection: Review of cross-cultural and intracultural evidence.* Manuscript submitted for publication.

Rohner, R. P. (in press). Acceptance and rejection. In D. Levinson, J. Ponzetti, & P. Jorgensen (Eds.), *Encyclopedia of human emotions.* New York: Mac-Millan.

Rohner, R. P., & Brothers, S. A. (in press). Perceived parental rejection, psychological maladjustment, and borderline personality disorder. *Journal of Emotional Abuse.*

Rohner, R. P., & Chaki-Sircar, M. (1988). *Women and children in a Bengali village.* Hanover, NH: University Press of New England.

Veneziano, R. A., & Rohner, R. P. (1998). Perceived paternal warmth, paternal involvement, and youths' psychological adjustment in a rural, biracial southern community. *Journal of Marriage and the Family, 60*, 335–343.

Young, M. H., Miller, B. E., Norton, M. C., & Hill, J. E. (1995). The effect of parental supportive behaviors on life satisfaction of adolescent offspring. *Journal of Marriage and the Family, 57*, 813–822.

Recommended Reading

Biller, H. B. (1993). Fathers and families: Paternal factors in child development. Westport, CT: Auburn House.

Booth, A., & Crouter, A. C. (Eds.). (1998). Men in families: When do they get involved? What difference does it make? Mahwah, NJ: Erlbaum.

Lamb, M. E. (Ed.). (1997). The role of the father in child development. New York: John Wiley & Sons.

Rohner, R. P. (1986). (See References)

Ronald P. Rohner, Center for the Study of Parental Acceptance and Rejection, School of Family Studies, University of Connecticut, Storrs, Connecticut

From *Current Directions in Psychological Science*, October 1998, pp. 157-161. © 1998 by Ronald P. Rohner and the American Psychological Society. Reprinted by permission of Blackwell Publishers.

The Moral Development of Children

It is not enough for kids to tell right from wrong. They must develop a commitment to acting on their ideals. Enlightened parenting can help

by William Damon

With unsettling regularity, news reports tell us of children wreaking havoc on their schools and communities: attacking teachers and classmates, murdering parents, persecuting others out of viciousness, avarice or spite. We hear about feral gangs of children running drugs or numbers, about teenage date rape, about youthful vandalism, about epidemics of cheating even in academically elite schools. Not long ago a middle-class gang of youths terrorized an affluent California suburb through menacing threats and extortion, proudly awarding themselves points for each antisocial act. Such stories make *Lord of the Flies* seem eerily prophetic.

What many people forget in the face of this grim news is that most children most of the time do follow the rules of their society, act fairly, treat friends kindly, tell the truth and respect their elders. Many youngsters do even more. A large portion of young Americans volunteer in community service—according to one survey, between 22 and 45 percent, depending on the location. Young people have also been leaders in social causes. Harvard University psychiatrist Robert Coles has written about children such as Ruby, an African-American girl who broke the color barrier in her school during the 1960s. Ruby's daily walk into the all-white school demonstrated a brave sense of moral purpose. When taunted by classmates, Ruby prayed for their redemption rather than cursing them. "Ruby," Coles observed, "had a will and used it to make an ethical choice; she demonstrated moral stamina; she possessed honor, courage."

All children are born with a running start on the path to moral development. A number of inborn responses predispose them to act in ethical ways. For example, empathy—the capacity to experience another person's pleasure or pain vicariously—is part of our native endowment as humans. Newborns cry when they hear others cry and show signs of pleasure at happy sounds such as cooing and laughter. By the second year of life, children commonly console peers or parents in distress.

Sometimes, of course, they do not quite know what comfort to provide. Psychologist Martin L. Hoffman of New York University once saw a toddler offering his mother his security blanket when he perceived she was upset. Although the emotional disposition to help is present, the means of helping others effectively must be learned and refined through social experience. Moreover, in many people the capacity for empathy stagnates or even diminishes. People can act cruelly to those they refuse to empathize with. A New York police officer once asked a teenage thug how he could have crippled an 83-year-old woman during a mugging. The boy replied, "What do I care? I'm not her."

A scientific account of moral growth must explain both the good and the bad. Why do most children act in reasonably—sometimes exceptionally—moral ways, even when it flies in the face of their immediate self-interest? Why do some children depart from accepted standards, often to the great harm of themselves and others? How does a child acquire mores and develop a lifelong commitment to moral behavior, or not?

The Six Stages of Moral Judgment

Growing up, children and young adults come to rely less on external discipline and more on deeply held beliefs. They go through as many as six stages (grouped into three levels) of moral reasoning, as first argued by psychologist Lawrence Kohlberg in the late 1950s (*below*). The evidence includes a long-term study of 58 young men interviewed periodically over two decades. Their moral maturity was judged by how they analyzed hypothetical dilemmas, such as whether a husband should steal a drug for his dying wife. Either yes or no was a valid answer; what mattered was how the men justified it. As they grew up, they passed through the stages in succession, albeit at different rates (*bar graph*). The sixth stage remained elusive. Despite the general success of this model for describing intellectual growth, it does not explain people's actual behavior. Two people at the same stage may act differently. —W.D.

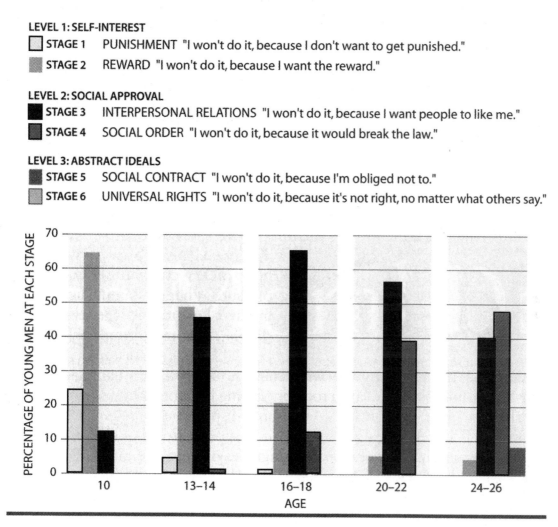

LEVEL 1: SELF-INTEREST
STAGE 1   PUNISHMENT   "I won't do it, because I don't want to get punished."
STAGE 2   REWARD   "I won't do it, because I want the reward."

LEVEL 2: SOCIAL APPROVAL
STAGE 3   INTERPERSONAL RELATIONS   "I won't do it, because I want people to like me."
STAGE 4   SOCIAL ORDER   "I won't do it, because it would break the law."

LEVEL 3: ABSTRACT IDEALS
STAGE 5   SOCIAL CONTRACT   "I won't do it, because I'm obliged not to."
STAGE 6   UNIVERSAL RIGHTS   "I won't do it, because it's not right, no matter what others say."

Edward Bell

Psychologists do not have definitive answers to these questions, and often their studies seem merely to confirm parents' observations and intuition. But parents, like all people, can be led astray by subjective biases, incomplete information and media sensationalism. They may blame a relatively trivial event—say, a music concert—for a deep-seated problem such as drug dependency. They may incorrectly attribute their own problems to a strict upbringing and then try to compensate by raising their children in an overly permissive way. In such a hotly contested area as children's moral values, a systematic, scientific approach is the only way to avoid wild swings of emotional reaction that end up repeating the same mistakes.

The Genealogy of Morals

The study of moral development has become a lively growth industry within the social sciences. Journals are full of new findings and competing models. Some theories focus on natural biological forces; others stress social influence and experience; still others, the judgment that results from children's intellectual development. Although each theory has a different emphasis, all recognize that no single cause can account for either moral or immoral behavior. Watching violent videos or playing shoot-'em-up computer games may push some children over the edge and leave others unaffected. Conventional wisdom dwells on lone silver bullets, but scientific understanding must be built on an appreciation of the complexity and variety of children's lives.

Biologically oriented, or "nativist," theories maintain that human morality springs from emotional dispositions that are hardwired into our species. Hoffman, Colwyn Trevar—then of the University of Edinburgh and Nancy Eisenberg of Arizona State University have established that babies can feel empathy as soon as they recognize the existence of others—sometimes in the first week after birth. Other moral emotions that make an early appearance include shame, guilt and indignation. As Harvard child psychologist Jerome S. Kagan has described, young children can be outraged by the violation of social expectations, such as a breach in the rules of a favorite game or rearranged buttons on a piece of familiar clothing.

Nearly everybody, in every culture, inherits these dispositions. Mary D. Ainsworth of the University of Virginia reported empathy among Ugandan and American infants; Norma Feshbach of the University of California at Los Angeles conducted a similar comparison of newborns in Europe, Israel and the U.S.; Millard C. Madsen of U.C.L.A. studied sharing by preschool children in nine cultures. As far as psychologists know, children everywhere start life with caring feelings toward those close to them and adverse reactions to inhumane or unjust behavior. Differences in how these reactions are triggered and expressed emerge only later, once children have been exposed to the particular value systems of their cultures.

In contrast, the learning theories concentrate on children's acquisition of behavioral norms and values through observation, imitation and reward. Research in this tradition has concluded that moral behavior is context-bound, varying from situation to situation almost independently of stated beliefs. Landmark studies in the 1920s, still frequently cited, include Hugh Hartshorne and Mark May's survey of how children reacted when given the chance to cheat. The children's behavior depended largely on whether they thought they would be caught. It could be predicted neither from their conduct in previous situations nor from their knowledge of common moral rules, such as the Ten Commandments and the Boy Scout's code.

Later reanalyses of Hartshorne and May's data, performed by Roger Burton of the State University of New York at Buffalo, discovered at least one general trend: younger children were more likely to cheat than adolescents. Perhaps socialization or mental growth can restrain dishonest behavior after all. But the effect was not a large one.

The third basic theory of moral development puts the emphasis on intellectual growth, arguing that virtue and vice are ultimately a matter of conscious choice. The best-known cognitive theories are those of psychologists Jean Piaget and Lawrence Kohlberg. Both described children's early moral beliefs as oriented toward power and authority. For young children, might makes right, literally. Over time they come to understand that social rules are made by people and thus can be renegotiated and that reciprocity in relationships is more fair than unilateral obedience. Kohlberg identified a six-stage sequence in the maturation of moral judgment [see box, "The Six Stages of Moral Judgment"]. Several thousand studies have used it as a measure of how advanced a person's moral reasoning is.

Conscience versus Chocolate

Although the main parts of Kohlberg's sequence have been confirmed, notable exceptions stand out. Few if any people reach the sixth and most advanced stage, in which their moral view is based purely on abstract principles. As for the early stages in the sequence, many studies (including ones from my own laboratory) have found that young children have a far richer sense of positive morality than the model indicates. In other words, they do not act simply out of fear of punishment. When a playmate hogs a plate of cookies or refuses to relinquish a swing, the protest "That's not fair!" is common. At the same time, young children realize that they have an obligation to share with others—even when their parents say not to. Preschool children generally believe in an equal distribution of goods and back up their beliefs with reasons such as empathy ("I want my friend to feel nice"), reciprocity ("She shares her toys with me") and egalitarianism ("We should all get the same"). All this they figure out through confrontation with peers at play. Without fairness, they learn, there will be trouble.

In fact, none of the three traditional theories is sufficient to explain children's moral growth and behavior. None captures the most essential dimensions of moral life: character and commitment. Regardless of how children develop their initial system of values, the key question is: What makes them live up to their ideals or not? This issue is the focus of recent scientific thinking.

Like adults, children struggle with temptation. To see how this tug of war plays itself out in the world of small

"Could You Live with Yourself?"

In a distressed neighborhood in Camden, N.J., social psychologist Daniel Hart of Rutgers University interviewed an African-American teenager who was active in community service:

How would you describe yourself?

I am the kind of person who wants to get involved, who believes in getting involved. I just had this complex, I call it, where people think of Camden as being a bad place, which bothered me. Every city has its own bad places, you know. I just want to work with people, work to change that image that people have of Camden. You can't start with adults, because they don't change. But if you can get into the minds of young children, show them what's wrong and let them know that you don't want them to be this way, then it could work, because they're more persuadable.

Is there really one correct solution to moral problems like this one?

Basically, it's like I said before.You're supposed to try to help save a life.

How do you know?

Well, it's just—how could you live with yourself? Say that I could help save this person's life—could I just let that person die? I mean, I couldn't live with myself if that happened. A few years ago my sister was killed, and… the night she was killed I was over at her house, earlier that day. Maybe if I had spent the night at her house that day, maybe this wouldn't have happened.

You said that you're not a bad influence on others. Why is that important?

Well, I try not to be a bad role model. All of us have bad qualities, of course; still, you have to be a role model even if you're a person walking down the street. You know, we have a society today where there are criminals and crooks. There are drug users. Kids look to those people. If they see a drug dealer with a lot of money, they want money, too, and then they're going to do drugs. So it's important that you try not to be a bad influence, because that can go a long way. Even if you say, oh, wow, you tell your little sister or brother to be quiet so Mom and Dad won't wake so you won't have to go to school. And they get in the habit of being quiet [laughs], you're not going to school, things like that. So when you're a bad influence, it always travels very far.

Why don't you want that to happen?

Because in today's society there's just really too much crime, too much violence. I mean everywhere. And I've even experienced violence, because my sister was murdered. You know, we need not to have that in future years, so we need to teach our children otherwise.

children, my colleagues and I (then at Clark University) devised the following experiment. We brought groups, each of four children, into our lab, gave them string and beads, and asked them to make bracelets and necklaces for us. We then thanked them profusely for their splendid work and rewarded them, as a group, with 10 candy bars. Then the real experiment began: we told each group that it would need to decide the best way to divide up the reward. We left the room and watched through a one-way mirror.

Before the experiment, we had interviewed participants about the concept of fairness. We were curious, of course, to find out whether the prospect of gobbling up real chocolate would overwhelm their abstract sense of right and wrong. To test this thoroughly, we gave one unfortunate control group an almost identical conundrum, using cardboard rectangles rather than real chocolate—a not so subtle way of defusing their self-interest. We observed groups of four-, six-, eight- and 10-year-old children to see whether the relationship between situational and hypothetical morality changed with age.

The children's ideals did make a difference but within limits circumscribed by narrow self-interest. Children given cardboard acted almost three times more generously toward one another than did children given chocolate. Yet moral beliefs still held some sway. For example, children who had earlier expressed a belief in merit-based solutions ("The one who did the best job should get more of the candy") were the ones most likely to advocate for merit in the real situation. But they did so most avidly when they themselves could claim to have done more than their peers. Without such a claim, they were easily persuaded to drop meritocracy for an equal division.

Even so, these children seldom abandoned fairness entirely. They may have switched from one idea of justice to another—say, from merit to equality—but they did not resort to egoistic justifications such as "I should get more because I'm big" or "Boys like candy more than girls, and I'm a boy." Such rationales generally came from children who had declared no belief in either equality or meritocracy. Older children were more likely to believe in fairness and to act accordingly, even when such action favored others. This finding was evidence for the reassuring proposition that ideals can have an increasing influence on conduct as a child matures.

Do the Right Thing

But this process is not automatic. A person must adopt those beliefs as a central part of his or her personal identity. When a person moves from saying "People should be honest" to "I want to be honest," he or she becomes more likely to tell the truth in everyday interactions. A person's use of moral principles to define the self is called the person's moral identity. Moral identity determines not merely what the person considers to be the right course of action but also why he or she would decide: "I myself must take this course." This distinction is crucial to understanding the variety of moral behavior. The same basic ideals are widely shared by even the youngest members of society; the difference is the resolve to act on those ideals.

Most children and adults will express the belief that it is wrong to allow others to suffer, but only a subset of them will conclude that they themselves must do something about, say, ethnic cleansing in Kosovo. Those are the ones who are most likely to donate money or fly to the Balkans to help. Their concerns about human suffering are central to the way they think about themselves and their life goals, and so they feel a responsibility to take action, even at great personal cost.

In a study of moral exemplars—people with long, publicly documented histories of charity and civil-rights work—psychologist Anne Colby of the Carnegie Foundation and I encountered a high level of integration between self-identity and moral concerns. "People who define themselves in terms of their moral goals are likely to see moral problems in everyday events, and they are also likely to see themselves as necessarily implicated in these problems," we wrote. Yet the exemplars showed no signs of more insightful moral reasoning. Their ideals and Kohlberg levels were much the same as everyone else's.

Conversely, many people are equally aware of moral problems, but to them the issues seem remote from their own lives and their senses of self. Kosovo and Rwanda sound far away and insignificant; they are easily put out of mind. Even issues closer to home—say, a maniacal clique of peers who threaten a classmate—may seem like someone else's problem. For people who feel this way, inaction does not strike at their self-conception. Therefore, despite commonplace assumptions to the contrary, their moral knowledge will not be enough to impel moral action.

The development of a moral identity follows a general pattern. It normally takes shape in late childhood, when children acquire the capacity to analyze people—including themselves—in terms of stable character traits. In childhood, self-identifying traits usually consist of action-related skills and interests ("I'm smart" or "I love music"). With age, children start to use moral terms to define themselves. By the onset of puberty, they typically invoke adjectives such as "fairminded," "generous" and "honest."

Some adolescents go so far as to describe themselves primarily in terms of moral goals. They speak of noble purposes, such as caring for others or improving their communities, as missions that give meaning to their lives. Working in Camden, N.J., Daniel Hart and his colleagues at Rutgers University found that a high proportion of so-called care exemplars—teenagers identified by teachers and peers as highly committed to volunteering—had self-identities that were based on moral belief systems. Yet they scored no higher than their peers on the standard psychological tests of moral judgment. The study is noteworthy because it was conducted in an economically de-prived urban setting among an adolescent population often stereotyped as high risk and criminally inclined [*see box*, "Could You Live with Yourself?"].

At the other end of the moral spectrum, further evidence indicates that moral identity drives behavior. Social psychologists Hazel Markus of Stanford University and Daphne Oyserman of the University of Michigan have observed that delinquent youths have immature senses of self, especially when talking about their future selves (a critical part of adolescent identity). These troubled teenagers do not imagine themselves as doctors, husbands, voting citizens, church members—any social role that embodies a positive value commitment.

How does a young person acquire, or not acquire, a moral identity? It is an incremental process, occurring gradually in thousands of small ways: feedback from others; observations of actions by others that either inspire or appall; reflections on one's own experience; cultural influences such as family, school, religious institutions and the mass media. The relative importance of these factors varies from child to child.

Teach Your Children Well

For most children, parents are the original source of moral guidance. Psychologists such as Diana Baumrind of the University of California at Berkeley have shown that "authoritative" parenting facilitates children's moral growth more surely than either "permissive" or "authoritarian" parenting. The authoritative mode establishes consistent family rules and firm limits but also encourages open discussion and clear communication to explain and, when justified, revise the rules. In contrast, the permissive mode avoids rules entirely; the authoritarian mode irregularly enforces rules at the parent's whim—the "because I said so" approach.

Although permissive and authoritarian parenting seem like opposites, they actually tend to produce similar patterns of poor self-control and low social responsibility in children. Neither mode presents children with the realistic expectations and structured guidance that challenge them to expand their moral horizons. Both can foster habits—such as feeling that mores come from the outside—that could inhibit the development of a moral identity. In this way, moral or immoral conduct during adulthood often has roots in childhood experience.

As children grow, they are increasingly exposed to influences beyond the family. In most families, however, the parent-child relationship remains primary as long as the child lives at home. A parent's comment on a raunchy music lyric or a blood-drenched video usually will stick with a child long after the media experience has faded. In fact, if salacious or violent media programming opens the door to responsible parental feedback, the benefits can far outweigh the harm.

How Universal Are Values?

The observed importance of shared values in children's moral development raises some of the most hotly debated questions in philosophy and the social sciences today. Do values vary from place to place, or is there a set of universal values that guides moral development everywhere? Do children growing up in different cultures or at different times acquire fundamentally different mores?

Some light was shed on the cultural issue by Richard A. Shweder of the University of Chicago and his colleagues in a study of Hindu-Brahmin children in India and children from Judeo-Christian backgrounds in the U.S. The study revealed striking contrasts between the two groups. From an early age, the Indian children learned to maintain tradition, to respect defined rules of interpersonal relationships and to help people in need. American children, in comparison, were oriented toward autonomy, liberty and personal rights. The Indian children said that breaches of tradition, such as eating beef or addressing one's father by his first name, were particularly reprehensible. They saw nothing wrong with a man caning his errant son or a husband beating his wife when she went to the movies without his permission. The American children were appalled by all physically punitive behavior but indifferent to infractions such as eating forbidden foods or using improper forms of address.

Moreover, the Indians and Americans moved in opposite directions as they matured. Whereas Indian children restricted value judgments to situations with which they were directly familiar, Indian adults generalized their values to a broad range of social conditions. American children said that moral standards should apply to every-

one always; American adults modified values in the face of changing circumstances. In short, the Indians began life as relativists and ended up an universalists, whereas the Americans went precisely the other way.

Percentage of Kids with Enough Problems to Warrant Psychiatry

1976 ▇▇▇▇▇ 10%
1989 ▇▇▇▇▇▇▇▇▇ 18.2%
   0 2 4 6 8 10 12 14 16 18

KIDS THESE DAYS are likier to need mental health services, judging from parents' reports of behavioral and emotional problems

It would be overstating matters, however, to say that children from different cultures adopt completely different moral codes. In Schweder's study, both groups of children thought that deceitful acts (a father breaking a promise to a child) and uncharitable acts (ignoring a beggar with a sick child) were wrong. They also shared a repugnance toward theft, vandalism and harming innocent victims, although there was some disagreement on what constitutes innocence. Among these judgments may be found a universal moral sense, based on common human aversions. It reflects core values—benevolence, fairness, honesty—that may be necessary for sustaining human relationships in all but the most dysfunctional societies.

A parallel line of research has studied gender differences, arguing that girls learn to emphasize caring, whereas boys incline toward rules and justice. Unlike the predictions made by culture theory, however, these gender claims have not held up. The original research that claimed to find gender differences lacked proper control groups. Well-designed studies of

American children—for example, those by Lawrence Walker of the University of British Columbia—rarely detect differences between boys' and girls' ideals. Even for adults, when educational or occupational levels are controlled, the differences disappear. Female lawyers have almost the same moral orientations as their male counterparts; the same can be said for male and female nurses, homemakers, scientists, high school dropouts and so on. As cultural theorists point out, there is far more similarity between male and female moral orientations within any given culture than between male and female orientations across cultures.

Generational differences are also of interest, especially to people who bemoan what they see as declining morality. Such complaints, of course, are nothing new [see "Teenage Attitudes," by H. H. Remmers and D. H. Radler; [&smallcaps]Scientific American[&stop], June 1958; and "The Origins of Alienation," by Urie Bronfenbrenner; [&smallcaps]Scientific American[&stop], August 1974]. Nevertheless, there is some evidence that young people today are more likely to engage in antisocial behavior than those a generation ago were. According to a survey by Thomas M. Achenbach and Catherine T. Howell of the University of Vermont, parents and teachers reported more behavioral problems (lying, cheating) and other threats to healthy development (depression, withdrawal) in 1989 than in 1976 (*above*). (The researchers are now updating their survey.) But in the long sweep of human history, 13 years is merely an eye blink. The changes could reflect a passing problem, such as overly permissive fashions in child rearing, rather than a permanent trend.

—*W.D.*

EDWARD BELL; SOURCE; THOMAS M. ACHENBACH AND CATHERINE T. HOWELL

One of the most influential things parents can do is to encourage the right kinds of peer relations. Interactions with peers can spur moral growth by showing children the conflict between their preconceptions and social reality. During the debates about dividing the chocolate, some of our subjects seemed to pick up new—and more informed—ideas about justice. In a follow-up study, we confirmed that the peer debate had heightened their awareness of the rights of others. Children who participated actively in the debate, both expressing their opinions and listening to the viewpoints of others, were especially likely to benefit.

In adolescence, peer interactions are crucial in forging a self-identity. To be sure, this process often plays out in cliquish social behavior: as a means of defining and shoring up the sense of self, kids will seek out like-minded peers and spurn others who seem foreign. But when kept within reasonable bounds, the in-group clustering generally evolves into a more mature friendship pattern. What can parents do in the meantime to fortify a teenager who is bearing the brunt of isolation or persecution? The most important message they can give is that cruel behavior reveals something about the perpetrator rather than about the victim. If this advice helps the youngster resist taking the treatment personally, the period of persecution will pass without leaving any psychological scars.

Some psychologists, taking a sociological approach, are examining community-level variables, such as whether various moral influences—parents, teachers, mass media and so on—are consistent with one another. In a study of 311 adolescents from 10 American towns and cities, Francis A. J. Ianni of the Columbia University Teachers College noticed high degrees of altruistic behavior and low degrees of antisocial behavior among youngsters from communities where there was consensus in expectations for young people.

Everyone in these places agreed that honesty, for instance, is a fundamental value. Teachers did not tolerate cheating on exams, parents did not let their children lie and get away with it, sports coaches did not encourage teams to bend the rules for the sake of a win, and people of all ages expected openness from their friends. But many communities were divided along such lines. Coaches espoused winning above all else, and parents protested when teachers reprimanded their children for cheating or shoddy schoolwork. Under such circumstances, children learned not to take moral messages seriously.

Ianni named the set of shared standards in harmonious communities a "youth charter." Ethnicity, cultural diversity, socioeconomic status, geographic location and population size had nothing to do with whether a town offered its young people a steady moral compass. The notion of a youth charter is being explored in social interventions that foster communication among children,

parents, teachers and other influential adults. Meanwhile other researchers have sought to understand whether the specific values depend on cultural, gender or generational background [see box, "How Universal Are Values?"].

Unfortunately, the concepts embodied in youth charters seem ever rarer in American society. Even when adults spot trouble, they may fail to step in. Parents are busy and often out of touch with the peer life of their children; they give kids more autonomy than ever before, and kids expect it—indeed, demand it. Teachers, for their part, feel that a child's nonacademic life is none of their business and that they could be censured, even sued, if they intervened in a student's personal or moral problem. And neighbors feel the same way: that they have no business interfering with another family's business, even if they see a child headed for trouble.

Everything that psychologists know from the study of children's moral development indicates that moral identity—the key source of moral commitment throughout life—is fostered by multiple social influences that guide a child in the same general direction. Children must hear the message enough for it to stick. The challenge for pluralistic societies will be to find enough common ground to communicate the shared standards that the young need.

Further Reading

THE MEANING AND MEASUREMENT OF MORAL DEVELOPMENT. Lawrence Kohlberg. Clark University, Heinz Werner Institute, 1981.

THE EMERGENCE OF MORALITY IN YOUNG CHILDREN. Edited by Jerome Kagan and Sharon Lamb. University of Chicago Press, 1987.

THE MORAL CHILD: NURTURING CHILDREN'S NATURAL MORAL GROWTH. William Damon. Free Press, 1990.

ARE AMERICAN CHILDREN'S PROBLEMS GETTING WORSE? A 13-YEAR COMPARISON. Thomas M. Achenbach and Catherine T. Howell in *Journal of the American Academy of Child and Adolescent Psychiatry*, Vol. 32, No. 6, pages 1145–1154; November 1993.

SOME DO CARE: CONTEMPORARY LIVES OF MORAL COMMITMENT. Anne Colby. Free Press, 1994.

THE YOUTH CHARTER: HOW COMMUNITIES CAN WORK TOGETHER TO RAISE STANDARDS FOR ALL OUR CHILDREN. William Damon. Free Press, 1997.

The Author

WILLIAM DAMON remembers being in an eighth-grade clique that tormented an unpopular kid. After describing his acts in the school newspaper, he was told by his English teacher, "I give you an A for the writing, but what you're doing is really shameful." That moral feedback has stayed with him. Damon is now director of the Center on Adolescence at Stanford University, an interdisciplinary program that specializes in what he has called "the least understood, the least trusted, the most feared and most neglected period of development." A developmental psychologist, he has studied intellectual and moral growth, educational methods, and peer and cultural influences on children. He is the author of numerous books and the father of three children, the youngest now in high school.

Playing With God

The mother of an eight-year-old thinks religion only becomes meaningful when its meaning is discovered by her child. The child declares she does not believe in religion or God, but believes in nature and science. With the exception of Christmas, the parents admit they rarely take their daughter to church. When they do, she complains they are ruining her Christmas. The parents are told they cannot impart their understanding of religion onto their daughter and that their daughter subconsciously understands spirituality.

by Tracy Cochran

"RELIGION ISN'T FOR ME," announced my eight-year-old daughter, Alexandra, as we ate dinner together one January night. "I think of it like an old spider on the wall. I know that it's there but I try to ignore it."

Alexandra took a bite of pasta and studied my reaction.

"When I pray it's usually just for ordinary things, like 'Please, please, let me get an A on this test,'" she added.

Since Christmas, Alexandra had been making provocative statements about religion and prayer.

"I don't believe in God, I believe in Nature," my daughter continued. "Everything comes from Nature. We are Nature, Mommy. Church makes everything seem boring. Even a nice song like 'Jingle Bells' sounds really slow in church." "Jiiiinnnnglllle Bellllls…. "Alexandra lowered her voice and sang a kind of funeral dirge to underline her point. .

On Christmas Day, my husband and I had taken Alexandra to Mass at St. Patrick's Cathedral. We rarely took Alexandra to church, but we had wanted her to see thousands of people from around the world praying together and solemnly rejoicing about the appearance of the miraculous on earth. I was trying to delicately engineer an impression that would lead her to suspect there is a finer intelligence or reality behind the world of appearances. But Alexandra hated the cathedral that day. She found it crowded and cold, and wailed that we were ruining Christmas for her by bringing her there.

A wise man once said that trying to impart your understanding to others by talking is like trying to fill them up with bread by looking at them. Since Christmas, Alexandra had been struggling to give me bread. She has reminded me that kids know how to touch this finer

world inside themselves although they rarely call this intimate connection prayer.

That January night I asked Alexandra if she ever thought about where the universe came from, big questions like that.

"Of course, but that's science!" she exclaimed. "I love science so much I would rather go to school naked than not be able to study it."

It is becoming clear to me that "science" to my little daughter isn't a strictly intellectual discipline but a license to explore with all her senses and imagination. The "scientific" ideas and questions that catch fire for her—"Is every atom made up of matter?" "What if you could make a machine that could look into a dog's brain? Would it even be worth it?"—are fresh and generative. Shot through with a sense of wonder at creation, Alexandra's "science" is akin to our most ancient way of being spiritual. Like other children who speak but aren't yet too adept at arguing for their own feelings and beliefs, my daughter has been inhabiting her body and the natural world with a sense of deep connection and curiosity. In his collection of essays, Living By Wonder, the educator Richard Lewis describes this childhood state as the time of "the incandescent virtues of 'why?'"

AT THE CHRISTMAS Mass, a big, stern-looking priest, one of many serving Communion that day, came and stood in the aisle a few feet from our pew. The faithful flowed forward, including Alexandra's grandmother, who had accompanied us. A young Mexican wearing a red hooded sweatshirt over a battered leather jacket followed Alexandra's grandmother. He was followed by a willowy matron in a fur coat, who was in turn followed by a tiny old woman dressed in black.

"The Body of Christ, the Body of Christ," the priest repeated as he held up the Communion wafers. Some people reached out with cupped hands like small children. Others opened their mouths to be fed in the traditional infant-like pose of surrender to a greater power. Alexandra slumped at the end of the pew and sighed and glowered. "It's just that I don't really feel comfortable anywhere there aren't plants and animals," she explained to me later. After the Mass, I took her up to inspect the life-size creche near the altar. I told her the Christmas story again, picturing it as a kind of time-release capsule of higher truth that would take effect in the future. I was providing Alexandra with a cosmic vision, with food for prayer. She asked me how the wise men picked Jesus to be this "big deal baby." I told her the wise men followed an unusual star that shone over the manger.

"I know about the star," said Alexandra. "But a star is as big as the sun, so that's like saying the sun is over your house. It's not really over your house, it's over the whole earth."

As we walked up an aisle toward the cathedral's main entrance, my husband pointed to a gaunt, haunted portrait of Christ above an altar tiered with flickering candles. He explained to Alexandra that this face was based on marks that were left on the Shroud of Turin.

"Excuse me?" asked Alexandra. "Has anybody seriously looked at this man? Like, maybe he could use a shave or something?"

I knew Alexandra was trying to provoke me, but there was a visceral question under her words that galvanized my attention. I wondered how any child could feel a connection to this tortured-looking man who lived two thousand years ago.

I thought of telling her that Jesus loved children, or that she could try to feel a connection by saying his name in her heart. But these answers felt cheap. Alexandra regarded me with a calm, grave expression. She looked very small and very present in this cold, cavernous, crowded place.

"They kept calling Jesus 'the king,'" Alexandra continued. "How can one baby be the king of the whole world?"

"He didn't call himself a king," I said. "He called himself the son of man. He wanted to show us that we can all be like him."

"Then why did he want to be worshipped in a huge, fancy place like this?"

"I'm not sure he would have wanted to be worshipped like this," I replied.

"Then what are we doing here?"

Brought to a full stop, I asked Alexandra where she would like to celebrate Christmas.

"In the African savannah surrounded by animals," she said." Only I wouldn't make the animals celebrate. They should be what they are and I would observe them."

Alexandra lit up as she spoke of this. It occurred to me that I had been too busy trying to teach Alexandra to stop and listen to her. As she talked, I remembered that the heart of prayer was the experience of being seen and heard by a loving, boundlessly accepting attention.

MONTHS BEFORE Christmas, while spending a weekend at the wooded upstate New York community of the Omega Institute, I had watched from a distance as a young camp counselor led Alexandra and a group of other children through the woods blindfolded. They were identifying different kinds of trees by hugging them and smelling them. When Alexandra took her turn she looked so radiant, so deeply engaged in the life around her that I knew, as I had the first moment I laid eyes on my daughter, that she was already part of that other world that I was trying so hard to lead her to. She knew innately how to feel her way into the heart of things.

In Living By Wonder, Lewis describes how children are able to "fuse with the object of their play." According to him, children innately seek to understand the world around them by drawing on their own sensations and feelings, their own bodily understanding of growth and change. Imagination in children, according to Lewis, is their ability to project their inner images and experience on to the world as a way of sympathetically knowing.

"Did the tree hug you back?" I had asked Alexandra.

"I don't like it when you talk that way," she'd answered, although she knows that I've caught her saying hello to things as if they were alive.

In The Spell of the Sensuous, philosopher David Abram describes the way indigenous people have preserved our innate "carnal, sensorial empathy" with the natural world. More in touch with their bodies and "animal senses" than modern city dwellers, indigenous people are more aware that the natural world around us is awake and speaking. I have seen that children also have this capacity to listen to the world around them with their "animal bodies," and they don't stop at the natural world. They fuse their sensations with their earliest feelings of well-being (and fear of abandonment) to know the One behind the world.

Although Alexandra would never use these words, there's a chance that when she was hugging trees she was finding God in the flesh of life. I know this because once I was a kid and risked playing at prayer.

When I was a little girl, there was a game I played when I couldn't sleep. Although I never thought of it as a prayer or used these words, it was my way of seeking God. I would peel off my blankets and slip down to the cold hardwood floor (I remember doing this mostly in the winter). The first few moments on the floor were my leap of faith. Freezing and feeling utterly exposed and alone, I thought of all the people and other beings who had no beds, no blankets, no shelter at all. These thoughts were a ritual that always made me feel gratitude or a stab of empathy. They made me feel connected to the rest of the world. I would also feel brave in a special way, as if I were daring to venture out on my own. I was not only dipping into dangerously big subjects, I was risking being seen by the unknown.

As I lay there a shift always took place. The labels I had about "cold" and "hard" gave way. I noticed that the polished hardwood was soft in its own way, more giving than stone or steel. As I listened to the wind blowing outside my bedroom window (the winter temperatures in Watertown, New York, often hit twenty and even thirty below zero), I imagined what it was like outside, and truly valued that I was in a warm, life-saving shelter. As I broke through the isolation of my thoughts and sank into the experience of my body, I began to sense that everything in the world had emerged from a mystery. Why was there a world and not nothing? As a child I couldn't help but ask the question with my whole being, and as I asked it I felt vibrantly alive and present in a living world.

I would scramble back up to my bed and experience its incredible softness, wondering how I could have been numb to it before. I would pull up the sheet, savoring its smoothness. I would pull up the blankets and quilt one at a time, feeling unimaginably rich and relaxed and provided for. Even the air that touched my face was luxurious. I felt cradled in a benevolent, listening silence, and I knew without words that I had drawn closer to God by going deep within myself. It was a state that I would recapture many years later in moments of meditation and prayer.

Not all imaginary play expresses an impulse to prayer, of course. I played another game in which I was a deadly, superintelligent black panther named Striker. Striker liked to crouch in trees and stalk the other kids who came to play in my backyard. Like a fairy tale, this game let me play with some of my wildest energies. My prayer game, on the other hand, harbored the wish to see and be seen by a finer, larger intelligence.

Recently, Alexandra and I heard Kaddish recited for the first time. The prayer was so exalted, so utterly above sentimental condolence that it occurred to me that, as tradition says, it really may have been given to man by the angels. I resolved to read Alexandra the Beatitudes and the Psalms, and to teach her the Lord's Prayer.

I still have to restrain myself, in other words, from the impulse to drag Alexandra to the threshold of sacred truth. Yet on a deeper level I know that I have to let her find her own way. I try to remember now that what becomes truly meaningful to any one of us are those truths which we have discovered inside ourselves.

Still, there is a reciprocal exchange between Alexandra and me. A few nights ago, there was a new development. I found Alexandra curled up in bed with a book of Bible stories.

"I'm not religious, you know," she said, studying me over the top of the book. "But could you just let me read for five more minutes?"

TRACY COCHRAN is co-author of *Transformations: Awakening to the Sacred in Ourselves* (Bell Tower Books) and a contributing editor of *Tricycle: The Buddhist Review*.

UNIT 5
Cultural and Societal Influences

Unit Selections

Key Points to Consider

- Alcohol and drug use among adults and teenagers is nothing new. What is new about the research on the outcomes of early use of drugs and alcohol? Did you experiment with or use drugs or alcohol as a teenager or young adult? Why or why not? What sort of peer pressure or media influences might have had an impact on you?

- Do you think that some children are born to be violent? What cultural factors may exacerbate violence? Does our society or government have an obligation to reduce media violence?

- If family breakdown is related to numerous problems for children, should public policy be designed to help reduce the enormous number of children living in poverty in our country?

- Have you ever had contact with or known anyone with autism? Based on "The Early Origins of Autism," what information or assurances might you give to parents of an autistic child for future prognosis?

- Advances in cognitive and brain research have done much to raise awareness and understanding of dyslexia. Based on the reading, what sort of interventions seem to benefit those with dyslexia?

- How would you react and what might you do if your child was summarily kidnapped from you in a country without the formal legal, political, and criminal justice system that we are accustomed to in the United States?

 **Links: www.dushkin.com/online/**
These sites are annotated in the World Wide Web pages.

Ask NOAH About: Mental Health
http://www.noah-health.org/english/illness/mentalhealth/mental.html

Association to Benefit Children (ABC)
http://www.a-b-c.org

Children Now
http://www.childrennow.org

Council for Exceptional Children
http://www.cec.sped.org

National Black Child Development Institute
http://www.nbcdi.org

Prevent Child Abuse America
http://www.preventchildabuse.org

Social scientists and developmental psychologists have come to realize that children are influenced by a multitude of social forces that surround them. In this unit we present articles to illuminate how American children are influenced by broad factors such as economics, culture, politics, and the media. These influences also affect the family, which is a major context of child development, and many children are now faced with more family challenges than ever. In addition, analysis of exceptional or atypical children gives the reader a more comprehensive account of child development. Thus, articles are presented on special challenges of development, such as poverty, youth, violence, latchkey children, sexual abuse, autism, and child depression.

What will children and life be like in the new millennium? Author Jerry Adler offers a fascinating take on both past history and future possibilities in a wide-ranging article, "Tomorrow's Child." He cites amazing technological and medical advances, economic opportunities, and cultural forces as playing pivotal roles in shaping the child of the future.

With today's hectic pace and multiple demands it comes as no surprise that adults and teenagers face many everyday stresses and challenges. Unfortunately, some young adults turn to abusing alcohol, and the research in "Getting Stupid" documents studies indicating that teenagers who drink are se-

riously compromising their memory, intellectual, and brain functioning.

At no time in recorded history have we witnessed more children killing children. In "Why the Young Kill," Sharon Begley describes research showing that both biological factors and environmental influences play powerful roles in predisposing some children to becoming murderers.

Some children all around the world are faced with challenges such as severe poverty, sexual, physical abuse, and kidnapping. Such children are often misunderstood and mistreated and pose special challenges to parents, teachers, and society. Are schools and families prepared to deal with them? To do so, teachers and parents need more and better information. These issues are discussed in "The Effects of Poverty on Children," "Effects of Maltreatment and Ways to Promote Children's Resiliency," and "A Mother-and-Child Reunion." Two other areas in which researchers, parents, and educators continue to struggle to understand and help include coping with an autistic child or a child struggling with dyslexia. "The Early Origins of Autism" by researcher Patricia Rodier describes some cutting edge research honing in on the cause of this difficult disorder, while "Dyslexia and the New Science of Reading" provides illustrative information on dyslexia and promising new techniques for helping children learn in spite of this condition.

TOMORROW'S CHILD

Amazing medical advances, great economic opportunities, earlier schooling and many new kinds of Barbie dolls are among the wonders in store for the first Americans of a new century.

BY JERRY ADLER

SHE WILL BE CONCEIVED, ALMOST CERTAINLY, sometime in the next six months, and will tumble headfirst into the world nine months later, wholly unconscious of her uniqueness as the first American of the millennium. Escaping by a stroke of the clock the awful burden of the present century, she (or he) will never hear the screams at Dachau or see the sky burst into flames over Hiroshima; the cold war will be as remote as the epic of Gilgamesh. For that matter, even the re-runs of "Barney" will bear the musty reek of the classics. Some things are eternal, though, and present trends indicate that sometime in the next century the average American girl could have more Barbie dolls than she has classmates. Grandchild of baby boomers! The very phrase boggles the mind—although not so much, perhaps, as the fact that of the 8.9 million American children who will be born in the year 2000, at least 70,000 of them are expected to still be alive in 2100.

First, though, they'll survive being dropped on their heads in the delivery room when the Y2K computer bug shuts off the electricity. To each century belongs its own terrors, and also its own pleasures. The child born in the year 2000 may face epidemics of previously unknown tropical diseases, but he also may be able to eat broccoli Jell-O instead of broccoli. And the toy industry may come to the rescue of lonely kids with a doll designed to remind them of their mothers. "We have so many latchkey children in search of a human connection," muses marketing consultant Faith Popcorn. "They'll be able to carry their mother around in doll form!" A lot has been written lately about the future as the venue for abstract breakthroughs in science, technology and medicine, but much less on the concrete questions of how Americans will actually live in it.

Babies born as early as 19 weeks after conception may survive, thanks to a technology enabling them to breathe through a liquid.

The millennium baby will be born into a nation of approximately 275 million, the third largest in the world, and still growing; the midrange estimate of the Census Bureau is that the population will reach 323 million by 2020 and 394 million by midcentury. Where will all those people live? Mostly in California, Texas and Florida, which among them will account for almost three out of 10 Americans by 2025. They will be squeezed onto proportionately less land: the median lot size of a new single-family house will almost certainly continue the slow, steady drop of the last 20 years. Children born in the year 2000 will live, on average, twice as long as those born in 1900. But they will live in bigger houses; the median floor area will reach 2,000 square feet any year now, a 25 percent increase since 1977. "The 800-square-foot Levittown house—that's a big family room now," says Columbia University historian Kenneth T. Jackson.

The cohort born circa 2000 should also benefit from what some economists are calling "the great asset sell-off" of the 21st century—the liquidation of family homes as the baby boomers start retiring in the second and third decades. "Younger Americans will get some great deals" on real estate, says Teresa Ghilarducci, a specialist in economic forecasting at Notre Dame. And, she adds, "it will be a great time to look for and get great jobs." But boomers will also be liquidating their investments, so stock-market values will stagnate. Except in some favored sun-belt locales, families moving out will create what Ghilarducci ominously calls "suburban wastelands." Downtown neighborhoods that haven't gentrified by then will be just out of luck.

The salient economic fact in the child's life may be the growing gap between the haves and have-nots, says Robert Litan, director of economic studies at the Brookings Institution. As disparities of wealth and income continue to widen, he says, "we could find ourselves living in a winner-take-all society. If people don't see economic opportunity, they drop out" of civil society. These trends will play themselves out in an America increasingly populated by minorities. By 2050, the Census Bureau projects an American population that is one-quarter black, Asian or Native

American and one-quarter Hispanic. How the nation fares in the next century will depend on whether those changes widen the socioeconomic gap between races or help close it. And meanwhile, which of the children born in the year 2000 will be chosen for the Harvard class of 2022—bearing in mind that by the time they enroll, the projected cost of a Harvard education will be more than $320,000?

There are a few things we can say with some assurance. Millennium babies will be about the same size as their parents. The long-term trend among Caucasians toward greater size is a factor of better nutrition, but as everyone knows, Americans are already maxed out when it comes to food consumption. Children born in the year 2000 will, however; live longer than ever: 73 years, on average, for a boy, and almost 80 for a girl—approximately double the average life expectancy of a newborn at the turn of the last century. And the figures are expected to rise steadily throughout the first half of the century. Those averages, though, conceal a wide disparity among different races. Whites, interestingly, are about in the middle; the category of Asians and Pacific Islanders will live the longest; blacks the shortest. It is a depressing statistic that a black male born in 2000 will have a life expectancy of 64.6 years—actually *less* than for an older brother born in 1995.

Some of the improvement in life span will come from reducing already low rates of infant death. Dr. James Marks of the Centers for Disease Control estimates that the mortality rate for newborns, around eight per 1,000 live births, could drop to as little as one per 1,000. Premature births account for many newborn deaths, but in the next decade, says bioethicist Arthur Caplan of the University of Pennsylvania, doctors will perform the astonishing feat of keeping alive babies born as early as 19 or 20 weeks after conception, weighing only eight ounces. Preemies younger than about 24 weeks now almost invariably succumb to the failure of their underdeveloped lungs, but techniques are now being developed to allow them to breathe oxygen from a liquid solution until they can sustain themselves in the air.

Even more impressive are advances forecast for in utero surgery. Already doctors can remove fetal tumors and correct conditions such as diaphragmatic hernia—a hole in the diaphragm that can cause serious lung problems. But standard open surgery on a living fetus is a very high-risk procedure. Within the next decade, surgeons will be performing these operations

with the help of tiny cameras mounted on needle-like probes, according to Dr. Michael Harrison, head of the Fetal Treatment Center at the University of California, San Francisco. Ultimately, he expects, doctors will be able to do anything on a fetus that can be done after birth. "Heart repairs? We're working on them day and night [in animals]," Harrison says. "It hasn't been done in humans yet, but we will be there in the next century."

A new theory will change our attitudes abour child rearing— we don't know what it is yet, but there always is one

The road map to the 21st century is being written now in the Human Genome Project, the monumentally ambitious attempt to catalog the entire complement of a normal person's DNA. When it's completed, in about 2003, researchers will be able to identify the genes responsible for many of mankind's most intractable afflictions—such as cystic fibrosis, muscular dystrophy and congenital immune deficiency. As a first step, doctors will be able to diagnose these diseases in utero, and parents will have the chance—and, consequently, the burden—of deciding whether to end the pregnancy. (Some of these tests are already in use.) But by the early years of the next century doctors will perform the equivalent of alchemy, curing disease by directly tinkering with patients' DNA. They will synthesize normal copies of the defective gene, or altered genes that counteract it, and attach them to a "vector" such as a benign virus to carry them into the patient's cells. In combination with Harrison's fetal-surgery techniques, it may be possible to cure congenital conditions even before birth.

For most babies born in the year 2000, smoking and overeating obviously will be a bigger threat to health than birth defects. Childhood obesity "is up dramatically since the '80s," says Marks of the CDC, and is expected to increase among kids who lift a finger only to click a mouse button. But routine genetic screening early in the next century will make a difference there, too, by identifying the health risks

specific to each individual. The public-health lesson of this century is that people generally change their lifestyles only under the threat of death, which is why those born in the future will probably not have to sit through so many public-service exhortations about fitness from Arnold Schwarzenegger. Instead, doctors will tell them which particular risks they run, and what they have to do to stay alive—including, for example, the nutritional supplements that will do them the most good. On smoking, diet and exercise the advice is probably going to be pretty much the same as it is now—except that there are always people who will live a long time no matter what they eat. One of the great pleasures of living in the next century may be finding out you're one of them.

In terms of psychological health, a new theory will revolutionize parents' attitudes toward child rearing. No one knows what the new theory will be, but there always is one. The 20th century's succession of mutually contradictory panaceas (more structure; more freedom; it doesn't make a difference) shouldn't obscure the point that until about the 1940s, "most parents didn't give much thought to child development at all," says Jerome Singer, a Yale child psychologist. "From a parenting point of view, children are better off today, and will be better off in the next few decades. Parents realize children need attention and oversight of what's going on in their lives, and those beliefs are penetrating into the lower socioeconomic groups."

And if kids persist in being maladjusted, there will be lots more ways to treat them. Caplan foresees radical new therapies that will rely on virtual-reality simulators (so the patient can practice, say, controlling his aggression in a mock situation) and brain scans that will tell the therapist on the spot whether the patient was learning. With this technique, he says, "you could look for change in real time," a boon to patients and insurance companies alike. There also will be many more problems to treat. The frontier of therapy in the next century will be "sub-syndromal" conditions such as mild depression, social phobias and anxieties. "We'll be treating emotional disabilities that we don't even label today," says Dr. Solomon H. Snyder, who heads the department of neuroscience at Johns Hopkins University. The debates over Prozac and Ritalin, which some authorities suspect are being prescribed indiscriminately, prefigure what will be two of the most important questions in 21st-century medical ethics: How far should we go in "enhancing" people who are essentially normal? And who will pay for it?

The reading wars will continue, with increasing reliance on computers, but kids will still be put to bed with 'Goodnight Moon'

And periodically someone will invent the one and only best method to teach reading, rendering all other techniques hopelessly obsolete. It might well involve computers; there is already a burgeoning market for what's called "lapware," software aimed at children under a year old, who do their computing while sitting on Mommy's lap. "I've seen some that attempt to teach kids to associate letters and sounds with colors," says a very dubious David Elkind, a professor of child development at Tufts University. "That's a skill most children don't have until they're 4 or 5." Whatever the new movement is, it will provoke an equally strong reaction as soon as parents discover that it doesn't automatically turn their toddlers into John Updike. "The reading wars"—basically pitting old-fashioned phonics against everything else—"have been going on for a century and a half, so what chance do we have of ending them by the year 2000?" says Timothy Shanahan, a professor of education at the University of Illinois-Chicago.

The truth, well known to researchers, is that most kids can learn to read with almost any method, and will do it by themselves if left alone with a pile of books. And there will still be books in the next century. As births increased in the 1980s, the number of new children's titles published annually doubled, even as families started buying

computers for the first time. Paula Quint, president of the Children's Book Council, expects that as births level off over the next few years the number of new titles will hold steady at about 5,000 a year. A few of these may even turn into classics, but it's safe to say that in the next century and beyond, kids will still be put to bed with "Goodnight Moon."

The change that is likely to make a real difference in the lives of millennium kids is a mundane one: the slow adoption of universal pre-K education. Most of the kids who attend preschool now are from relatively well-off families, even though research shows that the programs most benefit poor children. A few states, in search of a morally unassailable use of gambling proceeds, are dedicating them to providing free programs for 4-year-olds. "In 10 years," predicts Anne Mitchell, a consultant on early-childhood programs, "free preschool will be commonplace."

And in so many other ways, the year 2000 will be a great time to be born. Kids will have terrifically cool ethnic names like Pilar, Selena or Kai—although there may also be a countertrend, fueled by millennial religious fervor, for Biblical names like Isaiah and Elijah. Their mothers are more likely to breast-feed them than has been true for a generation (a quarter of all mothers nursed their children for at least six months last year, up from about 5 percent in 1971). And they will be able, if their parents don't mind, to run around in diapers until they're almost 4. Recognizing a trend toward later toilet training (and bigger kids), Procter & Gamble recently introduced Pampers in size 6, for toddlers 35 pounds and over. Of course, kids who are kept in diapers until the age of 4 can only help drive up the cost of raising them, which, according to U.S. Department of Agriculture statistics, will amount to approximately $250,000 for the first 18 years of a millennium baby's life.

Inevitably, part of that sum will toward the purchase of Barbie dolls. In the

early 1980s, most girls were content with one Barbie; the average collection is now up to 10 and likely to rise in the future as Mattel expands the line into infinity—adding just this year, for example, Chilean, Thai, Polish and Native American Barbies. Last year Mattel added a wheelchair Barbie, and a spokeswoman suggests "there may be more dolls with other disabilities in the future."

Yes, the kid of the future will be, if anything, even more pampered and catered to than the fabled baby boomers themselves, at least in part because there's so much money to be made off them. Leaving the house at 7:30 in the morning for 12-hour days of school, restaurants and shopping, they will require ever-more-elaborate "urban survival clothes," like the currently popular cargo pants in whose capacious pockets one can stow a meatball grinder, a palmtop computer and a jar of The Limited's most exciting new cosmetic product, fruit-scented antibacterial glitter gel. In what marketing guru Popcorn regards as one of the most significant social trends of the next millennium, "cross-aging," kids will be more like adults (and vice versa): "We're going to see health clubs for kids, kids as experts on things like the Internet, and new businesses, like Kinko's for Kids, to provide professional quality project presentations." The travel market of the future will increasingly be geared to kids, and not just at theme parks—24 million business trips included children in 1996, up 160 percent from 1991. So, to anyone who may have wondered whether it was right to bring a child into the uncertain world of the 21st century, it's fair to say, your fears are groundless.

The next millennium is going to be great for kids.

It's the adults who will miss the 1990s.

With PAT WINGERT, KAREN SPRINGEN, ELIZABETH ANGELL *and* MICHAEL MEYER

getting *stupid*

New research indicates that teenagers who drink too much may
lose as much as 10 percent of their brainpower—the difference
between passing and failing in school… and in life

By Bernice Wuethrich

Sarah, a high school senior, drinks in moderation, but many of her friends do not. At one party, a classmate passed out after downing more than 20 shots of hard liquor and had to be rushed to a local emergency room. At another party a friend got sick, so Sarah made her drink water, dressed her in a sweatshirt to keep her warm, and lay her in bed, with a bucket on the floor. Then she brushed the girl's long hair away from her face so that it wouldn't get coated with vomit. "Every weekend, drinking is the only thing people do. Every single party has alcohol," says Sarah. (The names of the teenagers in these stories have been changed to protect their privacy.)

THE MOST RECENT STATISTICS FROM the U.S. Substance Abuse and Mental Health Services Administration's National Household Survey on Drug Abuse indicate that nearly 7 million youths between the ages of 12 and 20 binge-drink at least once a month. And despite the fact that many colleges have cracked down on drinking, Henry Wechsler of the Harvard School of Public Health says that two of every five college students still binge-drink regularly. For a male that means downing five or more drinks

in a row; for a female it means consuming four drinks in one session at least once in a two-week period.

Few teens seem to worry much about what such drinking does to their bodies. Cirrhosis of the liver is unlikely to catch up with them for decades, and heart disease must seem as remote as retirement. But new research suggests that young drinkers are courting danger. Because their brains are still developing well into their twenties, teens who drink excessively may be destroying significant amounts of mental capacity in ways that are more dramatic than in older drinkers.

Scientists have long known that excessive alcohol consumption among adults over long periods of time can create brain damage, ranging from a mild loss of motor skills to psychosis and even the inability to form memories. But less has been known about the impact alcohol has on younger brains. Until recently, scientists assumed that a youthful brain is more resilient than an adult brain and could escape many of the worst ills of alcohol. But some researchers are now beginning to question this assumption. Preliminary results from

several studies indicate that the younger the brain is, the more it may be at risk. "The adolescent brain is a developing nervous system, and the thins you do to it can change it," says Scott Swartzwelder, a neuropsychologist at Duke University and the U.S. Department of Veterans Affairs.

Teen drinkers appear to be most susceptible to damage in the hippocampus, a structure buried deep in the brain that is responsible for many types of learning and memory, and the prefrontal cortex, located behind the forehead, which is the brain's chief decision maker and voice of reason. Both areas, especially the prefrontal cortex, undergo dramatic change in the second decade of life.

Swartzwelder and his team have been studying how alcohol affects the hippocampus, an evolutionarily old part of the brain that is similar in rats and humans. Six years ago, when Swartzwelder published his first paper suggesting that alcohol disrupts the hippocampus more severely in adolescent rats than in adult rats, "people didn't believe it," he says. Since then, his research has shown that the adolescents brain is more easily damaged in the struc-

Jason, 19

DRINKING HISTORY: First drink: age 14, at a party with 18-year-olds. Now drinks three or four times a week.
MOST ALCOHOL EVER CONSUMED: "In school we play beer for beer. I think I got up to 17 beers. One night when I was 15, I had 14 shots of whatever there was, until my friend got really sick and I had to take care of her."
AFTEREFFECTS: "I have been sick from drinking, but I have never blacked out. My social life affects my schoolwork, but drinking does not."

Terry, 19

DRINKING HISTORY: First drink: age 13, stole wine from liquor cabinet. Drinks about two or three times a week.
MOST ALCOHOL EVER CONSUMED: nine shots of liquor.
AFTEREFFECTS: "I have been sick many times, but I always remember what I did. Sometimes if I know I've had too much to drink, it feels better to get it out of my system. If I felt that my drinking was at all hindering my work, I would stop."

Sofia, 18

DRINKING HISTORY: First drink: age 14, "Kahlua in warm milk to help me sleep." Now drinks "once every couple of weeks."
MOST ALCOHOL EVER CONSUMED: "I'm not sure. I drink until I'm buzzed, stop until my buzz wears off, then maybe have more. I've never had enough to be out of control or even be hungover."
AFTEREFFECTS: "I'm a pretty conscientious student, and I don't drink enough to let it affect my schoolwork."

Stanley, 19

DRINKING HISTORY: First drink: age 14, at a friend's house. Now drinks every weekend.
MOST ALCOHOL EVER CONSUMED: two 40 oz. beers and three shots of liquor.
AFTEREFFECTS: "I've been sick and blacked out. After a night of drinking I don't get out of bed until 12:00 or 1:00 p.m. So I'm unable to do all my schoolwork."

Cindy, 18

DRINKING HISTORY: First drink: age 14, at a party. "In high school I drank every weekend."
MOST ALCOHOL EVER CONSUMED: three shots vodka, four shots rum, two screwdrivers, one strawberry daiquiri, and one beer.
AFTEREFFECTS: "In high school I had all B 's and A – 's. I don't drink that much in college, and I have a B/B – average. Go figure. I put more effort into my college work though because I'm not rushing out at 6 o'clock to get a good six hours in of drinking."

Joe, 19

DRINKING HISTORY: First drink: age 4, sipped father's beer and didn't like it. Now drinks once every week or two.
MOST ALCOHOL EVER CONSUMED: 10 mixed drinks.
AFTEREFFECTS: "I've vomited on three occasions because of alcohol. That's it though. Drinking has not affected my schoolwork."

tures that regulate the acquisition and storage of memories.

Learning depends on communication between nerve cells, or neurons, within the hippocampus. To communicate, a neuron fires an electrical signal down its axon, a single fiber extending away from the cell's center. In response, the axon releases chemical messengers, called neurotransmitters, which bind to receptors on the receiving branches of neighboring cells. Depending on the types of neurotransmitters released, the receiving cell may be jolted into action or settle more deeply into rest.

But the formation of memories requires more than a simple firing or inhibition of nerve cells. There must be some physical change in the hippocampal neurons that represents the encoding of new information. Scientists believe that this change occurs in the synapses, the tiny gaps between neurons that neurotransmitters traverse. Repeated use of synapses seems to increase their ability to fire up connecting cells. Laboratory experiments on brain tissue can induce this process, called long-term potentiation. Researchers assume that something similar takes places in the intact living brain, although it is impossible to observe directly. Essentially, if the repetitive neural reverberations are strong enough, they burn in new patterns of synaptic circuitry to encode memory, just as the more often a child recites his ABCs, the better he knows them.

Swartzwelder's first clue that alcohol powerfully disrupts memory in the adolescent brain came from studying rat hippocampi. He found that alcohol blocks long-term potentiation in adolescent brain tissue much more than in adult tissue.

Next, Swartzwelder identified a likely explanation. Long-term potentiation—and thus memory formation—relies in large part on the action of a neurotransmitter known as glutamate, the brain's chemical kingpin of neural excitation. Glutamate strengthens a cell's electrical stimulation when it binds to a docking port called the NMDA receptor. If the receptor is blocked, so is long-term potentiation, and thus memory formation. Swartzwelder found that exposure to the equivalent of just two beers inhibits the NMDA receptors in the hippocampal cells of adolescent rats, while more than twice as much is required to produce the same effect in adult rats. These findings led him to suspect that alcohol consumption might have a dramatic impact on the ability of adolescents to learn. So he set up a series of behavioral tests.

The younger the brain, the *more it may be at risk*

First, Swartzwelder's team dosed adolescent and adult rats with alcohol and ran them through maze-learning tests. Compared with the adult rats, the adolescents failed miserably. To see whether similar results held true for humans, Swartzwelder recruited a group of volunteers aged 21 to 29 years old. He couldn't use younger subjects because of laws that forbid drinking before age 21. He chose to split the volunteers into two groups: 21 to 24 years old and 25 to 29 years old. "While I couldn't argue that these younger folks are adolescents, even in their early twenties their brains are still developing," Swartzwelder says. After three drinks, with a blood-alcohol level slightly below the National Highway Traffic Safety Administration's recommended limit—.08 percent—the younger group's learning was impaired 25 percent more than the older group's.

Intrigued by these results, Swartzwelder's colleague Aaron White, a biological psychologist at Duke, set out to discover how vulnerable the adolescent brain is to long-term damage. He gave adolescent and adult rats large doses of alcohol every other day for 20 days—the equivalent of a 150-pound human chugging 24 drinks in a row. Twenty days after the last binge, when the adolescent rats had reached adulthood, White trained them in a maze-memory task roughly akin to that performed by a human when remembering the location of his car in a parking garage.

Both the younger and older rats performed equally well when sober. But when intoxicated, those who had binged as adolescents performed much worse. "Binge alcohol exposure in adolescence appears to produce long-lasting changes in brain function," White says. He suspects that early damage caused by alcohol

could surface whenever the brain is taxed. He also suspects that the NMDA receptor is involved, because just as alcohol in the system inhibits the receptor, the drug's withdrawal overstimulates it—which can kill the cell outright.

During the fall semester last year, at least 11 college students died from alcohol-related causes—at California State University at Chico, Colgate University in New York, Old Dominion University in Virginia, the University of Michigan, Vincennes University in Kentucky, Washington and Lee University in Virginia, and Washington State University. No one knows how many other students were rushed to emergency rooms for alcohol poisoning, but at Duke, 11 students had visited local ERs in just the first three weeks of school, and in only one night of partying, three students from the University of Tennessee were hospitalized.

STUDENTS WHO DRINK HEAVILY sometimes joke that they are killing a few brain cells. New research suggests that this is not funny. Some of the evidence is anatomical; Michael De Bellis at the University of Pittsburgh Medical Center used magnetic resonance imaging to compare the hippocampi of subjects 14 to 21 years old who abused alcohol to the hippocampi of those who did not. He found that the longer and the more a young person had been drinking, the smaller his hippocampus. The average size difference between healthy teens and alcohol abusers was roughly 10 percent. That is a lot of brain cells.

De Bellis speculates that the shrinkage may be due to cell damage and death that occurs during withdrawal from alcohol. Withdrawal is the brain's way of trying to get back to normal after prolonged or heavy drinking. It can leave the hands jittery, set off the classic headache, generate intense anxiety, and even provoke seizures, as neurons that had adjusted to the presence of alcohol try to adjust to its absence. Because alcohol slows down the

transmission of nerve signals—in part by stopping glutamate from activating its NMDA receptors—nerve cells under the influence react by increasing the number and sensitivity of these receptors. When drinking stops, the brain is suddenly struck with too many hyperactive receptors.

Hyperactive receptors *can cause cell death*

Mark Prendergast, a neuroscientist at the University of Kentucky, recently revealed one way these hyperactive receptors kill brain cells. First, he exposed rat hippocampal slices to alcohol for 10 days, then removed the alcohol. Following withdrawal, he stained the tissue with a fluorescent dye that lit up dead and dying cells. When exposed to an alcohol concentration of about .08 percent, cell death increased some 25 percent above the baseline. When concentrations were two or three times higher, he wrote in a recent issue of *Alcoholism: Clinical and Experimental Research,* the number of dead cells shot up to 100 percent above the baseline.

Prendergast says that the younger brain tissue was far more sensitive. Preadolescent tissue suffered four to five time more cell death than did adult tissue. In all cases, most of the death occurred in hippocampal cells that were packed with NMDA receptors. To home in on the cause, he treated another batch of brain slices with the drug MK-801, which blocks NMDA receptors. He reasoned that if overexcitability during alcohol withdrawal was causing cell death, blocking the receptors, should minimize the carnage. It did, by about 75 percent.

Now Prendergast is examining what makes the receptors so lethal. By tracking radioactive calcium, he found that the overexcited receptors open floodgates that allow calcium to swamp the cell. Too much calcium can turn on suicide genes that cause the neuron to break down its own membrane. Indeed, that is exactly what Prendergast observed during alcohol withdrawal: Overactive receptors opened wide, and the influx of calcium became a raging flood.

Prendergast says that four or five drinks may cause a mild withdrawal. And, according to Harvard's Wechsler, 44 percent of college students binge in this manner. More alarming, 23 percent of them consume 72 percent of all the alcohol that college students drink.

Chuck was 15 the first time he binged— on warm beers chugged with friends late at night in a vacant house. Six years later, celebrating his 21st birthday, he rapidly downed four shots of vodka in his dorm room. Then he and his friends drove through the snowy night to a sorority party at a bar, where he consumed another 16 drinks. Chuck's friends later told him how the rest of the night unfolded. He danced in a cage. He spun on the floor. He careened around the parking lot with a friend on his back. Halfway home, he stumbled out of the car and threw up. A friend half carried him home down frozen roads at 2 a.m. "I don't remember any of this," Chuck says. But he does remember the hangover he lived with for two days, as his brain and body withdrew from booze.

RECENT HUMAN STUDIES SUPPORT a conclusion Prendergast drew from his molecular experiments: The greatest brain damage from alcohol occurs during withdrawal. At the University of California at San Diego and the VA San Diego Health Care System, Sandra Brown, Susan Taper, and Gregory Brown have been following alcohol-dependent adolescents for eight years. Repeated testing shows that problem drinkers perform more poorly on tests of cognition and learning than do nondrinkers. Furthermore, "the single best predictor of neuropsychological deficits for adolescents is withdrawal symptoms," says principal investigator Sandra Brown.

The psychologists recruited a group of 33 teenagers aged 15 and 16, all heavy drinkers. On average, each teen had used alcohol more than 750 times—the equivalent of drinking every day for two and a half years. Bingeing was common: The teens downed an average of eight drinks at each sitting. The researchers matched drinkers with nondrinkers of the same gender and similar age, IQ, socioeconomic background, and family history of alcohol use. Then, three weeks after the drinkers had their last drink, all the teens took a two-hour battery of tests.

The teens with alcohol problems had a harder time recalling information, both verbal and nonverbal, that they had learned 20 minutes earlier. Words such as *apple* and *football* escaped them. The performance difference was about 10 percent. "It's not serious brain damage, but it's the difference of a grade, a pass or a fail," Tapert says. Other tests evaluated skills needed for map learning, geometry, or science. Again, there was a 10 percent difference in performance.

"The study shows that just several years of heavy alcohol use by youth can adversely affect their brain functions in ways that are critical to learning," Sandra Brown says. She is following the group of teenagers until they reach age 30, and some have already passed 21. "Those who continue to use alcohol heavily are developing attentional deficits in addition to the memory and problem-solving deficits that showed up early on," Brown says. "In the past we thought of alcohol as a more benign drug. It's not included in the war on drugs. This study clearly demonstrates that the most popular drug is also an incredibly dangerous drug."

Brown's research team is also using functional magnetic resonance imaging to compare the brain function of alcohol abusers and nondrinkers. Initial results show that brains of young adults with a history of alcohol dependence are less active

than the brains of nondrinkers during tasks that require spatial working memory (comparable to the maze task that White conducted on rats). In addition, the adolescent drinkers seem to exhibit greater levels of brain activity when they are exposed to alcohol-related stimuli. For instance, when the drinkers read words such as *wasted* or *tequila* on a screen, the nucleus accumbens—a small section of the brain associated with craving—lights up.

The nucleus accumbens is integral to the brain's so-called pleasure circuit, which scientists now believe undergoes major remodeling during adolescence. Underlying the pleasure circuit is the neurotransmitter dopamine. Sex, food, and many drugs, including alcohol, can all induce the release of dopamine, which creates feelings of pleasure and in turn encourages repetition of the original behavior. During adolescence, the balance of dopamine activity temporarily shifts away from the nucleus accumbens, the brain's key pleasure and reward center, to the prefrontal cortex. Linda Spear, a developmental psychobiologist at Binghamton University in New York, speculates that as a result of this shift in balance, teenagers may find drugs less rewarding than earlier or later in life. And if the drugs produce less of a kick, more will be needed for the same effect. "In the case of alcohol, this may lead to binge drinking," she says.

When Lynn was a freshman in high school, she liked to hang out at her friend John's apartment. More often than not, his father would be drinking beer. "He was like, 'Help yourself,'" Lynn says. Friends would come over and play drinking games until four or five in the morning. The longer the games continued, the tougher the rules became, doubling and tripling the number of drinks consumed. One night, Lynn came home drunk. Her mother talked her through her options, sharing stories of relatives who had ruined their lives drinking. Lynn struggled with her choices. A year later she still drinks, but she's kept a pact with her girlfriends to stop bingeing.

DURING ADOLESCENCE, THE PREFRONtal cortex changes more than any other part of the brain. At around age 11 or 12, its neurons branch out like crazy, only to be seriously pruned back in the years that follow. All this tumult is to good purpose. In the adult brain, the prefrontal cortex executes the thought processes adolescents struggle to master: the ability to plan ahead, think abstractly, and integrate information to make sound decisions.

Now there is evidence that the prefrontal cortex and associated areas are among those most damaged in the brains of bingeing adolescents. Fulton Crews, director of the Center for Alcohol Studies at the University of North Carolina at Chapel Hill, has studied the patterns of cell death in the brains of adolescent and adult rats after four-day drinking bouts. While both groups showed damage in the back areas of the brain and in the frontally located olfactory bulb, used for smell, only the adolescents suffered brain damage in other frontal areas.

That youthful damage was severe. It extended from the rat's olfactory bulb to the interconnected parts of the brain that process sensory information and memories to make associations, such as "This smell and the sight of that wall tell me I'm in a place where I previously faced down an enemy." The regions of cell death

in the rat experiment corresponded to the human prefrontal cortex and to parts of the limbic system.

The limbic system, which includes the hippocampus, changes throughout adolescence, according to recent work by Jay Giedd at the National Institute of Mental Health in Bethesda, Maryland. The limbic system not only encodes memory but is also mobilized when a person is hungry or frightened or angry; it helps the brain process survival impulses. The limbic system and the prefrontal cortex must work in concert for a person to make sound decisions.

Damage to the prefrontal cortex and the limbic system is especially worrisome because they play an important role in the formation of an adult personality. "Binge drinking could be making permanent long-term changes in the final neural physiology, which is expressed as personality and behavior in the individual," Crews says. But he readily acknowledges that such conclusions are hypothetical. "It's very hard to prove this stuff. You can't do an experiment in which you change people's brains."

Nonetheless, evidence of the vulnerability of young people to alcohol is mounting. A study by Bridget Grant of the National Institute on Alcohol Abuse and Alcoholism shows that the younger someone is when he begins to regularly drink alcohol, the more likely that individual will eventually become an alcoholic.

Grant found that 40 percent of the drinkers who got started before age 15 were classified later in life as alcohol dependent, compared with only 10 percent of those who began drinking at age 21 or 22. Overall, beginning at age 15, the risk of future alcohol dependence decreased by 14 percent with each passing year of abstention.

The study leaves unanswered whether early regular drinking is merely a marker of later abuse or whether it results in long-term changes in the brain that increase the later propensity for abuse. "It's got to be both," Crews says. For one thing, he points out that studies of rats and people have shown that repeated alcohol use makes it harder for a person—or a rat—to learn new ways of doing things, rather than repeating the same actions over and over again. In short, the way alcohol changes the brain makes it increasingly difficult over time to stop reaching for beer after beer after beer.

Ultimately, the collateral damage caused by having so many American adolescents reach for one drink after another may be incalculable. "People in their late teens have been drinking heavily for generations. We're not a society of idiots, but we're not a society of Einsteins either," says Swartzwelder. "What if you've compromised your function by 7 percent or 10 percent and never known the difference?"

From *Discover*, magazine, March 2001, pp. 56-63, by Bernice Wuethrich © 2001. Reprinted with permission of Discover magazine.

WHY THE YOUNG KILL

Are certain young brains predisposed to violence? Maybe—but how these kids are raised can either save them or push them over the brink. The biological roots of violence.

BY SHARON BEGLEY

THE TEMPTATION, OF COURSE, IS TO SEIZE on one cause, one single explanation for Littleton, and West Paducah, and Jonesboro and all the other towns that have acquired iconic status the way "Dallas" or "Munich" did for earlier generations. Surely the cause is having access to guns. Or being a victim of abuse at the hands of parents or peers. Or being immersed in a culture that glorifies violence and revenge. But there isn't one cause. And while that makes stemming the tide of youth violence a lot harder, it also makes it less of an unfathomable mystery. Science has a new understanding of the roots of violence that promises to explain why not every child with access to guns becomes an Eric Harris or a Dylan Klebold, and why not *every* child who feels ostracized, or who embraces the Goth esthetic, goes on a murderous rampage. The bottom line: you need a particular environment imposed on a particular biology to turn a child into a killer.

It should be said right off that attempts to trace violence to biology have long been tainted by racism, eugenics and plain old poor science. The turbulence of the 1960s led some physicians to advocate psychosurgery to "treat those people with low violence thresholds," as one 1967 letter to a medical journal put it. In other words, lobotomize the civil-rights and antiwar protesters. And if crimes are disproportionately committed by some ethnic groups, then finding genes or other traits common to that group risks tarring millions of innocent people. At the other end of the political spectrum, many conservatives view biological theories of violence as the mother of all insanity defenses, with biology not merely an explanation but an excuse. The conclusions emerging from interdisciplinary research in neuroscience and psychology, however, are not so simple-minded as to argue that violence is in the genes, or murder in the folds of the brain's frontal lobes. Instead, the picture is more nuanced, based as it is on the discovery that experience rewires the brain. The dawning realization of the constant back-and-forth between nature and nurture

has resurrected the search for the biological roots of violence.

Early experiences seem to be especially powerful: a child's brain is more malleable than that of an adult. The dark side of the zero-to-3 movement, which emphasizes the huge potential for learning during this period, is that the young brain also is extra vulnerable to hurt in the first years of life. A child who suffers repeated "hits" of stress—abuse, neglect, terror—experiences physical changes in his brain, finds Dr. Bruce Perry of Baylor College of Medicine. The incessant flood of stress chemicals tends to reset the brain's system of fight-or-flight hormones, putting them on hair-trigger alert. The result is the kid who shows impulsive aggression, the kid who pops the classmate who disses him. For the outcast, hostile confrontations—not necessarily an elbow to the stomach at recess, but merely kids vacating en masse when he sits down in the cafeteria—can increase the level of stress hormones in his brain. And that can have dangerous consequences. "The early environment programs the nervous system to make an individual more or less reactive to stress," says biologist Michael Meaney of McGill University. "If parental care is inadequate or unsupportive, the [brain] may decide that the world stinks—and it better be ready to meet the challenge." This, then, is how having an abusive parent raises the risk of youth violence: it can change a child's brain. Forever after, influences like the mean-spiritedness that schools condone or the humiliation that's standard fare in adolescence pummel the mind of the child whose brain has been made excruciatingly vulnerable to them.

In other children, constant exposure to pain and violence can make their brain's system of stress hormones unresponsive, like a keypad that has been pushed so often it just stops working. These are the kids with antisocial personalities. They typically have low heart rates and impaired emotional sensitivity. Their signature is a lack of empathy, and their sensitivity to the world around them is practically nonexistent. Often they abuse animals: Kip Kinkel, the 15-year-old who killed his parents and shot 24 schoolmates last May, had a history of this; Luke Woodham, who killed three schoolmates and wounded seven at his high school in Pearl, Miss., in 1997, had previously beaten his dog with a club, wrapped it in a bag and set it on fire. These are also the adolescents who do not respond to punishment: nothing hurts. Their ability to feel, to react, has died, and so has their conscience. Hostile, impulsive aggressors usually feel sorry afterward. Antisocial aggressors don't feel at all. Paradoxically, though, they often have a keen sense of injustices aimed at themselves.

Inept parenting encompasses more than outright abuse, however. Parents who are withdrawn and remote, neglectful and passive, are at risk of shaping a child who (absent a compensating source of love and attention) shuts down emotionally. It's important to be clear about this: inadequate parenting short of Dickensian neglect generally has little ill effect on most children. But to a vulnerable baby, the result of neglect can be tragic. Perry finds that neglect impairs the development of the brain's cortex, which controls feelings of belonging and attachment. "When there are experiences in early life that result in an underdeveloped capacity [to form relationships]," says Perry, "kids have a hard time empathizing with people. They tend to be relatively passive and perceive themselves to be stomped on by the outside world."

RISK FACTORS

Having any of the following risk factors doubles a boy's chance of becoming a murderer:

- **Coming from a family with a history of criminal violence**
- **Being abused**
- **Belonging to a gang**
- **Abusing drugs or alcohol**

Having any of these risk factors, in addition to the above, triples the risk of becoming a killer:

- **Using a weapon**
- **Having been arrested**
- **Having a neurological problem that impairs thinking or feeling**
- **Having had problems at school**

These neglected kids are the ones who desperately seek a script, an ideology that fits their sense of being humiliated and ostracized. Today's pop culture offers all too many dangerous ones, from the music of Rammstein to the game of Doom. Historically, most of those scripts have featured males. That may explain, at least in part, why the murderers are Andrews and Dylans rather than Ashleys and Kaitlins, suggests Deborah Prothrow-Smith of the Harvard School of Public Health. "But girls are now 25 percent of the adolescents arrested for violent crime," she notes. "This follows the media portrayal of girl superheroes beating people up," from Power Rangers to Xena. Another reason that the schoolyard murderers are boys is that girls tend to internalize ostracism and shame rather than turning it into anger. And just as girls could be the next wave of killers, so could even younger children. "Increasingly, we're seeing the high-risk population for lethal violence as being the 10- to 14-year-olds," says Richard Lieberman, a school psychologist in Los Angeles. "Developmentally, their concept of death is still magical. They still think it's temporary, like little Kenny in 'South Park'." Of course, there are loads of empty, emotionally unattached girls and boys. The large majority won't become violent. "But if they're in a violent environment," says Perry, "they're more likely to."

There seems to be a genetic component to the vulnerability that can turn into anti-

social-personality disorder. It is only a tiny bend in the twig, but depending on how the child grows up, the bend will be exaggerated or straightened out. Such aspects of temperament as "irritability, impulsivity, hyperactivity and a low sensitivity to emotions in others are all biologically based," says psychologist James Garbarino of Cornell University, author of the upcoming book "Lost Boys: Why Our Sons Turn Violent and How We Can Save Them." A baby who is unreactive to hugs and smiles can be left to go her natural, antisocial way if frustrated parents become exasperated, withdrawn, neglectful or enraged. Or that child can be pushed back toward the land of the feeling by parents who never give up trying to engage and stimulate and form a loving bond with her. The different responses of parents produce different brains, and thus behaviors. "Behavior is the result of a dialogue between your brain and your experiences," concludes Debra Niehoff, author of the recent book "The Biology of Violence." "Although people are born with some biological givens, the brain has many blank pages. From the first moments of childhood the brain acts as a historian, recording our experiences in the language of neurochemistry."

There are some out-and-out brain pathologies that lead to violence. Lesions of the frontal lobe can induce apathy and distort both judgment and emotion. In the brain scans he has done in his Fairfield, Calif., clinic of 50 murderers, psychiatrist Daniel Amen finds several shared patterns. The structure called the cingulate gyrus, curving through the center of the brain, is hyperactive in murderers. The CG acts like the brain's transmission, shifting from one thought to another. When it is impaired, people get stuck on one thought. Also, the prefrontal cortex, which seems to act as the brain's supervisor, is sluggish in the 50 murderers. "If you have violent thoughts that you're stuck on and no supervisor, that's a prescription for trouble," says Amen, author of "Change Your Brain/ Change Your Life." The sort of damage he finds can result from head trauma as well as exposure to toxic substances like alcohol during gestation.

Children who kill are not, with very few exceptions, amoral. But their morality is aberrant. "I killed because people like me are mistreated every day," said pudgy, bespectacled Luke Woodham, who murdered three students. "My whole life I felt outcasted, alone." So do a lot of adolescents. The difference is that at least some of the recent school killers felt emotionally or physically abandoned by those who should love them. Andrew Golden, who was 11 when he and Mitchell Johnson, 13, went on their killing spree in Jonesboro, Ark., was raised mainly by his grandparents while his parents worked. Mitchell mourned the loss of his father to divorce.

Unless they have another source of unconditional love, such boys fail to develop, or lose, the neural circuits that control the capacity to feel and to form healthy relationships. That makes them hypersensitive to perceived injustice. A sense of injustice is often accompanied by a feeling of abject powerlessness. An adult can often see his way to restoring a sense of self-worth, says psychiatrist James Gilligan of Harvard Medical School, through success in work or love. A child usually lacks the emotional skills to do that. As one killer told Garbarino's colleague, "I'd rather be wanted for murder than not wanted at all."

THAT THE LITTLETON MASSACRE ENDED in suicide may not be a coincidence. As Michael Carneal was wrestled to the ground after killing three fellow students in Paducah in 1997, he cried out, "Kill me now!" Kip Kinkel pleaded with the schoolmates who stopped him, "Shoot me!" With suicide "you get immortality," says Michael Flynn of John Jay College of Criminal Justice. "That is a great feeling of power for an adolescent who has no sense that he matters."

The good news is that understanding the roots of violence offers clues on how to prevent it. The bad news is that ever more children are exposed to the influences that, in the already vulnerable, can produce a bent toward murder. Juvenile homicide is twice as common today as it was in the mid-1980s. It isn't the brains kids are born with that has changed in half a generation; what has changed is the ubiquity of vio-

lence, the easy access to guns and the glorification of revenge in real life and in entertainment. To deny the role of these influences is like denying that air pollution triggers childhood asthma. Yes, to develop asthma a child needs a specific, biological vulnerability. But as long as some children have this respiratory vulnerability—and some always will— then allowing pollution to fill our air will make some children wheeze, and cough, and die. And as long as some children have a neurological vulnerability—and some always will—then turning a blind eye to bad parenting, bullying and the gun culture will make other children seethe, and withdraw, and kill.

With ADAM ROGERS, PAT WINGERT *and* THOMAS HAYDEN

The Effects of Poverty on Children

Abstract

Although hundreds of studies have documented the association between family poverty and children's health, achievement, and behavior, few measure the effects of the timing, depth, and duration of poverty on children, and many fail to adjust for other family characteristics (for example, female headship, mother's age, and schooling) that may account for much of the observed correlation between poverty and child outcomes. This article focuses on a recent set of studies that explore the relationship between poverty and child outcomes in depth. By and large, this research supports the conclusion that family income has selective but, in some instances, quite substantial effects on child and adolescent well-being. Family income appears to be more strongly related to children's ability and achievement than to their emotional outcomes. Children who live in extreme poverty and who live below the poverty line for multiple years appear, all other things being equal, to suffer the worst outcomes. The timing of poverty also seems to be important for certain child outcomes. Children who experience poverty during their preschool and early school years have lower rates of school completion than children and adolescents who experience poverty only in later years. Although more research is needed on the significance of the timing of poverty on child outcomes, findings to date suggest that interventions during early childhood may be most important in reducing poverty's impact on children.

Jeanne Brooks-Gunn
Greg J. Duncan

In recent years, about one in five American children—some 12 to 14 million—have lived in families in which cash income failed to exceed official poverty thresholds. Another one-fifth lived in families whose incomes were no more than twice the poverty threshold.[1,2] For a small minority of children—4.8% of all children and 15% of children who ever became poor—childhood poverty lasted 10 years or more.[3]

Income poverty is the condition of not having enough income to meet basic needs for food, clothing, and shelter. Because children are dependent on others, they enter or avoid poverty by virtue of their family's economic circumstances. Children cannot alter family conditions by themselves, at least until they approach adulthood. Government programs, such as those described by Devaney, Ellwood, and Love in this journal issue, have been developed to increase the likelihood that poor children are provided basic necessities. But even with these programs, poor children do not fare as well as those whose families are not poor.[4]

What does poverty mean for children? How does the relative lack of income influence children's day-to-day lives? Is it through inadequate nutrition; fewer learning experiences; instability of residence; lower quality of schools; exposure to environmental toxins, family violence, and homelessness; dangerous streets; or less access to friends, services, and, for adolescents, jobs? This article reviews recent research that used longitudinal data to examine the relationship between low-income poverty and child outcomes in several domains.

Hundreds of studies, books, and reports have examined the detrimental effects of poverty on the well-being of children. Many have been summarized in recent reports such as *Wasting America's Future* from the Children's Defense Fund and *Alive and Well?* from the National Center for

Children in Poverty.[5] However, while the literature on the effects of poverty on children is large, many studies lack the precision necessary to allow researchers to disentangle the effects on children of the array of factors associated with poverty. Understanding of these relationships is key to designing effective policies to ameliorate these problems for children.

This article examines these relationships and the consequences for children of growing up poor. It begins with a long, but by no means exhaustive, list of child outcomes (see Table 1) that have been found to be associated with poverty in several large, nationally representative, cross-sectional surveys. This list makes clear the broad range of effects poverty can have on children. It does little, however, to inform the discussion of the causal effects of income poverty on children because the studies from which this list is derived did not control for other variables associated with poverty. For example, poor families are more likely to be headed by a parent who is single, has low educational attainment, is unemployed, has low earning potential and is young. These parental attributes, separately or in combination, might account for some of the observed negative consequences of poverty on children. Nor do the relationships identified in the table capture the critical factors of the timing, depth, and duration of childhood poverty on children.[6,7]

This article focuses on studies that used national longitudinal data sets to estimate the effects of family income on children's lives, independent of other family conditions that might be related to growing up in a low-income household. These studies attempt to isolate the effect of family income by taking into account, statistically, the effects of maternal age at the child's birth, maternal education, marital status, ethnicity, and other factors on child outcomes.[2,8] Many used data on family income over several years and at different stages of development to estimate the differential effects of the timing and duration of poverty on child outcomes. The data sets analyzed include the Panel Study of Income Dynamics (PSID), the National Longitudinal Survey of Youth (NLSY), Children of the NLSY (the follow-up of the children born to the women in the original NLSY cohort), the National Survey of Families and Households (NSFH), the National Health and Nutrition Examination Survey (NHANES), and the Infant Health and Development Program (IHDP). These rich data sets include multiple measures of child outcomes and family and child characteristics.

This article is divided into four sections. The first focuses on the consequences of poverty across five child outcomes. If income does, in fact, affect child outcomes, then it is important not only to identify these outcomes but also to describe the pathways through which income operates. Accordingly, in the second section, five pathways through which poverty might operate are described. The third section focuses on whether the links between poverty and outcomes can reasonably be attributed to income rather than

other family characteristics. The concluding section considers policy implications of the research reviewed.

Effects of Income on Child Outcomes

Measures of Child Well-Being

As illustrated in Table 1, poor children suffer higher incidences of adverse health, developmental, and other outcomes than non-poor children. The specific dimensions of the well-being of children and youths considered in some detail in this article include (1) physical health (low birth weight, growth stunting, and lead poisoning), (2) cognitive ability (intelligence, verbal ability, and achievement test scores), (3) school achievement (years of schooling, high school completion), (4) emotional and behavioral outcomes, and (5) teenage out-of-wedlock childbearing. Other outcomes are not addressed owing to a scarcity of available research, a lack of space, and because they overlap with included outcomes.

While this review is organized around specific outcomes, it could also have been organized around the various ages of childhood.[9–11] Five age groups are often distinguished—prenatal to 2 years, early childhood (ages 3 to 6), late childhood (ages 7 to 10), early adolescence (ages 11 to 15), and late adolescence (ages 16 to 19). Each age group covers one or two major transitions in a child's life, such as school entrances or exits, biological maturation, possible cognitive changes, role changes, or some combination of these. These periods are characterized by relatively universal developmental challenges that require new modes of adaptation to biological, psychological, or social changes.[10]

Somewhat different indicators of child and youth well-being are associated with each period. For example, grade retention is more salient in the late childhood years than in adolescence (since most schools do not hold students back once they reach eighth grade[12]). Furthermore, low income might influence each indicator differently. As an illustration, income has stronger effects on cognitive and verbal ability test scores than it has on indices of emotional health in the childhood years.

Physical Health

Compared with nonpoor children, poor children in the United States experience diminished physical health as measured by a number of indicators of health status and outcomes (see Table 1). In the 1988 National Health Interview Survey, parents reported that poor children were only two-thirds as likely to be in excellent health and almost twice as likely to be in fair or poor health as nonpoor children. These large differences in health status between poor and nonpoor children do not reflect adjustment for potentially confounding factors (factors, other than income, that may be associated with living in poverty) nor do they distinguish between long- or short-term poverty or the timing of poverty. This sec-

Table 1

Selected Population-Based Indicators of Well-Being for Poor and Nonpoor Children in the United States

Indicator	Percentage of Poor Children (unless noted)	Percentage of Nonpoor Children (unless noted)	Ratio of Poor to Nonpoor Children
Physical Health Outcomes (for children between 0 and 17 years unless noted)			
Reported to be in excellent health[a]	37.4	55.2	0.7
Reported to be in fair to poor health[a]	11.7	<+>6.5	1.8
Experienced an accident, poisoning, or injury in the past year that required medical attention[a]	11.8	14.7	0.8
Chronic asthma[a]	4.4	4.3	1.0
Low birth weight (less than 2,500 grams)[b]	1.0	>0.6	1.7
Lead poisoning (blood lead levels 10 u/dl or greater)[c]	16.3	4.7	3.5
Infant mortality[b]	1.4 deaths per 100 live births	0.8 death per 100 live births	1.7
Deaths During Childhood (0 to 14 years)[d]	1.2	0.8	1.5
Stunting (being in the fifth percentile for height for age for 2 to 17 years)[e]	10.0	5.0	2.0
Number of days spent in bed in past year[a]	5.3 days	3.8 days	1.4
Number of short-stay hospital episodes in past year per 1,000 children[a]	81.3 stays	41.2 stays	2.0
Cognitive Outcomes			
Developmental delay (includes both limited and long-term developmental deficits) (0 to 17 years)[a]	5.0	3.8	1.3
Learning disability (defined as having exceptional difficulty in learning to read, write, and do arithmetic) (3 to 17 years)[a]	8.3	6.1	1.4
School Achievement Outcomes (5 to 17 years)			
Grade repetition (reported to have ever repeated a grade)[a]	28.8	14.1	2.0
Ever expelled or suspended[a]	11.9	6.1	2.0
High school dropout (percentage 16- to 24-year olds who were not in school or did not finish high school in 1994)[f]	21.0	9.6	2.2
Emotional or Behavioral Outcomes (3 to 17 years unless noted)			
Parent reports child has ever had an emotional or behavioral problem that lasted three months or more[g]	16.4	12.7	1.3
Parent reports child ever being treated for an emotional problem or behavioral problem[a]	2.5	4.5	0.6
Parent reports child has experienced one or more of a list of typical child behavioral problems in the last three months[h] (5 to 17 years)	57.4	57.3	1.0
Other			
Female teens who had an out-of-wedlock birth[i]	11.0	3.6	3.1
Economically inactive at age 24 (not employed or in school)[j]	15.9	8.3	1.9
Experienced hunger (food insufficiency) at least once in past year[k]	15.9	1.6	9.9
Reported cases of child abuse and neglect[l]	5.4	0.8	6.8
Violent crimes (experienced by poor families and nonpoor families)[m]	5.4	2.6	2.1
Afraid to go out (percentage of family heads in poor and nonpoor families who report they are afraid to go out in their neighborhood)[n]	19.5	8.7	2.2

Note: This list of child outcomes reflects findings from large nationally representative surveys that collect data on child outcomes and family income. While most data comes from the 1988 National Health Interview Survey Child Health Supplement, data from other nationally representative surveys are included. The rates presented are from simple cross-tabulations. In most cases, the data do not reflect factors that might be important to child outcomes other than poverty status at the time of data collection. The ratios reflect rounding. *(Notes continued on next page.)*

(Notes continued from previous page)

[a] Data from the 1988 National Health Interview Survey Child Health Supplement (NHS-CHS),a nationwide household interview survey. Children's health status was reported by the adult household member who knew the most about the sample child's health,usually the child's mother. Figures calculated from Dawson,D.A. Family structure and children's health: United States,1988. Vital Health and Statistics,Series 10,no. 178. Hyattsville,MD: U.S. Department of Health and Human Services,Public Health Service,June 1991; and Coiro,M.J.,Zill,n.,and Bloom,B. Health of our nation's children. Vital Health and Statistics,Series 10,no. 191. Hyattsville,MD: U.S. Department of Health and Human Services,Public Health Service,December 1994.

[b] Data from the National Maternal and Infant Health Survey,data collected in 1989 and 1990,with 1988 as the reference period. Percentages were calculated from the number of deaths and number of low birth weight births per 1,000 live births as reported in Federman,M.,Garner,T.,Short,K.,et al. What does it mean to be poor in America? Monthly Labor Review (May 1996) 119,5:10.

[c] Data from the NHANES III,1988-1991. Poor children who lived in families with incomes less than 130% of the poverty threshold are classified as poor. All other children are classified as nonpoor.

[d] Percentages include only black and white youths. Percentages calculated from Table 7 in Rogot,E. A mortality study of 1.3 million persons by demographic,social and economic factors: 1979-1985 follow-up. Rockville,MD: National Institutes of Health,July 1992.

[e] Data from NHANES II,1976-1980. For more discussion,see the Child Indicators article in this journal issue.

[f] National Center for Education Statistics. Dropout rates in the United States: 1994. Table 7,Status dropout rate,ages 16-24,by income and race ethnicity: October 1994. Available online at: http://www.ed.gov/NCES/pubs/r941007.html.

[g] Data from the NHIS-CHS. The question was meant to identify children with common psychological disorders such as attention deficit disorder or depression,as well as more severe problems such as autism.

[h] Data from the NHIS-CHS. Parents responded "sometimes true," "often true," or "not true" to a list of 32 statements typical of children's behaviors. Each statement corresponded to one of six individual behavior problems--antisocial behavior,anxiety,peer conflict/social withdrawal,dependency,hyperactivity,and headstrong behavior. Statements included behaviors such as cheating or lying,being disobedient in the home,being secretive,and demanding a lot of attention. For a more complete description,see Section P-11 of the NHIS-CHS questionnaire.

[i] Data from the Panel Study of Income Dynamics (PSID). Based on 1,705 children ages 0 to 6 in 1968; outcomes measured at ages 21 to 27. Haveman,R.,and Wolfe,B. Succeeding generations: On the effect of investments in children. New York: Russell Sage Foundation,1994,p. 108,Table 4,10c.

[j] Data from the PSID. Based on 1,705 children ages 0 to 6 in 1968; outcomes measured at ages 21 to 27. In Succeeding generations: On the effect of investments in children. Haveman,R.,and Wolfe,B. New York: Russell Sage Foundation,1994,p. 108,Table 4,10d. Economically inactive is defined as not being a full-time student,working 1,000 hours or more per year; attending school part time and working 500 hours; a mother of an infant or mother of two or more children less than five years old; a part-time student and the mother of a child less than five years old.

[k] Data from NHANES III,1988-1991. Figures reflect food insufficiency,the term used in government hunger-related survey questions. For a more in-depth discussion,see Lewit,E.M.,and Kerrebrock,N. Child indicators: Childhood hunger. The Future of Children (Spring 1997) 7,1:128-37.

[l] Data from Study of National Incidence and Prevalence of Child Abuse and Neglect: 1988. In Wasting America's future. Children's Defense Fund. Boston: Beacon Press,1994,pp. 5-29,87,Tables 5-6. Poor families are those with annual incomes below $15,000.

[m] Data from the National Crime Victimization Interview Survey. Results are for households or persons living in households. Data were collected between January 1992 and June 1993 with 1992 as the reference period. Percentages are calculated from number of violent crimes per 1,000 people per year. Reported in Federman,M.,Garner,T.,Short,K.,et al. What does it mean to be poor in America? Monthly Labor Review (May 1996) 119,5:9.

[n] Data from the Survey of Income and Program Participation. Participation data collection and reference periods are September through December 1992. Reported in Federman,M.,Garner,T.,Short,K.,et al. What does it mean to be poor in America?<%2> Monthly Labor Review (May 1996) 119,5:9.

tion reviews research on the relationship of poverty to several key measures of child health, low birth weight and infant mortality, growth stunting, and lead poisoning. For the most part, the focus is on research that attempts to adjust for important confounding factors and/or to address the effect of the duration of poverty on child health outcomes.

Birth Outcomes

Low birth weight (2,500 grams or less) and infant mortality are important indicators of child health. Low birth weight is associated with an increased likelihood of subsequent physical health and cognitive and emotional problems that can persist through childhood and adolescence. Serious physical disabilities, grade repetition, and learning disabilities are more prevalent among children who were low birth weight as infants, as are lower levels of intelligence and of math and reading achievement. Low birth weight is also the key risk factor for infant mortality (especially death within the first 28 days of life), which is a widely accepted indicator of the health and well-being of children.[13]

> ## Poverty status had a statistically significant effect on both low birth weight and the neonatal mortality rate for whites but not for blacks

Estimating the effects of poverty alone on birth outcomes is complicated by the fact that adverse birth outcomes are more prevalent for unmarried women, those with low levels of education, and black mothers—all groups with high poverty rates. One study that used data from the NLSY to examine the relationship between family income and low birth weight did find, however, that among whites, women with family income below the federal poverty level in the year of birth were 80% more likely to have a low birth weight baby as compared with women whose family incomes were above the poverty level (this study statistically controlled for mothers' age, education, marital status, and smoking status). Further analysis also showed that the duration of poverty had an important effect; if a white woman was poor both at the time when she entered the longitudinal NLSY sample and at the time of her pregnancy (5 to 10 years later), she was more than three times more likely to deliver a low birth weight infant than a white woman who was not poor at both times. For black women in this sample, although the odds of having a low birth weight baby were twice the odds for white mothers, the probability of having a low birth weight baby was not related to family poverty status.[14]

Other studies that used county level data to examine the effects of income or poverty status and a number of pregnancy-related health services on birth outcomes for white and black women also found that income or poverty status had a statistically significant effect on both low birth weight and the neonatal mortality rate for whites but not for blacks.[15,16]

Growth Stunting

Although overt malnutrition and starvation are rare among poor children in the United States, deficits in children's nutritional status are associated with poverty. As described more fully in the Child Indicators article in this journal issue, stunting (low height for age), a measure of nutritional status, is more prevalent among poor than nonpoor children. Studies using data from the NLSY show that differentials in height for age between poor and nonpoor children are greater when long-term rather than single-year measures of poverty are used in models to predict stunting. These differentials by poverty status are large even in models that statistically control for many other family and child characteristics associated with poverty.[17]

Lead Poisoning

Harmful effects of lead have been documented even at low levels of exposure. Health problems vary with length of exposure, intensity of lead in the environment, and the developmental stage of the child—with risks beginning prior to birth. At very young ages, lead exposure is linked to stunted growth,[18] hearing loss,[19] vitamin D metabolism damage, impaired blood production, and toxic effects on the kidneys.[20] Additionally, even a small increase in blood lead above the Centers for Disease Control and Prevention (CDC) current intervention threshold (10 µg/dL) is associated with a decrease in intelligence quotient (IQ).[21]

Today, deteriorating lead-based house paint remains the primary source of lead for young children. Infants and toddlers in old housing eat the sweet-tasting paint chips and breathe the lead dust from deteriorating paint. Four to five million children reside in homes with lead levels exceeding the accepted threshold for safety,[22] and more than 1.5 million children under six years of age have elevated blood lead levels.[23]

Using data from NHANES III (1988–1991), one study found that children's blood lead levels declined as family income increased.[23] All other things being equal, mean blood lead levels were 9% lower for one- to five-year-olds in families with incomes twice the poverty level than for those who were poor. Overall blood levels were highest among one- to five-year-olds who were non-Hispanic blacks from low-income families in large central cities. The mean blood lead level for this group, 9.7 µg/dL, was just under the CDC's threshold for intervention and almost three times the mean for all one- to five-year-olds.

Cognitive Abilities

As reported in Table 1, children living below the poverty threshold are 1.3 times as likely as nonpoor children to experience learning disabilities and developmental delays. Reliable measures of cognitive ability and school achievement for young children in the Children of the NLSY and IHDP data sets have been used in a number of studies to examine the relationship between cognitive ability and poverty in detail.[6,24–26] This article reports on several studies that control for a number of potentially important family characteristics and attempts to distinguish between the effects of long- and short-term poverty.

The effects of long-term poverty on measures of children's cognitive ability were significantly greater than the effects of short-term poverty.

A recent study using data from the Children of the NLSY and the IHDP compared children in families with incomes less than half of the poverty threshold to children in families with incomes between 1.5 and twice the poverty threshold. The poorer children scored between 6 and 13 points lower on various standardized tests of IQ, verbal ability, and achievement.[25] These differences are very large from an educational perspective and were present even after controlling for maternal age, marital status, education, and ethnicity. A 6- to 13-point difference might mean, for example, the difference between being placed in a special education class or not. Children in families with incomes closer to, but still below, the poverty line also did worse than children in higher-income families, but the differences were smaller. The smallest differences appeared for the earliest (age two) measure of cognitive ability; however, the sizes of the effects were similar for children from three to eight. These findings suggest that the effects of poverty on children's cognitive development occur early.

The study also found that duration of poverty was an important factor in the lower scores of poor children on measures of cognitive ability. Children who lived in persistently poor families (defined in this study as poor over a four-year span) had scores on the various assessments six to nine points lower than children who were never poor.[25] Another analysis of the NLSY that controlled for a number of important maternal and child health characteristics showed that the effects of long-term poverty (based on family income averaged over 13 years prior to testing of the child) on measures of children's cognitive ability were significantly greater than the effects of short-term poverty (measured by income in the year of observation).[26]

A few studies link long-term family income to cognitive ability and achievement measured during the school years. Research on children's test scores at ages seven and eight found that the effects of income on these scores were similar in size to those reported for three-year-olds.[25] But research relating family income measured during adolescence on cognitive ability finds relatively smaller effects.[27] As summarized in the next section, these modest effects of income on cognitive ability are consistent with literature showing modest effects of income on schooling attainment, but both sets of studies may be biased by the fact that their measurement of parental income is restricted to the child's adoles-

cent years. It is not yet possible to make conclusive statements regarding the size of the effects of poverty on children's long-term cognitive development.

School Achievement Outcomes

Educational attainment is well recognized as a powerful predictor of experiences in later life. A comprehensive review of the relationship between parental income and school attainment, published in 1994, concluded that poverty limited school achievement but that the effect of income on the number of school years completed was small.[28] In general, the studies suggested that a 10% increase in family income is associated with a 0.2% to 2% increase in the number of school years completed.[28]

Several more recent studies using different longitudinal data sets (the PSID, the NLSY and Children of the NLSY) also find that poverty status has a small negative impact on high school graduation and years of schooling obtained. Much of the observed relationship between income and schooling appears to be related to a number of confounding factors such as parental education, family structure, and neighborhood characteristics.[28–30] Some of these studies suggest that the components of income (for example, AFDC) and the way income is measured (number of years in poverty versus annual family income or the ratio of income to the poverty threshold) may lead to somewhat different conclusions. But all the studies suggest that, after controlling for many appropriate confounding variables, the effects of poverty per se on school achievement are likely to be statistically significant, yet small. Based on the results of one study, the authors estimated that, if poverty were eliminated for all children, mean years of schooling for all children would increase by only 0.3% (less than half a month).[30]

For low-income children, a $10,000 increase in mean family income between birth and age 5 was associated with nearly a full-year increase in completed schooling.

Why do not the apparently strong effects of parental income on cognitive abilities and school achievement in the early childhood years translate into larger effects on completed schooling? One possible reason is that extrafamilial environments (for example, schools and neighborhoods) begin to matter as much or more for children than family conditions once children reach school age. A second possible reason is that school-related achievement depends on both ability and behavior. As is discussed in the Emotional and Behavioral Outcomes section, children's behavioral problems, measured either before or after the transition into school, are not very sensitive to parental income differences.

A third, and potentially crucial, reason concerns the timing of economic deprivation. Few studies measure income from early childhood to adolescence, so there is no way to know whether poverty early in childhood has noteworthy effects on later outcomes such as school completion. Because family income varies over time,[31] income measured during adolescence, or even middle childhood, may not reflect income in early childhood. A recent study that attempted to evaluate how the timing of income might affect completed schooling found that family income averaged from birth to age 5 had a much more powerful effect on the number of school years a child completes than does family income measured either between ages 5 and 10 or between ages 11 and 15.[7] For low-income children, a $10,000 increase in mean family income between birth and age 5 was associated with nearly a full-year increase in completed schooling. Similar increments to family income later in childhood had no significant impact, suggesting that income may indeed be an important determinant of completed schooling but that only income during the early childhood years matters.

Emotional and Behavioral Outcomes

Poor children suffer from emotional and behavioral problems more frequently than do nonpoor children (see Table 1). Emotional outcomes are often grouped along two dimensions: externalizing behaviors including aggression, fighting, and acting out, and internalizing behaviors such as anxiety, social withdrawal, and depression. Data regarding emotional outcomes are based on parental and teacher reports. This section reviews studies that distinguish between the effects of long- and short-term poverty on emotional outcomes of children at different ages.

One study of low birth weight five-year-olds using the IHDP data set found that children in persistently poor families had more internalizing and externalizing behavior problems than children who had never been poor. The analysis controlled for maternal education and family structure and defined long-term poverty as income below the poverty threshold for each of four consecutive years. Short-term poverty (defined as poor in at least one of four years) was also associated with more behavioral problems, though the effects were not as large as those for persistent poverty.[6]

Two different studies using the NLSY report findings consistent with those of the IHDP study. Both found persistent poverty to be a significant predictor of some behavioral problems.[26,32] One study used data from the 1986 NLSY and found that for four- to eight-year-olds persistent poverty (defined as a specific percentage of years of life during which the child lived below the poverty level) was positively related to the presence of internalizing symptoms (such as dependence, anxiety, and unhappiness) even after controlling for current poverty status, mother's age, educa-

tion, and marital status. In contrast, current poverty (defined by current family income below the poverty line) but not persistent poverty was associated with more externalizing problems (such as hyperactivity, peer conflict, and headstrong behavior).[32]

Problematic emotional outcomes are associated with family poverty; however, the effects of poverty on emotional outcomes are not as large as its effects on cognitive outcomes.

The second study used NLSY data from 1978–1991 and analyzed children ages 3 to 11. On average children living in long-term poverty (defined by the ratio of family income to the poverty level averaged over 13 years) ranked three to seven percentile points higher (indicating more problems) on a behavior problem index than children with incomes above the poverty line. After controlling for a range of factors including mother's characteristics, nutrition, and infant health behaviors, the difference remained though it dropped in magnitude. This study also found that children who experienced one year of poverty had more behavioral problems than children who had lived in long-term poverty.[26]

The above studies demonstrate that problematic emotional outcomes are associated with family poverty. However, it is important to note that the effects of poverty on emotional outcomes are not as large as those found in cognitive outcomes. Also these studies do not show that children in long-term poverty experience emotional problems with greater frequency or of the same type as children who experience only short-term poverty. These studies analyzed data for young children. Few studies have examined the link between emotional outcomes and poverty for adolescents. One small study of 7th- to 10th-graders in the rural Midwest did not find a statistically significant relationship between poverty and emotional problems, either internalizing or externalizing.[33] Self-reporting by the adolescents rather than maternal reporting, as used in the data sets on younger children, may account for the differences found in the effects of income on emotional outcomes in this study as compared with the previously reviewed research. It may also be that younger children are more affected by poverty than older children.

These findings point to the need for further research to improve understanding of the link between income and children's emotional outcomes.

Teenage Out-of-Wedlock Childbearing

The negative consequences for both mothers and children associated with births to unwed teen mothers make it a source of policy concern.[34] Although the rate of out-of-wedlock births among poor teens is almost three times as high as the rate among those from nonpoor families (see Table 1), the literature on linkages between family income and out-of-wedlock childbearing is not conclusive. A recent review of the evidence put it this way: "[P]arental income is negative and usually, but not always, significant.... The few reports of the quantitative effects of simulated changes in variables suggest that decreases in parental income... will lead to small increases in the probability that teen girls will experience a nonmarital birth."[28]

> A child's home environment accounts for a substantial portion of the effects of family income on cognitive outcomes in young children.

A recent study, which used data from the PSID to investigate factors in teen out-of-wedlock births, found that variations in income around the poverty threshold were not predictive of a teenage birth but that the probability of a teenager's having an out-of-wedlock birth declined significantly at family income levels above twice the poverty threshold.[35] The duration and timing of poverty had no effect on the probability of a teen out-of-wedlock birth. These findings are somewhat different from those reported for cognitive outcomes and school achievement. In the case of

cognitive outcomes for young children, the variation in income mattered most to children at very low levels of income; for school achievement, the timing and duration of poverty seemed to have important differential effects on outcomes.

Why should poverty status matter more for schooling than for childbearing? This difference is consistent with the more general result that parental income appears more strongly linked with ability and achievement than with behavior. The factors influencing teenage out-of-wedlock childbearing are less well understood than the factors influencing schooling completion: interventions have generally been much less successful in altering teen birthrates than in keeping teens in school.[36,37]

Pathways Through Which Poverty Operates

The research reviewed thus far suggests that living in poverty exacts a heavy toll on children. However, it does not shed light on the pathways or mechanisms by which low income exerts its effects on children. As the term is used in this discussion, a "pathway" is a mechanism through which poverty or income can influence a child outcome. By implication, this definition implies that a pathway should be causally related to both income and at least one child outcome. Exploration of these pathways is important for a more complete understanding of the effects of poverty on children; moreover, exploration of pathways can lead to the identification of leverage points that may be amenable to policy intervention and remediation in the absence of a change in family income.

©Steven Rubin

Research on the size and strength of the pathways through which income might influence child health and development is still scanty. In this section, five potential pathways are discussed: (1) health and nutrition, (2) the home environment, (3) parental interactions with children, (4) parental mental health, and (5) neighborhood conditions. Space limitations preclude a discussion of other potential pathways such as access to and use of prenatal care, access to pediatric care, exposure to environmental toxins, household stability, provision of learning experiences outside the home, quality of school attended, and peer groups. Further, few studies have tested pathway models using these variables.

Health and Nutrition

Although health is itself an outcome, it can also be viewed as a pathway by which poverty influences other child outcomes, such as cognitive ability and school achievement. As discussed previously poor children experience increased rates of low birth weight and elevated blood lead levels when compared with nonpoor children. These conditions have, in turn, been associated with reduced IQ and other measures of cognitive functioning in young children and, in the case of low birth weight, with increased rates of learning disabilities, grade retention, and school dropout in older children and youths.

A 1990 analysis indicated that the poverty-related health factors such as low birth weight, elevated blood lead levels, anemia,[38] and recurrent ear infections and hearing loss contributed to the differential in IQ scores between poor and nonpoor four-year-olds.[39] The findings suggest that the cumulative health disadvantage experienced by poor children on these four health measures may have accounted for as much as 13% to 20% of the difference in IQ between the poor and nonpoor four-year-olds during the 1970s and 1980s.[39]

As discussed in the Child Indicators article in this journal issue, malnutrition in childhood (as measured by anthropometric indicators) is associated with lower scores on tests of cognitive development. Deficits in these anthropometric measures are associated with poverty among children in the United States, and the effects can be substantial. One recent study found that the effect of stunting on short-term memory was equivalent to the difference in short-term memory between children in families that had experienced poverty for 13 years and children in families with incomes at least three times the poverty level.[26]

Home Environment

A number of studies have found that a child's home environment—opportunities for learning, warmth of mother-child interactions, and the physical condition of the home—accounts for a substantial portion of the effects of family income on cognitive outcomes in young children. Some large longitudinal data sets use the HOME scale as a measure of the home environment. The HOME scale is made up of items that measure household resources, such as reading materials and toys, and parental practices, such as discipline methods. The HOME scale has been shown to be correlated with family income and poverty, with higher levels of income associated with improved home environments as measured by the scale.[7,40]

Parents who are poor are likely to be less healthy, both emotionally and physically, than those who are not poor.

Several studies have found that differences in the home environment of higher- and lower-income children, as measured by the HOME scale, account for a substantial portion of the effect of income on the cognitive development of preschool children and on the achievement scores of elementary school children.[6,26,37] In one study, differences in the home environment also seemed to account for some of the effects of poverty status on behavioral problems. In addition, the provisions of learning experiences in the home (measured by specific subscales of the HOME scale) have been shown to account for up to half of the effect of poverty status on the IQ scores of five-year-olds.[37,41]

Parental Interactions with Children

A number of studies have attempted to go beyond documentation of activities and materials in the home to capture the effects of parent-child interactions on child outcomes. Much of the work is based on small and/or community-based samples. That work suggests that child adjustment and achievement are facilitated by certain parental practices. There is also some evidence that poverty is linked to lower-quality parent-child interaction and to increased use of harsh punishment. This research suggests that parental practices may be an important pathway between economic resources and child outcomes.

Evidence of such a parental-practice pathway from research using large national data sets of the kind reviewed in this article is less consistent. One NLSY-based study found that currently poor mothers spanked their children more often than nonpoor mothers and that this harsh behavior was an important component of the effect of poverty on children's mental health.[32] Mothers' parenting behavior was not, however, found to be an important pathway by which persistent poverty affected children's mental health. A more recent study using the National Survey of Families and Households found that the level of household income was only weakly related to effective parenting and that differences in parent practices did not account for much of the association between poverty and child well-being.[42]

Among adolescents, family economic pressure may lead to conflict with parents, resulting in lower school grades, reduced emotional health, and impaired social relation-ships.[33,43] Other work suggests that it may be income loss or economic uncertainty due to unemployment, underemployment, and unstable work conditions, rather than poverty or low income per se, that is a source for conflict between parents and teens leading to emotional and school problems.[33,44]

Parental Mental Health

Parents who are poor are likely to be less healthy, both emotionally and physically, than those who are not poor.[45] And parental irritability and depressive symptoms are associated with more conflicted interactions with adolescents, leading to less satisfactory emotional, social, and cognitive development.[43,46,47] Some studies have established that parental mental health accounts for some of the effect of economic circumstances on child health and behavior. Additionally, poor parental mental health is associated with impaired parent-child interactions and less provision of learning experiences in the home.[33,41,48]

> Low income may lead to residence in extremely poor neighborhoods characterized by social disorganization and few resources for child development.

Neighborhood Conditions

Another possible pathway through which family income operates has to do with the neighborhoods in which poor families reside. Poor parents are constrained in their choice of neighborhoods and schools. Low income may lead to residence in extremely poor neighborhoods characterized by social disorganization (crime, many unemployed adults, neighbors not monitoring the behavior of adolescents) and few resources for child development (playgrounds, child care, health care facilities, parks, after-school programs).[49,50] The affluence of neighborhoods is associated with child and adolescent outcomes (intelligence test scores at ages 3 and 5 and high school graduation rates by age 20) over and above family poverty.[37,51] Neighborhood residence also seems to be associated with parenting practices, over and above family income and education.[52] Neighborhood effects on intelligence scores are in part mediated by the learning environment in the home.[52,53] Living in neighborhoods with high concentrations of poor people is associated with less provision of learning experiences in the homes of preschoolers, over and above the links seen between family income and learning experiences.

A key issue that has not been fully explored is the extent to which neighborhood effects may be overestimated because neighborhood characteristics also reflect the choices of neighborhood residents. One study that examined the effects of peer groups (as measured by the socioeconomic status of students in a respondent's school) on teenage pregnancy and school dropout behavior found that while student body socioeconomic status seemed to be an important predictor of both dropout and teen pregnancy rates, it did not appear to be related to those outcomes in statistical models that treated this peer characteristic as a matter of family choice.[54]

How Much Does Income Cause Child Outcomes?

It may seem odd to raise this question after summarizing evidence indicating that family income does matter—across the childhood and adolescent years and for a number of indicators of well-being. However, these associations have been demonstrated when a relatively small set of family characteristics are controlled through statistical analyses. It is possible, therefore, that other important family characteristics have not been controlled for and that, as a result of this omission, the effects of income are estimated incorrectly.... Distinguishing between the effects on children of poverty and its related events and conditions is crucial for public policy formulation. Programs that alter family income may not have intended benefits for children if the importance of family income has been mismeasured.

Despite the evidence reviewed in this article and elsewhere, there is an important segment of the population who believes that income per se may not appreciably affect child outcomes. This viewpoint sees parental income mainly as a proxy for other characteristics such as character (a strong work ethic) or genetic endowment that influence both children and parents. A recent book by Susan Mayer, *What Money Can't Buy: The Effect of Parental Income on Children's Outcomes*,[55] presents a series of tests to examine explicitly the effects of income on a set of child outcomes. In one test, measures of income *after* the occurrence of an outcome are added to statistical models of the effects of income and other characteristics on a child outcome. The idea behind this test is that unanticipated future income can capture unmeasured parental characteristics but cannot have caused the child outcome. The inclusion of future income frequently produced a large reduction in the estimated impact of prior parent income. Mayer also tries to estimate the effects on children of components of income (for example, asset income) that are independent of the actions of the family. Although these tests provide some support for the hypothesis that family income may not matter much for child outcomes, even Mayer admits that these statistical procedures are not without their problems. For example, prior income and future income are highly correlated, and if parents take reasonable expectations of future income into consideration in making decisions regarding the well-being of children, then the assumption that child outcomes are independent of future income, which underlies the first test, is violated.

A second approach to the problem that omitted variables may bias the estimation of the effects of income and poverty on children looks at siblings within families. Siblings reared in the same family share many of the same unmeasured family characteristics. Thus, comparing children at the same age within families makes it possible to look at the income of the family at different time points (for example, if a firstborn was five years of age in 1985 and the second child was five years of age in 1988, it is possible to look at their achievement levels at this age and the average family income between 1980 and 1985 for the firstborn and between 1983 and 1988 for the second child). One study that used this approach found that sibling differences in income were associated with sibling differences in completed schooling, which gave support to the notion that family income matters.[7]

Perhaps the most convincing demonstration of the effects of income is to provide poor families with income in the context of a randomized trial. In four Income Maintenance/Negative Income Tax Experiments in the 1960s and 1970s, experimental treatment families received a guaranteed minimum income. (These experiments are discussed in more detail in the article by Janet Currie in this journal issue.) Substantial benefits resulting from increased income effects were found for child nutrition, early school achievement, and high school completion in some sites but not in others. These results might be viewed as inconclusive; however, since the site with the largest effects for younger children (North Carolina) was also the poorest, one interpretation of the results is that income effects are most important for the very poorest families.[56,57]

Conclusion

The evidence reviewed in this article supports the conclusion that family income can substantially influence child and adolescent well-being. However, the associations between income and child outcomes are more complex and varied than suggested by the simple associations presented in Table 1. Family income seems to be more strongly related to children's ability and achievement-related outcomes than to emotional outcomes. In addition, the effects are particularly pronounced for children who live below the poverty line for multiple years and for children who live in extreme poverty (that is, 50% or less of the poverty threshold). These income effects are probably not due to some unmeasured characteristics of low-income families: family income, in and of itself, does appear to matter.

The timing of poverty is also important, although this conclusion is based on only a small number of studies. Low income during the preschool and early school years exhibits the strongest correlation with low rates of high school completion, as compared with low income during the childhood and adolescent years.[7,58][&stop] Poor-quality schooling, which is correlated with high neighborhood poverty, may exacerbate this effect.[59] These findings suggest that early childhood interventions may be critical in reducing the impact of low income on children's lives.

The pathways through which low income influences children also suggest some general recommendations. Nutrition programs, especially if they target the most undernourished poor, may have beneficial effects on both physical and cognitive outcomes. Lead abatement and parental education programs may improve cognitive outcomes in poor children residing in inner-city neighborhoods where lead is still an important hazard.

Because about one-half of the effect of family income on cognitive ability is mediated by the home environment, including learning experiences in the home, interventions might profitably focus on working with parents. An example is the Learningames curriculum in which parents are provided instruction, materials, and role playing in learning experiences.[60] Other effective learning-oriented programs might also be pursued.[61–63]

Finally, income policies (as discussed by Robert Plotnick in this journal issue) and in-kind support programs (as discussed by Devaney, Ellwood, and Love in this journal issue) can have immediate impact on the number or children living in poverty and on the circumstances in which they live. Most important, based on this review, would be efforts to eliminate deep and persistent poverty especially during a child's early years. Support to families with older children may be desirable on other grounds, but the available research suggests that it will probably not have the same impact on child outcomes as programs focused on younger children.

The authors would like to thank the National Institute of Child Health and Human Development Research Network on Child and Family Well-being for supporting the writing of this article. The Russell Sage Foundation's contribution is also appreciated as is that of the William T. Grant Foundation, and the Canadian Institute for Advanced Research. The authors are also grateful for the feedback provided by Linda Baker, Pamela K. Klebanov, and Judith Smith and would like to thank Phyllis Gyamfi for her editorial assistance.

Notes

1. Hernandez, D.J. *America's children: Resources from family government and the economy.* New York: Russell Sage Foundation, 1993.

2. Duncan, G.J., and Brooks-Gunn, J., eds. *Consequences of growing up poor.* New York: Russell Sage Foundation, 1997.

3. Duncan, G.J., and Rodgers, W.L. Longitudinal aspects of childhood poverty. *Journal of Marriage and the Family* (November 1988) 50,4:1007–21.

4. Chase-Lansdale, P.L., and Brooks-Gunn, J., eds. *Escape from poverty: What makes a difference for children?* New York: Cambridge University Press, 1995.

5. Children's Defense Fund. *Wasting America's future.* Boston: Beacon Press, 1994; Klerman, L. *Alive and well?* New York: National Center for Children in Poverty, Columbia University, 1991.

6. Duncan, G.J., Brooks-Gunn, J., and Klebanov, P.K. Economic deprivation and early-childhood development. *Child Development* (1994) 65,2:296–318.

7. Duncan, G.J., Yeung, W., Brooks-Gunn, J., and Smith, J.R. How much does childhood poverty affect the life chances of children? *American Sociological Review,* in press.

8. Hauser, R., Brown, B., and Prosser W. *Indicators of children's well-being.* New York: Russell Sage Foundation, in press.

9. Brooks-Gunn, J., Guo, G., and Furstenberg, F.F., Jr. Who drops out of and who continues beyond high school?: A 20-year study of black youth. *Journal of Research in Adolescence* (1993) 37,3:271–94.

10. Graber, J.A., and Brooks-Gunn, J. Transitions and turning points: Navigating the passage from childhood through adolescence. *Developmental Psychology* (1996) 32,4:768–76.

11. Rutter, M. Beyond longitudinal data: Causes, consequences, changes and continuity. *Journal of Counseling and Clinical Psychology* (1994) 62,5:928–90.

12. Guo, G., Brooks-Gunn, J., and Harris, K.M. Parents' labor-force attachment and grade retention among urban black children. *Sociology of Education* (1996) 69,3:217–36.

13. For a review of the causes and consequences of low birth weight in the United States, see Shiono, P., ed. Low Birth Weight. *The Future of Children* (Spring 1995) 5,1:4–231.

14. Starfield, B., Shapiro, S., Weiss, J., et al. Race, family income, and low birth weight. *American Journal of Epidemiology* (1991) 134,10:1167–74.

15. Corman, H., and Grossman, M. Determinants of neonatal mortality rates in the U.S.: A reduced form model. *Journal of Health Economics* (1985) 4,3:213–36.

16. Frank, R., Strobino, D., Salkever, D., and Jackson, C. Updated estimates of the impact of prenatal care on birthweight outcomes by race. *Journal of Human Resources* (1992) 27,4:629–42.

17. Miller, J., and Korenman, S. Poverty and children's nutritional status in the United States. *American Journal of Epidemiology* (1994) 140,3:233–43.

18. Schwartz, J., Angle, C., and Pitcher, H. Relationship between childhood blood lead levels and stature. *Pediatrics* (1986) 77,3:281–88.

19. Schwartz, J., and Otto, D. Lead and minor hearing impairment. *Archives of Environmental Health* (1991) 46,5:300–05.

20. Agency for Toxic Substances and Disease Registry. *The nature and extent of lead poisoning in the US.: A report to Congress.* Washington, DC: U.S. Department of Health and Human Services, 1988, Section II, p. 7.

21. Schwartz, J. Low level lead exposure and children's IQ: A meta-analysis and search for threshold. *Environmental Research* (1994) 65,1:42–55.

22. Ronald Morony, Deputy Director, U.S. Department of Housing and Urban Development, Office of Lead-Based Paint Abatement and Poisoning Prevention, Washington, DC. Personal communication, November 20, 1996.

23. Brody, D.J., Pirkle, L., Kramer, R., et al. Blood lead levels in the U.S. population. *Journal of the American Medical Association* (1994) 272,4:277–81.

24. Brooks-Gunn, J., McCarton, C.M., Casey, P.H., et al. Early intervention in low birth weight premature infants: Results through age 5 years from the Infant Health and Development Program. *Journal of the American Medical Association* (1994) 272,16: 1257–62.

25. Smith, J.R., Brooks-Gunn, J., and Klebanov, P. The consequences of living in poverty for young children's cognitive and verbal ability and early school achievement. In *Consequences of growing up poor.* G.J. Duncan and J. Brooks-Gunn, eds. New York: Russell Sage Foundation, 1997.

26. Korenman, S., Miller, J.E., and Sjaastad, J.E. Long-term poverty and child development in the United States: Results from the National Longitudinal Survey of Youth. *Children and Youth Services Review* (1995)17,1/2:127–51.

27. Peters. E., and Mullis, N. The role of the family and source of income in adolescent achievement. In *Consequences of growing up poor:* G. Duncan and J. Brooks-Gunn, eds. New York: Russell Sage Foundation, 1997.

28. Haveman, R., and Wolfe, B. The determinants of children's attainments: A review of methods and findings. *Journal of Economic Literature* (1995) 33,3:1829–78.

29. Teachman, J., Paasch, K.M., Day, R., and Carver, K.P. Poverty during adolescence and subsequent educational attainment. In *Consequences of growing up poor:* G. Duncan and J. Brooks-Gunn, eds. New York: Russell Sage Foundation, 1997.

30. Haveman, R., and Wolfe, B. *Succeeding generations: On the effect of investments in children.* New York: Russell Sage Foundation, 1994.

31. Duncan, G.J. Volatility of family income over the life course. In *Life-span development and behavior.* Vol. 9. P. Baltes, D. Featherman, and R.M. Lerner, eds. Hillsdale, NJ: Erlbaum, 1988, pp. 317–58.

32. McLeod, J.D., and Shanahan, M.J. Poverty, parenting and children's mental health. *American Sociological Review* (June 1993) 58,3:351–66.

33. Conger, R.D., Conger, K.J., and Elder, G.H. Family economic hardship and adolescent adjustment: Mediating and moderating processes. In *Consequences of growing up poor:* G. Duncan and J. Brooks-Gunn, eds. New York: Russell Sage Foundation, 1997.

34. Hotz, V.J., McElroy, S.W., and Sanders, S.G. Costs and consequences of teenage childbearing. *Chicago Policy Review.* Internet: http://www.spc.uchicago.edu/cpr/Teenage_Child.htm.

35. Haveman, R., Wolfe, B., and Wilson, K. Childhood poverty and adolescent schooling and fertility outcomes: Reduced form and structural estimates. In *Consequences of growing up poor.* G.J. Duncan and J. Brooks-Gunn, eds. New York: Russell Sage Foundation, 1997.

36. U.S. Department of Health and Human Services. *Report to Congress on out-of-wedlock childbearing.* PHS-95–1257. Hyattsville, MD: DHHS, September 1995.

37. Brooks-Gunn, J., Duncan, G.J., Klebanov, P.K., and Sealand, N. Do neighborhoods influence child and adolescent behavior? *American Journal of Sociology* (1993) 99,2:335–95.

38. Iron-deficiency anemia is an important health problem that was traditionally identified with child poverty. Iron-deficiency anemia has been associated with impaired exercise capacity, increased susceptibility to lead absorption, and developmental and behavioral problems; see Oski, F. Iron deficiency in infancy and childhood. *The New England Journal of Medicine.* (July 15, 1993) 329,3:190–93. The importance of iron-deficiency anemia and its sequelae among poor children in the United States today is unclear. Increased use of iron-fortified foods and infant formulas along with their provision through public nutrition programs such as the Special Supplemental Food Program for Women, Infants, and Children (see the article by Devaney, Ellwood, and Love in this journal issue) have contributed to a dramatic decline in anemia; see Yip, R., Binkin, N.J., Fleshood, L., and Trowbridge, F.L. Declining prevalence of anemia among low-income children in the U.S. *Journal of American Medical Association* (1987) 258,12:1623. Between 1980 and 1991, the prevalence of anemia among infants and children through age five declined from 7% to 3%. Still, low-income children participating in public health programs have a higher-than-average

prevalence of anemia; see Yip, R., Parvanta, I., Scanlon, K., et al. Pediatric Nutrition Surveillance System—United States, 1980–1991. *Morbidity and Mortality Weekly Report* (November 1992) 41,SS-7:1–24. In part, this is because risk of anemia is a criterion for enrollment in these programs and also because these low-income children have low iron levels.

39. Goldstein, N. *Explaining socioeconomic differences in children's cognitive test scores.* Working Paper No. H-90-1. Cambridge, MA: Malcolm Wiener Center for Social Policy, John F. Kennedy School of Government, Harvard University, 1990.

40. Garrett, P., Ng'andu, N., and Ferron, J. Poverty experience of young children and the quality of their home environments. *Child Development* (1994) 65,2:331–45.

41. Bradley, R.H. Home environment and parenting. In *Handbook of parenting:* M. Bornstein, ed. Hillsdale, NJ: Erlbaum, 1995.

42. Hanson, T., McLanahan, S., and Thomson, E. Economic resources, parental practices, and child well-being. In *Consequences of growing up poor:* G.J. Duncan and J. Brooks-Gunn, eds. New York: Russell Sage Foundation, 1997.

43. Conger, R.D., Ge, S., Elder, G.H., Jr., et al. Economic stress, coercive family process and developmental problems of adolescents. *Child Development* (1994) 65,2:541–61.

44. McLoyd, V.C. The impact of economic hardship on black families and children: Psychological distress, parenting, and socioemotional development. *Child Development* (1990) 61,2:311–46.

45. Adler, N.E., Boyce, T., Chesney, M.A., et al. Socioeconomic inequalities in health: No easy solution. *Journal of the American Medical Association* (1993) 269:3140–45.

46. Liaw, F.R., and Brooks-Gunn, J. Cumulative familial risks and low birth weight children's cognitive and behavioral development. *Journal of Clinical Child Psychology* (1995) 23,4:360–72.

47. McLoyd, V.C., Jayaratne, T.E., Ceballo, R., and Borquez, J. Unemployment and work interruption among African American single mothers. Effects on parenting and adolescent socioemotional functioning. *Child Development* (1994) 65,2:562–89.

48. Brooks-Gunn, J., Klebanov, P.K., and Liaw, F. The learning, physical, and emotional environment of the home in the context of poverty: The Infant Health and Development Program. *Children and Youth Services Review* (1995)17,1/2.251–76.

49. Wilson, W.J. *The truly disadvantaged. The inner city, the underclass, and public policy.* Chicago: University of Chicago Press, 1987.

50. Sampson, R., and Morenoff, J. Ecological perspectives on the neighborhood context of urban poverty: Past and present. In *Neighborhood poverty: Conceptual, methodological, and policy approaches to studying neighborhoods.* Vol. 2. J. Brooks-Gunn, G. Duncan, and J.L. Aber, eds. New York: Russell Sage Foundation, in press.

51. Brooks-Gunn, J., Duncan, G.J., and Aber, J.L., eds. *Neighborhood poverty: Context and consequences for children.* Vol. 1. New York: Russell Sage Foundation, in press.

52. Klebanov, P.K., Brooks-Gunn, J., and Duncan, G.J. Does neighborhood and family poverty affect mother's parenting, mental health and social support? *Journal of Marriage and Family* (1994) 56,2:441–55.

53. Klebanov, P.K., Brooks-Gunn, J., Chase-Lansdale, L., and Gordon, R. The intersection of the neighborhood and home environment and its influence on young children. In *Neighborhood poverty: Context and consequences for children.* Vol. 1. J. Brooks-Gunn, G.J. Duncan, and J.L. Aber, eds. New York: Russell Sage Foundation, in press.

54. Evans, W.N., Oates, W.E., and Schwab, R.M. Measuring peer group effects: A study of teenage behavior. *Journal of Practical Economy* (1992) 100,5:966–91.

55. Mayer S.E. *What money can't buy: The effect of parental income on children's outcomes.* Cambridge, MA: Harvard University Press, 1997.

56. Kershwa, D., and Fair, J. *The New Jersey income maintenance experiment.* Vol. I. New York: Academic Press, 1976.

57. Salkind, N.J., and Haskins, R. Negative income tax: The impact on children from low-income families. *Journal of Family Issues* (1982) 3,2:165–80.

58. Baydar, N., Brooks-Gunn, J., and Furstenberg, E.F., Jr. Early warning signs of functional illiteracy: Predictors in childhood and adolescence. *Child Development* (1993) 64,3:815–29.

59. Alexander, K.L., and Entwisle, D.R. Achievement in the first 2 years of school: Patterns and processes. *Monographs of the Society for Research in Child Development* (1988) 53,2:1–153.

60. Sparling, J.J., and Lewis, J. *Partner for learning.* Lewisville, NC: Kaplan, 1984.

61. Olds, D.L., and Kitzman, H. Review of research on home visiting for pregnant women and parents of young children. *The Future of Children* (Winter 1993) 3,3:53–92.

62. Brooks-Gunn, J., Denner, J., and Klebanov, P.K. Families and neighborhoods as contexts for education. In *Changing populations, changing schools: Ninety-fourth yearbook of the National Society for the Study of Education, Part II.* E. Flaxman and A. H. Passow, eds. Chicago, IL: National Society for the Study of Education, 1995, pp. 233–52.

63. Brooks-Gunn, J. Strategies for altering the outcomes of poor children and their families. In *Escape from poverty: What makes a difference for children?* P.L. Chase-Lansdale and J. Brooks-Gunn, eds. New York: Cambridge University Press, 1996.

Jeanne Brooks-Gunn, *Ph.D., is Virginia and Leonard Marx professor of child development and education, and is director of the Center for Young Children and Families at Teachers College, Columbia University.*

Greg J. Duncan, *Ph.D., is a professor of education and social policy, and is a faculty associate at the Institute for Policy Research, Northwestern University.*

From *The Future of Children*, Summer/Fall 1997, pp. 55–71. © 1997 by the Center for the Future of Children of the David and Lucile Packard Foundation. Reprinted by permission. *The Future of Children* journals and executive summaries are available free of charge by faxing mailing information to: Circulation Department (650) 948-6498.

Effects of
*M*altreatment
and Ways To Promote Children's Resiliency

Barbara Lowenthal

Each year, about four million American children are exposed to traumatic events (Schwartz & Perry, 1994) such as physical, sexual, and emotional abuse; neglect; accidents; severe injuries; and natural disasters. Children may develop posttraumatic stress disorder as a result, leaving them vulnerable to phobias, conduct and behavioral difficulties, anxiety disorders, depression, and other neuropsychiatric disorders. This article will focus on the effects of maltreatment, including abuse and neglect, on young children. The author will discuss possible neurological, psychological, and cognitive consequences, as well as interventions that can promote resiliency in children. As concerned professionals, we need to advocate both for methods of preventing abuse and neglect, and for interventions that will assist maltreated children.

Neurological Effects of Abuse and Neglect

Recent research provides information about the neurology and development of the brain during the first years of life. At birth, the brain is the most immature organ in the human body; it will continue to develop as a result of both genetics and environmental experiences, which can have both positive or negative effects (Terr,

1991). Different areas of the brain are responsible for specific functions (Terr, 1991). The frontal lobe is responsible for abstract thought. Systems in the limbic area regulate affect, emotion, and the attachment process. Other systems in the brain stem regulate the heart rate, blood pressure, and states of arousal (Tauwer, 1989).

> As concerned professionals, we need to advocate both for methods of preventing abuse and neglect, and for interventions that will assist maltreated children.

The brain houses millions of nerve cells or neurons, which are connected to each other by synapses. These synapses, or

pathways, compose the "wiring" of the brain (Neuberger, 1997), and allow the various regions of the brain to communicate with each other. Brain development after birth consists of a continuous process of wiring the connections among neurons. While new synapses form, those that are not used will be "pruned." A child's brain will develop 1,000 trillion synapses during the first year of life. By age 10, however, the pruning process occurs more frequently than does the formation of new synapses (Nash, 1997). At that point, the child has about 500 trillion synapses, a figure that remains somewhat constant through adulthood.

A young child's neurodevelopment can be disrupted in two ways: through a lack of sensory experiences, which are necessary for the brain's optimal development (Stermer, 1997), and through abnormally active neurons, caused by such negative experiences as maltreatment and neglect (Perry, 1993). Negative environmental events can result in the malfunctioning of those regions of the brain responsible for the regulation of affect, empathy, and emotions. Continual abuse and neglect also can disrupt infants' attachment process with their caregivers, and, consequently, lead children to mistrust their environments (Nash, 1997).

Humans' so-called fight-or-flight response to stress, which prepares individuals to defend themselves against perceived dangers, may actually make the brain malfunction. Under the stress of the fight-or-flight response, the body exhibits a faster heart rate as well as increased production of a steroid hormone called cortisol. High levels of cortisol can kill brain cells and reduce the number of synapses. Studies of adults who experienced continuous abuse as children indicate that the prolonged stress of maltreatment results in a shrinkage of those regions of the brain responsible for memory, learning, and the regulation of affect and emotional expression (Neuberger, 1997). Other studies show that the brains of maltreated children can be 20 to 30 percent smaller than those of their nonmaltreated peers (Perry, 1993).

Maltreated youngsters' brains tend to be attuned to danger. At the slightest threat, these children will track anxiously any signs of further abusive attacks. Such early experiences of stress form templates in the brain in which the fear responses become fixed; thus, their brains become organized purely for survival. The resulting state of constant alert may help them avoid further maltreatment, but it also degrades their development. These youngsters are at great risk for emotional, behavior, learning, and physical difficulties (Herman, 1992; Terr, 1990). Other potential long-term effects include fewer opportunities for comfort, support, and nurturance.

Other ways that abused children cope with fears are "freezing" and dissociative responses. Because physical flight often is not possible for very young children, they freeze when they have no control over threatening events. The freezing response allows a child time to process and evaluate the stressor. Some caretakers, however, often interpret a freezing response as noncompliance to their instructions, which, if frustration arises, may open the door to further mistreatment. The brain's organization may be further altered if the additional maltreatment lasts long enough. Eventually, youngsters feel anxious and frustrated all the time, even when experiences are nonthreatening. As a result, children may be irritable, hypervigilant, hyperactive, or aggressive; they also might be prone to throwing tantrums and showing a regression in their development (James, 1994).

Dissociation, another common response to maltreatment, occurs when individuals separate their painful experience from conscious awareness. It protects maltreated children against the overwhelming emotions and thoughts connected to their traumatic experiences. When carried to an extreme, however, this response can result in amnesia and hallucinations (Herman, 1992; Terr, 1991). Children also may exhibit personality and self-identity disorders.

Psychological Effects of Abuse and Neglect

The psychological effects of abuse and neglect may include the disregulation of affect, the avoidance of intimacy, provocative behaviors, and disturbances in the attachment process.

> Studies of adults who experienced continuous abuse as children indicate that the prolonged stress of maltreatment results in a shrinkage of those regions of the brain responsible for memory, learning, and the regulation of affect and emotional expression.

Disregulation of Affect. Maltreated children often have difficulty in regulating affect and emotions. They may have intrusive and intensely emotional memories of their maltreatment, which they attempt to control by avoiding displays of their feelings. Sometimes, the only way to identify their emotions is through physiological responses, such as increased heart rates and perspiration. Although these children appear capable of describing other people's feelings, they cannot describe their own.

Avoidance of Intimacy. Survivors of child abuse and neglect tend to avoid intimate relationships, because they believe that getting close to someone else increases their vulnerability and lack of control (James, 1994). Intimacy, in fact, represents a threat, rather than nurturance and love. To avoid intimacy, children may withdraw, avoid eye contact, be hyperactive, or exhibit inappropriate behaviors.

Provocative Behaviors. If maltreated children are unable to find relief through numbing their feelings, they may instead act provocatively and aggressively. They may inflict harm on others, commit self-mutilation or even suicide, and otherwise behave in antisocial ways. Apparently, the underlying purpose behind these provocative and emotional acts is to produce the numbing responses that can lessen their extreme anxieties.

Disturbances in the Attachment Process. Attachment is the bond that young children form with their primary caregivers—usually, their parents (Hanson & Lynch, 1995). Early relationships help shape the development of the child's personality and social-emotional adjustment (Thurman & Widerstrom, 1990). The attachment process is important, as it affects the child's ability to cope with stress, regulate emotions, benefit from social supports, and form nurturing and loving relationships. Maltreated children's attachment processes are disrupted, however (Barnett, 1997). Usually, a caregiver and infant form close, secure emotional bonds, as evident by infants' demonstrably strong preferences for their primary caregivers, and by the enjoyment and comfort that they derive from that closeness. Parents show their attachment in their desire to nurture, comfort, and protect their babies, and by acting uneasy and sad when separated. Because the attachment process promotes a sense of security, trust, and self-esteem, it also furthers the infants' desire to explore and learn from their environments. While secure attachments help children in all areas of development, they are essential in establishing self-identity and self-worth (Moroz, 1993).

Abuse and neglect can impede the attachment process and diminish children's feelings of security and trust in their caregivers. Maltreated children may feel unworthy or unloved, and they may view the world as a dangerous place. When caregivers are neglectful, uncaring, or abusive, children become more vulnerable to stressors, and will have difficulty forming intimate and positive relationships. The children often become angry and resentful toward their caregivers, a feeling that may transfer to other relationships in their lives (Zeanah, 1993).

Effects on Cognition and Learning. Child abuse may adversely affect children's ability to learn. On average, abused, maltreated, or neglected children score lower on cognitive measures and demonstrate poorer school achievement compared to their non-abused peers of similar socioeconomic backgrounds (Barnett, 1997; Vondra, Barnett, & Cicchetti, 1990). Children with uncaring parents or caregivers will learn to view themselves as unworthy, unlovable, and incompetent in school-related and cognitive tasks. Abuse often leads to a loss of self-esteem and a lack of motivation to achieve at school.

Even at a very early age, maltreated children have difficulty adapting to their child care and preschool environments. Abused toddlers respond more negatively, in contrast with non-abused peers, to their mirror images, and they make fewer positive statements about themselves (Vondra, Allen, & Cicchetti, 1990). A study by Erickson, Stroufe, and Pianta (1989) found that physically abused preschoolers were more angry and noncompliant, compared to their non-abused classmates of similar socioeconomic backgrounds. The maltreated children also were more impulsive and disorganized, and were less successful on pre-academic tasks. They lacked the necessary social and work skills for age-appropriate adjustment in their preschool and kindergarten classes. Almost half of the physically abused youngsters were referred for special education or retention by the end of their kindergarten year. Similarly, emotionally abused young children displayed more disruptive, noncompliant behavior and a lack of persistence in their schoolwork, compared to their non-abused peers.

The behavior of the sexually abused children studied by Erickson, Stroufe, and Pianta (1989) was characterized by extreme anxiety, inattentiveness, and difficulty in following directions. Their social behaviors ranged from withdrawal to extreme aggression; consequently, they often were rejected by their classmates. These children commonly depended much more than their peers did on adults, appearing to have a strong need for their teachers' affection and approval. Their dependent behaviors seemed to reflect their roles as victims at home.

Neglected children, compared to children suffering from other forms of abuse, appeared to have the most severe problems, based on a number of investigations (Eckenrode, Laird, & Doris, 1993; Mash & Wolfe, 1991). They were the least successful on cognitive tasks in kindergarten; they were more anxious, inattentive, apathetic; and they had more difficulty concentrating on pre-academic work. Socially, they exhibited inappropriate behaviors and were not accepted by their peers. These youngsters rarely displayed positive affect, humor, or joy. A majority of these neglected children were retained or referred for special education (because of possible learning disabilities and/or social-emotional difficulties) at the end of kindergarten. The lack of stimulation at home might have been an important factor contributing to their poor performances. A lack of opportunities to learn social and pre-academic skills becomes obvious at school.

> On average, abused, maltreated, or neglected children score lower on cognitive measures and demonstrate poorer school achievement compared to their non-abused peers of similar socioeconomic backgrounds.

All types of maltreated children, as they get older, demonstrate more cognitive deficits and are considered more at-risk for school failure and to drop out than their non-maltreated peers (Kurtz, Gaudin, Wodarski, & Howing, 1993; Reyome, 1993). Teachers rated the abused children as being more overactive, inattentive, and impulsive than their non-abused classmates. They appeared less motivated to achieve at school and had difficulty learning. All types of maltreated children behave similarly, because forms of abuse often overlap. In other words, children may suffer from more than one type of abuse, such as a combination of emotional, sexual, and physical maltreatment.

Two studies compared the characteristics of physically abused, sexually abused, and neglected school-age children (Eckenrode, Laird, & Doris, 1993; Kurtz, Gaudin, Wodarski, & Howing, 1993). The physically abused students had significant school problems. Their performance was poor in all academic subjects, especially so in mathematics and language skills. They appeared to be underachievers and were more likely to be retained than their non-maltreated classmates. As adolescents, they were more likely to drop out of school. Both teachers and parents reported that these children had significantly more behavioral problems than their non-abused peers.

Neglect was associated with the poorest academic achievement among the groups of maltreated students. Teachers reported that these pupils were performing below grade level, and that their rate of school absenteeism was nearly five times that of the comparison group of non-neglected students. Neglect appears to have a greater long-term impact on academic performance than other forms of abuse. The neglected children's adaptive functioning ability, however, was within normal limits. Perhaps these children learned the survival skills out of necessity, because of the lack of care in their homes. Sexually abused children, on the other hand, were similar to nonabused youngsters in terms of academic achievement and in the number of discipline problems. They did not differ significantly in any area of academic performance. Although sexual abuse has negative social-emotional consequences, its effects on academic achievement were not evident in these studies. No matter what type of abuse, however, school personnel must intervene—to help prevent further maltreatment, and to assist these children with their learning problems.

Interventions To Prevent Maltreatment and Promote Resiliency

Abused and neglected children are at high risk for psychological, neurological, and cognitive impairments. Children already may have developed problems by the time they are identified as being maltreated. Consequently, we need to pay greater attention to measures that promote resiliency, including home visits, and to the presence of alternate caregivers, social support interventions, and therapeutic programs.

Availability of Alternate Caregivers. Alternate caregivers must step in when children have been abused by their parents or other primary caregivers. These caregivers may be grandparents, other relatives, foster or adoptive parents, and teachers. Alternate caregivers can provide abused or neglected children with the safety, dedication, and nurturance they need to recover from their traumas.

Therapeutic caregiving can help prevent either the fight-or-flight response or dissociation from becoming "fixed" in children's brains. Thus, children can develop a sense of trust, and remain open to positive learning and emotional experiences. Therapeutic caregiving requires, among other attributes, the ability to acknowledge the child's pain; the ability to recognize that some anti-social behaviors are reflections of painful experiences; an understanding of the child's need to process and integrate these experiences; a willingness to be a part of a treatment team; and a strong belief that caregivers' actions will help the youngster, even if the benefits are not immediately apparent. Caregivers must help these children develop positive self-images (Moroz, 1993). Children need warmth, nurturance, empathy, stability, and a sense of belonging in order to promote their resiliency.

Social Support Interventions. Social support can "include the emotional, physical, informational, instrumental and material aid provided by others to maintain health and well-being, promote adoptions of life events and foster development in an adaptive manner" (Dunst, Trivette, & Deal, 1988, p. 28). Informal support may be provided by family members, friends, and neighbors, as well as by religious organizations and peer support groups. Formal support systems include home visiting programs, parenting classes, and mental health services.

Informal Support Systems. Some of the parents or primary caregivers who abuse their children have suffered from their own maltreatment as children. Poverty and unemployment may increase the likelihood of abuse. Informal support from families, friends, and community members, in the form of providing child care, respite care, counsel during a job search, transportation, or financial aid, for example, can greatly help. Taking advantage of such informal support can help dysfunctional families to end the cycle of abuse and to function more positively (Barnett,

> All types of maltreated children, as they get older, demonstrate more cognitive deficits and are considered more at-risk for school failure and to drop out than their non-maltreated peers.

Formal Support Systems. Formal community support systems, such as family therapy, are available (Daro, 1993; Manly, Cicchetti, & Barnett, 1994). Such services may supply basic needs, such as food, clothing, and shelter. The programs that teach basic parenting skills are particularly helpful. Such programs also help reduce family stress and pathology (Barnett, Manley, & Cicchetti, 1993).

Intervention Programs for Child Victims. Intervention services, including child care and preschool classes that specialize in the treatment of neglected and abused young children, are increasingly available. Many challenges must be overcome when assisting maltreated children, who may have a combination of language, cognitive, and social-emotional delays (Barnett, 1997). A National Clinical Evaluation study examined the outcomes of 19 separate projects (Daro, 1993) that trained teachers to use therapeutic techniques with maltreated young children, ages 18 months to 8 years. About 70 percent of the abused children demonstrated improvements in their adaptive, cognitive, and social-emotional skills.

Culp, Little, Lefts, & Lawrence (1991) described therapeutic projects that provided services such as play therapy, speech and language therapy, occupational and physical therapies, and home visits. The curriculum was designed to foster children's positive relationships with adults and peers, to increase their abilities to regulate emotions, and to improve self-esteem. Court-mandated services for the

maltreating parents consisted of comprehensive group and individual therapy, and home visits by professionals. Positive outcomes were documented for both the maltreated children and their parents. The results of these studies indicate that abused children and their caretakers require individualized treatments for special problems. The duration of treatment also had an effect on the outcomes. Maltreating parents who were in therapy for 18 months made more improvements in their interactions with the children than did parents who were in treatment for shorter periods of time (Culp, Little, Letts, & Lawrence, 1991). Home visits appeared to help parents manage their stress levels, which, in turn, helped to head off further maltreatment. Other preventive measures consisted of mental health services, which enabled some parents to relieve emotional problems.

Conclusion

Abuse and neglect have many possible negative neurological, psychological, and cognitive effects on young children. More research on childhood traumas and on therapeutic techniques that assist the child victims is needed, and should be advocated by concerned professionals, families, and citizens.

References

Barnett, D. (1997). The effects of early intervention on maltreating parents and their children. In M. J. Guralnick (Ed.), *The effectiveness of early intervention* (pp. 147–170). Baltimore: Brookes.

Barnett, D., Manley, J. T., & Cicchetti, D. (1993). Defining child maltreatment: The interface between policy and research. In D. Cicchetti & S. Toth (Eds.), *Child abuse, child development, and social policy* (pp. 7–73). Norwood, NJ: Ablex.

Barnett, D., Vondra, J. I., & Shonk, S. (1996). Relations among self perceptions, motivation, and school functioning of low income maltreated and non-maltreated children. *Child Abuse and Neglect, 20,* 397–410.

Culp, R. E., Little, V., Letts, D., & Lawrence, H. (1991). Maltreated children's self-concept. Effects of a comprehensive treatment program. *American Journal of Orthopsychiatry, 61,* 114–121.

Daro, D. (1993). Child maltreatment research: Implications for program design. In D. Cicchetti & S. Toth (Eds.),

Child abuse, child development, and social policy (pp. 331–367). Norwood, NJ: Ablex.

Dunst, C., Trivette, C., & Deal, A. (1988). *Enabling and empowering families.* Cambridge, MA: Brookline Books.

Eckenrode, J., Laird, M., & Doris, J. (1993). School performance and disciplinary problems among abused and neglected children. *Developmental Psychology, 29,* 53–62.

Erickson, M. F., Stroufe, L. A., & Pianta, R. (1989). The effects of maltreatment on the development of young children. In D. Cicchetti & V. Carlson (Eds.), *Child maltreatment: Theory and research on the causes and consequences of child abuse and neglect* (pp. 647–684). New York: Cambridge University Press.

Hanson, M. J., & Lynch, E. W. (1995). *Early intervention: Implementing child and family services for infants and toddlers who are at-risk or disabled.* Austin, TX: Pro-Ed.

Herman, J. (1992). *Trauma and recovery.* New York: Basic Books.

James, B. (1994). *Handbook for treatment of attachment-trauma problems in children.* New York: Lexington Books.

Kurtz, P.D., Gaudin, J. M., Wodarski, J. S., & Howing, P. T. (1993). Maltreatment and the school-aged child: School performance consequences. *Child Abuse and Neglect, 17,* 581–589.

Mash, E. J., & Wolfe, D. A. (1991). Methodological issues in research in child abuse. *Criminal Justice and Behavior, 18,* 8–29.

Moroz, K. J. (1993). *Supporting adoptive families with special needs children—A handbook for mental health professionals.* Waterbury, VT: The Vermont Adoptions Project, U.S. Department of Health and Human Services Grant #90–CO–0484.

Nash, J. J. (1997, February 3). Fertile minds. *Time,* 48–56.

Neuberger, J. J. (1997). Brain development research: Wonderful window of opportunity to build public support for early childhood education. *Young Children, 52,* 4–9.

Perry, B. D. (1993). Medicine and psychotherapy: Neurodevelopment and neurophysiology of trauma. *The Advisor, 6,* 13–20.

Reyome, N. D. (1993). A comparison of the school performance of sexually abused, neglected, and non-maltreated children. *Child Study Journal, 23,* 17–38.

Schwartz, E. D., & Perry, B. D. (1994). The post-traumatic response in children and adolescents. *Psychiatric Clinics of North America, 17,* 311–326.

Stermer, J. (1997, July 31). Home visits give kids a chance. *Chicago Tribune, 16.*

Tauwer, C. L. (1989). Critical periods of brain development. *Infants and Young Children, 1,* VII–VIII.

Terr, L. (1990). *Too scared to cry: Psychic trauma in childhood.* New York: Harper and Row.

Terr, L. C. (1991). Childhood traumas: An outline and overview. *American Journal of Psychiatry, 148,* 10–20.

Thurman, S. K., & Widerstrom, A. H. (1990). *Infants and young children with special needs.* Baltimore: Brookes.

Vondra, J. I., Barnett, D., & Cicchetti, D. (1990). Self concept, motivation, and competence among preschoolers from maltreating and comparison families. *Child Abuse and Neglect, 14,* 525–540.

Zeanah, C. H., Jr. (1993). *Handbook of infant mental health.* New York: Guilford Press.

Barbara Lowenthal is Professor, Department of Special Education, Northeastern Illinois University, Chicago, Illinois.

From *Childhood Education*, Summer 1999, pp. 204-209. © 1999 by the Association for Childhood Education International, 17904 Georgia Avenue, Suite 215, Olney, MD 20832. Reprinted by permission.

The Early Origins of Autism

New research into the causes of this baffling disorder is focusing on genes that control the development of the brain

by Patricia M. Rodier

Autism has been mystifying scientists for more than half a century. The complex behavioral disorder encompasses a wide variety of symptoms, most of which usually appear before a child turns three. Children with autism are unable to interpret the emotional states of others, failing to recognize anger, sorrow or manipulative intent. Their language skills are often limited, and they find it difficult to initiate or sustain conversations. They also frequently exhibit an intense preoccupation with a single subject, activity or gesture.

These behaviors can be incredibly debilitating. How can you be included in a typical classroom if you can't be dissuaded from banging your head on your desk? How can you make friends if your overriding interest is in calendars? When children with autism also suffer from mental retardation—as most of them do—the prognosis is even worse. Intensive behavioral therapy improves the outcome for many patients, but their symptoms can make it impossible for them to live independently, even if they have normal IQs.

I became involved in the search for autism's causes relatively recently—and almost by accident. As an embryologist, I previously focused on various birth defects of the brain. In 1994 I attended a remarkable presentation at a scientific conference on research into birth defects. Two pediatric ophthalmologists, Marilyn T. Miller of the University of Illinois at Chicago and Kerstin Strömland of Goteborg University in Sweden, described a surprising outcome from a study investigating eye motility prob-

lems in victims of thalidomide, the morning-sickness drug that caused an epidemic of birth defects in the 1960s. The study's subjects were adults who had been exposed to the drug while still in the womb. After examining these people, Miller and Strömland made an observation that had somehow eluded previous researchers: about five percent of the thalidomide victims had autism, which is about 30 times higher than the rate among the general population.

When I heard these results, I felt a shock of recognition, a feeling so powerful that I actually became dizzy and began to hyperventilate. In the effort to identify autism's causes, researchers had long sought to pinpoint exactly when the disorder begins. Previous speculation had focused on late gestation or early postnatal life as the time of origin, but there was no evidence to back up either hypothesis. The connection with thalidomide suddenly threw a brilliant new light on the subject. It suggested that autism originates in the early weeks of pregnancy, when the embryo's brain and the rest of its nervous system are just beginning to develop. Indeed, Miller and Strömland's work convinced me that the mystery of autism could soon be solved.

Genetic Factors

At least 16 of every 10,000 babies are born with autism or one of its related disorders [*see "The Spectrum of Autism Disorders"*]. Since autism was first identified in 1943, scientists have made great strides in describing its symptoms. The biologi-

cal basis for autism, however, has been elusive - an unfortunate circumstance, because such an understanding could enable researchers to identify the leading risk factors for autism and possibly to design new treatments for the condition.

At least 16 of every 10,000 babies are born with autism or one of its related disorders

By examining the inheritance of the disorder, researchers have shown that autism runs in families, though not in a clear-cut way. Siblings of people with autism have a 3 to 8 percent chance of being diagnosed with the same disorder. This is much greater than the 0.16 percent risk in the general population but much less than the 50 percent chance that would characterize a genetic disease caused by a single dominant mutation (in which one faulty gene inherited from one parent is sufficient to cause the disorder) or the 25 percent chance that would characterize a single recessive mutation (in which a copy of the faulty gene must be inherited from each parent). The results fit best with models in which variants of several genes contribute to the outcome. To complicate matters further, relatives of people with autism may fail to meet all the criteria for the disorder but still have some of its symptoms. Although these relatives may have some of the gene variants linked to autism—whatever they may be—for some reason the

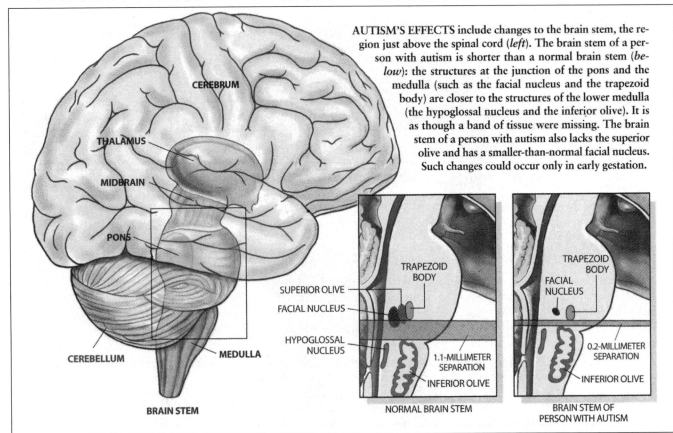

AUTISM'S EFFECTS include changes to the brain stem, the region just above the spinal cord (*left*). The brain stem of a person with autism is shorter than a normal brain stem (*below*): the structures at the junction of the pons and the medulla (such as the facial nucleus and the trapezoid body) are closer to the structures of the lower medulla (the hypoglossal nucleus and the inferior olive). It is as though a band of tissue were missing. The brain stem of a person with autism also lacks the superior olive and has a smaller-than-normal facial nucleus. Such changes could occur only in early gestation.

TERESE WINSLOW

genetic factors are not fully expressed in these individuals.

Studies of twins in the U.K. confirm that autism has a heritable component but suggest that environmental influences play a role as well. For example, if genetic factors alone were involved, monozygotic (identical) twins, who share the same genes, should have a 100 percent chance of sharing the same diagnosis. Instead, when one twin has autism, the second twin has only a 60 percent chance of being diagnosed with the same disorder. That twin also has an 86 percent chance of having some of autism's symptoms. These figures indicate that other factors must modify the genetic predisposition to the disorder.

The Embryology of Autism

Several environmental risk factors are already known. In utero exposure to rubella (German measles) or to birth defect-causing substances such as ethanol and valproic acid increases the chances that autism will develop. People with certain genetic diseases, such as phenylketonuria and tuberous sclerosis,

also have a greater chance of developing autism. None of these factors, however, is present frequently enough to be responsible for many cases. Furthermore, most exposures to diseases or hazardous substances would be likely to affect both members of a pair of twins rather than just one. Some of the environmental influences must be more subtle than those identified so far. Researchers do not know how the multiple factors combine to make some people display symptoms while allowing others to escape them. This variation makes the search for autism's causes especially difficult.

In their 1994 study Miller and Strömland added another environmental contributor to autism: thalidomide exposure in utero. All their subjects—Swedish adults born in the late 1950s and early 1960s– exhibited some of the malformations for which thalidomide is infamous: stunted arms and legs, misshapen or missing ears and thumbs, and neurological dysfunctions of the eye and facial muscles. Because scientists know which organs of the embryo are developing at each stage of pregnancy, they can pin-

point the exact days when a malformation can be induced: the thumb is affected as early as day 22 after conception, the ears from days 20 to 33, and the arms and legs from days 25 to 35. What made the new study so exciting for me was Miller and Strömland's discovery that most of the thalidomide victims with autism had anomalies in the external part of their ears but no malformations of the arms or legs. This pattern indicated that the subjects had been injured very early in gestation—20 to 24 days after conception—before many women even know they are pregnant.

For embryologists, nothing tells us so much about *what* happened to an embryo as knowing *when* it happened. In the case of thalidomide-induced autism, the critical period is much earlier than many investigators would have guessed. Very few neurons form as early as the fourth week of gestation, and most are motor neurons of the cranial nerves, the ones that operate the muscles of the eyes, ears, face, jaw, throat and tongue. The cell bodies of these neurons are located in the brain stem, the region between the spinal

Thalidomide Timeline

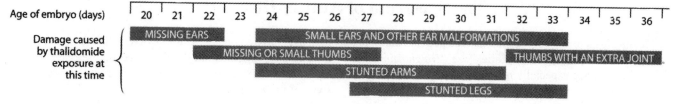

BIRTH DEFECTS caused by thalidomide vary depending on when the mother was exposed to the drug.

cord and the rest of the brain. Because these motor neurons develop at the same time as the external ears, one might predict that the thalidomide victims with autism would also suffer from dysfunctions of the cranial nerves. Miller and Strömland confirmed this prediction—they found that all the subjects with autism had abnormalities of eye movement or facial expression, or both.

The next logical question was, "Are the cases of autism after thalidomide exposure similar to cases of unknown cause, or are they different?" Aside from their behavioral symptoms, people with autism have often been described not only as normal in appearance but as unusually attractive. They are certainly normal in stature, with normal-to-large heads. The few studies that have tested nonbehavioral features of people with autism, however, have concluded that there are indeed minor physical and neurological anomalies in many cases, and they are the same ones noted in thalidomide-induced autism. For example, minor malformations of the external ears—notably posterior rotation, in which the top of the ear is tilted backward more than 15 degrees–are more common in children with autism than in typically developing children, children with mental retardation or siblings of children with autism. Dysfunctions of eye movement had been associated with autism before the thalidomide study, and lack of facial expression is one of the behaviors used to diagnose the condition.

The Neurobiology of Autism

Is it possible that all the symptoms of autism arise from changes in the function of the cranial nerves? Probably not. It is more likely that the nerve dysfunctions in people with autism reflect an early brain in-

jury that not only affects the cranial nerves but also has secondary effects on later brain development. That is, the injury to the brain stem might somehow interfere with the proper development or wiring of other brain regions, including those involved in higher-level functions such as speech, resulting in the behavioral symptoms of autism. Or perhaps the ear malformations and cranial nerve dysfunctions are only side effects of an injury that we don't understand. Whatever the true situation may be, the anomalies in patients with autism of unknown cause were much the same as the anomalies in the thalidomide victims with autism. The conclusion was clear: many cases of autism, if not all, are initiated very early in gestation.

The region of the brain implicated by the thalidomide study—the brain stem—is one that has rarely been considered in studies of autism or in studies of other kinds of congenital brain damage, for that matter. On a simplistic level, neurobiologists associate the brain stem with the most basic functions: breathing, eating, balance, motor coordination and so forth. Many of the behaviors disturbed in autism, such as language, planning and interpretation of social cues, are believed to be controlled by higher-level regions of the brain, such as the cerebral cortex and the hippocampus in the forebrain.

Yet some symptoms common in autism—lack of facial expression, hypersensitivity to touch and sound, and sleep disturbances—do sound like ones more likely to originate in the brain regions associated with basic functions. Furthermore, the most consistently observed abnormality in the brains of people with autism is not a change in the forebrain but a reduction in the number of neurons in the cerebellum, a large processing center of the hindbrain that has long been known to have critical functions in the control of muscle movement.

One reason for scientists' confusion about the brain regions involved in autism may be that our assumptions about where functions are controlled are shaky. For example, the laboratory group led by Eric Courchesne of the University of California at San Diego has shown that parts of the cerebellum are activated during certain tasks requiring high-level cognitive processing. Another difficulty is that the symptoms of autism are so complex. If simpler behavioral abnormalities could be shown to be diagnostic of the disorder, researchers might have a better chance of identifying their source in the nervous system [see "A Simpler Symptom of Autism"].

Many cases of autism, if not all, are initiated very early in gestation.

In 1995 our research team had the opportunity to follow up on the thalidomide study by examining the brain stem of a person with autism. The tissue samples came from the autopsy of a young woman who had suffered from autism of unknown cause; she had died in the 1970s, but fortunately the samples of her brain tissue had been preserved. When we examined the woman's brain stem, we were struck by the near absence of two structures: the facial nucleus, which controls the muscles of facial expression, and the superior olive, which is a relay station for auditory information. Both structures arise from the same segment of the embryo's neural tube, the organ that develops into the central nervous system. Counts of the facial neurons in the woman's brain showed only about 400 cells, whereas counts of facial neurons in a control brain showed 9,000.

Overall, the woman's brain was normal in size; in fact, it was slightly heavier than the average brain. I hypothesized

The Spectrum of Autism Disorders

Adiagnosis of autism requires that the patient exhibit abnormal behaviors in three categories [see "Diagnostic Categories"] and have especially notable deficits in the category of social interaction. In addition, clinicians have identified several related disorders that share some of the behavioral features of autism but have different emphases or additional symptoms. For example, Pervasive Development Disorder, Not Otherwise Specified (PDD-NOS) denotes patients who miss fulfilling the autism creiteria in one of the three categories. As is true of autism, PDD-NOS includes patients with the whole range of IQs. Asperger syndrome is used to describe patients with normal IQs and no evidence of language delay. Two much rarer diagnoses are Childhood Disintegrative Disorder, in which normal early development is followed by regression to severe disability, and Rett syndrome, a progressive neurological disorder that occurs only in females.

Although many scientists have long known that autism is an inherited disease, recently family studies by Peter Szatmari's group at McMaster University in Ontario suggest that it is the spectrum of symptoms that runs in families, rather than a single diagnosis. For example, a child with autism may have a brother with asperger syndrome, or a woman with autism may have a nephew with PDD-NOS. These family studies strongly suggest that at least three of the diagnoses—autism, PDD-NOS, and Asperger sundrome—arise from some of the same inherited factors. —P.M.R.

Diagnostic Categories

Impairment of Social Interaction: Failure to use eye contact, facial expression or gestures to regulate social interaction; failure to seek comfort; failure to develop relationships with peers.

Impairment of Communication: Failure to use spoken language, without compensating by gesture; deficit in initiating or sustaining a converstation, despite adequate speech; aberrant language (for example, repeating a question instead of replying).

Restricted and Repetitive Interests and Behaviors: Abnormally intense preoccupation with one subject or activity; distress over change; insistence on routines or rituals with no purpose; repetitive movements, such as hand flapping.

that the brain stem was lacking only the specific neurons already identified—those in the facial nucleus and the superior olive—and to test that idea I decided to measure the distances between a number of neuroanatomical landmarks. I was surprised to discover that my hypothesis was absolutely wrong. Although the side-to-side measures were indeed normal, the front-to-back measures were astonishingly reduced in the brain stem of the woman with autism. It was as though a band of tissue had been cut out of the brain stem, and the two remaining pieces had been knit back together with no seam where the tissue was missing.

For the second time in my life, I felt a powerful shock of recognition. I heard a roaring in my ears, my vision dimmed, and I felt as though my head might explode. The shock was not generated by the unexpected result but by the realization that! had seen this pattern of shortening before, in a paper that showed pictures of abnormal mouse brains. When I retrieved the article from the stacks of papers on my office floor, I found that the correspondence between the brain I had been studying and the mouse brains described in the article was even more striking than I had remembered. Both cases exhibited shortening of the brain stem, a smaller-than-normal facial nucleus and the absence of a superior olive. Additional features of the mice were clearly related to other anomalies associated with autism: they had ear malformations and lacked one of the brain structures controlling eye movement.

What had altered the brains of these mice? It was not exposure to thalidomide or any of the other environmental factors associated with autism but the elimination of the function of a gene. These were transgenic "knockout" mice, engineered to lack the expression of the gene known as *Hoxa1* so that researchers could study the gene's role in early development. The obvious question was, "Could this be one of the genes involved in autism?"

The literature supported the idea that *Hoxa1* was an excellent candidate for autism research. The studies of knockout mice showed that *Hoxa1* plays a central role in development of the brain stem. Groups in Salt Lake City and London had studied different knockout strains with similar results. They found that the gene is active in the brain stem when the first neurons are forming—the same period that Miller and Strömland had identified as the time when thalidomide caused autism. *Hoxa1* produces a type of protein called a transcription factor, which modulates the activity of other genes. What is more, *Hoxa1* is not active in any tissue after early embryogenesis. If a gene is active throughout life, as many are, altered function of that gene usually leads to problems that increase with age. A gene active only during development is a better candidate to explain a congenital disability like autism, which seems to be stable after childhood.

Hoxa1 is what geneticists call a "highly conserved" gene, meaning that the sequence of nucleotides that make up its DNA has changed little over the course of evolution. We assume that this is a characteristic of genes that are critical to survival: they suffer mutations as other genes do, but most changes are likely to be fatal, so they are rarely passed on to subsequent genera-

A Simpler Symptom of Autism

Scientists at York University and the Hospital for Sick Children in Toronto have recently identified an autism-related behavior that is much simpler than the array of behaviors that have traditionally been used to diagnose the condition. Susan Bryson and her doctoral student Reginald Landry have found that children with autism respond abnormally to a task involving their reactions to visual stimuli. Because this mental activity is probably mediated by a primitive part of the brain—most likely the brain stem or the cerebellum, or both—the discovery has important implications for the neurobiology of autism. Bryson and Landry's work could also help clinicians develop a simpler way to test children for the disorder.

In their study Bryson and Landry observed the reactions of two groups of children, those with autism and those without it, as they watched lights flashing on video screens [*see illustration*]. The children ranged in age from four to seven. In the first test, each child was placed in front of a three-screen panel, and a flashing light appeared on the middle screen. This stimulus prompted the children to focus their eyes on the flashes (a). Then the middle screen went blank, and a flashing light ap-

peared on the far-right or the far-left screen of the panel. Both groups of children shifted their eyes to that screen (b). In the second test, however, the lights on the middle screen kept flashing while the lights appeared on the other screen. The children without autism shifted focus on the new stimulus (c), but the children with autism remained "stuck" on the first stimulus and failed to turn their eyes to the new one (d). The two tests were repeated many times for each child.

Bryson and Landry found that children with other kinds of brain damage are perfectly normal in their ability to disengage from one stimulus and focus on another. Children with autism, however, repeatedly fail to disengage from the first stimulus, even if they are highly intelligent. Researchers suspect that this ability is a low-level brain function because it typically appears in infants—as early as three to four months after birth—and in children with low IQs. Animals also orient themselves toward new stimuli, so scientists could conceivably use a similar test in animal studies to verify whether genetic manipulations or toxicologic exposures have produced this symptom of autism.   —*P.M.R.*

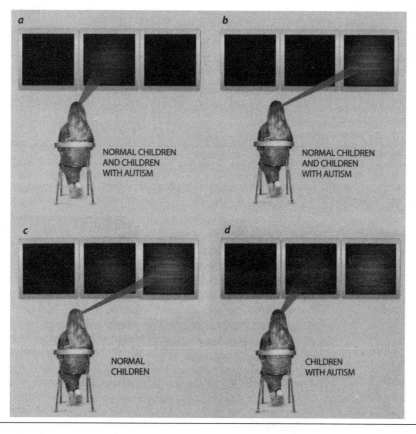

tions. Although many other genes appear in several forms—for example, the genes that encode eye color or blood type—highly conserved genes are not commonly found in multiple versions (also known as polymorphic alleles, or allelic variants). The fact that no one had ever discovered a

variant of *Hoxa1* in any mammalian species suggested that my colleagues and I might have trouble finding one in cases of autism. On the other hand, it seemed likely that if a variant allele could be found, it might well be one of the triggers for the development of the disorder.

Zeroing in on *HOXA1*

The human version of the gene, labeled as *HOXA1*, resides on chromosome 7 and is relatively small. It contains just two protein-coding regions, or exons, along with regions that regulate the level of protein production or do nothing at all. Deviations from the normal sequence in any part of a gene can affect its performance, but the vast majority of disease-causing variations are in the protein-coding regions. Thus, we began the search for variant alleles by focusing on the exons of HOXA1. Using blood samples from people with autism and from subjects in a control group, we extracted the DNA and looked for deviations from the normal sequence of nucleotides.

The good news is that we have identified two variant alleles of HOXA1. One has a minor deviation in the sequence of one of the gene's exons, meaning that the protein encoded by the variant gene is slightly different from the protein encoded by the normal gene. We have studied this newly discovered allele in detail, measuring its prevalence among various groups of people to determine if it plays a role in causing autism. (The other variant allele is more difficult to investigate because it involves a change in the physical structure of the gene's DNA.) We found that the rate of the variant allele among people with autism was significantly higher than the rate among their family members who do not have the disorder and the rate among unrelated individuals without the disorder. The differences were much greater than would be expected by chance.

The bad news is that, just as the family studies had predicted, HOXA1 is only one of many genes involved in the spectrum of autism disorders. Furthermore, the allele that we have studied in detail is variably expressed—its presence does not guarantee that autism will arise. Preliminary data indicate that the variant allele occurs in about 20 percent of the people who do not have autism and in about 40 percent of those who do. The allele approximately doubles the risk of developing the condition. But in about 60 percent of people with autism, the allele is not present, meaning that other genetic factors must be contributing to the disorder.

To pin down those factors, we must continue searching for other variants in HOXA1, because most genetic disorders result from many different deviant alle-

les of the same gene. Variations in other genes involved in early development may also predispose their carriers to autism. We have already discovered a variant allele of HOXB1, a gene on chromosome 17 that is derived from the same ancestral source as HOXA1 and has similar functions in the development of the brain stem, but its effect in autism appears to be minor. Other investigators are scrutinizing candidate regions on chromosome 15 and on another part of chromosome 7. Although researchers are focusing on alleles that increase the risk of autism, other alleles may decrease the risk. These could help explain the variable expression of the spectrum of autism-related disorders.

Even a minimal understanding of the genetic basis of autism would be of great value. For example, researchers could transfer the alleles associated with autism from humans to mice, engineering them to be genetically susceptible to the disorder. By exposing these mice to substances suspected of increasing the risk of autism, we would be able to study the interaction of environmental factors with genetic background and perhaps compile an expanded list of substances that women need to avoid during early pregnancy. What is more, by examining the development of these genetically engineered mice, we could learn more about the brain damage that underlies autism. If researchers can determine exactly what is wrong with the brains of people with autism, they may be able to suggest drug therapies or other treatments that could ameliorate the effects of the damage.

Devising a genetic test for autism—similar to the current tests for cystic fibrosis, sickle cell anemia and other diseases—would be a much more difficult task. Because so many genes appear to be involved in the disorder, one cannot accurately predict the odds of having a child with autism by simply testing for one or two variant alleles in the parents. Tests might be developed, however, for the siblings of people with autism, who often fear that their own children will inherit the disorder. Clinicians could look for a set of

well-established genetic risk factors in both the family member with autism and the unaffected sibling. If the person with autism has several high-risk alleles, whereas the sibling does not, the sibling would at least be reassured that his or her offspring would not be subject to the known risks within his or her family.

Nothing will make the search for autism's causes simple. But every risk factor that we are able to identify takes away some of the mystery. More important, new data spawn new hypotheses. Just as the thalidomide results drew attention to the brain stem and to the HOXA1 gene, new data from developmental genetics, behavioral studies, brain imaging and many other sources can be expected to produce more welcome shocks of recognition for investigators of autism. In time, their work may help alleviate the terrible suffering caused by the disorder.

Further Information

AUTISM IN THALIDOMIDE EMBRYOPATHY: A POPULATION STUDY. K. Strömland, V. Nordin, M. Miller, B. Åkerström and C. Gillberg in *Developmental Medicine and Child Neurology*, Vol. 36, No. 4, pages 351–356; April 1994.

EMBRYOLOGICAL ORIGIN FOR AUTISM: DEVELOPMENTAL ANOMALIES OF THE CRANIAL NERVE MOTOR NUCLEI. P. M. Rodier, J. L. Ingram, B. Tisdale, S. Nelson and J. Romano in *Journal of Comparative Neurology*, Vol. 370, No. 2, pages 247–261; June 24, 1996.

THINKING IN PICTURES: AND OTHER REPORTS FROM MY LIFE WITH AUTISM. Temple Grandin. Vintage Books, 1996.

More information on autism is available at the Web page of the National Alliance for Autism Research at www.naar.org

PATRICIA M. RODIER is professor of obstetrics and gynecology at the University of Rochester. She has studied injuries to the developing nervous system since she was a postdoctoral fellow in embryology at the University of Virginia, but she began to investigate autism only after hearing the results of the thalidomide study. Rodier has assembled a group of scientists from many disciplines at six institutions to study the genetic and environmental causes of the disorder and says that working with experts from other fields is rejuvenating.

Dyslexia

AND THE NEW SCIENCE OF READING

Millions of otherwise bright children struggle with words, but recent brain research shows there's hope—if parents and teachers know what to look for

BY BARBARA KANTROWITZ AND ANNE UNDERWOOD

The first thing Kathryn Nicholas will tell you about her 11-year-old son Jason is that he's a bright, curious kid who can build elaborate machines out of Legos and remember the code names and payloads of bombers. "He has a phenomenal desire to see how things work," she says proudly. But reading, for Jason, was a train wreck. In first grade he was assigned to special-education classes with three mildly retarded children. Two years later, despite extra help, he still couldn't decipher a sentence, and his mother was worried that he would soon become so discouraged that he would give up trying. Then she heard about Virginia Wise Berninger, an educational psychologist at the University of Washington who studies dyslexia, a disorder that makes learning to read extremely difficult. As part of her ongoing research, Berninger tested Jason and then invited

him to a summer program for dyslexic boys. The kids didn't just play letter games. They did science experiments, studied biodiversity, met with a geneticist and radiologist from the university—and learned to read words relating to the science they were studying. Berninger explained that their brains weren't defective, just different. She told them that Einstein had trouble in school, too, until he found one that emphasized individual thinking and discouraged rote memorization. At the end of the program, Jason went up to her and asked earnestly, "Can you help me get into a school like Einstein's?"

Unfortunately, there are no schools like that around the Nicholas home in Kent, Wash. But Jason did make dramatic gains during that summer program in 1997. What's more, he's maintained them. He'll never be a great speller. He still stumbles

over new words in a text. But he's an honors student in his sixth-grade class and continues to amaze his mom every day with his creativity. "I look at kids like Jason and think God gave them other things to compensate," says his mother. "They think differently, and come up with creative ideas we've never thought of. They have a gift, even though the world sees it as a disability." Indeed, famous and successful dyslexics include Tom Cruise, artist Robert Rauschenberg and Olympian Dan O'Brien.

Jason is one of the lucky ones—and not just because he's smart and creative. Until recently, dyslexia and other reading problems were a mystery to most teachers and parents. As a result, too many kids passed through school without mastering the printed page. Some were treated as mentally deficient; many were left functionally illiterate, unable to ever meet their potential. But in the last several years, says Yale researcher Sally Shaywitz, "there's been a revolution in what we've learned about reading and dyslexia." Scientists like Shaywitz and Berninger are using a variety of new imaging techniques to watch the brain at work. Their experiments have shown that reading disorders are most likely the result of what is, in effect, faulty wiring in the brain—not laziness, stupidity or a poor home environment. There's also convincing evidence that dyslexia is largely inherited; scientists have identified four chromosomes that may be involved. Dyslexia is now considered a chronic problem for some kids, not just a "phase." Scientists have also discarded another old stereotype, that almost all dyslexics are boys. Studies indicate that many girls are affected as well—and not getting help.

At the same time, educational researchers have come up with innovative teaching strategies for kids who are having trouble learning to read. New screening tests are pinpointing children at risk before they get discouraged by years of frustration and failure. And educators are trying to get the message to parents that they should be on the alert for the first signs of potential problems (box).

Jean Urban

Then: School administrators told Jean Urban's mother not to worry when the child couldn't grasp phonics in first grade. She was clearly smart, as her math grades showed. Finally, in second grade, her mom insisted on testing her for learning disabilities.

Now: With special training Urban, now 10 and in fifth grade, is making progress and says she's "pretty good at reading." She is part of a study at Yale that will see whether the special training is actually changing how her brain works.

It's an urgent mission. Mass literacy is a relatively new social goal. A hundred years ago people didn't need to be good readers in order to earn a living. But in the Information Age, no one can get by without knowing how to read well and understand increasingly complex material. These skills don't come easily to about 20 percent of kids. Not all of these youngsters

are dyslexic. Researchers now think that dyslexia represents the low end of a continuum of reading ability. The teaching strategies that help dyslexics, those most severely disabled, are also helping kids who require only a little extra attention.

Matthew Schafir

finally got help thanks to his mother, Peggy

Then: From kindergarten on, reading was a struggle, even after years of tutoring and testing. Desperate, Schafir's mom took him to a clinic seven hours from their home. To save money, mother and son lived in a tent for part of the time Matthew got intensive intervention.

Now: His reading level went from second to fifth grade in six weeks. At 14, Matthew reads at grade level, but still needs help with spelling and writing. His mom, meanwhile, is now working to bring the latest reading research to schools in Richmond, Ind.

These dramatic changes come none too soon. For years people thought dyslexia was a vision problem, in which children reversed letters. The misconception is rooted in the earliest research. Dyslexia was first described 100 years ago by W. Pringle Morgan, a general practitioner in Sussex, England. In 1896 he published an article in the British Medical Journal about a 14-year-old boy named Percy who was "quick at games and in no way inferior to others of his age"—except that he was unable to read. Because Percy and others like him had problems with written words, not with spoken language, it was assumed that the problem was visual. Dyslexia was turned over to ophthalmologists, who tried to teach dyslexic kids by using outsized letters and words.

This didn't help at all because most dyslexics see as well as anyone else. But they do have trouble pulling words apart into their constituent sounds, what scientists call phonemes. These are the smallest discernible segments of speech; there are more than 40 of them in the English language. To understand how this process works, Shaywitz uses the example of the word "cat," which is made up of three phonemes: "kuh," "aah" and "tuh." Most people understand this, but dyslexics can only hear "cat"—one sound. As a result, they can't sound out words, the first step in reading. Most people race through this

sounding-out phase and the process becomes an automatic, essentially unconscious, part of reading. Dyslexics get stuck at the starting gate because they can't make the connection between the symbol and the sound.

Researchers are getting a clearer picture of why this is happening by using new imaging techniques. Brain scans are now showing that when dyslexics try to decipher words, certain areas in the back of the brain are underactivated, while other areas in the front are overactivated. In the September issue of the American Journal of Neuroradiology, Berninger and her colleague Todd Richards reported on a study in which they scanned the brains of six dyslexic and seven nondyslexic boys performing three different tasks: telling two musical tones apart, distinguishing real spoken words from nonsense and picking out rhyming syllables. The only difference was in the rhyming task. Dyslexics scored significantly lower and scans showed that regions in the front of their brains were in overdrive. This suggests that dyslexics have to work much harder to analyze sound patterns. The sounding-out process wasn't efficient.

Charles Schwab

at the Schwab Foundation for Learning

Then: Discount broker Charles Schwab struggled in school with reading. At Stanford, he flunked English "once or twice" and failed French. He never knew his problem was dyslexia, though, until his son was diagnosed with it. He established the foundation in San Mateo, Calif., in 1987 to provide information on learning disabilities (800-230-0988).

Now: "Out of the closet" as a dyslexic, he reads three or four newspapers a day, "but only the front page and business section," he says. "I read the same subject matter all the time so I'm good at it."

Shaywitz and her husband, Bennett (co-directors of the NICHD-Yale Center for the study of Learning and Attention), are using functional magnetic resonance imaging (fMRI) to track blood flow through the brain. The areas that receive the most blood are working the hardest. Last year they reported in the Proceedings of the National Academy of Sciences that they saw a similar pattern of increased activity in the front of the brain, an area that's known to

THE ANATOMY OF A READING DISABILITY

Sally and Bennett Shaywitz at Yale have used brain scans to show that dyslexics have too little activity in the back of the brain and increased activity in the front

LETE JEAT

The fMRI machine: Gauges the brain's activity while the child reads words off a screen. The child answers questions like this one: do these nonsense words (left) rhyme?

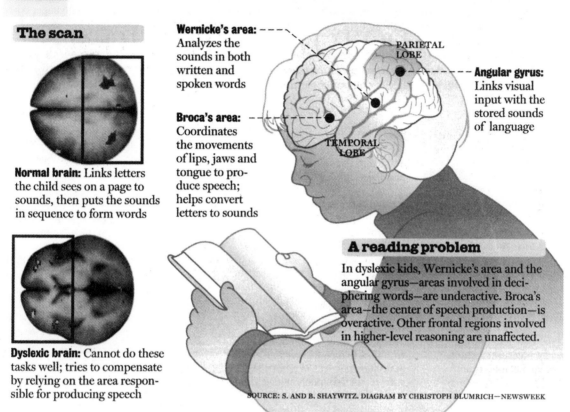

The scan

Normal brain: Links letters the child sees on a page to sounds, then puts the sounds in sequence to form words

Dyslexic brain: Cannot do these tasks well; tries to compensate by relying on the area responsible for producing speech

Wernicke's area: Analyzes the sounds in both written and spoken words

Broca's area: Coordinates the movements of lips, jaws and tongue to produce speech; helps convert letters to sounds

PARIETAL LOBE

Angular gyrus: Links visual input with the stored sounds of language

TEMPORAL LOBE

A reading problem

In dyslexic kids, Wernicke's area and the angular gyrus—areas involved in deciphering words—are underactive. Broca's area—the center of speech production—is overactive. Other frontal regions involved in higher-level reasoning are unaffected.

SOURCE: S. AND B. SHAYWITZ. DIAGRAM BY CHRISTOPH BLUMRICH—NEWSWEEK

---

govern speech production. "What we believe is that dyslexics are trying to find another way to get at the sound of the word," says Sally Shaywitz, perhaps by saying words under their breaths. This could be one cause of dyslexia: inefficient pathways in the brain.

Because of this research, scientists now have a much better understanding of how we process written language. What they're realizing is that learning to read is not a natural process like learning to speak. "Speech is a biologically hard-wired ability," says Reid Lyon, chief of the child development and behavior branch of the National Institute for Child Health and Human Development (NICHD). "Almost all humans acquire it in the same way. They coo, then they babble, use single words, then put two words together." Scientists

John Corcoran

is proud that at last he can read to his grandchildren

Then: By sixth grade John Corcoran, a severe dyslexic, still couldn't spell "cat" and could tell MEN from WOMEN on restroom doors only because one was longer. Still illiterate as an adult, he taught social studies in high school—by using movies for lessons, inviting guest speakers and having students grade papers.

Now: At 48, he registered for a public-library literacy program. That was a start, but the real improvement came when he began treating the dyslexia explicitly. Now 60, he published "The Teacher Who Couldn't Read" in 1994.

estimate that the ability to use speech is at least 100,000 years old while written language is only about 5,000 years old. Because written language is so new, learning it is not in our genes; we have to be taught.

Which reading method works best? The answer is a lot more complicated than the much-ballyhooed "reading wars" of the last decade, in which proponents of whole language or phonics each claimed the true path to literacy. The often highly politicized debate distracts from the real issue, that both methods are failing too many kids. Instead, experts say, reading needs to be taught in a carefully sequenced way that includes pieces of both these methods, plus much more. It must be based on solid research and geared to the needs of individual kids. No single strategy will work for everyone who's having trouble, researchers say. "People can respond differently to a similar deficit," says Georgetown University neuroscientist Guinevere Eden. "Some can draw on other skills." The right method for a particular child depends on the severity of the problem and the age at which a youngster is diagnosed.

Everyone agrees that early intervention is the most effective. Researchers suspect there's a window between the ages of 5 and 7 when the underlying skills of reading are most easily learned. "If kids are at risk, we can address it with 30 minutes of intervention a day at the kindergarten level," says Lyon. "By the time children are 8 or 9, it takes at least two hours a day of special training." The key is finding those at risk early. One new screening test, developed by Barbara Foorman and her colleagues at the University of Texas-Houston Medical School, asks kindergartners to give the sounds for specific letters and sets of letters. Kids who have trouble get more specific diagnostic testing. This fall, Foorman's two-minute test, called the Texas Primary Reading Inventory, will be used in 89 percent of the state's school districts. Marilyn Jager Adams, a researcher at the Harvard Graduate School of Education, has also developed a two-minute screen, currently being tested in Kansas schools. It checks kindergartners for basic skills and tests higher-level abilities, such as fluency and word recognition, as children progress.

In the future, we may be able to spot problems even earlier. Two researchers at the University of Louisville, Victoria and Dennis Molfese, have studied the brainwaves of infants and compared them to the reading skills of the same kids at 8. In a report released earlier this year, the Molfeses said they found that infants who later had reading problems responded slightly more slowly to a series of taped syllables—perhaps because they were not processing sounds efficiently.

No one really knows how the Molfeses' findings fit into the larger picture. Some researchers think these delays correlate with another key predictor of reading trouble, the lack of a skill called "rapid naming," quickly retrieving the names of very familiar letters and numbers. "What you're measuring," says Joseph Torgesen, an educational psychologist at Florida State University, "is how fast a child can make a connection between a visual symbol and its spoken equivalent." That skill is essential to reading. Maryanne Wolf, director of the Center for Reading and Language Research at Tufts University, believes sound differentiation and naming speed could be

separate causes of dyslexia, what she calls a "double deficit."

One program that has been proved effective is the Lindamood Phoneme Sequencing program (LiPS), which makes students identify how sounds feel while saying them. Consonants are given names according to the motions involved in making them. For example, "P" is a "lip popper" because the lips start together and then come apart. This gives students another way to recognize letter sounds. One reason this may work is it helps dyslexics get past their initial obstacle, their inability to break words down. They may not be able to distinguish the constituent sounds in a word, but they can feel their mouths making distinct and separate motions. Researchers are now trying to find out whether this kind of training can produce changes in the brains of dyslexics.

In selecting a program for their kids, Shaywitz advises parents and teachers to look for programs that emphasize breaking words down into sounds—what researchers call "phoneme awareness." "Dyslexic kids need very intense and specific help" in this area, she says. The second key ingredient is learning the letters that go with those sounds—or phonics, which Lyon calls "nonnegotiable… You have to learn it." The final essential is constant practice, using interesting stories to develop fluency, vocabulary and comprehension. While these are elements of any good reading program, the difference is in the increased intensity and explicitness for dyslexics.

Researchers are using this information, gleaned from the new brain research, to revolutionize the way reading is taught to all students. The main obstacle is that many classroom teachers are woefully undertrained in the newest techniques. "Teaching reading *is* rocket science," says Louisa Moats, NICHD researcher. "Our profession has underestimated how much and what kind of training teachers need." For the last two years, Moats has been working with some Washington, D.C., public schools with a large number of students who may be at risk because they come from low-income homes, and haven't had much exposure to books. Their curriculum includes lots of rhyming, songs and games, as well as hands-on activities. By the end of the first year, administrators were amazed to find that almost all of their kindergartners were starting to read.

Until more kids get that chance, much of the burden will continue to fall on parents. But there's a lot they can do even be-

fore their kids are in school. Language games like pig Latin (igpay atinlay) enhance the ability to manipulate sounds in words. Another good tool: just about anything by Dr. Seuss, because of the rhyming and wordplay in the texts. Of course, this is no guarantee of success, but research consistently shows that kids who are exposed to rhymes are more likely to hear the individual sounds of language. When their kids start kindergarten, parents should be alert for signs that the children are falling behind. Getting help isn't always easy; parents have to be aggressive advocates.

Susan Hall, now president of the Illinois branch of the International Dyslexia Association and coauthor (with Louisa Moats) of "Straight Talk About Reading," started on that path five years ago when her son Brandon was in first grade. She knew something was wrong because he wouldn't talk about school and seemed much too eager to get home when she picked him up at the end of the day. So she volunteered as a parent aide. What she saw was disturbing. "The children were supposed to read aloud," she recalls. "When I heard the first child, I knew she could read a lot better than my child could read. When his turn came, he was devastated. That enabled me to open the door and talk about what was bothering him."

Hall asked to have Brandon tested at school, but, she says, "they said they couldn't possibly do it because he wasn't a year behind yet"—a requirement in many districts that costs kids valuable time. Finding a good diagnostician proved difficult. After two tutors didn't work out, Hall decided to study on her own. A Harvard M.B.A., she quit working and made fixing Brandon's problems her cause. "The first year, I took three graduate courses in reading at our local teachers college, flew around the country to attend 10 conferences and read 25 books on the subject." She was impressed with the speakers at an International Dyslexia Association conference and took Brandon to a tutor who used their approach. It helped, but Brandon still had problems. Finally, "at a huge cost to my family," Hall took Brandon to a Lindamood clinic in California, where he finally made a breakthrough. Brandon, now in sixth grade, is a pretty good reader, his mother says, "but his troubles continue in writing, spelling, French and oh, yes—we still have algebra ahead."

Hall gave Brandon what dyslexic kids need most—the emotional support to stay positive about school. But her experiences have left her frustrated and angry—feelings shared by many other parents who

WHAT PARENTS CAN DO TO HELP THEIR KIDS

Experts are getting better at identifying what's normal and what's not for beginning readers. While kids develop at different speeds, this list can provide an idea of what to watch for on the path to literacy. Parents who notice significant problems should seek expert help.

SCHOOL LEVEL	TYPICAL DEVELOPMENT	POSSIBLE SIGNS OF TROUBLE	HOW TO HELP
Ages 3-4, preschool	Listens to stories; knows that words are read in books; can identify some alphabet letters (like those in their own name); tries to write.	Doesn't know how to hold a book; can't differentiate between squiggles and letters; unable to recognize own name; has limited vocabulary.	Read books aloud; teach songs with rhyming words; write down children's spoken words and read them back; avoid workbooks.
Kindergarten	Can rhyme spoken words and blend sounds to make words (e.g., "m-m-m" plus "an" makes "man"); connects some sounds and letters.	Unable to distinguish individual sounds that make up words (e.g., the "kuh-aah-tuh" in "cat"); slow to name familiar objects and colors.	Emphasize rhyme in games, songs, books; by middle of year, seek testing in "phonemic awareness" if no improvement occurs.
1st and 2d grades	Learns to read simple text aloud; with practice, reads more complex books with comprehension and accuracy; counts syllables in words.	Complains that reading is easier for everyone else; has no idea how to decode unknown words; falls significantly behind peers; avoids reading.	Become your child's advocate; lobby for phonemic-awareness testing and intensive instruction with solid research base.
2d and 3d grades	Begins to read independently, silently and for pleasure; rereads sentences when meaning is unclear; learns to correctly spell simple words; reads aloud with expression.	Starts to withdraw, exhibits other troubling behavior; seems to guess at unknown words in an irrational way; focuses so much on decoding words that meaning is lost.	Seek out professional help and support groups that can offer resources,, referrals; encourage activities where child can succeed while reading struggle continues.

COMPILED BY PAT WINGERT; SOURCES: NATIONAL RESEARCH COUNCIL, NATIONAL ASSN. FOR THE EDUCATION OF YOUNG CHILDREN

were left to find an answer on their own. "This is just way too difficult," she says. "You do what you think is best and hope that research doesn't come out later showing you should have done something else. We have got to make this process a whole lot easier." That's a goal shared by everyone involved in unraveling the mysteries of dyslexia—researchers, teachers, parents and most of all, the kids themselves.

—*With* PAT WINGERT

A Mother-and-Child Reunion

Africa's wars have dislocated thousands of children. Our writer Nadya Labi finds hope in one mother's tale

IT IS A CUSTOM IN SOME PARTS OF WEST AFRICA TO PLANT a seed when a child is born. The seed is buried deep in the ground along with the umbilical cord. It takes root, slowly growing into the sturdiness of a coconut or a mango or a kola-nut tree. The tree is the certificate that proves this child existed in this village. It is stability in a region that has been rent by war for more than a decade. In its shade, no fighting, no hurt should come.

In Coyah, a town in Guinea blessed with springs of the purest water, Ibrahim and Marie ignored the tradition. Not defiantly but without thought, because Aisha was their first child and they were distracted by worries. No one was buying the beds Ibrahim built, and refugees from Liberia and Sierra Leone were spilling into the country, carrying with them tales of brutality.

Life seemed full of grace nearly a decade ago, when Ibrahim caught sight of a slim schoolgirl at the local Muslim academy. Marie carried herself with such ease that Ibrahim, 22 years eager, proposed on the spot. She demurred at first, but later, over her guardian uncle's opposition, she married him.

Marie began to grow full at the waist two years later. Secretly she hoped for a girl. The bellyache came and passed—the labor lasted not even an hour—and she called the baby Aisha. Aisha was a lively child with huge brown eyes and a flashing smile. She ate whatever Marie prepared, whether it was a stew of pounded cassava leaves or a soup of ground peanuts; but like all children, she loved sweets, and would charm her mother into buying her cakes at the market. She slept in the same bed with her mother, always staying close. And when her little sister came along, she nicknamed her Bobo.

When Aisha was five, Marie left her daughter in the care of her husband's aunt while she visited nearby Conakry for a few days. While she was away a woman named Fatim appeared in the village. She told everyone that she was Marie's sister and settled in. Then, the day Marie was to return, Fatim roused Aisha, promising the child good-

ies if she came along quietly. When the neighbors asked Aisha where she was going, she responded lightly, "I'm going to get some fried doughnuts."

Aisha didn't return. It was the kind of disappearance that is all too common in this part of West Africa, where war and chaos are as routine as the peace of an American suburb. Children disappear, sometimes kidnapped like Aisha by traders who sell them into slavery, sometimes split accidentally from their parents at refugee camps or nabbed by passing soldiers to join the fight. Thousands of children have been separated from their families by the civil war that started in Liberia in 1989, spread to Sierra Leone in 1991 and has now infected Guinea. Children with no parents and no protection roam the streets of Conakry.

The situation is worsening. Guinea became the battlefield last fall as rebels from all three countries attacked and burned the refugee camps that line the country's southern borders. Everyone ran whichever way seemed away from the sounds of gunfire: south to Liberia, north to Guinea's interior and south to Sierra Leone. The 460,000 refugees, added to tens of thousands of newly displaced natives, amounted to a crisis.

The refugees in Parrot's Beak, a region in southeastern Guinea that borders Sierra Leone, inhabit a lush tropical splendor that belies encroaching danger. The Revolutionary United Front, the rebels in Sierra Leone who mutilate civilians to instill fear—double arm amputations are a favored tactic—may be approaching if U.N. troops push them to the north. Humanitarian agencies hope to transfer the refugees by truckloads to Guinea's interior—an ambitious plan that is sure to tear apart more families. "You cannot avoid separation," says Alfonse Munyanza, who works for the U.N. High Commissioner for Refugees. "You can minimize it, but there is no exodus that is done with people smiling." There are things that can be done by donors in other countries to help stitch these families back together. But for now, West Africa is filled

VICTIMS OF WAR

Mariama Jalloh

AGE: 14; HOME: SIERRA LEONE

Mariama was raped at age 11. She was reunited with family in April.

Some rebels took me and carried me from my house. My mother and father were there. The rebels had guns. They said because I'm beautiful and a girl. They took six of my half sisters also. I heard them yelling.

I shouted. I was afraid. I started bleeding. My belly was hurting. It was one after the other. There were three of them. I can't remember how long it went on. I was dragged outside by the rebels and told to go away. They said go home, but I could not walk by then. I saw a gentleman in the streets who knew me. He took me on his back to my house. My mother and father took me to the doctor.

A week later my big brother was killed. Rumors started flying that the rebels were cutting [off] hands. We started running to the national stadium. I began to be afraid. I didn't see my mother. I started thinking the rebels would catch me again. Since I couldn't find my parents, I started crying. I heard boats were going to Guinea. I took a *pam-pam* [a boat that can hold 159 to 200 people]. The trip took two days. I didn't eat. I didn't drink. I didn't sleep. When the boat landed, I had nobody.

Lucy Jalloh

AGE: 60ISH; HOME: SIERRA LEONE

Lucy is a foster mother who has taken care of four refugee children.

It was April 1991. I heard the rebels were coming. The town was panicked. I had a local restaurant, selling rice and sauce. Everyone was running. One boy came to where I was and sat beside the pot. Then three girls put down their baskets and came to me. I asked them, "What happened?" They said, "We came to sell leaves. Because of the problem on the ground, we would like you to take us wherever you want to go. We are little children." Everybody headed to Guinea.

This one here. She was this small [the size of a toddler]. I take her to be the same as my own daughter. I don't want her to go far. We eat together. We take a bath together. She doesn't give me problems.

I gave birth to six children, and five died. My breast milk was not good. I nursed them, and all five died. The first at birth, the second when it was crawling, the third began to walk…The problem was my breasts. The last one, I pounded rice and gave her powdered rice with medicine. The way my belly hurt when I gave birth to my children. That's the same pain that this child's parent had.

with parents and children searching desperately for one another.

When the bad woman came for Aisha, she didn't understand what had happened. One day there was food and Bobo and Mamma, braiding her hair, washing her, cuddling her. And then nothing except angry shouts in a strange tongue and hard hands. Hands that landed on her backside and her face, hitting her if she cried or walked too slowly or asked for food or just because. She walked with the woman, who talked about doughnuts that never appeared. She walked and walked until she ended up in a strange place where no one spoke Susu. She spent her days cleaning and helping with domestic tasks. The time passed.

Then they started walking again. The woman took her to a store with big bales of dried fish and posters of a big man in a yellow robe, the President. They went to sleep and woke to an angry man shouting. He didn't want them dozing on his fish. The angry man took them to another place. Then the bad woman left.

Aisha tried to keep quiet so the bad woman wouldn't come back. She stayed with the angry man and his wife and children. She began to feel very bad and hot all over. She didn't eat. She didn't play. She just kept very quiet in the corner.

A CHILD WITHOUT AN identity cannot be found. In the refugee camps and the streets of Guinea there is no tree that locates a child and acts as an address. It is for humans to find the roots of a lost child.

After Aisha's disappearance, Marie refused to eat for a week. Ibrahim went to all the mosques in the area, offering sacrifices for his daughter's return. He gave 5,000 kola nuts and 5,000 Guinean francs to each mosque that he visited. He asked all the local radio stations to publicize Aisha's disappearance. After six months and six mosques, he ran out of money and hope. Marie, for her part, believed her daughter had died.

The International Rescue Committee specializes in this kind of detective work from the other end of the equation—starting with the child. Since 1999 it has identified more than 1,600 separated children in Guinea. "The family is the best guarantor for the protection of these children," says Jacqueline Botte, the country program director for child tracing. If no biological relatives can be found, the IRC places the children with foster families or, as a last resort, at a transit center. But blood and memory exert a special pull. Kids separated from their families for as long as 10 years want to go home—home to the community of their earliest remembrance.

The journey back usually begins at a mosque or a church or a camp, when the names of children—and whatever scraps of information can be ascertained—are read over a loudspeaker. At an outdoor mosque in Conakry on a recent Friday, an IRC worker, Sheku Conteh, intoned the names of some 30 children. A lizard scurried up a tree whose base was ringed with well-worn plastic sandals and sneakers, while a woman performed her ablutions with a kettle. The men stood barefoot on a makeshift dais; women wearing scarves on their heads sat on the ground behind them; all listened intently. "If you don't know anything, it's O.K.," Conteh blared out. "But if you know something, anything, about this child, this is a big, big blessing."

The blessing of a reunion begins with the business of tiny scraps. A man faintly recalls the name of a child and thinks he might know the family. A woman remembers seeing a child with bright eyes heading off with that woman who sold cassava leaves. And with this small scrap, the IRC teams begin to try to undo a heartbreak. The work is painstaking, as it takes days and perhaps weeks to check out every lead.

By the time Esther Touré, an IRC worker, collected Aisha in Kissidougou, in southeastern Guinea, the child was running a fever from malaria. She barely spoke except at night, when she would cry out in her nightmares and wet her bed. She had been found only because the storekeeper with whom she had been abandoned called the local police. Amid the tidal wave of refugees moving from place to place, Aisha had been parked for a crucial moment in the vicinity of someone who cared enough to help her. Esther took Aisha back to Guéckédou, about an hour's drive south, where she and her family spoke Susu. She gave Aisha peppermints to gain her trust. Finally, one day Esther asked, "Who is your mother?" and Aisha responded, "My mother is Marie."

The word went out. On the radio stations in Kindia, Forécariah and Coyah, every place in Guinea where Susu is spoken, the announcement was made that a young girl named Aisha whose mother was Marie had been found. Ibrahim's brother Mamadouba heard the news. He went to the station to look at the accompanying picture of the girl. It was Aisha.

The family sent Mamadouba, the most educated of them all, to Guéckédou with a family picture of Aisha, her birth certificate and Marie's identification card. As he approached Esther's house, Mamadouba saw Aisha eating at the table and shouted her name. She continued eating. He showed Esther the papers, but she was wary. Why didn't the girl respond? She refused to let him take Aisha. He wept in disappointment.

Marie and Ibrahim were desperate. They pressed the IRC for Aisha's return. Esther decided to bring Aisha to Coyah to find out if Aisha's mother had truly been located.

This time there could be no mistake. As the IRC jeep approached the yard, Marie flew to meet it. She rushed for her daughter with no thought of the metal tonnage heading toward her. She raced to the vehicle as it braked to a

THE BOY SOLDIER

Mohamed Kamara

AGE: 17; HOME: SIERRA LEONE
Mohamed was kidnapped by Sierra Leonean rebels and made to kill.

There was smoke everywhere. My mother was sleeping deeply. She didn't wake up. I tried to move her, but she was too fat. I woke my stepfather, but it was too late. The fire was inside the room. I ran away.

Lieutenant "Cuthand" took me. He said I should join them. He caught me and drugged me with brown-brown [a form of cocaine]. I felt bad. Then they gave me a gun. They gave me an ax. I cut off hands. I killed. Many times. I thought about my mom. My eyes were red, and I wasn't feeling good, but I kept on destroying. I kept thinking about my mother. When I thought about her, I would cry remembering all the things she did for me. She paid my school fees and, when I was sick, took me to the hospital. Anything I wanted, my mother gave me.

I was afraid. Lieutenant "Blood" told me if I didn't cut off people's hands, then my own hand would be cut off. I cut off the ear and gave the ear to the person to eat instead of killing the person. I didn't want to do it, but when I turned around the other guys were looking at me. The people ate the ears. No one refused because I had a gun. I was with the rebels for four years.

Last year I escaped from the port in Freetown. I saw friends from school. I tore off my uniform. They asked me for money. I didn't have any. I said that I would bail out water for them. That's how I came to Guinea. I stayed in the streets with my friends. I didn't eat. I didn't wash. I begged for drink. When I came here (to an IRC center in Conakry), I have forgotten those things, thanks be to God.

I don't feel guilty. But the side effects of the drugs bother me. My head hurts when the sun is hot and I think about it.

halt and slammed into the door. So as not to be knocked over, Esther took Aisha out the other side.

Aisha began to run. She met Marie's waiting arms and cried, "*Oh, N'Gah.*" Oh, my mother.

Weeping, Marie responded, "*Woh, M'Deeh.*" Oh, my daughter.

ESCAPING FROM THE DARKNESS

Drugs like Prozac, Paxil and Luvox can work wonders for clinically depressed kids. But what about the long-term consequences?

By HOWARD CHUA-EOAN

MEGAN KELLAR IS BUBBLY AND BOUNC-ing and lip-synching to the Backstreet Boys. *Get down, get down and move it all around!* The sixth-grader is dancing to the synthesized bubble-gum beat at a talent show at the John Muir Elementary School in Parma, Ohio. *Get down, get down and move it all around!* There is nothing down about Megan, even as she gets down in front of the audience. Her mother remembers a similar effervescence half a dozen years ago. "She'd be singing to herself and making up songs all the time," says Linda Kellar. And sure enough, that part of her is still there. "Megan's such a happy child," the mother of a girl on Megan's baseball team remarked to Linda. Yes, Linda agreed, but there's something you ought to know. Megan is clinically depressed and on the antidepressant Paxil. Says Linda: "She couldn't believe it."

Six years ago, Linda wouldn't have believed that her daughter was clinically depressed either. But shortly after her parents separated, Megan stopped singing. When other kids came over to play, she would lie down in the yard and just watch. At Christmas she wouldn't decorate the tree. Linda thought her daughter was simply melancholy over her parents' split and took her to see a counselor. That seemed to help for a while. Then for about eight months, when Megan was 10, she cried constantly and wouldn't go to school. She lost her appetite and got so weak that at one point she couldn't get out of bed. When a doctor recommended Paxil in conjunction with ther-

apy, Linda recoiled. "I did not want to put my baby on an antidepressant," she says. Then she relented because, she says, "Megan wasn't living her childhood." Linda noticed changes in just two weeks. Soon Megan was singing again. "She's not drugged or doped," says Linda. "She still cries when she sees *Old Yeller* and still has moody days." But, as Megan says, "I'm back to normal, like I used to be."

Megan Kellar shares her kind of normality with hundreds of thousands of other American kids. Each year an estimated 500,000 to 1 million prescriptions for antidepressants are written for children and teens. On the one hand, the benefits are apparent and important. Experts estimate that as many as 1 in 20 American preteens and adolescents suffer from clinical depression. It is something they cannot outgrow. Depression cycles over and over again throughout a lifetime, peaking during episodes of emotional distress, subsiding only to well up again at the next crisis. And as research increasingly shows, depression is often a marker for other disorders, including the syndrome that used to be called manic depression and is now known as bipolar disorder. If undetected and untreated in preteens, depressive episodes can lead to severe anxiety or manic outbursts not only in adulthood but as early as adolescence.

On the other hand, come the questions. How do we tell which kids are at risk? Has science fully apprised us of the effects on kids of medication designed for an adult brain? Have we set out on a path that will

produce a generation that escapes the pain only to lose the character-building properties of angst?

TO MEDICATE OR NOT TO MEDICATE? THE dilemma can be traced back to 1987, when the FDA approved Prozac as the first of a new class of antidepressants known as selective serotonin reuptake inhibitors (SS-RIs). Prozac had none of the more serious side effects and risks of the earlier antidepressants and worked faster to control depressive symptoms. Prozac and the other SSRIs (they now include Zoloft, Paxil, Luvox and Celexa) had one other advantage over the older, tricyclic antidepressants: children responded to them. One of the few recent studies on the subject showed that among depressed children ages 8 to 18, 56% improved while on Prozac, in contrast to 33% on a placebo. Says Dr. David Fassler, chair of the American Psychiatric Association's Council on Adolescents and Their Families: "Physicians have a lot of experience using the medications with adult patients with good results, and recent research increases their general level of comfort in using them with children and adolescents."

But which kids?

Not so long ago, many psychiatrists argued that children and young teens could not get depressed because they were not mature enough to internalize their anger. Today, says Fassler, "we realize that depression does occur in childhood and adolescence and that it occurs more often in children than we previously realized."

Still, depression is slightly harder to diagnose in adolescents than in adults, and not because teens are expected to be moodier and more withdrawn. They are less likely to realize that they are depressed and thus less likely to seek help. "Younger kids also have more difficulty expressing their feelings in words," says Dr. Boris Birmaher, a child psychiatrist at the University of Pittsburgh. "When kids become depressed, they become irritable, act out, have temper tantrums and other behavioral problems. It's hard to ascertain that these are the symptoms of depression unless you ask them questions in a language they can understand."

> ## "I would have sold my house... to get Nick taken care of."
>
> SUSAN DUBUQUE,
> author and mother

Furthermore, the very definition of being a child—what makes him survive and grow—is being able to move up and down emotionally, having a basic elasticity. Says Dr. Peter Jensen, child and adolescent psychiatrist at the National Institute of Mental Health: "A child is more fluid and plastic than an adult. A child may look depressed one day because his dog died but seem O.K. three days later."

But if parents live in a world of family mood swings, that doesn't mean they are prepared to put their own child on mind-altering drugs. That prospect can lead to major soul searching: Will they be thought less of as parents? And if they do agree to antidepressants, will the child still be the one they know?

Donna Mitchell was told her daughter, eight-year-old Sawateos, had attention-deficit hyperactivity disorder, but she also showed signs of serious depression and anxiety, which are often found in combination. Mitchell's first reaction was, "I can pray this away. I thought, Listen, nobody in my family is going on drugs. That's an insult. I figured all we needed was family talks." But two years after the diagnosis, Mitchell has agreed to put her child on the ADHD drug Ritalin. She still resists the idea of antidepressants. It's her preteen daughter who's making the case for doing it. "Mama, it's in our genes," Sawateos tells her.

All this may help explain why it is so hard for the people closest to children to detect that anything is really wrong. Studies show that parents consistently miss the signs of depression. In one survey by researchers at Ball State and Columbia universities, 57% of teens who had attempted suicide were found to be suffering from major depression. But only 13% of the parents of suicides believed their child was depressed.

Diagnosis is critical because depressed children tend to develop increasingly severe mental disorders and in some cases psychosis as teens and adults. Three studies on children who were depressed before puberty show that as adults they had a higher rate of antisocial behavior, anxiety and major depression than those who experienced their first depressive episode as teens. "Prepubertal depression does occur, and those who get it are more susceptible to [the] mania [of bipolar disorder] later," says Dr. John March, director of the program on pediatric psychopharmacology at Duke University. "The earlier you get it, the more likely you will develop chronic depressive and anxiety symptoms."

So how do psychiatrists pick out kids who are depressed from those who are simply moody? In his book *"Help Me, I'm Sad,"* Fassler lists a number of physical symptoms in three age groups—preschool-

ers, young school-age children and adolescents. Among preschoolers, the signs include frequent, unexplained stomachaches, headaches and fatigue. Depressed school-age children frequently weigh 10 lbs. less than their peers, may have dramatic changes in sleep patterns and may start speaking in an affectless monotone. Adolescents go through eating disorders, dramatic weight gains or losses, promiscuity, drug abuse, excessive picking at acne, and fingernail biting to the point of bleeding.

Fassler cautions that none of these symptoms may ever be present and a whole constellation of more subjective manifestations must be considered. Adults and adolescents share many of the same warning signs—low self-esteem, tearfulness, withdrawal and a morbid obsession with death and dying. Among adolescents, however, depression is often accompanied by episodes of irritability that, unlike mood swings, stretch for weeks rather than days.

Dr. Elizabeth Weller, professor of psychiatry and pediatrics at the University of Pennsylvania, has developed techniques for detecting depression in kids. First she establishes a rapport with a child. Then she asks, for example, whether he still has fun playing softball or whether it is taking him longer to finish his homework—both of which are ways to figure out whether the child has lost motivation and concentration. Crying is another marker for depression, but Weller says boys rarely admit to it. So she asks them how often they *feel* like crying.

> ## "Depression occurs in children more often than we realized."
>
> DAVID FASSLER,
> psychiatrist

WHAT KIDS ARE TAKING

The most commonly prescribed antidepressants for children are not approved in the U.S. for those under 18, but anecdotal reports show that they appear to be safe and work well for this group. Some manufacturers of these drugs are currently conducting studies of their effect on depressed children.

	Prozac	Zoloft	Paxil	Luvox	Celexa
Approved for adults with	■ Depression ■ Bulimia ■ Obsessive-Compulsive Disorder	■ Depression ■ Obsessive-Compulsive Disorder ■ Panic Disorder	■ Depression ■ Obsessive-Compulsive Disorder ■ Panic Disorder ■ Social Phobia (approval pending)	■ Obsessive-Compulsive Disorder	■ Depression
Characteristics	Remains in body for at least two weeks. Makes some patients agitated, anxious	Remains in body for one week	Has sedating effect on many patients	Also approved for use in children with OCD	Produces fewer adverse reactions with other drugs

She then quizzes parents and teachers for other signs. Parents can tell her if a child no longer cares about his appearance and has lost interest in bathing or getting new clothes. Teachers can tell her whether a child who used to be alert and active has turned to daydreaming or has lost a certain verve. As Weller puts it, "Has the bubble gone out of the face?"

There are several other complicating factors. Some psychiatrists believe depression in younger children often appears in conjunction with other disorders. "Many depressed kids," notes Fassler, "are initially diagnosed with ADHD or learning disabilities. We need to separate out the conditions and treat both problems." But there's a chicken-and-egg problem here: antisocial behavior or a learning disability can lead a child to become isolated and alienated from peers and thus can trigger depression. And depression can further interfere with learning or bring on antisocial behavior.

But does a diagnosis of depression in a child require medication? Consider Nancy Allee's 10-month journey with SSRIs and other drugs. At 12, she was as bubbly as Megan Kellar is now. She soon developed "a five-month-long headache" and started having nightmares. After about a year in counseling, things seemed to be going better and, her mother Judith says, "we terminated it so as not to make it a way of life." A few months later, Nancy became hostile and rebellious but nothing that Judith considered "out of the bounds for a normal teenager." Then, "without any warning, she [took an] overdose" of her migraine medication, was hospitalized and depression was diagnosed. While Judith thought the overdose was out of the blue, Nancy says, "I'd had depression for a long time. If I'd had bad thoughts, I'd always had them and kind of grew up with them. I was always very bubbly, even when I was depressed. A lot of people didn't notice it. To me, suicide had always been an option."

Nancy was put on Zoloft. When that didn't work, the doctor added Paxil and then several other drugs. But there was a panoply of side effects: her hands would shake, she would bang her head against the wall. A voracious reader, she became too withdrawn and listless to pick up a book. There were times she couldn't sleep, but on one occasion she slept 72 hours straight.

"I was seeing five different doctors, and it was overkill," says Nancy. "At one point, I was taking 15 pills in the morning and 15 in the evening. I wound up burying my medication in the backyard. I didn't

want to take it anymore." Then Nancy was tested for allergies, a process that required her to be medication free. "It was like the sky was blue again," says Nancy, who at 18 is still off drugs but sees a counselor occasionally. "The colors came back. It was a total change from the medication stupor. Everything wasn't peachy, but I was able to appreciate doing things again."

HOW TO SPOT A DEPRESSED CHILD

The key thing to watch for is drastic changes in teen behavior. Other red flags to consider:

- **DIFFICULTY MAINTAINING RELATIONSHIPS** May become antisocial, reject friends or refuse to take part in school and family events
- **REDUCED PHYSICAL ACTIVITY** May suffer from lethargy or appear to drag self around
- **MORBID OR SUICIDAL THOUGHTS** May seek out games, music, art or books with death-related themes
- **LOW SELF-ESTEEM** May feel that they are worthless and that their peers, teachers and family disapprove of them
- **SELF-DESTRUCTIVE BEHAVIOR** May harm their body by, for example, biting fingernails to the point of bleeding
- **PROBLEMS AT SCHOOL** Grades may drop or classroom troublemaking rise
- **CHANGES IN SLEEP PATTERNS** May either have restless nights or sleep away the day

Preschoolers

- Frequent unexplained stomachaches, headaches, or fatigue
- Overactivity or excessive restlessness
- A sad appearance
- Low tolerance for frustration
- Irritability
- Loss of pleasure in activities
- Tendency to portray the world as bleak

Most psychiatrists, despite their enthusiasm for the new antidepressants, write

prescriptions for only six months to a year and taper the dosage toward the end. Even Fassler admits, "We try to use medication for the minimum amount of time possible. And with a younger child, we're more cautious about using medication because we have less research concerning both the effectiveness and the long-term consequences and side effects." Says Michael Faenza, president of the National Mental Health Association: "I feel very strongly that no child should be receiving medication without counseling. Medication is just one spoke in the wheel."

The lack of science about the effects of these drugs on childhood development is the reason the FDA has required all manufacturers of SSRIs that treat depression to conduct studies on the subject. Says Dr. Peter Kramer, professor of psychiatry at Brown University and author of *Listening to Prozac:* "Anyone who thinks about this problem is worried about what it means to substantially change neurotransmission in a developing brain. We don't know if these kids would compensate on their own over time and if by giving them these medicines we are interfering with that compensatory mechanism."

Until we know more, some argue, the risks of such medication are just too great, if only because of the message it sends to children. Says Dr. Sidney Wolfe, director of Public Citizen's Health Research Group: "We are moving into an era where any quirk of a personality is fair game for a drug. On one hand, we are telling kids to just say no to drugs, but on the other hand, their pediatricians are saying, 'Take this. You'll feel good.'"

Teen rebellion can put a twist on even that, however. One New York couple, becalmed by antidepressants themselves and openly concerned about the depression of their 18-year-old, were castigated by their son for their "weakness" and dependence on Prozac. His argument: your drugs change who you really are. In place of their drugs, the young man argued for his "natural" remedy: marijuana.

Indeed, pot and alcohol are common forms of self-medication among depressed teens. Weller estimates that about 30% of her teen patients have used pot or alcohol after a depressive episode, most of them at the urging of friends who said smoking and drinking would make them feel better. A high school social worker in Minnesota decided to look into the case of a troubled girl who was still a freshman at 17. The girl admitted she smoked pot as a constant habit but did not understand why she craved it so

The Danger of Suppressing Sadness

What if Holden Caulfield had been taking Prozac?

CONSIDERING HIS WEALTH OF SYMPTOMS—lethargy, forgetfulness, loss of interest in friends and studies—can there be any doubt that Holden Caulfield, the dropout hero of J.D. Salinger's 1950s masterpiece *The Catcher in the Rye*, would be on Luvox, Prozac or a similar drug if he were a teenager today? No doubt whatsoever. A textbook teen depressive by current standards, Caulfield would be a natural candidate for pharmaceutical intervention, joining a rising number of adolescents whose moodiness, anxiety, and rebelliousness are being interpreted as warning signs of chemical imbalances. Indeed, if Caulfield had been a '90s teen, his incessant griping about "phonies" and general hostility toward mainstream society might have been nipped in the neurological bud. The cultural consequences? Incalculable.

With the stroke of countless pens on thousands of prescription pads, the American coming-of-age experience—the stuff of endless novels, movies and pop songs—could gradually be rendered unrecognizable. Goodbye Salinger, Elvis and Bob Dylan; hello psychopharmacology. "The kids in my school traded Zoloft and Prozac pills the way kids used to trade baseball cards," says Stephen Morris, an Episcopal priest and former chaplain at a Texas parochial school. Of course, this school experience doesn't prove that schoolyards everywhere have turned into bustling prescription-drug bazaars. But Morris, who headed a schoolwide committee called Addressing Behaviors of Concern, recalls that "the problems we focused on were not dramatically different from my own youthful experiences." At least three-quarters of the time, says Morris, the kids in question were placed on medication in what he saw as the beginning of a vicious cycle that frequently worsened the original problem. "Challenges that teachers used to handle are being handed over to psychiatrists. Instead of dealing with kids inside the classroom, they yank them out, put them on drugs and stick them back in with glazed eyes a few days later. No wonder the kids end up as outcasts."

Such outcasts may someday form their own majority, if this trend continues. The pain and confusion of growing up, once considered the proper subject of gloomy poetry read under the blankets and angry rock songs rehearsed in the garage, can now mean a quick ticket to the doctor's office. And it doesn't take a lot of acting up for a restless teenager to attract professional attention. On a website sponsored by Channel One, a television network for school-age youth, a recent posting written with the help of the National Association for Mental Illness classified the following behaviors as possible symptoms of manic depression in teens: "increased talking—the adolescent talks too much," "distractibility," unrealistic highs in self-esteem—for example, a teenager who feels specially connected to God."

That last one is a doozy. And heartbreaking. Could it be that Cassie Bernal, who bravely professed her religious faith while staring down the barrel of a gun at the height of the Columbine massacre, was not so much a hero and a martyr as an untreated candidate for lithium? For the education establishment to go on red alert at the first sign of spirituality in their students would be a devastating development.

What is happening here? For better or worse, an institutional drug culture has sprung up in the hallways of All-American High, mimicking the one already established among depressed adults. As was pointed out in the May issue of *Harper's* magazine, the line between illicit, feel-good drugs such as marijuana and amphetamines and legal mood-altering substances such as Luvox, Wellbutrin, and Effexor is a blurry one. Many of the same optimistic claims—enhanced concentration, decreased anxiety, a renewed capacity for feeling pleasure—are made for both types of magic bullet, whether they are bought on the street or in a pharmacy. A profoundly mixed message is being sent to teens when certain substances are demonized for promoting the same subjective states touted on the labels of other compounds. Adolescents, who are famously alert to hypocrisy among their elders, will surely be the first to catch this irony.

At least one hopes so. Teenage skepticism—Holden Caulfield's bitter gift for discerning inconsistencies in the solemn pronouncements of adults—may be one of the troubling traits on the medicators' target list. A pill that tones down youthful b.s. detectors would certainly be a boon to parents and teachers, but how would it enrich the lives of teenagers? Even if such a pill improved their moods—helping them to stick to their studies, say, and compete in a world with close to zero tolerance for unproductive monkeying around—would it not rob them (and the rest of us) of a potent source of social criticism, political idealism and cultural change? The trials and tribulations of growing up yield wisdom for all involved, both kids and parents. The young pose a constant challenge to the old, often an uncomfortable one, almost always an unexpected one, but meeting that challenge with hastily filled prescriptions may be bad medicine for everybody.

For teens who need medication just to function or lessen the real dangers they might pose to others or themselves, the new medications may truly be miraculous. I know from my own experience with clinical depression (contracted as an adult and treated with a combination of therapy and drugs) that such diseases are real and formidable, impossible to wish away. But for kids in the murky emotional borderlands described in books like *The Catcher in the Rye*, antidepressants, stimulants and sedatives aren't a substitute for books and records, heroes and antiheroes. "I get bored sometimes," Holden Caulfield says, "when people tell me to act my age. Sometimes I act a lot older than I am—I really do—but people never notice it. People never notice anything."

Maybe if people start noticing first and medicating second, more of today's confused young Caulfields will stand a chance of maturing into Salingers.

much. A psychological evaluation found the girl was suffering from clinical depression as well as ADHD. She was prescribed an antidepressant, which had striking results. It not only elevated her mood and

helped her focus but also reduced her desire for pot and tobacco.

"IT USED TO BE SAID THAT ADOLESCENCE is the most common form of psychosis,"

says Kramer, the man who helped make Prozac famous. Then he turns serious. "But if a child has a prolonged period of depressive moods, he needs to be evaluated for depression." Even if little is known about the long-term effects of SSRIs on young bodies, most doctors in the field argue that the drugs are a blessing to kids in pain. Says Duke's March, who is doing a comparative study of the benefits of Prozac and cognitive-behavior therapy: "My clinical experience is that it's worse to risk a major mental illness as a child than to be on medication. If you weigh the risks against the benefits, the benefits are probably going to win."

Susan Dubuque of Richmond, Va., is convinced of the benefits. Her son Nick went through "seven years of testing hell." At seven, ADHD was diagnosed and he was put on Ritalin. "When he was 10 years old, he didn't want a birthday party because he just couldn't deal with it," she recalls. Then, his mother says, Nick "bottomed out and became suicidal, and one day I found him in a closet with a toy gun pointed at his head, and he said, 'If this was real, I'd use it.'" The next day she saw a psychologist who had recently evaluated Nick and was told, "If you don't get him help, next time he'll be successful." Nick was found to be suffering from clinical depression and took a series of antidepressants. "I was worried about my son's killing himself," says Susan, who was called by clinicians a "histrionic mother" and a "therapy junkie," as she spent $4,000 on drugs and therapy for her son. "I would have sold my house if that was what it would have taken."

Nick is better now, and has co-authored a book with his mom: *Kid Power Tactics for Dealing with Depression*. Susan is happy to have her son back safe—even though there is some stress. "It's so much fun to have an obnoxious 15-year-old," she says, "and I mean *normal* obnoxious."

—**Reported by Jodie Morse/New York, Alice Park/Washington and James Willwerth/ Los Angeles**

Index

Index

Test Your Knowledge Form

We encourage you to photocopy and use this page as a tool to assess how the articles in *Annual Editions* expand on the information in your textbook. By reflecting on the articles you will gain enhanced text information. You can also access this useful form on a product's book support Web site at *http://www.dushkin.com/online/*.

NAME: _____ DATE: _____

TITLE AND NUMBER OF ARTICLE:
_____

BRIEFLY STATE THE MAIN IDEA OF THIS ARTICLE:
_____

_____

LIST THREE IMPORTANT FACTS THAT THE AUTHOR USES TO SUPPORT THE MAIN IDEA:

_____

WHAT INFORMATION OR IDEAS DISCUSSED IN THIS ARTICLE ARE ALSO DISCUSSED IN YOUR TEXTBOOK OR OTHER READINGS THAT YOU HAVE DONE? LIST THE TEXTBOOK CHAPTERS AND PAGE NUMBERS:

_____

LIST ANY EXAMPLES OF BIAS OR FAULTY REASONING THAT YOU FOUND IN THE ARTICLE:

_____

LIST ANY NEW TERMS/CONCEPTS THAT WERE DISCUSSED IN THE ARTICLE, AND WRITE A SHORT DEFINITION:

We Want Your Advice

ANNUAL EDITIONS revisions depend on two major opinion sources: one is our Advisory Board, listed in the front of this volume, which works with us in scanning the thousands of articles published in the public press each year; the other is you—the person actually using the book. Please help us and the users of the next edition by completing the prepaid article rating form on this page and returning it to us. Thank you for your help!

ANNUAL EDITIONS: Child Growth and Development 02/03

ARTICLE RATING FORM

Here is an opportunity for you to have direct input into the next revision of this volume.
We would like you to rate each of the articles listed below, using the following scale:

1. **Excellent: should definitely be retained**
2. **Above average: should probably be retained**
3. **Below average: should probably be deleted**
4. **Poor: should definitely be deleted**

Your ratings will play a vital part in the next revision.
Please mail this prepaid form to us as soon as possible.
Thanks for your help!

RATING	ARTICLE
	1. The End of Nature Versus Nurture
	2. How Old Is Too Old to Have a Baby?
	3. Fetal Psychology
	4. The World of the Senses
	5. Kids, Start Your Engines
	6. The Quest for a Super Kid
	7. Evolution and Developmental Sex Differences
	8. Categories in Young Children's Thinking
	9. Do Young Children Understand What Others Feel, Want, and Know?
	10. Giftedness: Current Theory and Research
	11. The First Seven . . . and the Eighth: A Conversation With Howard Gardner
	12. Parental Engagement That Makes a Difference
	13. Where the Boys Are
	14. A Sense of Self
	15. Emotional Intelligence: What the Research Says
	16. Babies, Bonds, and Brains
	17. What Ever Happened to Play?
	18. The Company They Keep: Friendships and Their Developmental Significance
	19. The Adjustment of Children From Immigrant Families
	20. Contemporary Research on Parenting: The Case for Nature and Nurture
	21. What Matters? What Does Not? Five Perspectives on the Association Between Marital Transitions and Children's Adjustment
	22. American Child Care Today
	23. Do Working Parents Make the Grade?
	24. Father Love and Child Development: History and Current Evidence
	25. The Moral Development of Children
	26. Playing With God
	27. Tomorrow's Child
	28. Getting Stupid
	29. Why the Young Kill
	30. The Effects of Poverty on Children

RATING	ARTICLE
	31. Effects of Maltreatment and Ways to Promote Children's Resiliency
	32. The Early Origins of Autism
	33. Dyslexia and the New Science of Reading
	34. A Mother-and-Child Reunion
	35. Escaping From the Darkness

(Continued on next page)

BUSINESS REPLY MAIL
FIRST-CLASS MAIL PERMIT NO. 84 GUILFORD CT

POSTAGE WILL BE PAID BY ADDRESSEE

McGraw-Hill/Dushkin
530 Old Whitfield Street
Guilford, Ct 06437-9989

ABOUT YOU

Name

Date

_____

Are you a teacher? ☐   A student? ☐
Your school's name

_____

Department

_____

Address   City   State   Zip

_____

School telephone #

_____

YOUR COMMENTS ARE IMPORTANT TO US!

Please fill in the following information:
For which course did you use this book?

_____

Did you use a text with this ANNUAL EDITION?   ☐ yes ☐ no
What was the title of the text?

_____

What are your general reactions to the *Annual Editions* concept?

_____

Have you read any pertinent articles recently that you think should be included in the next edition? Explain.

_____

Are there any articles that you feel should be replaced in the next edition? Why?

_____

Are there any World Wide Web sites that you feel should be included in the next edition? Please annotate.

_____

May we contact you for editorial input?   ☐ yes ☐ no
May we quote your comments? ☐ yes ☐ no